UltraAge

EVERYWOMAN'S GUIDE
TO FACING THE FUTURE

UltraAge

MARY SPILLANE

VICTORIA McKEE

MACMILLAN

First published 1999 by Macmillan

an imprint of Macmillan Publishers Ltd
25 Eccleston Place, London SW1W 9NF
Basingstoke and Oxford

Associated companies throughout the world

ISBN 0 333 71736 8

9 8 7 6 5 4 3 2 1

A CIP catalogue record for this book is available from the British Library.

A full list of picture credits appears on pages 433–4.

Designed by First Edition
Typeset by The Florence Group, Stoodleigh, Devon
Photographic reproduction by Speedscan Ltd, Basildon, Essex
Printed and bound in Italy by New Interlitho S.p.a., Milan

This book is dedicated to our children,

ANNA and LUCY, DANIEL and JESSICA,

our closest link with immortality . . .

Contents

7 Doing It In Style 254

• What are you trying to project? • Ruts and mistakes are inevitable
• The rut quiz • What it takes • Face your own wardrobe – *Capsules easiest to swallow* • Put your money where your life is • Make peace with your body shape • Pulling a look together – *Colour co-ordination – Accessorizing – You first, outfit second – Underpinning – Think trends not fads – Adapt and update – Help at hand – Avoid a second adolescence*

8 Keeping Pace at Work 282

• Working smarter • Changing attitudes with attitude • Refuse to be another statistic • Women at work: New Images • Prepare your pension • Old dogs can learn new tricks • Still sharp • Decline in working skills not inevitable • The seven ages of skills • It's official: Life begins at forty-five • Fifties and beyond: Prime Time • Don't let work stress you out • Image matters • Don't let your attitude or your arteries (or your hairstyle) harden • Different for the boys • Working it out • Loving your work is loving yourself • Keep on going to keep going strong

9 Healthy Body 310

• All ageing is not equal • Simple living, simple pleasures • Ageing achievers and underachievers • Exercise: it's got to be joyful • Don't just talk. Walk yourself fitter • Make it social • Look East • Variety is the spice of life • Use it or lose it • Essential exercises • What works • Listen to your body • The food dilemma • Is simply eating less the key to longevity? • Weight and shape: is there a correlation? • Mirror, mirror • We each need our own lifediet • Power foods • Super supplements • Super extras • Natural foods and herbal supplements

10 An Ageless Mind and Spirit 346

• The Ultimate Age defiers • New seekers • Brain fitness • Age cannot wither an active brain • Memory tricks • Train that brain! • Mind over matter • Why we forget • Brain games • Feed your head • Age with attitude • Don't clutter your mind or your life • Go for goals • The role of religion

• Therapy – new opiate of the masses? • Beating a retreat • Make your own luck and longevity

11 *The Pleasure Principle*   *374*

12 *Future Perfect?*   *394*

Introduction

We just HAD to do this book ... two anxious Baby Boomers in their mid-forties shouting, 'Hold on – what's happening?'

Sure, numerous books on ageing have been written by learned doctors, scientists, psychologists and academics. We are none of those things – although we have consulted many of them for this book and are very grateful for their generosity with their fascinating opinions as well as their research.

This is not an elitist beauty bible for 'high maintenance women' detailing expensive products and fashionable philosophies or therapies that require huge outlays of cash, and credibility (although we do consider some).

Nor is it just for – and about – the fortunate few who, by the luck of nature or nurture are naturally 'Superyoung', as defined by Dr David Weeks – one of many specialists in the field who have kindly shared their expertise with us.

The good news is that there's plenty that can be done to hold back the ravages usually associated with age.

UltraAge is for real women who may be looking and feeling their real age – or worse – but who want to change that fact and slow the clock down, if not send it into reverse. We hope it will be your resource guide to ageing confidently, joyfully and in style.

It was written by two working mothers who have little time or patience for pampering. We are blessed and burdened with family responsibilities, have juggled demanding careers and domestic responsibilities across two decades as well as trying to develop ourselves along the way. In that we are no different than many women of our generation.

Through our work – as an image consultant and a health journalist – and personal experiences we were both discovering a lot about the ageing process. Through our friendship we found we had the right combination of skills to examine the issues of ageing from different perspectives. We hope this means giving you a broader, more balanced view than many other books that promote one treatment or one theory or showcase unrealistic role models blessed with flawless genes and an unlimited bank balance.

We both yearned for 'the vision thing' to help us avoid the pitfalls of 'the age thing', but didn't have a lifetime – more like the odd lunchtime – in which to seek it. We didn't know exactly what we were looking for, but knew that a lot of other women were looking for it, too. One thing was certain: we didn't want to become yet two more moaning, menopausal matrons who couldn't laugh at themselves and keep life – and the horizon ahead – in perspective.

Curious to discover whether achieving longevity and a healthy old age were to any degree in our control or genetically pre-determined – 'in our stars or in ourselves' – we set out to see if there was any chance for those of us without lucky genes who have burned the candle at both ends up until mid-life. (We were cheered to be told, by some one who had lived long enough to know, that 'a person without a past doesn't have much future'!)

Is it possible to reset our biological clocks or, if not, to rejuvenate ourselves physically, emotionally and spiritually in order to get the most out of the years to come? The answer is yes – to a considerable degree, with more advances predicted for every additional year we can hang on in there. Things are changing so fast, the frontiers of science pushed forward so quickly, that even while writing this book new reports came out daily.

While the only sure alternative to ageing at the moment is death, the good news is that there's plenty that can be done to hold back the ravages usually associated with age which, we are thrilled to have found, need not be inevitable. Better still, this doesn't need to involve spending a fortune – or too much time obsessing!

If you're like us you don't have the time or inclination to grow your own organic food, squeeze your own carrot juice, be 'born again', search for your 'inner child' or imbibe expensive elixirs promising eternal youth. We assure you we're not keen to shoot up with growth hormones, live on a severely restricted diet or clone ourselves for spare parts – although we thought you'd like to know about some of these 'cutting-edge' concepts in the new field known as 'anti-ageing medicine'. We've even presented some ideas we find laughable, and hope that you will enjoy laughing at them too, since laughter is one of the best age defiers around! Our determination to investigate all the new possibilities came from a desire to be able to look ahead ourselves with enthusiasm rather than dread. We don't want to fight age, we want to work cooperatively with it, to age as healthily and actively as we can.

'Getting older is a certainty unless you die so you might as well get used to it.'

The words of the great and still gorgeous Catherine Deneuve at fifty-four seem to sum up our view admirably: 'I have a reasonable attitude towards my appearance. I think it's right to fight for some things, but I don't want to swim against the tide, the flow of time. I want to control it a little, of course, but I don't want to be in denial.'

We also applaud the absolutely fabulous Joanna Lumley's assertion that 'Getting older is a certainty unless you die so you might as well get used to it. It's all to do with looks, isn't it? Vanity. Pathetic, puerile vanity. You get wiser as you get older, but no one seems to give a jot.'

In our quest for knowledge we have visited anti-ageing clinics and menopause specialists and one of us even tried cosmetic surgery (despite the other's best efforts to stop her!) and played guinea pig in the HRT game of roulette. From these experiences, and from the experts we have consulted and the case studies we present, we hope you will draw inspiration, and maybe even a positive anti-ageing plan tailored to your personal aspirations.

In this book we share our findings with you. Some of them we've worked out for ourselves; others come from listening to feminists and earth mothers, beauties, businesswomen and brainy types who have formed their own philosophies for coping with ageing. We were eager to understand what fuels the spark of life and liveliness that keeps some people going strong long after their contemporaries have retired into a doddery dotage. We want to help other women, along with ourselves

and our daughters, to find out how to kindle our own spark and find the right fuels to keep it going.

Many women to whom we spoke were finding themselves up against a barrier more formidable than the 'glass ceiling' and worried about what, if anything, was on the other side. Others had successfully made the transition from outgrown youth and found a new vigour and serenity with age. You'll learn from them, as we did, practical ways to enhance and extend your own earning power as well as the value of your life's currency.

The internationally known experts to whom we are particularly grateful because they have acted as special consultants to us are Drs Thomas Crook (brain and memory), Vincent Giampapa (cosmetic surgery and anti-ageing medicine), Ronald Klatz (anti-ageing medicine), Ronald Marks (dermatology), Michael Perring (anti-ageing medicine), Dawn Skelton (anti-ageing exercises), Jan Stanek (cosmetic surgery), David Weeks (the 'Superyoung'), Professors Cary Cooper (stress and occupational health) and Craig Sharp (exercise physiology), Mr Joseph Jordan (consultant gynacologist), Daniel Field (hairdresser and colourist), Patrick Holford (nutritionist), Philip Kingsley (trichologist) and Lizzie Webb (exercise expert). You can read more about them, as well as the work of many others, in this book.

We hope you will be intrigued, as we are, by all the options, present and possible, that might help the human race realize its potential to live to well over a century in the coming millennium. But even if that prospect daunts you, as it does us, why not strive to improve the quality of every day with some of the easy, low-cost changes we recommend that don't require a radical change of life?

ADVICE TO THE READER

Before following any medical or dietary advice contained in this book, it is recommended that you consult your doctor if you suffer from any health problems or special conditions or are in any doubt as to its suitability.

1
Facing It

'If youth but knew, and old age
only could.'

HENRY ESTIENNE (1531–98)

Ageing: Time to Redefine

Ageing: it's been going on a long time but never before has the subject been so compelling, even sexy. In the third millennium, ageing will be one of the top hot issues facing not only policy-makers worried about meeting the burgeoning pension demands of the Baby-Boomer generation, but also scientists, sociologists, the medical profession, and a panoply of industries from health and beauty to technology and travel. The United Nations fittingly designated 1999 'The UN Year of the Older Person' as a gateway to a 'millennium of maturity', with an increasingly long-lived population which has greater expectations of age than ever before.

Sure, one day we'll die, but we want it to be later than our parents, and we want to grow older differently than they or their parents did. We see no reason why we shouldn't remain fit, happy and prosperous at eighty, ninety, a hundred and beyond – as the scientists of our generation are, increasingly, assuring us we can!

Ageing is hot because the 'can-do, let's sort the problem' generation is mid-life and viewing the horizon. This is the first generation that has grown up having the technology to change what they don't like about themselves from cosmetic surgery for each real or imagined imperfection to laser treatments for everything from short sightedness to wrinkles. So it's tempting, if a trifle arrogant, to regard ageing as a 'treatable condition' as specialists in the burgeoning new field of 'anti-ageing medicine' are now calling it.

This same generation created 'youth culture' and made being a free-wheeling flower-child groovy in the '60s. So not surprisingly it intends to make the menopausal and, eventually, the geriatric, hip (even with replacements) in the 2000s!

But for the moment we are no longer just young and don't like it. We were the ones who concurred with Pete Townshend of The Who that you could never trust anyone over thirty. But now, in our forties and fifties, we are trying to remain *integral* because just being viable isn't enough. We are used to having our opinions heard and we must keep contributing and shaping them, even if it is only to lead the way for younger generations nipping at our heels. Some of us have the sensation of teetering on the brink of an abyss and feel real panic or despair while many are seeking alternatives, or 'solutions' to feeling less than fulfilled because of simply getting older.

Freud said that, 'No one believes in his own death . . . in the unconscious everyone is convinced of his own immortality.' So it is with ageing. As Simone de Beauvoir put it, 'When it seizes our own personal life we are dumbfounded.' And the shock is compounded when the horrified features looking back at us from the mirror are those of our mother – or, worse still, our father! – particularly to a generation which protested we'd never be like our parents, and certainly never grow old as they did.

Dr Ronald Klatz, founder and president of the American Academy of Anti-Ageing Medicine reflects, 'The Baby Boomers said "No" to Vietnam and now they're saying "No" to ageing!' His research and books tell us how using nutrients, antioxidants and hormones can hold the ravages of age at bay.

> *'The Baby Boomers said "No" to Vietnam and now they're saying "No" to ageing!'*
>
> DR RONALD KLATZ

The whole anti-ageing movement is dedicated to the proposition that ageing is a treatable condition, that its negative aspects, the falling off in function and vitality, are actually due to disease and deficiencies which can be prevented or put right rather than to an inevitable decline. It is certainly an exciting thought.

But we hold that having a positive attitude towards the process is probably ultimately more important than all the pills and potions, surgery and therapies which claim to slow it down. We are not saying 'No' to ageing as we are two women who, like most, are pragmatists. Yet we do want to redefine what ageing means for those of us who will grow old in the twenty-first century.

Never before has a generation had such a good chance of being able to do just that. The fact that there is a new medical speciality known as 'anti-ageing medicine' – and numerous 'longevity' associations boasting thousands of members internationally – shows just how serious the urge to hold back time, or some of its more depressing effects, has become. Gerontology – traditionally the medicine of coping with old age – may eventually be replaced by this school of medicine, which is aimed at prolonging youthful and vigorous life. Gerontology was always known as the Cinderella speciality because it attracted so little funding and prestige. Anti-ageing medicine may prove to be its Fairy Godmother.

What Does Thirty or Fifty Really Look Like?

Even before the advent of the anti-ageing movement, people of fifty had begun looking and feeling like thirty-five-year-olds used to – or trying to do so. But that's not enough for some. They want to be thirty-five again, to have the energies, enzymes and waistlines of a thirty-five-year-old. Women in their fifties, and even sixties (like Britain's Elizabeth Buttle) are demanding the right to have babies even if they have to borrow younger women's eggs to do so. They want to look lithe and to be limber in leotards, still wear the jeans (but with added Lycra and stretchable waistlines, please) they grew up in and not succumb to the ageing styles or frame of mind that their mothers slipped into at that age.

On her fiftieth birthday, Germaine Greer called herself 'a chronic adolescent', saying she had 'grown old without ever having grown up. At fifty, with a thickening waistline and grizzled hair, jowls that show a pronounced tendency to droop and an intermittent sciatica that shoots down my right leg like lightning, you'd think I was becoming a solid citizen, but I am as much of a ratbag as ever,' she boasted, posing on a Harley-Davidson.

The impact of the media on our mindset has made the quest for the mythical Fountain of Youth a greater priority than it was in the days of the explorer Ponce de Leon. Hollywood stars perpetuate myths of perfection. Julie Christie found that she couldn't keep up with the rest of them without succumbing to a facelift at fifty-seven. 'I fought against it because it was not something I wanted to do but, I mean, my jawline isn't exactly the one I was born with,' she said in an interview to promote the film *Afterglow*, a title which seemed to sum up the way she looked after her surgery. With commendable candour she confessed, 'It is hard as the face changes and your mind isn't changing at the same pace as your body. The realization that youth is no longer yours takes quite a long time because you've spent all your life being young and nobody tells you what it's like not to be.'

I wasn't going to wait until fifty-seven like Julie Christie, and opted for surgical help in my forties, as you will read in Chapter Six. This was not in a mad pursuit of youth but to correlate my sad, drooping face with a still bounding inner spirit. Thus Baby Boomers are taking pre-emptive strikes at ageing. Surgical treatments and non-surgical

techniques (Chapter Six), hormone replacement (Chapter Four), anti-oxidants and new exercise regimes (Chapter Nine), alternative thera-pies and retreats (Chapter Ten), training for new careers (Chapter Eight), swapping or rejuvenating their partners along with themselves (Chapter Eleven) are all part of the arsenal.

Older women make up the largest part of the population, and our cohort is growing faster than any other group on the planet! According to the US Census Bureau there are now 310 million females over the age of sixty against men of the same age who number 251 million. By 2025 there will be a whopping 645 million women over sixty, with men predicted to number a mere 546 million. 'This has a huge implication for society,' according to the Bureau. 'Older women are more likely to be widowed, to live alone and to live in poverty.' The fastest growing age group is the over eighties. They now number 42 million, compared with 23 million men. By 2025 there will 100 million women over eighty (62 million men). Elderly women will emerge as a hugely influential sector of the electorates of most Western countries (according to the *American Journal of Foreign Affairs* in 1998).

Pushing Back the Clock is Not Politically Correct – Yet

There are many who resist the notion that you can 'turn back the clock' and argue that this relentless pursuit of youth is a massive conspiracy of multi-national beauty and diet businesses, the media and the enter-tainment industry. We are constantly bombarded with idealized images we can't possibly hope to live up to – and nor should we. It is this that causes lovely young women (and even many older ones) to turn anorexic and allows cowboy cosmetic surgeons to make millions altering perfectly good noses and chins or suctioning fat out of buttocks that don't really have any to spare. It is this that makes the cosmetics and slimming industries the mega-billion buckers they are today, with new products launched seemingly daily to feed off our insecurities and promising the impossible soon . . . for only £30, £50 or £100 a month.

There will be some who will rail against advice that after a certain age a woman is advised not to wear white leather or expose her cleavage before 8 p.m.; or that it's time to pack up the pearlized eyeshadow along with trainers (apart from when working out) and halter tops.

What a difference two decades makes! Some of us get leaner and more sinewy with age, others fill out a bit. Look what my passion for running has done to accelerate things (being energetic in Boston, 1978, and at the end of a 20-mile cliff run in 1997), while Victoria's ageing is far less obvious – although she says only her hair is the same (relaxing in Naples, 1970, and in Cornwall, 1998).

How dare we, you cry. What about Vivienne Westwood, Dolly Parton, Joan Collins, Goldie Hawn, Shirley MacLaine, Edna O'Brien, Molly Parkin, not to mention countless other mature beauties who can happily defy such conventions?

We hail them with you, but insist that you do a reality check on your own life and the people you need or want to influence. Most of us still have to get along with co-workers and go to the supermarket, and don't want to appear eccentric or larger than life. You will find plenty of scope in our suggestions and we leave it to you to decide what's best for you. We will poke fun, and possibly insult some of your sensibilities. But we didn't want to write another academic tome that takes itself too seriously. If you can't have a laugh at yourself (and we have plenty of laughs at our own expense) then you will get older faster!

Face It, Don't Fake It

'He who fears death dies many times before his time' goes an ancient proverb. In the same way, those that fear ageing will die a thousand small deaths if they see each new wrinkle as another nail in the coffin rather than as a mark of experience. You might try to fake your age, but eventually you'll have to face it. That first grey hair, the wrinkle that doesn't go away when you stop laughing, crêpey skin on your neck and hands, and ebbing energy levels all seem harbingers of things to come, some better, a lot worse. You realize that you can't accomplish what you used to: a minor injury doesn't heal as quickly; you notice an aching in your joints in certain weather; you come into a room and forget why you're there; it takes you a while to unstiffen when you get out of bed in the morning. Suddenly, you realize you are moving like your grandmother once did!

Sue, a woman Victoria sometimes swims with, was thrilled to hear about this book. 'Because it is traumatic, ageing,' she said as they side-stroked alongside each other. Sue, a woman in her mid-fifties, and enjoying early retirement from a teaching career, looked fit and happy. But she told of her inner turmoil about growing old, and how frightening it was, and how horrified she was 'to look in the mirror and see my mother'. A sixty-two-year-old who overheard the conversation chirped in, 'What's all this sighing about?' Gesturing to the baby grand-daughter she'd been swimming with she said, 'She won't have to suffer with arthritis and stiff joints and the things I have from getting down on my knees to scrub and carrying heavy bags of groceries because I didn't have a car.' That may be so, but her granddaughter will have to contend with a more sedentary, computer-centred life, with a diet of chemical compounds calling themselves food, and whatever new stresses manifest themselves in the twenty-first century. The main benefit her granddaughter will enjoy is improved awareness of what causes the deteriorations we associate with age and which are avoidable aspects that can be prevented or, at least, postponed.

Ageing Through the Ages

Men have traditionally worried about getting old because it meant loss of strength and status – the young buck ousting the old stag as leader of the pack. Women have always worried about getting old because it meant loss of the beauty and fertility that were their main stock in trade in society. So, while Julius Caesar was kept from feeling his age by Cleopatra, and covered his baldness with laurel wreaths, the Egyptian queen was anxiously oiling her hair and bathing in asses' milk to keep her skin supple. Her milk baths probably worked because the lactic acid present in milk would act as an exfoliant, leaving the skin softer and more glowing. That is why there are several new beauty products on the market which make use of milk proteins (Marie Antoinette preferred red wine to keep wrinkles at bay, and a new cosmetic range makes use of this ingredient).

Queen Elizabeth I – the reputedly 'Virgin' queen who used her femininity as one of the prime weapons in her powerful arsenal – was petrified, it seems, of looking old even as she welcomed every year of her long life. It was possibly thoughts of her make-up, reputed to be several inches thick towards the end of her life to cover her wrinkles, that prompted Shakespeare to have Hamlet tell the skull of Yorrick, 'Now get you to my lady's chamber, and tell her, let her paint an inch thick, to this favour she must come; make her laugh at that . . .' Queen Elizabeth would not have been amused.

Despite her ferocious jealousy of younger women in her court, she kept a sharp mind into her seventies, and loved nothing more than honing it with political wheeler-dealing. She was, in many ways, not unlike the twentieth-century political icon Margaret Thatcher, who was

known to be captivating to many men while she wielded power in her sixties and seventies.

Aristophanes' play *Ecclesiazusae* was one of the first and bravest to portray women needing erotic love when they are old. In the play, the women take over the government of Athens and introduce a law decreeing that no young man can enjoy his girlfriend without first giving sexual services to any elderly woman who is attracted to him. This, along with other marvellous literary references to love in old age, has been gathered by gerontologist Dr Hamilton Gibson (aged eighty-three) in his book *Love in Later Life*. He also dredged up a wonderful poem, celebrating the charms of older women, by Philodemus, translated thus:

> Charito is more than sixty
> Yet her hair is still a dense forest,
> No brassiere holds up the marble cones
> Of her high-pointed breasts.
> Her unwrinkled flesh exhales ambrosia
> And myriads of teasing charms. . . .

But Chaucer and Shakespeare have been more harsh on older women with the former (in *The Merchant's Tale*) saying '. . . Old beef is no so good as tender veal. I'll have no woman thirty years of age – that's only fodder, bean straw for a cage.'

Shakespeare, despite his sensitive understanding of human nature is cruel on the subject of mature love: Hamlet says to his mother Gertrude, '. . . at your age, the heyday in the blood is tame, it's humble and waits upon judgement . . .' and blames her for succumbing to Claudius's sexual advances. He also mocks Polonius, Lancelot Gobbo and other old characters, but by and large aged men have enjoyed some respect in society and literature while women were reviled as witches or laughed at as pantomime dames.

The film *Sunset Boulevard*, turned into a popular musical by Andrew Lloyd Webber, poignantly illustrates society's fear and horror of the older woman – particularly if she is predatory, with an eye for younger men. But today both roles for older women (look at the successes of actresses such as Meryl Streep, Glenn Close, Judi Dench and Helen Mirren) and the role of older women in society is changing thanks to advances in appearance, aspirations and attitude.

Goldie Hawn (at 24 and 50) keeps us laughing with her belief that getting older is more than all right.

Tina Turner (at 32 and 57) proved that women can not only survive a destructive marriage but thrive as a result.

From model to actress to fashion muse to fashion arbiter, Catherine Deneuve (at 23 and 54) revels as the doyenne of European beauty.

Fashions have come and gone while Lauren Bacall (at around 20 and at 73) has an inimitable – and indomitable – style that remains timeless.

Ageing is an Attitude Thing

Dr Ronald Klatz predicts that within thirty years the human race has the potential to be on the verge of immortality, or at least to live to its potential of over one hundred years – as long as we don't kill ourselves off first through war or environmental havoc, that is.

But for the time being ageing is one of the few certainties in life unless you die young. So when you consider the alternative it may not seem so bad. As the well-known Euro-TV personality, agony aunt and animal expert Katie Boyle, still bubbly and beautiful in her sixties, put it, 'You've got to look at it all as life's rich pageant, and take things like the menopause in your stride.' Katie is far from a let-it-all-hang-out earth mother. Her hair is blonde and bouffant, her maquillage always immaculate, and although she hasn't had cosmetic surgery on her face she had no qualms about resorting to it to reduce her painfully large bosom. And when she gains more than five pounds she makes sure she does something about it. That's sensible body maintenance and personal pride, not panic about getting older.

'No disease . . . is more lethal than the boredom that follows retirement. The body goes into a state of rapid deterioration when it loses its reason for being.'

NORMAN COUSINS

Some years ago, Pat York, the American photographer wife of English actor Michael York, compiled a book she called *Going Strong*, consisting of portraits and interviews with seventy-five over seventy-five-year-olds who were still very much in the mainstream. Some are still going strong at the time of writing. Not all of them looked young, but all were active, vigorous and very much in possession of all their marbles.

One thing in common among the impressive international list, which included fashion designer Sir Hardy Amies, philanthropist Brooke Astor, comedian George Burns, libel lawyer Peter Carter-Ruck, novelist Barbara Cartland, television chef Julia Child, Professor John Kenneth Galbraith, actor Sir John Geilgud, public relations guru Eleanor Lambert, author and historian Elizabeth (Countess of) Longford, veteran film critic Dilys Powell and sculptor and ceramicist Beatrice Wood was their love of what they did. The amazing thing was that most of them were still involved in careers that had engrossed them all their lives. This positive attitude towards their work helped to keep

them going. As the late Norman Cousins wrote, 'No disease . . . is more lethal than the boredom that follows retirement . . . The body goes into a state of rapid deterioration when it loses its reason for being . . .'

It's the looking forward not backward that characterizes UltraAgers. You've got to keep looking forward to work and fun to keep pace with the real world. A rich fantasy life may also help if you are past the age of actualizing your dreams. Beatrice Wood, who died at 105, said that her 'dream lover' visited her each night when she was in bed and that he helped to keep her young! 'When we're completely free of any kind of desire, I think the will to live ceases,' she observed. Wood's three key precepts to successful ageing were to focus on the present, to realize that few things are worth getting agitated about, and to keep the mind open to new learning and experiences. That probably had every bit as much to do with her longevity as the fact that she was a small eater, a vegetarian, and physically active; attributes explored later in this book.

The Labels are Changing

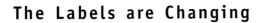

The language and the labels of old age are being fine-tuned. We resist becoming 'wrinklies' or pensioners. 'I'm the oldest of the Baby Boomers,' President Clinton declared. 'I'm what you'd call near elderly.' According to the insurance actuaries this group covers forty- to sixty-year-olds. Some would say that President Clinton was simply enjoying adultescence, another new phase in the phrases of life that Boomers have coined. Other Americans, increasingly sensitive about getting their jargon spot-on and as inoffensive as possible (hence, often ending up with bland politically correct euphemisms), banter with categories like the 'almost old' as well as the 'older Americans'. The American Association of Retired Persons (AARP) currently avoids 'senior citizens', an improvement on previous labels, in favour of 'the mature market', a term which would be more approved of by the ageing activist movement known as The Grey Panthers, who walk softly but carry big sticks!

Whatever the political, economic or demographic umbrella, being the right side of (i.e. over) forty means belonging to the First World's sexiest cohort. Gail Sheehy's *New Passages* has been the most lyrical tract yet in redefining age cohorts. She uses phrases like the flourishing

forties, the flaming fifties, serene sixties, uninhibited eighties, nobility of the nineties and celebratory centenarians. She's helped us look forward to moving on from 'middlescence' in our forties into the 'age of mastery' in the fifties, followed by the 'age of integrity' in our sixties to finally reach 'coalescence'. Doesn't it all sound wonderful? Can you wait to be in these enlightened, fulfilling new phases? There is plenty to look forward to, as we hope you will feel from reading this book, as well as Sheehy's and others listed in our bibliography. It's better to be over the hill than under it!

Ageism: The Buck Stops With You

It won't do you any good to be the most wonderful-looking seventy-something on your street if you feel useless and cast aside in society. Yet many older people do today, thanks to mandatory retirement ages and patronizing treatment of 'pensioners'.

Across the First World the projected number of young people is due to fall over the next twenty-five years. As the Baby Boom genera-tion ages and the smaller cohorts born in the '70s and '80s enter the job market, the percentage of the population within working age will fall as a proportion of the total population, causing governments worries about pension schemes, health services and how a smaller working population is going to support a larger, non-working one.

We will make it fashionable to be old in the early twenty-first century!

We could argue that it is the attitudes to ageing and ageing workers that must alter, rather than pensions. And the quickest way to start changing those attitudes is to start to change them in yourself and in your own expectations for old age. It is ridiculous to force active, ener-getic, forward-looking people to retire at sixty or sixty-five if they don't want to – just as it can be cruel to force young parents or burned-out forty-five-year-olds to stay on a relentless treadmill without enough time to enjoy their families or to re-charge their batteries.

It is up to us to change rigid attitudes and, as the biggest ever cohort of forty-somethings moves inexorably into late middle age, there are signs that we can. More companies are becoming receptive to flexitime and part-time working as a way to keep skilled employees, and to keep

them fresh. As corporations 'downsize' they typically become aware of the advantages of using experienced freelance workers, consultants or 'interim managers' for specialist tasks, in order to keep their core work-force at a reasonable size.

A word of consolation: If you are easing into 'old age' in the first quarter of the next millennium then you will be in good company. The largest social group will be ageing with you, and that should cause a huge attitude shift towards oldies. Baby Boomers created the trend towards peace, love and flower power in the '60s and '70s, towards Yuppification and parenthood in the '80s, towards New Age mysticism and millennial seeking in the '90s. We will make it fashionable to be old in the early twenty-first century! We will have more company, and more help, than our mothers and grandmothers. And we will have the bene-fits of hundreds of books, written by bewildered Boomers struggling with the process themselves and sharing their thoughts and triumphs.

How Old Are You Really?

A good place to start is to find out your age . . . not the one on your birth certifi-cate but the one you are in terms of attitude, health, fitness and image. Answer the following questions with true or false to see how close the age you identify with – your real age – is to your chronological age.

1. I feel puffed when I have to walk up a flight of stairs. *True/False*

2. The music my children like always sounds too loud yet when I am watching television I have to turn up the volume to hear it properly. *True/False*

3. I am not the least bit interested in knowing who is top of the charts these days. *True/False*

4. The print in the telephone directory and on food and medicine pack-aging is too small to read. *True/False*

5. When I've been a bit piggy with food for a time I find it hard to get back on track eating sensibly. *True/False*

6. Watching television makes me drowsy, and is particularly good for encouraging catnaps. *True/False*

7. I have trouble opening bottles and jars. *True/False*

8. Elasticized waistbands on skirts and trousers are wonderfully practical and stylish. *True/False*

9. I don't feel confident driving at night. *True/False*

10. Facial hair is a fact of life after a certain age. *True/False*

11. Taking vitamins is for hypochondriacs. *True/False*

12. After a long walk or a game of tennis/golf, my muscles and joints seize up and really ache for a day or two afterwards. *True/False*

13. When it's icy outside I tend to stay indoors rather than risk a fall. *True/False*

14. I am not really aware of the frequency of my bowel movements. *True/False*

15. The only websites in my home are those created by spiders. *True/False*

16. I find it more difficult to lose weight these days even though I stick religiously to a low-calorie diet. *True/False*

17. My skin feels dry most of the year. *True/False*

18. Forgetfulness happens to everyone. There is little to be done about it after a certain age. *True/False*

19. I have been developing freckles in the last few years which don't fade when my suntan does. *True/False*

20. I am slower on the keyboard (or with my knitting needles) than I was. *True/False*

21. I've never tried line dancing or yoga. *True/False*

22. I've read the same newspaper for years. *True/False*

23. A dinner party is always preferable to a night club. *True/False*

24. Racy novels are for the lonely and unfulfilled. *True/False*

25. Jogging, skiing, or scuba diving should never be started after fifty. *True/False*

26. I never forget a face but the name that goes with it is easy to forget. *True/False*

27. There's little point in travelling abroad until you have fully explored your own backyard. *True/False*

28. Bits of food seem to get stuck in between my teeth all the time. *True/False*

29. Foreplay is embarrassing in a long-term relationship. *True/False*

30. There is saggy skin beneath my chin. *True/False*

31. I wouldn't pay to have a bone density test. *True/False*

32. If I pinch the back of my hand it takes a while for the skin to drop back. *True/False*

33. I have to conserve my energy and miss my old 'get up and go'. *True/False*

34. Cosmetic dentistry is for celebrities. *True/False*

35. I don't like being massaged and wouldn't massage myself let alone others. *True/False*

36. I have to urinate more frequently than I used to. *True/False*

37. Swimming is enough exercise for me. *True/False*

38. Talking to plants and pets is an early sign of dementia. *True/False*

39. I would choose CNN over MTV any day. *True/False*

40. It is unseemly to belly laugh in public. *True/False*

41. If a body-pierced punk sat next to me on a flight, train, or bus I would move seats. *True/False*

42. Cocktail parties are a strain on the ears as well as the back. *True/False*

43. Varicose veins are normal later in life. *True/False*

44. Make-up is a waste of money after mid-life. *True/False*

45. Long hair is ageing on women. *True/False*

46. Medical advice when you aren't ill is indulgent. *True/False*

47. My feet and ankles tend to swell after a long day. *True/False*

48. The prospect of sex doesn't excite me. I'd prefer a good book or movie any day. *True/False*

49. My toes and fingers go numb very quickly in cold weather. *True/False*

50. I am sleeping a lot less than I used to. *True/False*

Your Score

0 to 10 True Answers

You are an UltraAger interested in new places and people and in charge of your own health and image as you age. This book will show you how to continue to look after yourself and how to pursue new adventures regardless of your age.

10 to 25 True Answers

You are as old as your birth certificate and stuck in a few ruts. Explore ways to break loose of traditions and routines and re-invent your future. How you age is a matter of what you choose to do now about your health and lifestyle. The steps you take after reading this book could knock ten years – at least – off your age.

25 to 40 True Answers

You are older than you need to be both in image and in spirit. Who says your adventures are over or that you can't go salsa dancing or windsurfing? Your body is as lax as your spirit. Let's see if we can re-charge your batteries and make you feel young and energetic again.

40 to 50 True Answers

You might have your eye on a Zimmer frame but there is hope for you yet, simply because you are reading this book. *Don't put it down* until you find ten new ways to feel younger and more positive about living. Take this quiz again, once you finish reading *UltraAge*, and see how much younger you are.

ANALYSE YOUR ANSWERS TO THE QUIZ

1. Good that you are taking the stairs instead of a lift, but huffing and puffing conveys that you aren't as fit as you need to be. Consider how you can walk more every day, not at a leisurely ramble but power-walking. See Chapter Nine for details.

2. Hearing deterioration is a fact of life and will begin earlier for Baby Boomers who rocked around the clock at concerts and discos and latterly blasted their Walkman stereos too high for too long. Read more about hearing loss in Chapter Three.

3. Okay, so today's music might not be your cup of tea. But asking kids' opinions of some of their favourite pop stars and groups will ensure you are a 'golden oldie'. Keeping your children and grand-children interested in you means maintaining an interest in them and their lives. See Chapters Ten and Eleven for more tips on improving relationships.

4. Visual impairment may come quicker to those of us who read excessively or spend too many hours in front of our computers. Read more (with your specs) in Chapter Three and check Chapter Nine to see if you are getting the extra help needed from your food and supplements.

5. The idea of sensible eating sounds so boring. Why not rethink your attitude towards food as fuel while still allowing scope for regular treats (Chapter Eleven). You might never want to 'pig out' again.

6. Sleep patterns can alter as we age but your catnaps could cause insomnia. Read more in Chapters Three and Nine.

7. Stiff joints and physical weakness can make the simplest task, like opening a jar, a performance. Read how you can improve your manual dexterity and strength without having to wear a leotard and lift barbells. See Chapter Nine.

8. Elasticated waistbands are comfy but can be very ageing unless you know how to choose and wear them. See Chapter Seven for tips.

9. Vision difficulties, e.g. night blindness and macular degeneration, require coping skills along with antioxidants. See Chapter Three to see if it is time for a trip to an ophthalmologist (a medical doctor with an eye speciality) for treatment.

10. After the menopause those prickly hairs can start sprouting every-where you don't want them. But you don't need to just sit there

stroking your whiskers. See Chapter Five for ways to deal with facial hair.

11. Vitamins stand for vitality. Read the latest research on what's best for your lifestyle (Chapter Nine) and what the anti-ageing gurus recommend (Chapter Twelve).

12. Tendonitis and bursitis are two afflictions of the occasionally active but unfit. Read how to avoid stiff muscles and aching joints by keeping yourself limber and active. See Chapter Nine.

13. Breaks and fractures are synonymous with osteoporosis. Bone thinning starts in the menopause. Discover if you are a likely candidate. Read on for what you can do now to strengthen, and even improve, your bones. See Chapter Four.

14. Your digestive system is a harbinger of your health. Monitor it regularly. For more advice see Chapter Nine.

15. Even if you can't afford an Internet link at home, it's worth checking out a friend's computer or your local library to tune in and link up with the world. As we all might be working well beyond traditional retirement ages, keeping pace with technology will keep you learning and earning. For more details on work see Chapter Eight.

16. Weight gain changes as we age and requires new approaches depending upon where you are with the menopause or beyond and what your lifestyle requires. See Chapter Nine for advice.

17. Dry skin can result from a variety of factors. If yours is dry year-round you are looking older than you are. See Chapter Five for help.

18. The forgetful oldie is a stereotype that doesn't need to be you. See what you can do with your diet to keep razor sharp along with some brain teasing exercises in Chapter Ten.

19. Age or sun spots were caused years ago. Read more about them in Chapter Three and learn about new remedies in Chapter Five.

20. There are more than one hundred kinds of arthritis, some of which are linked to our immune systems and hormones. Learn how to tackle it in Chapter Three.

21. If you haven't been dancing in the last year you are becoming an old fogey. Get your dancing shoes ready and learn why you will be younger as a result in Chapters Nine and Eleven.

22. Limiting knowledge and views from a small coterie of pals, the same newspaper or breakfast TV programme means that you might not be flexing your brain enough. Learn why debating (not arguing)

and keeping informed keeps you employable (Chapter Eight) as well as good company (Chapter Eleven).

23. Indeed, a dinner party might be easier on the nerves than a bop at a club, but trying new experiences keeps you young. Learn why in Chapters Ten and Eleven.

24. Racy fiction may stimulate your fantasies and be all you need to help you feel sensuous if not down right sexy. Learn why sex is one of the keys to longevity in Chapter Twelve along with the possibilities if you are foot-loose and fancy-free in Chapter Eleven.

25. If you are fit enough there is no reason why you can't explore new sports and adventures. Learn how in Chapter Nine.

26. Memory loss may be linked to your diet – see Chapter Nine. Learn more about keeping track of things in Chapter Ten.

27. Travel broadens the mind and needn't require a re-mortgage on the house. Do some research to learn about the adventures that you might try to feel more alive and fulfilled.

28. Our teeth not only give away our age but their condition can possibly damage our health. Read more in Chapter Three.

29. Learn how to spice up your relationship without kinky underwear or embarrassing appliances. See Chapter Eleven.

30. Saggy skin can be minimized with make-up (Chapter Five) or annihilated with cosmetic surgery. See Chapter Six.

31. A bone-density test is an investment in your long-term health. Read why in Chapter Four.

32. Your hands state your age but also the kind of woman you are. Do yours give out the message you want? See Chapters Five and Six.

33. Loss of energy is not a prerequisite of older age. Lots of twenty-somethings are more sluggish than their grandparents. Read how to keep vibrant via diet and exercise in Chapter Nine.

34. A beautiful smile is as important to you as it is to your friends. Does yours let you down due to bad teeth? See Chapters Five and Nine for suggestions.

35. Massage, whether self-administered or provided by a friend, is both relaxing and pleasurable. Learn the necessary touch techniques in Chapter Eleven.

36. Kidney and bladder difficulties may result from childbirth and cause both embarrassment and discomfort for women. Exercise and diet can provide real improvement. See Chapters Two and Nine.

37. Swimming is wonderful, all-over exercise but it cannot prevent bone loss. Learn more in Chapters Four and Nine.

38. A touch of eccentricity is welcome in all women liberated from earlier duties and roles. Learn how to do what you want in Chapter Ten.

39. To keep in tune with the times means not getting stuck in a rut. Learn how to keep pace with younger workmates in Chapters Eight and Ten.

40. Laughter is essential to good health. Learn how to give and get more laughs in your life in Chapters Ten and Eleven.

41. Welcome the opportunity to speak to anyone different and to expand your horizons regardless of your age. It's one of the secrets of longevity. See Chapters Ten and Twelve.

42. Asking others to constantly repeat themselves makes us tedious company. How to prevent hearing loss can be found in Chapter Three.

43. Varicose veins can be prevented and dealt with. Learn more in Chapters Three and Six.

44. Make-up is worthwhile both in terms of time and money, but it doesn't need to cost a lot to look terrific. See Chapter Five.

45. If your hair is an asset, you can wear it however you want. Learn how to make the most of yours in Chapters Two and Five.

46. Don't hesitate to get advice on feeling well. Maybe you need alternative guidance to feel in peak condition. See Chapters Nine and Ten.

47. Bloating and water retention can be endemic to the menopause. Learn how to treat these conditions in Chapter Four.

48. Do whatever tickles your fancy, be it making love or tending your garden. Pleasure is the key to a long and happy life. Learn why in Chapter Eleven.

49. Poor circulation can be painful and prevent you from enjoying life. Learn the causes and treatments in Chapter Three.

50. Sleep disorders are pervasive. Learn how to get the rest you need in Chapter Three.

2

The Seven Ages of Women

'Every age has its pleasures, its style of wit,
and its own ways.'

NICOLAS BOILEAU-DESPREAUX (1636–1711)

A Woman for All Seasons

At every age and stage of adult life we can hear, if we are alert for it, 'Time's winged chariot hurrying near'. If we don't get into a flap but prepare ourselves adequately for the future, it is less likely to land heavily on us, crushing our egos and self-image in the process. Helen Gurley Brown, editor of the youth-orientated magazine *Cosmopolitan* in America until she was seventy-three, and advocate of 'Having It All', says she began writing her book *The Late Show* when she suddenly realized that she was taking ageing so badly because she 'expected to go on forever being the *jeune fille*, [a] little waif-girl right into my nineties'.

If you haven't been aware of the whisper of Time's wings, that chariot can swoop in on you so suddenly that the shock can be brutal. Enjoying each stage of life while being aware of what you can do to maximize your health and enjoyment in the next is the way to ensure that that chariot stays well behind you until you are ready for it to scoop you up and carry you away in comfort.

Here we discuss the 'seven ages of women': up to the twenties (for ageing-discussion purposes there is little point in going through adolescent acne and angst); the thirties; the forties; the fifties; the sixties; the seventies, and the eighties and beyond. We asked leading experts in areas that impact on ageing to give us their view of what happens, for good and bad, during these seven life stages, and what steps we can take to prepare for what is predictable and to prevent the preventable. We won't cross-reference every point here – you can use the index at the back of the book to find where we give you more detailed information about most of these topics, for instance, in the chapters that discuss diet, exercise, beauty and cosmetic surgery. Sometimes just being informed and aware of what is likely to happen is enough to help you cope. If you allow it to stress you unduly it's much more likely to age you prematurely (See Stress in Chapter Three.)

Like Dickens' Ghost of Christmas Yet To Come, we will be showing you some frightening images of what *might* be, but not necessarily what *will* be if you are lucky or determined enough. Just because wrinkles tend to start appearing in earnest in the forties doesn't mean yours will, and just because muscle tone is generally lost in the fifties doesn't mean that you can't still look fantastic, particularly if you follow our concensus of advice.

At birth a man in Britain has a life expectancy of 74.1 years, a woman of 79.4. But when the man reaches 40 he has a life expectancy of 75.9 years, and a woman of 40 can expect to live until she is 80.5 years old. By the age of 50 a man can expect to live until he is 76.7 years old, but a 50-year-old woman has a projected lifespan of 81.2 years. At 60 these figures go up to 78.3 for men and 82.3 for women. By the time a man and woman reach the age of 70 he can expect to live until he's 81.4 years old, she until she's 84.6. A man of 80 should enjoy 6.5 more years of life and a woman of 80 to live to 88.5.

Don't feel bad if you've already marred your twenties by over-enthusiastic sun-tanning, or your thirties by yo-yo dieting. There is the chance to improve your health and fitness in every decade, and even ninety-year-olds showed considerable improvement in muscle mass and tone after twelve weeks on a suitable exercise programme. Remember, you may not have a model figure or a wrinkle-free face, but the very fact that you've already lived into your forties, fifties, or sixties gives you a much better than average chance of living into your seventies, eighties or nineties. With every year you've survived, the chances of you living to a ripe old age increase (see below), and with advances in medicine and knowledge there is an ever greater chance of living longer the longer you live!

Slowing the Ageing Process

Don't also feel that you have to follow every piece of advice from every expert. The authors certainly don't, and in some instances we may be reporting on options of surgery, hormonal therapy or 'anti-ageing' remedies that we ourselves wouldn't contemplate – at least not at the moment. Some of the experts even conflict on certain points, with the anti-ageing specialist recommending AHA (alpha hydroxy acid) skin peels at an early age and the dermatologist disagreeing about the benefits. We just want you to know the choices that are open to you. You might completely shun a surgical solution, or moan at exercise or diet suggestions. Our message is to take up what inspires you, and save other ideas for if and when they might seem more relevant. Bear in mind also that research in this field is advancing fast, so today's daring, 'cutting-edge' therapy may be commonplace, or completely discounted, tomorrow.

However, we're absolutely not advising that you should become obsessive about producing an anti-ageing plan or become paranoid at

every sign of age. The stress of that would only age you even quicker. But you might be forewarned, we hope, and therefore forearmed, against some of the odder effects of age – like the fact that the composition of your breast tissue will change and that your voice will grow more reedy as your hormone levels drop. (Can't you tell a lot about most people's age on the phone? Men's voices become higher and more piping as their testosterone levels lower, women's gruffen without oestrogen.) Or like the fact that your nose and earlobes will actually grow longer with age – and what to do about it! – or that a weak platysma muscle (what?) in the neck is a dead give-away that you're on the wrong-side of forty.

Your Expert Advisers

Let us first introduce you to the experts we have most closely consulted for this decade-by-decade guide.

Dr David Weeks is a clinical neuropsychologist at the Jardine Clinic of the Royal Edinburgh Infirmary in Scotland, and expert on the 'Superyoung', the title of his book (Hodder & Stoughton, 1998) and the subject of years of research into 3,500 people who looked and felt considerably younger than their age. He is also an expert on brain fitness and has developed mind-games to help prevent mental abilities declining with age. The biggest tip he gave us is, 'Try to learn something new every day, not just every decade. Don't let a single day go by without having some sort of new or joyful experience.' He also advocates the importance of powerful interests in work and hobbies, which most of his 'Superyoung' had benefited from. 'Remember also that ageing isn't linear: it doesn't affect all the body's systems equally,' he warns. 'Ageing is accelerated by anxiety, fear, anger and hate.'

Professor Cary J. Cooper, our stress expert, is an American who is professor of occupational psychology at the University of Manchester's Institute of Science and Technology (UMIST) in England, and who is internationally respected for his research on stress at home and in the workplace. He believes that the forties are the crunch point in women's lives, a critical transition stage, a literal change of life even for those who aren't yet undergoing the biological change of life. 'I think the forties are the worst time for women,' he says. 'Beyond that it gets better!'

Joseph Jordan, consultant gynaecologist, is a Fellow of the Royal College of Obstetricians and Gynaecologists and director of the Birmingham and Midland Women's Hospital Trust in Britain. Internationally known as a pioneer and leading practitioner of many gynaecological techniques, he is also an expert in hormone replacement therapy (HRT), and was involved (with Professor John Studd) in opening the first HRT clinic available on Britain's National Health Service in 1972. He believes HRT is not only safe but a boon for post-menopausal women – his own mother only came off it at eighty-three. But he knows that making the choice each woman is happy with is crucial, rather than relying on general principles for everyone – a philosophy we strongly support. 'You have to consider the woman as a whole,' he believes. Too many gynaecologists, women complain, seem to think of their patients as wombs without views. He has found that 'a positive attitude' is possibly the most important factor in recovering from health problems.

Professor Craig Sharp is professor of sports science at England's Brunel University. He has worked with Olympians and leading sportspeople of all kinds to improve their performance and potential, and is the exercise physiologist we consulted. He says, 'A leading question to ask is, "How old would you think you were if you didn't know how old you are?" I'd predict the disparity between theory and fact in the answer would give an indication of the exercise level of the individual.' He believes that while we cannot escape our genetic programming – at least not yet – 'a great deal can be done to minimize the detraining aspects of ageing by modest exercise programmes which embrace some conditioning in strength and flexibility as well as the more commonly prescribed and performed aerobic exercises.' He comforts us with the fact that from 'one hundred metres to 10,000 metres, men and women of eighty respectively take only fifty-five per cent and seventy-five per cent longer to cover the distance than they did at forty, while there is a virtual plateau in performance between the ages of twenty and forty.'

'How old would you think you were if you didn't know how old you are?'

Dr Michael Perring is our British anti-ageing specialist, a pioneer in his field, who runs the Optimal Health centres in London specializing in the type of anti-ageing programmes more commonly seen in the US. Whereas Dr Weeks' philosophy is 'use it or you lose it', Dr Perring's prescription is 'lose it and I'll replace it for you'. He is also a sex therapist who is aware of the sexual problems which can be encountered in each decade. He believes that 'You must find a way to continue to have a sensual life even if you are on your own,' and that in old age, 'A woman can gain a lot of power if she has the confidence to be freed from the constraints of convention.'

Dr Vincent Giampapa is our American anti-ageing specialist and consultant on cosmetic surgery. He runs the Longevity Institutes International and is one of the founding members of the American Academy of Anti-Ageing Medicine. He makes use of a full range of techniques from hormone replacement therapy for men and women to prescribing the 'nutrient precursors' which stimulate the body to produce more of the hormones lost with age. He uses the latest anti-ageing surgery only as a last resort. Unlike some anti-ageing specialists he believes that 'You have to be careful not to take too much of any hormone at too early a stage in case the body cuts back on producing its own.' He is also an advocate of exercise and relaxation techniques for naturally stimulating the body to produce the substances it needs to stay youthful and flexible.

'A woman can gain a lot of power if she has the confidence to be freed from the constraints of convention.'

Philip Kingsley and Daniel Field are the experts we turned to for advice on hair. The former is a leading trichologist with clinics in London, New York and Singapore, and clients who include Sigourney Weaver, Sean Connery (!) and Ivana Trump. Author of *The Complete Hair Book* and *Hair, an Owner's Handbook*, he believes that 'feeding your head' (as Jefferson Airplane advised, Boomers will recall) is a vital part of creating healthy hair. Daniel Field is one of Britain's best known hairdressers and colourists with salons from Soho to Scotland and a range of organic hair products reflecting his interest in the environment. He believes that 'You should never try to persuade people that they should change their hairstyle just because they are "of a certain age".'

Professor Ronald Marks is professor of dermatology at the University of Wales in Cardiff and also clinical professor of dermatology at the University of Miami in Florida. Author of *The Sun and Your Skin* and *Skin Disease in Old Age* he is a consultant to The Body Shop International and an independent thinker who states that 'You don't need to be rich to have good skin because some of the best products are very basic,' and often the least expensive. He advises us not to be fooled by fancy

packaging (although we will argue that in some instances you're paying for scientific research which you may well consider worth the price), and that in order to protect our own packaging we have to stop worshipping the sun and instead be wary of the damage it can do.

Patrick Holford is the founder director of the Institute of Optimum Nutrition, an independent educational charity for researching and exploring 'what we need in the way of nutrition for "superhealth" to reach our highest potential,' as he puts it. 'There's very little independent information on nutrition so it's very important to check out the sources funding your information' (like meat, butter and sugar manufacturers sponsoring nutrition information for schools, or 'nutrition foundations' financed by the manufacturers of popular snack products). 'The reason we're called independent is that we don't accept funding from food or drug companies.' His philosophy on ageing and nutrition, expressed in his two books *The Optimum Nutrition Bible* and *100 % Health* (Piatkus, 1997 and 1998), is that 'the primary mechanism for ageing is to do with the balance between oxidants and antioxidants'.

The Twenties: Living for Today

Enjoy it, babes, because this is the last unwrinkled period in your life. You can gain and lose weight without being left with saggy skin and stretch marks. You can party all night and still look great the next day. You can forget to remove your make-up, not need moisturizer, and scrub your face with soap and water. Your hair should be lustrous, and it's a safe bet that your bottom and boobs are as pert as they're ever going to be. Physically, if not mentally, you're at the prime age for parenthood, even if not quite at your prime in other areas.

Yet body image is one of the biggest stress factors for young women during this period – part of the baggage of unresolved childhood issues that can linger on into adulthood like the puppy fat that can give the face less interesting definition than it will attain in its thirties. 'One quarter of women won't have sorted out their childhood and adolescent problems by the time they reach their twenties, and it can be ageing to have these things which can turn into personality disorders or neuroses hanging over you,' says Dr Weeks. Mothers facing menopause and middle-aged spread can become infuriated at the way their late teen and twenty-something daughters are for ever complaining

of imaginary face and figure faults on their (to others) seemingly flaw-less bodies.

I'M GONNA LIVE FOR EVER!

Risk and sensation-seeking are also dangers at this age. 'Experimenting with drugs, drink and cigarettes puts lots of strain on the system,' Dr Weeks notes. Few of his Superyoung ever smoked! Because we feel at this age as if we're going to live for ever, the vague threat of lung or skin cancer or substance addiction at some future date doesn't bother us. Some women in their twenties pierce, tattoo and otherwise muti-late their beautiful bodies, unable to conceive of a time when they may not want sixteen holes in one ear or 'Damian' scrawled across their stomach.

Smoking is not only most likely to be a major temptation at this time, but also a major risk – thanks to the long-term effects. Recent surveys have shown how many women believe that smoking helps them keep their weight down: this is a very dangerous trap to fall into. Smoking is likely to breed more health problems than being mildly overweight, being implicated in many studies with cancer of the cervix (the 'imma-ture' cervix is apparently vulnerable to cigarette toxins as well as to sexually transmitted diseases like the wart virus), not to mention pre-mature ageing and skin damage. For those who think they can ignore the health implications, remember that while at this age smoking may be seen to be socially acceptable, the ensuing wrinkles soon won't be!

Professor Cooper adds that 'the stresses of this age are about femi-ninity, developing an image of who you are and competing with men as well as looking for a man'. Women who are striving careerists in their twenties often discover they have a career but not a life by the time they're in their thirties, he warns. 'Get a life before you hit thirty or you'll regret it!'

A LITTLE OF THE RIGHT STUFF NOW PAYS HUGE DIVIDENDS LATER

Getting into good eating habits is vital during this decade, even if you're living in a bedsit or dormitory. But the motivation to do so often isn't strong if you're not overweight, as at this age the body can seem to survive, even thrive, on a diet of chocolate and cola, missed meals and salty or sugary snacks. But damage is being done even if you can't see it yet. The arteries of children as young as ten have been found to be furred up from fatty diets and sedentary habits due to their reliance on cars, televisions and computers. And you can't stock up early enough on calcium, since half of the adult bone mass is accumulated during adolescence, and it's better to acquire it long-term through a calcium-rich diet than in a last minute panic in your forties with calcium supplements. (Many other foods besides dairy foods are rich in calcium, such as broccoli and spinach, but you have to eat a fair bit of them.) The recommended calcium intake levels for young adults are beween 1,200 and 1,500 mg daily. (See Chapter Nine)

Vegetarianism is catching on among young people because it's 'New Age', cheap, politically correct and caring. In old age it can lead to a lower risk of heart disease, diabetes and cancers of the breast and colon. But there are risks of anaemia and malnutrition if a vegetarian diet is not carefully balanced by someone who understands the properties of different foods. And vegan diets, where all animal products such as eggs and cheese and milk are also off-limits, can be very dangerous to those who don't know what they're doing.

Gillian Anderson has challenged the daffy and hot-headed reputation of redheads with her cool portrayal of smart and sexy government agent Scully in the X-Files. Her milky complexion is testament to a diligent skin-care routine and use of a high factor sunscreen.

British news presenter Daljit Dhaliwal has won the hearts and minds of admirers worldwide to the extent that she has an international website fan club. All major media networks have found that a combination of female brains, beauty and ethnic mix attracts both advertisers and viewers. Daljit is a trailblazing role model for millions.

Young women can't live by vegetables and fruits alone, although they will benefit from eating a good deal of them – at least five portions of fresh vegetables and fruit a day are recommended for optimal health. It takes more effort to balance a vegetarian diet since sources of high quality protein are not as plentiful or obvious as they are for carnivores. Foods require balancing in order to create complete proteins providing you with the necessary amino acids to remain healthy. Plenty of beans, pulses and legumes should be eaten. Vegans must make sure to have plenty of nuts, nut butters, sesame seed pastes, sprouted seeds, and soya protein and milk or other plant milks, while non-vegans should supplement their vegetables with eggs, vegetarian cheese and other dairy products made either of cow's, sheep's, goat's or soya or other plant milk. Fish would also be helpful.

The tragic early death of vegetarian champion Linda McCartney at fifty-six and breast cancer in famous vegetarians like Carly Simon raised further questions about the health benefits of the meatless diet. However, a diet low in animal fat and high in soya protein is thought to have some positive effect on the risk of breast cancer, despite the sad case of Linda McCartney, and Japanese women who eat soya do have particularly low levels of the disease. Soya protein is a powerful phytoestrogen (plant oestrogen) which is thought to link on to oestrogen receptors in a way that may block them, acting somewhat like the anti-breast cancer drug Tamoxifen. But it just might be possible that a surfeit of soya while oestrogen levels are still high could overstimulate the breast, and we don't know about genetically modified soya. So we would advise a very varied vegetarian diet with nuts and pulses and lots of fresh vegetables in addition to soya and other plant proteins, rather than one that is totally dependent on ready prepared vegetarian dishes.

Professor Marks theorizes that 'Rotten Western diets are very bad for the skin, and we need to eat more fresh fruits and vegetables.' (See Chapters Four and Nine.) Drinking lots of still water (filtered, ideally) is advisable in order to maintain moisture in the tisues and flush out toxins.

FAKE THAT TAN

The single most important thing you can do to preserve your youthful appearance in this decade for the future is to stay out of the sun, our experts concur. Damage done on those 18–30 hot spot holidays will haunt you for the rest of your life. Dr Giampapa says you should use a sunscreen with UVA and B protection factors of at least SPF 15, but

some dermatologists who treat skin cancer suggest FACTOR 50 on your face! He says it's not too early to start using some AHA – alpha hydroxy acid (fruit acid) – face peels, Retin-A creams, or taking anti-oxidant vitamins. Professor Marks disagrees about the benefits of AHAs but agrees about the Retin-A, which he says can be used lifelong to 'promote proliferation of new blood vessels and connective tissue' and stimulate the production of cells in both the epidermis and dermis. He agrees also about the importance of sunscreen, and advises that even at this age it's not too early for a woman to wear a daily foundation make-up containing UVA and B filters. Although your skin can stand it at this age, the 'fresh and natural' look will leave you looking less fresh and more naturally wrinkled later. Besides, with today's bronzing powders and tanning creams being so effective you can easily look sun-kissed without the worry.

BODY-CONSCIOUS

Gynaecologically, a woman's biggest worries at this period are usually contraceptive. 'If avoiding pregnancy is important the Pill is, on balance, the best contraceptive,' says Joseph Jordan. 'But you should get by with the lowest oestrogen component, hopefully twenty micrograms, although for some that's not enough to control periods completely so you get irregular bleeding even though it acts as a contraceptive.' Unless she's in a long-standing relationship with someone she trusts (and, really, even if she isn't) a woman should advise her partner to use a sheath not only to protect against possible HIV infection and other STDs but also to guard against the risk of papilloma (wart) virus infection, which can affect the cervix and is linked to cervical cancer. Yet any cervical cancer scare you may have from a smear test taken during this decade is likely to be a false one, Mr Jordan says, as there are many false positives while the still immature cervix goes through changes. He advises waiting and having another test and examination by colposcopy – a telescope up your vagina.

Not all doctors, however, share Mr Jordan's confidence in oral contraceptives and some women are understandably wary having heard stories of death from blood clots, strokes, cervical and breast cancer being linked to the use of the Pill. Fortunately most of these stories were about earlier versions of the oral contraceptive, which were higher in oestrogen and not as well balanced as today's minimalist

versions. Recent research (published in the *New England Journal of Medicine*, 1998) has shown that the Pill can actually *reduce* the risk of ovarian cancer, while not increasing the risk of breast cancer in women who have inherited genes which predispose them to this disease. But all women should be aware of their own mother's and older sisters' experience with the Pill to be aware if there may be a genetic history of problems with taking added hormones. And with the additional worry about AIDS (scares about old-fashioned venereal diseases seem to have 'gonnorhoea with the wind'!) it is probably wise for all women except those in long-term monogamous relationships (and certainly those whose cervixes are still 'immature') to insist that their lover wears a condom. A feminine barrier method combined with the sheath can be as safe as the Pill and provide protection against more than pregnancy.

Chlamydia is, like the wart virus, a sexually transmitted disease. It is a major threat to fertility in this age range, particularly because, unlike other venereal diseases for which you can be checked at today's so-called 'genito-urinary clinics', it has very few symptoms. If you are sexually active it might be wise to be checked regularly, and 'any young woman with pelvic pain should always ask for a chlamydia check,' says Mr Jordan.

Girls are getting their periods earlier because they are increasing in size and body fat compared with the same age group in previous generations. This has nothing to do with when your menopause will begin, says Mr Jordan, but 'one danger is that between puberty and their twenties girls today are gaining body fat and tending to lose the aerobic fitness they had if they were fit as children,' warns Professor Sharp. 'This is also the age at which, unfortunately, they are dropping out of exercise *en masse*. Yet this is exactly the time when they should be caught in the 'exercise-for-life' habit and be involved in all sorts of sports. If sport is partaken in really seriously, though, young women may stop menstruating and can risk early osteoporosis (bone thinning – see Chapter Four).

HAIR TODAY . . .

Research for Daniel Field has shown that 'women who colour their hair in their twenties have more confidence than those who do not and generally earn more money!' (Whether this is cause or effect isn't clear.)

Since your hair is at its peak of condition in the twenties, and you don't want to spoil it, a 'semi or demi' colourant would be recommended rather than harsher permanent tints. This is also a time to experiment with 'hair mascara' and other products which just wash out and don't permeate the hair shaft. Philip Kingsley says that hair should be kept in its prime by frequent shampooing which, contrary to popular opinion, does not strip hair of its natural oils but actually 'remoisturizes'. At this age you can use pretty much any product, but your hair will tend to be oily, getting drier as you age.

UltraAge Prescriptions for the Twenties

Go for it! You can do anything you want. The world is your oyster and there's nothing you can't do if you set your mind to it. This is the time for adventure – backpacking around the world, working in a Third World country – and also the time to start turning your dreams into reality. Lots of varied sports and exercise, avoiding smoking, drugs and sun exposure without strong sunscreen, not drinking to excess, a varied fresh food diet, antioxidant vitamins if your diet isn't brilliant, regular cervical smears, chlamydia tests if necessary, care with contraception and protection from sexually transmitted diseases.

. . . GONE TOMORROW?

As Dr Perring notes, 'At this stage the hair has a particular lustre, the skin is at the peak of perfection, and all the curves are nicely rounded. A woman should revel in her skin and muscle tone and speed of response. But sexually she can look forward to her thirties, which will be her physical peak.'

The Thirties: Getting a Grip

The first fully adult decade, the first in which you are most likely to have your own home rather than be sharing 'digs', a proper job instead of just work and, if you've worked on getting a life in your twenties, possibly a partner and even children. You should feel as if you're in control of your own life and destiny at last, and confident about your body and your physical, professional and personal prowess.

'The big stress here is usually to do with the conflict between work and personal relationships, or between personal goals and family obligations,' says Dr David Weeks. The ticking of the biological clock can become unbearably loud, particularly for 'singletons' as the large number of thirty-something single professional women are now known, thanks to Bridget Jones. 'This stress can be very ageing, because frustration is the real killer,' says Dr Weeks. Other psychologically ageing factors in the thirties include not having found a suitable partner to nest and procreate with, or the revelation that your partner is wrong for you, or coming to terms with negative change in your relationship. 'If you don't acknowledge and deal with it at this age you may be stuck with it and it will lead to more frustration,' says Dr Weeks.

Another stress, notes Professor Cooper, 'is when women who may have even subconsciously relied on their looks suddenly wonder how much longer they'll be able to.' For in this decade come the initial facial lines and a slight loss of muscle tone, even though you're technically in your prime and, many people feel, have never looked better.

Björk, Iceland's most famous export, is renowned for her quirky musical talent as well as her creative, individual style. She credits living so close to nature as the key to keeping body and soul, not to mention her beauty, together.

WEIGHING IN

'This is the age to take note of any increase in body fat,' warns Professor Sharp. 'Remember that a woman eats about twenty tons of food between the ages of twenty-five and sixty-five yet should only put on about 24 lbs (11 kg) during that time. The body regulates itself wonderfully but it doesn't take a lot of change to make a difference. If you need to lose weight, think of making small changes over a long time, shedding a couple of pounds per month. That way the body doesn't go into starvation mode and drop its metabolic rate.' All types of exercise should be enjoyed, with a varied programme of aerobic and resistance activities.

But don't train too hard, because this can lead – as it does in many women athletes, to loss of periods, fertility problems and even early

osteoporosis. Fitness freaks can also turn into addicts when their daily workout goes from one to two hours. Rest days in between workouts are essential to remain in peak condition.

HORMONAL BALANCING ACT

Since hormones are considered by anti-ageing experts to be the source of life and youth, Doctors Giampapa and Perring would advise taking a baseline hormone and bone density test in your thirties, before both start to fluctuate around the menopause. For many women over thirty hormonal fluctuations manifest themselves in unsettling PMS, the precursor to menopausal symptoms. Both might at this stage start (if levels were low) to prescribe a few of the precursors that boost the body's natural production of what they consider the most essential anti-ageing hormone of all, human growth hormone (HGH), which lowers as we age. It is HGH which is largely responsible for giving us lean muscled bodies instead of flabby ones. Their patients might at this stage consider a little pregnenolone, one of the steroid chain with benefits in mental function, which would boost the body's supplies of dehydroepiandrosterone (DHEA), a testerone and HGH precurser, and progesterone for strong bones and a healthy libido. But Giampapa warns, 'You have to be careful not to take too much of any hormone or hormone precursor at this stage in case the body cuts back on producing its own.'

'You have to be careful not to take too much of any hormone or hormone precursor at this stage in case the body cuts back on producing its own.'

He would also suggest some 'phospholipids, which protect the cell membranes and act as transmitters to the brain' (see Chapter Twelve). Patrick Holford also recommends a steady supply of antioxidant vitamins A, C and E, and around 50 mg each of each B Vitamin.

From the mid-thirties onwards there are often changes in the menstrual patterns and perhaps a little more pain, says Mr Jordan. Premenstrual syndrome (PMS) can really rear its head now, as the symptoms are worse in women who have had children. While eighty per cent of women have some kind of pre-menstrual symptoms – breast tenderness, distended stomach, irritability – if you've got family problems and feel your own career or life slipping by, you might find that symptoms which felt manageable before seem suddenly unbearable. If

the symptom is fluid retention, a diuretic may help. For breast tenderness Mr Jordan recommends Evening Primrose Oil, for depression Vitamin B6. 'If none of these work, you could try extra progesterone, either a natural progesterone suppository, or a cream to be rubbed into the skin in the second half of the cycle, or tablets.' PMS is not a hormonal imbalance, he stresses, 'It's how a woman's individual system reacts to [hormones].'

A PREGNANT PAUSE . . .

There are many excellent books about pregnancy so we will defer to other sources for complete coverage of the subject. But there's no doubt that a woman who is healthy before conceiving and who eats healthily during pregnancy (and the list of what pregnant women can eat is shortening as the list of no-nos from alcohol to coffee to unpasteurized cheeses grows) and exercises gently during and immediately after her pregnancy should do better than others. If you're lucky you will even avoid stretch marks, saggy breasts and lifelong back problems this way. A healthy diet seems to have more to do with avoiding stretch marks than frantically smearing oil on your stomach, but lubrication can be helpful (although recent reports suggest that some products may be inadvisable for the baby's sake).

Never have the pressures been so great on the increasing number of women trying desperately to 'have it all'.

This becomes the prime decade for having children as career-minded mothers put having babies on the back burner, and increasing numbers of women are only contemplating conception as they turn forty.

Once you've had the baby, do you stay at home for six weeks, six months, six years, or should you be back at your desk in six days with a perfect figure and the perfect nanny? Never have the pressures been so great on the increasing number of women trying desperately to 'have it all', without time to stop and wonder, it sometimes seems, what 'it' is and what it all means.

Pregnancy can leave you with all sorts of things besides a delightful new addition to the family, including haemorrhoids, post-natal depression, crêpey skin, thinning hair and bad teeth. But all these are transient effects and should improve before your baby's sleeping through the night.

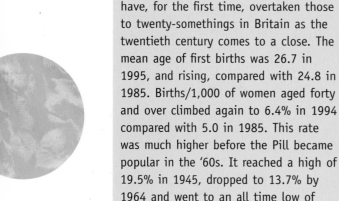

First births to thirty-something mothers have, for the first time, overtaken those to twenty-somethings in Britain as the twentieth century comes to a close. The mean age of first births was 26.7 in 1995, and rising, compared with 24.8 in 1985. Births/1,000 of women aged forty and over climbed again to 6.4% in 1994 compared with 5.0 in 1985. This rate was much higher before the Pill became popular in the '60s. It reached a high of 19.5% in 1945, dropped to 13.7% by 1964 and went to an all time low of 4.4% in 1977 before creeping up again. The difference is that these high figures were due to women unable to stop having babies before the advent of the Pill, as opposed to becoming late mothers from choice as they are now. Another big difference is that older mothers years ago were more likely to have problematic pregnancies than the better nourished, healthier, more youthful older mothers contemplating a first or subsequent pregnancy today.

If you've had your babies vaginally, you may suffer from some sort of stress incontinence if you haven't done your pelvic floor exercises diligently. 'That's why more and more women are requesting elective caesarians,' Mr Jordan has noticed. A lax pelvic floor can be a huge ageing factor which will detract greatly from your, and your partner's, enjoyment of sex. It can also lead to prolapse, which may have to be surgically corrected, and can necessitate a hysterectomy. Don't think it only happens to the old and fat. One beautiful, slim and seemingly fit thirty-six-year-old we know had to have her womb removed due to a prolapse after having three children.

It seems that whether or not you have children is not as important, to how you age as whether you are happy with your family or lack of it. Some 'women's diseases' are more common among women who haven't had children (ovarian and breast cancer), others in women who have (uterine). Having children fairly early in life, and breastfeeding them, both seem to afford some protection against breast cancer, although the reasons are not fully understood. But if you're having children during this decade, you're not yet considered to be having them 'early in life', even if you're no longer the 'elderly primagravida' you would have been back in the eighties, when Victoria was considered elderly for having her first child at twenty-nine.

THIRTY-SOMETHING THREATS

Cervical intraepithelial neoplasia (CIN), cancer of the cervix, is quite common in this decade but it can usually be cured if caught early

enough. If a woman's weight goes up substantially during this decade, she is more at risk of bladder problems when she gets older, of breast cancer and of cancer of the uterus. This is partly thought to be because fat stores oestrogen, which seems to be implicated in those types of cancer.

Anaemia in women of childbearing age, often overlooked, can be a cause of hair loss during this decade, says Mr Kingsley. He would test for haemoglobin levels in the blood after a period and prescribe a course of iron tablets and nutritional supplements (such as B Vitamins and folic acid), which would help the iron to be absorbed. He would also tell clients with this problem not to drink tea without milk, because what he calls 'the iron-binding capacity of the free tannin in tea can lead to less iron being stored in the tissues.'

Few thirty-somethings would have bared all with such rave reviews as talented Australian actress Nicole Kidman in her live performance of The Blue Room. *She admits to preferring the cooler weather, and slathers herself in sunscreen year-round.*

Mr Kingsley also sees many women in this age group whose hair loss, he believes, comes from the pressure they are under in their jobs or juggling work and home commitments. 'I can't tell them not to work so hard, but I can tell them to relax when they eat, have a drink, put their feet up from time to time and do some exercise,' he says. The right kind of exercise such as yoga, with its shoulder and headstands, can be good for the scalp and hair as it increases circulation in that area. But over-exercise can cause thinning hair, Mr Kingsley warns. Another possible cause of hair loss at

this age may be polycystic ovaries, which can be checked by ultrasound or magnetic resonance imaging (MRI) scans and treated, usually through keyhole surgery and usually without threat to fertility.

It is particularly important to get your nutritional balance right for healthy hair growth and for all sorts of reasons in this decade, particularly if you are 'eating for two', as you should be in terms of nutrients if not calories, before conception and during pregnancy and lactation.

NIPS AND TUCKS?

This is the decade in which you might opt for some laser resurfacing of your face to get rid of fine lines now creeping around the eyes and mouth, says Dr Giampapa, and when you should switch to non-soap-based cleansing milks and start moisturizing regularly, according to Professor Marks. But, unless you're gaga from sleepless nights with the kiddies, it may cheer you to know that you're at your peak mental capacity and, if you get any chance to test it out between feeds and nappy changes, in your physical and sexual prime. Your male partner, alas, has probably passed his.

It's supposed to be downhill from here – but after reading this book we hope you'll just experience gentle undulations!

> **UltraAge Prescription for the Thirties**
>
> This is the age to balance your life, your diet and your exercise routine, with so many elements to throw you off balance, particularly if you're heavily pregnant.

The Forties: The Transitional Time

THE CHANGE: EMOTIONAL

This is the decade of change of life for women, even if the average age at which periods stop is fifty-one. You may start feeling transitional from the time of your fortieth birthday, which can come as quite a shock for many because it sounds so old, and was about the total life expectancy around the turn of the last century. You may be going through all sorts of changes of life from perimenopausal mood swings and hot flushes to divorce and coming to terms with the fact that your partner of the past twenty years has turned to a younger woman to fool him into feeling that he's only as old as the woman he feels. As someone once said, 'Forty is the age when you realize your work isn't fulfilling, your marriage is a mistake, your children are dysfunctional and you're going to die.'

'But it can be a time of new freedom,' says Dr Weeks, 'when women feel free to become more individual.' In his study of eccentrics he noticed that most women didn't let their true eccentricity show until after they had raised their families, stopped being somebody's wife or mother, and started feeling able to be themselves. 'Women behaving badly' seems to start in the forties. But with more and more women today only starting families in their

'Women behaving badly' seems to start in the forties.

late thirties and early forties, this period of liberation is being pushed back towards the fifties. And there seems to be no good reason why women shouldn't start their families in their forties, as forty-year-olds today are, Mr Jordan notes, often as fit as twenty-somethings were a decade ago.

Professor Cooper says, 'This is the critical stage for women – a crunch point. Stresses can be about retaining femininity and attractiveness and about re-evaluating their lives and asking if they've made it and, if not, why not? It's a good time to stop and reflect on your life goals if you have them, and to create some if you don't or change those that need changing. This is the time to implement all the changes you want to see in the second half of your life.'

THE CHANGE: PHYSICAL

Dr Weeks has found that 'the more stable you are emotionally the less upset you will be by the advent of the menopause', although this does impact physically to some degree however well prepared you may be psychologically. He has noticed that 'The women who get on to HRT as early as possible seem to do better and avoid a lot of the negative physical symptoms.'

Mr Jordan sees many women in this decade who are 'tired, not coping well, off sex and so on, but if you measure the oestrogen levels they're totally normal. You just don't know what it's been before, and they're hard to get a baseline figure for because, depending on the time of month, they can vary from 100 units to 2,500.'

CHANGING MIND

You might experience some short-term memory loss at this time which can be very emotionally disturbing but which should be corrected by HRT, whether you decide to take combined oestrogen and progesterone or even just natural progesterone (see Chapter Four). Some of the brain fitness exercises in Chapter Ten might also help if you prefer not to take HRT – as would some of the nutritional supplements (PS and Q10) in Chapter Ten. The thing is not to panic, Dr Perring says. 'It's perfectly normal, and probably doesn't mean you're about to get Alzheimer's.' But it might mean that you've been neglecting your most important attribute, which needs exercising as much as the rest of your body.

Mid-life and motherhood have been made exotic thanks to Madonna realizing both. The in-your-face sexiness of her twenties and thirties has been replaced by a compelling self-assurance deriving from the absolute joy and devotion she has for her daughter. She will continue to be a defining role model for her own as well as younger generations.

CHANGING CONTRACEPTION

'The Pill can continue to be taken into the forties by women who are not overweight, have normal blood pressure and don't smoke,' says Mr Jordan. 'And women who have taken the Pill for any length of time are less likely to have cancer of the ovary. Pregnancy, lactation and the combined Pill are preventatives of this disease, which is impossible to screen for.' (However, see our earlier caveat about taking the Pill in your twenties.)

CHANGING WEIGHT

Fluctuations of weight at this point are more damaging than

they were, and particularly ageing as the skin's elasticity is affected. After forty people can look older when they lose weight, Dr Perring says, and it is more difficult to maintain muscle mass so buttocks as well as breasts, necks and under-arms start slipping. Watch out for piling on weight in the middle, as this pattern of weight gain has been associated with heart disease. A little 'middle-aged spread' may be inevitable, and may be Mother Nature's way of making oestrogen from fat cells to replace what the ovaries are no longer producing, but don't let a solid mass settle around your abdomen. Waist-whittling exercises, stretches and bends may help, but you should keep your weight down generally. Those who have gained weight around their middles should be particularly careful to avoid other cardiovascular risk factors such as smoking and a high-fat diet.

One of the most famous women in the world, Oprah Winfrey exemplifies inner and outer beauty. Able to laugh with others as well as at herself, Oprah has done plenty to build the self-esteem of women regardless of background or age.

CHANGING RELATIONSHIPS

Your forties may also herald a power shift in personal relationships. Dr Perring says, 'Women are peaking sexually in terms of the quality of their experience at this age while men of the same age are past it and just beginning to become aware of the tyre around their tummy and the bottleneck in their career.' You should be aware that the man in your life may be freaking out too at this age, feeling a failure if he hasn't achieved what he wanted to in life, or surprising himself by being discontented even if he has. Men's testosterone levels start to dwindle just as women's oestrogen and progesterone levels go down, and this

can cause irritability coupled with a lack of libido that can lead to many marital problems.

This is often a time when couples drift, or push themselves, apart, because each is silently crying out for help but the other is so wrapped up in their own problems they don't recognize the emergency signals. Make sure you take the time to look up from your own problems and try to understand and empathize with what your partner is going through. There are many clinics now which offer male HRT and assistance with impotence (other than Viagra) and other mid-life problems which can come between men and women at this stage of life. But men often feel the need to 'prove' themselves with a younger woman just when their partner most needs their emotional support.

Make sure you take the time to look up from your own problems and try to understand and empathize with what your partner is going through.

The good news is that most women not only maintain a healthy libido at this age, but find that it increases! The disappearance of sex drive in a woman is often due to depression, sometimes due to worrying about the loss of her youthful appearance, but a healthy woman who is happy with her body and her sexuality may find at this age that her own sex drive is becoming stronger while her male partner's weakens, hence the desire for a younger partner. She may find that it takes more and more effort to get a male of her own age aroused, which in itself can lead to feelings of insecurity in her – a vicious circle.

More bad news is that some women at this age lose some of the strength and quality of their orgasms, or their ability to achieve multiple ones. But HRT is said to be able to help to prevent this, but we're dubious of it being the panacea it's portrayed to be (see Chapter Four).

Feeling the approach of the menopause while your daughter is just reaching puberty can cause depression in some women who regard menstruation as an essential part of womanhood, Dr Perring has found. 'It can be very difficult.'

But there is wondrous joy to be experienced when a daughter blooms into womanhood. We have both experienced that pride, and for me the fact that middle-aged men can't seem to take their eyes off my elder daughter and hardly 'see' me when we are together only makes me proud. I feel confident I can hold my own with my personality and no longer need to rely on my youth or figure to work overtime. We only

wish we could give our daughters the confidence to know they are as beautiful as they are. It's one of Mother Nature's little tricks that she often doesn't give us the confidence to enjoy our looks until they are past their peak, and that beautiful young women often agonize constantly about their appearance.

CHANGING VISION

One sure way to spot an over-forty is the length at which they hold a paper away from their eyes to read it, or put on and take off spectacles when changing focal distances. This is because the eye tissues, like other parts of the body, are losing elasticity. Eye exercises started at this age might help – there are numerous books on the subject.

This is the age at which we need to begin to be tested regularly for glaucoma, a build-up of pressure in the eyes which can lead to blindness, and to know our blood pressure and cholesterol levels. If they're high, restrict salt and fat intake, try some autogenic (relaxation) exercises and look at your lifestyle generally, Dr Perring recommends.

The process of ageing isn't a steady decline but comes on us in jumps.

The process of ageing isn't a steady decline but comes on us in jumps. So you may not be imagining it if you stare at the mirror one day and see yourself as 'old', whereas the day before you saw yourself as young-ish. 'You can be forty for three years and then suddenly be forty-five because something precipitates the ageing process, like having an accident, an operation under general anaesthetic, or another stressful life event,' says Dr Perring. Some people, of course, stay thirty-nine for ever. You might be one of them.

HAIRY CHANGES

Your hair, too, is changing during this decade: its growth rate is slowing down, the diameter of individual hairs beginning to become slightly thinner, though the curlier your hair is the less this will show. You will probably notice quite a few white hairs, but at this time your skin tone becomes paler, too (see Chapter Five).

Mr Kingsley has found that many of the dyes you may resort to in order to cover up white hair may make your hair generally weaker and

'There is no such thing as grey hair,' says Philip Kingsley, 'just white ones which, when interspersed with your normally pigmented ones give that effect. Dark-haired people tend to notice them earlier than blondes. The exact mechanism that causes the pigments to change is still something of a mystery,' says Mr Kingsley, but he notes that 'some studies have shown that certain B Vitamins taken in large doses have begun to reverse the process of greying within three months. The hairs revert to white when the vitamins are stopped.' This could be why hair is rumoured, though not proven, to turn grey due to stress. (Marie Antoinette's was said to have turned white overnight at the prospect of meeting Madame La Guillotine; Mary Queen of Scots to have gone white very quickly during the lead-up to her execution; and the actress Julie Walters says hers went grey shortly after learning her daughter had leukaemia.) Stress uses up vital B Vitamins. It is not true that if you pull out a white hair two will grow in its place, but 'constant pulling can distort the hair follicle, resulting in more crinkly hair which gives the appearance of being coarser,' Mr Kingsley notes.

duller. He advises you to 'shampoo and condition your hair every day. You may worry that shampooing hair this frequently will cause dyed hair to lose its colour. However, your hair colour will fade gradually in any case, although more frequent washing may speed up the process a little. But it's better to shampoo it and, therefore, colour it more often than the reverse.' Shampooing is important because it exercises the scalp and hair follicles to encourage faster and healthier hair growth. Scalp massage can also be beneficial, and Mr Kingsley suggests you do this as often as possible, and at least once a week. Or maybe you could persuade someone to do it for you – even better!

THE CHANGING FACE

Wrinkles can become quite pronounced in forty-somethings, as both authors can attest. Collagen injections (see Chapter Six) are popular at this age for trying to plump them out, although many women reject or are allergic to the animal-based formula, and others tire of the regular six-monthly commitment required for maintenance. Laser resurfacing is growing in popularity as a method to eradicate wrinkles by 'burning' through them.

There are numerous expensive creams on the market that promise to relieve you of both wrinkles and a fair bit of money at the same

time. Professor Marks says that many wrinkle creams do work and are worth trying on the neck and facial lines. Inexpensive preparations such as the functionally named E-45 cream from your local chemist should do as well, he claims, as some of the fancier preparations with their posh packaging and formidably made-up saleswomen waiting to pounce when you enter a department store. Retin-A, available only on prescription in Britain, is probably a must by now, says Professor Marks, who feels it works best on early lines and is most beneficial with long-term use. Retin-A can cause skin irritation, 'But then you just modulate the use of it, or use a lower concentration,' he advises. 'It can be used for life and will improve self-repair of photo damage, which causes the main damage to the skin. The benefits are not controversial, but you may get to a certain point after six months or a year and stay there.'

It's important to protect hands, too, at this stage – either after years of washing dishes or from hot and cold weather sports such as swimming and skiing which can dry and chap the skin. Lipstick and foundation should always be worn, not just because they will probably make you look better as you lose the rosy glow of youth and start showing the effect of late nights and early mornings much more brutally, but because of the protection most of today's formulas give against UVA and B rays. (Make sure the ones you use do provide this.) But, all in all, most people wouldn't be too sad to retain the looks and vigour they have in their forties, the last decade you can kid yourself that you're still young, or at least in a youthful middle-age. The fifties hold more fear, but by all acccounts (although we haven't got there yet) they can be a fabulous time!

UltraAge Prescription for the Forties

Prepare for the upheavals this decade of change can bring in all areas of your life. Be aware of hormone levels, blood pressure, cholesterol and bone density levels which should be the targets for your age. This information is both variable and hard to get 'experts' to agree on. Blood pressure and cholesterol are easy enough to evaluate, but hormone levels and bone density are more difficult. For the latter, experts will only estimate what is 'good for your age', which is within a range. However, women really interested in their health wouldn't want to accept just being good for their ages, even if as 'safely' defined by the UN. I had to find out that my good-for-my-age bone density was also that of a twenty-something woman! Keep on taking or increase your antioxidants, and keep moisturizing and protecting your skin from the sun. Learn ways of dealing with grey hair that won't create greater hair problems. And exercise everything, from your bones to your brain!

The Fifties: Redefining

The fifties may seem a desolate dead end when viewed from below, or a gateway from the Second Age (middle age) to the Third, 'one foot in the grave' if you're being pessimistic, or pleasantly surprising, and, for many women truly the prime. 'For women the forties are the toughest decade,' says Dr Weeks. 'In the fifties it gets better!'

The American management consultant Sydney Rice Harrild, a fifty-something female herself, has dubbed the era from the fifties to the seventies 'Prime Time', a period when women are often unencumbered with family responsibilities, less likely to be desperately scrabbling up the career ladder but still in full possession of their physical faculties, and with an experienced, agile mind allied to a depth of lifelong learning. She advises we consider all the previous years simply as homework leading up to that time.

'This is a really good period for women. It can be the power decade.'

Once you've navigated your way through the mine-field the menopause can be (see Chapter Four) and, for the first time since you reached puberty, are no longer at the mercy of your fluctuating hormones, you may emerge stronger, with renewed energy and vigour. Many women are able, at last, to pour into work or personal projects, like landscaping a garden or working for a charity or training for a marathon, all those energies which were diffused in so many ways in their younger years trying to keep everybody else happy. A (female) management consultant observed to us, 'Men in their fifties are often time-serving at work. Women who've taken a career break return with new energy.'

THE POWER DECADE

At work it is, at least for the moment, the power decade for women. Most of the few women on the boards of major companies or who have reached positions of authority are in their fifties or older, like Marjorie Scardino of the Pearson Group, Yve Newbold, former company secretary of the Hanson Group, or Sarah Morrison, director of GEC, and women with political power such as US Secretary of State Madeleine Albright, former Irish President Mary Robinson, the British Speaker of the House of Commons Betty Boothroyd, or Jeanne Kirkpatrick, former US Ambassador to the UN. Elizabeth Dole might

be the first woman candidate for the US presidency, and at an age when she is entitled to be pensioned off, potting petunias.

But in the very near future, with more women crashing through the 'glass ceiling', positions of power will be reached earlier. This doesn't mean that women in their fifties will be pushed into early retirement: demographic changes mean that they will need to stay on in paid employment, consolidating their own achievements while, intentionally or not, acting as role models and even mentors to younger women.

Professor Cooper says, 'This is a really good period for women. It can be the power decade at work because they know where their career is going and have a great degree of autonomy. It's a good time to do what they want, unencumbered by kids and maybe even by a partner whose loss they have accepted. It's a 'Zeitgeist' for women, their time to do what they want. Enjoy it, go with it, but prioritize. It can be the ideal time to change your working pattern in your personal life. It may feel like your last decade to have a fling.

REDEFINING YOUR ROLE

'Stresses at this time come mainly from coming to terms with the changes in your life, not all of which you may have chosen,' Dr Weeks agrees. 'Adaptability is the most positive trait at this age. Women should be thinking ahead to a time when they may have fewer roles to juggle, about whether they want early retirement or to develop new areas of paid or unpaid work. "Empty nest syndrome" can be a problem even for women who've worked. This is the time when a lot of women have to accept a non-sex life, and if it's accepted it can be psychologically OK, but if they're frustrated by that it can be very sad.'

> 'Adaptability is the most positive trait at this age. Women should be thinking ahead to a time when they may have fewer roles to juggle...'

She is clearly a hardy personality who was working on turning the threat to her whole way of life to date into a challenge that she could rise to with renewed strength in the future. Indeed, the released mental energy which is liberated in many women of this age after their children are grown up is one of the reasons why they do so well at work and become the lifeblood of charities and volunteer organizations.

Margaret Cook, the former wife of British Foreign Secretary Robin Cook, divorced after nearly thirty years of marriage when her husband was very publicly discovered to have a mistress. She eloquently expressed the feelings of many other fifty-something women when she wrote, in an article in the English *Sunday Times* in 1998, 'Would I marry again? Almost certainly not. Men of fifty-plus tend to collect problems, regress emotionally, need to look after themselves. There is a theory that young women choose their mates according to the genes they wish their young to inherit. I've no doubt I submitted to this programming in my time. But I don't need to worry about that now: I am free to have unsuitable liaisons ... as dangerous as I like! Are there other positive outcomes? There are a lot of positive negatives, such as less shopping, less cooking, less tolerating ... less humouring ... less self-effacing. There is liberation, there is free time; and there is much released mental energy which I hope to direct into a creative channel.' Shortly after this, Margaret found a new partner via a dating agancy. Fifty-something ex-wives all over Britain cheered, 'Good on you, girl'.

LIFE INSURANCE POLICIES

Now is the age to start having regular mammograms, when the risk of acquiring breast cancer is considered greater than the risks from regular screening. This is not generally considered the case for younger women, whose breast tissue is denser and so may require higher doses of radiation for a meaningful X-ray. Breast cancer is more common in post menopausal women, hence the importance of screening.

If you're worried about breast cancer Mr Jordan says that 'The breast cancer in HRT users has been found to be of lower grade malignancy, less likely to spread to the lymph glands, and easier to treat [than that in non-users]. And if you stop taking oestrogen after no matter how long, within five years your risk of breast cancer goes back to what it would have been if you hadn't used it at all.' The development of SERMS (see page 158) should eventually take that worry away.

Some women at this age want hormone replacement therapy to correct problems which are not menopausal, he has found. 'A sympathetic look at the woman as a whole is necessary. You should find out what her family life is like – what her husband is doing, is he attracted to a younger woman; is she worrying about her lack of sexual attraction; are her kids getting pregnant or taking drugs? Often there are very good reasons for the depression that can occur at this age, yet the blame is usually put on the menopause.'

As well as making sure you have the necessary health checks at this age you should be thinking of other types of life insurance, and spend some time making a financial plan for the future in the event of retirement or ill health, as money worries can be a major source of stress for people who haven't thought about such things in advance and made adequate provision.

KICK START NEEDED

While women might think they should start taking it easy now and putting their feet up, the opposite is true. If anything, Professor Sharp says, they should be doing more weight-bearing exercise to keep their bones strong and to maintain muscle mass and minimize the middle-aged spread which occurs after menopause. But putting on a little bit of weight at this time may be Mother Nature's way of ensuring some extra oestrogen supplies, since fat cells store this vital hormone. The anti-ageing experts might at this stage recommend supplementing standard HRT with DHEA, progesterone, testosterone (yes!) and a human growth hormone (HGH) secretagogue such as lysine, an amino acid which should stimulate the body to produce more of its own growth hormone. (Injections of HGH should only come later, Dr Giampapa feels, when the body is unlikely to be adequately stimulated to produce its own.)

Why testosterone? Do women really need that? Yes, says Dr Giampapa. It is

Etched in the hearts of most middle-aged men as the desperate, desirable Lara in the hit '60s epic Dr Zhivago, *Julie Christie found that her career required the help of cosmetic surgery in her fifties despite her natural British resistance to all things 'artificial'. But unlike some of her contemporaries who have maybe gone 'too far', Christie remains a natural beauty.*

responsible to some degree for our libido, our drive, and it also helps to strengthen bones. Like HGH, it will help maintain lean tissue, which tends to diminish at this time. But these treatments, given in cream form where possible, are still very controversial. Few, however, would deny the possible benefits of antioxidant vitamins and a healthy diet.

Patrick Holford warns that 'You have to be careful with hormones. From DHEA you can make testosterone and oestrogen but not progesterone, so women who take it can make themselves more oestrogen-dominant, and unopposed oestrogen causes proliferation of cells causing fibroids, endometriosis and other problems.' At this stage a woman can easily have too much iron in her blood due to stopping menstruation, which can increase her risk of heart disease (see Chapter Three). 'Women's levels of ferritin – the way the body stores iron – in the blood go up dramatically post-menopausally, which is one explanation of why women's risk of cardio-vascular disease shoots up after the menopause,' says Patrick Holford. 'The probable reason is increased oxidation. Too much iron instead of being an antioxidant may actually oxidize or damage fats in the body. Rust shows how iron is involved in oxidation.'

CUT THE CALORIES

Diet at at this stage should be becoming significantly sparser, as older metabolisms burn off fewer calories and more of our intake is converted to fat. There is also a pile of evidence to indicate that eating sparingly in later life, if not throughout life, may help to ensure longevity (see Chapter Twelve). In experiments, rats who ate less were able to stay in the rat race longer, and many centenarians cite meagre rations among their health tips. Whether the diet should be vegetarian or meat-based, through, is open to debate, with Dr Giampapa recommending a nearly vegan one and Dr Ronald Klatz recommending one with substantial levels of animal protein. Some people react better to one than the other, but both should be moderate and well balanced with plenty of fruits and vegetables, nuts, seeds and wholegrains.

GET HEAVY WITH SKIN CARE

Skin care should be kicked into high gear during this decade says Professor Marks, with a richer emollient recommended at night for the fifty-five-plusses, gentle cleansing milks instead of soaps and continuing with the Retin-A. Wear foundations and lipsticks that keep out UVA and B rays. Special attention should be paid to hands to keep skin supple, and Retin-A may have some influence on keeping age spots at bay.

In this decade you'll lose considerable fat in the central third of the face, says Dr Giampapa, and lose much of the collagen that causes skin elasticity. Hence, among those who are not against surgical intervention, it is the age of the full facelift, as well as that at which women who have not previously had figure problems may go in for liposuction or liposculpture, he points out.

MEMORY BLOCKS

Memory losses may also be a problem if there is arteriosclerosis, due to drops in hormones. Hence the growing market in 'nutrient building blocks' such as phosphatidylserine (PS), one of the phospholipids produced from fatty acids, that are said to be able to 'turn back the clock on the non-diseased, ageing brain' as well as helping those with senile dementia and Alzheimer's (see Chapters Ten and Twelve).

CELEBRATE!

Many women are celebrating, rather than hiding, their fiftieth birthdays these days. We have been invited to many wonderful fiftieth birthdays by women proud of having reached that milestone half century. Hillary Clinton celebrated hers looking far better than she had at half that age, as many of her contemporaries do. There are so many 'fifty-plus and proud' celebrities such as the actresses Goldie Hawn, Cybill Shepherd and Helen Mirren – voted the 'sexiest woman on TV' in 1997 despite her advanced age – the model Lauren Hutton and the sexologist Shere Hite. Many more fifty-something females have been enjoying the active attentions of youthful lovers with Francesca Annis and Ralph Fiennes, Jill Gascoigne and Alfred Molina, just two of many such recent dramatic couplings. No longer are younger lovers considered 'toyboys': they're for real, and we'll be seeing more and more of them, pundits predict, as older women realize that their sex drives may be better matched by those of younger men.

Since Dr David Weeks discovered that many of his Superyoung had super young lovers, no wonder these fifty-something women look – and feel – so good for their age. And since men at this age may be wrapped up in the male menopause (which can now be treated with testosterone therapy) or impotent for a variety of reasons, from falling testosterone levels to taking beta blockers for high blood pressure, they're not such a good bet.

FERTILE IMAGININGS

Of course for some women menopausal symptoms don't begin until the fifties, and with fertility clinics offering treatment to women up to fifty-five, and sometimes older, it seems a late baby is still possible at this stage. In the future, of course, it will be created from our own eggs, extracted and frozen when we were in our twenties, at our prime where egg quality is concerned, and not carrying the high risk of Down's Syndrome that older ova do. Now most late pregnancies are from egg donors, but natural ones may still be possible, as Britain's Elizabeth Buttle almost had the world believing because we (like she) wanted to. But it is a spectacular enough accomplishment to bear a healthy baby at sixty! Having a youthful enough mindset to want a child at this age, and the energy to cope with a baby (let alone pregnancy and labour!) are probably in themselves indicators that you will be around for a long time to enjoy your late-life offspring.

We know several women who had their first child in their mid-forties or second families up to twenty years after starting their first, either with the same partner or a different one, and all agreed that the process was rejuvenating and

Unlike many women of her vintage, Whoopi Goldberg takes ageing as it comes and adapts her style accordingly.

energizing, if only because they were determined to prove to the world (and often to their younger partner) that they could cope.

The ability to conceive a child late in life was found, by researchers at Harvard University, to be one of the strongest predictors of longevity in women. It seems to be not so much producing the child that counts as having the youthful hormonal system that enables you to do so. The research was done among centenarians, a large proportion of whom proved to have had late pregnancies. So don't give up hope if you want a child at this age, you wild impetuous thing, but you may have to be realistic and realize it is unlikely to be genetically yours. That option will await your daughters (see Chapter Twelve).

> ## UltraAge Prescription for the Fifties
>
> Give your body and your life new definition as you rethink your role in the workplace, the family and society. Make sure you've got your 'life insurance policies' in place, from regular mammograms to financial planning. Get serious with skincare and flirt with the possibility of a surgical boost and/or a new (younger) lover!

The Sixties: Focusing on the Future

Time flies when you are having fun, and even when you aren't! Once you've forged through your fifties you'll probably soar through your sixties, as time really does seem to get faster all the time post-forty. Remember what a long time a year seemed when you were ten? Now it comes along at least six times as quickly in our perspective, and we can visualize next Christmas almost as soon as we're finished with this one. So, since time flies whether you're having fun or not, you might as well have fun!

GRAB YOUR CHANCES

Opportunities may decline in your sixties, says Professor Cooper, which can be depressing if you let it be, but you should be making positive plans for what you intend to do with the Third Age of your life, which seems always just around the next corner now. 'Women usually have more varied interests outside their main work than men, which is healthy, so they often don't have to work so hard at creating opportunities or cementing friendships as men do,' Professor Cooper notes. 'Men are often a disaster area at this age, and if you are partnered, you may

have a problem with your man if he's retired, trying to get him to focus. But stress can also come from seeing yourself as alone, without the status and support your work or family used to give you, or because of lack of prudent financial planning for retirement. Whether you're still working or not, this is a good time to join the local drama society, sign up for evening classes, or begin doing some work for charity because underemployment, like unemployment or retirement, can be a huge health hazard,' says Professor Cooper, 'and it's good to plan ahead.'

TAKE PRIDE: LOOKING AND FEELING GOOD

With active, attractive over-sixties role models such as Joan Collins, Jilly Cooper, Gloria Steinem, Sophia Loren, Shirley Bassey and the Duchess of Kent around, women who reached their first prime in the 1960s and who have taken the same sort of care of themselves can feel they're still in prime time in their sixties.

'Generally I find that women are looking younger and younger,' says Mr Jordan. 'But if you look at a group of women in their sixties who've used oestrogen for years and one that hasn't, most people would notice that the group on HRT looked fitter, healthier and much younger. Part of that, however, is because those women usually have a positive, proactive attitude about their health.' Many women who spurn HRT due to its side-effects yet take care of themselves could prove otherwise.

TAKE LIBERTIES

It doesn't do to get too hung up about your weight now, while keeping it within reasonable limits. 'You might look better about ten pounds or so heavier than you used to be,' says Mr Jordan. That's partly because a plumper face is probably less wrinkled, partly because fat cells produce some oestrogen.

'This can be a very liberating time for women in many ways, as Germaine Greer observed,' says Mr Jordan. 'It's just a pity she was so damning about oestrogen, which does so many things for women at this age, including keeping the vagina supple and lubricated and helping the bladder to stay elastic to prevent "urgency" and later incontinence.'

Greer, in her seminal work on menopause, *The Change* (Hamish Hamilton, 1991), says that 'Only when a woman ceases the fretful struggle to be beautiful can she turn her gaze outward, find the beautiful, and feed upon it. She can at last transcend the body that was what other people principally valued her for . . . It is quite impossible to explain to younger women that this new invisibility, like calm and indifference, is a desirable condition.' But Greer is far from invisible.

The actress Honor Blackman, known for her early sexpot roles in black leather in *The Avengers* on television and as Pussy Galore in the James Bond film *Goldfinger*, said at sixty-seven, while starring in the British television series *The Upper Hand* as the interfering and highly sexed mother of an advertising executive, 'From all points of view, this is a very good age to be!'

KEEP BODY CONSCIOUS

Even though in Britain women will stop being called for mammograms when they're sixty-five, Mr Jordan recommends that they still continue to have them every three years as they are entitled to do on Britain's National Health.

'Maintenance fitness is the key here,' says Professor Sharp. There is an accelerated post-menopausal fall-off in power and strength, he says. Between the ages of sixty-five and ninety, muscle power is lost more rapidly than strength, a decline of 3.5% per year for power compared with approximately 1.8% per year for strength. That is why you may still be able to pick up your grandchild even if you can't run for a bus like you used to. So he recommends 'Some aerobic work, regular walking plus a bit of strength work with weights, in the gym if possible, to counter the accelerated post-menopausal loss in strength. It is also important to work on flexibility to counter the loss in that area at this time. Yoga is particularly good for this.'

Exercise is essential to maintain youthful movement as well as a toned appearance. 'Goldie Hawn's splits and stretches are a prime example,' says Dr Perring. 'And physical activity of any kind naturally enhances hormone levels, particularly of HGH, which is responsible for maintaining lean tissue as people naturally tend to get flabbier when they get older.'

He and Dr Giampapa say that this is the first decade in which you might consider taking injections of human growth hormone (HGH) itself. You can read more about this in Chapter Twelve, but it is consid-

Highly acclaimed actresses Judi Dench reverted to her gamine cropped hairstyle, once a trademark in her twenties, thirty years on, proving that women can be stunningly cute at any age!

A role model to women of all ages and races, Maya Angelou is an accomplished writer and actress as well as being a powerful poet. She reduced us to tears with her moving autobiography and is a sell-out speaker wherever she travels worldwide.

ered the miracle anti-ageing hormone, worshipped by the anti-ageing industry in the US. HGH is synthesized these days, and no longer taken from corpses, but still at the time of writing has to be administered by subcutaneous injection. It has many potential side-effects if its use is not monitored carefully by a doctor, or if certain levels are exceeded. 'It could bring on diabetes, oedema, increased blood pressure and other problems,' Dr Perring acknowledges. It is available only on prescription and if he established, through tests, that a patient of this age was lacking in it and not making enough of her own, he would prescribe 'a low dose, twice a day, of half a unit with ten units over ten days and then four days off. But everybody has to find their own protocol.'

FACE FACTS

The demineralization of the facial bones can become evident during this decade, so Dr Giampapa performs a number of facial implants of

various kinds to improve structure. Chins, jaws and cheekbones can all be built up with various materials or with transplants of the patient's own fat. 'Skin maintenance should proceed as from fifty-five,' says Professor Marks.

STAY SENSUAL

'Women can still look wonderful during this decade,' says Dr Perring, 'as more and more of them are proving. There is no reason you shouldn't be having an active sex life if you have a partner, or a good sensual one, whether you do or not. You must find a way to continue to have a sensual life even if you are on your own.' Masturbation and same-sex relationships are two options open to women of this age who find themselves without a male partner, as so many do, but don't forget massage, cuddling grandchildren or stroking pets.

Interestingly enough, men who live longest tend to be married while long-lived women are not, women generally surviving their male partners. The reason for this statistic is that married men – at least of the generation studied so far – were generally taken care of by their wives while the wives had the added responsibility of caring for their husbands, often doing things according to his wishes rather than their own. So freedom from domestic demands, and living on someone else's schedule may be a blessing in disguise. That gives hope to all spinsters, divorcees and widows that perhaps you're luckier than your married friends, at least in the Third Age. But women who choose a younger partner, as so many more are doing, can hope to grow old with him.

The main thing is to make sure there's plenty of emotional contact, fun and laughter in your life at this stage and in the future.

> **UltraAge Prescription for the Sixties**
>
> Keep fit, keep alert and keep having fun. Worry less about what others think and enjoy thinking about what you need and want to do.

The Seventies: Bonus Years

You've had your biblically allotted three score years and ten and are *really old* now by most definitions. But in the enhanced lifespan envisioned by those who are reading this at twenty-, thirty- and forty-something, you may only be entering the Third Age at the end of this

decade, with the seventies still considered middle age, the forties youth. Or perhaps you are just 'near elderly', the term Bill Clinton bandied about. Merely by living this long you've earned yourself a bonus of five or six years more than you were due at birth, and you could be headed for a lot more. 'Although the average lifespan of women in the West is now seventy-six, I would say that the period we are biologically primed to reach is probably one hundred and twenty. The number who live to be one hundred doubles every ten years,' says Dr Perring.

But that's still a pipe dream for most of us, so let's consider the bleakest reality at the time of writing. Unless you're of the calibre of a candidate for the presidency of the United States, or have been irreplaceable at what you do for fifty years, like the redoubtable American film critic Pauline Kael, or are a writer like P. D. James or Barbara Cartland, or own your own business like Estée Lauder, you'll probably have been forced to retire by now. But you can keep on being an 'elder stateswoman' like Margaret Thatcher or the British Labour politician Barbara Castle.

Any children you have should be grown up and, in the current 'global village' described by Hillary Clinton, they may well be many miles away, together with any grandchildren (or great-grandchildren).

INDEPENDENCE IS THE KEY: BODY AND SPIRIT

'The dangers of this age are boredom and the loss of roles, and beginning to be unnecessarily psychologically dependent on younger people such as your children,' says Dr Weeks. Whereas during your fifties and sixties you were very likely learning what it was like not to have so many people dependent upon you, unless, of course, you had elderly parents of your own to deal with, in your seventies you may have to come to terms with starting to be more dependent on others. And seventy-year-old Boomers and beyond may well still have older relatives on hand who need their support! (See 'Caring', Chapter Three.)

Yet as independence of spirit is essential for successful ageing you should try to avoid letting others take charge of your life, deciding where you should live, who you should see and what you should eat. This is why so many indomitable oldies fight so hard to stay out of nursing homes, where statistics show they are more likely to die earlier than people of comparable ages living in their own homes. But there are many types of supervised, 'sheltered' living accommodations that offer assistance if you need it and leave you to your own devices if you don't. More are being built daily, many equipped with the latest state-of-the-art gadgets designed for ease of use by arthritic hands and stooped bodies, some tested by 'councils of elders' supplied by gerontology departments at universities.

MIRROR, MIRROR

If you saw your mother in your reflection on a bad day when you were in your forties or fifties, now you may be able – Oh, the horror of it! – to see your father, as some of the sexual characteristic distinctions between men and women begin to disappear at this stage of life, men's voices growing higher as women's gruffen due to the decrease in their sex hormones.

The seventies can see, according to Dr Giampapa (are you sitting down for this?), 'The complete loss of the youthful contours of the face, marked muscle and skin "ptosis" (sagging), and hair which has been thinning imperceptibly since your fifties increasingly now. There might even be a few whiskers on your chin because of the lack of female hormones, and you might have acquired a few witch-like warts on the end of your slightly lengthened nose. Your earlobes may be as dangly as your breasts, particularly if you've worn heavy earrings for years.

Loss of bone density, if you are prone to osteoporosis and have not taken measures to strengthen your bones with exercise and a calcium-rich diet or HRT, may suddenly become very marked. You will have shrunk significantly from your peak height in your thirties, and may have acquired the dreaded 'dowager's hump' that is a sign of bone demineralization coupled with bad posture. As many people of this age are unsure of themselves when out walking – although UltraAgers shouldn't be – they may walk with their heads down, looking at the ground, which hastens this process.

It's enough to send you straight to the whisky bottle – if your eyes, with their incipient cataracts, can see the reflection clearly. But you might not remember the reason you reached for it if arteriosclerosis has further clogged up the arteries to your brain.

But for UltraAgers who have followed a good programme of diet and exercise, kept mentally and physically active, these changes may

Women cheered around the world when the former dancer and actress Cyd Charisse took to the catwalk at 77 and strutted her stuff. She proves that style is indeed ageless.

occur much, much later than in your seventies, and many of them might not occur at all.

RESISTANCE REQUIRED

Victoria's yoga teacher tells an interesting story about her guru, B. K. S. Iyengar, founder of the Iyengar system of yoga, which is purely physical and therefore much loved in the West, and his pupil, Yehudi Menuhin, the great violinist. 'Mr Iyengar has two pictures of himself with Menuhin on his wall in India,' she claims. 'One shows him and Menuhin when they were both in their thirties, and Mr Iyengar is looking up at his pupil; another shows him and Menuhin when they were both nearly eighty. This time the yoga teacher is looking down at his pupil, who seems to have shrunk significantly compared with him.'

Although Sir Yehudi has also practised yoga and kept himself fitter than many of his age, he has clearly not done so with the single-minded dedication of Mr Iyengar. The yogi's spine, constantly stretched from spending many hours a day practising his demanding discipline, must not have shrunk as much as that of the violinist, who by virtue of his career has had to spend some of his time hunched over his instrument. The moral of this story? How you use your instrument, your body, over the coming years, is crucial to how well it will stand the test of time.

If you've exercised regularly without injuring yourself or being too rough on your joints, twisting your back in squash or tennis, or getting 'shin splints' from high impact aerobics, eaten the right food (see Chapter Nine), taken care of your complexion, kept your hormone levels high either with nutrient precursors, replacement ther-

apies or good habits coupled with fortunate genes, you can look in your seventies like people the generation before you did in their fifties. American bodybuilder Kathy Nelson does. Ms Nelson, who took up bodybuilding in her fifties, was a guest of honour at an anti-ageing conference, happy to show off her well-toned body in a bikini at seventy-one! Or maybe you'll just look like a very fit seventy-year-old but feel like a forty-year-old inside or, better still, a mischievous teenager.

STIMULATE YOUR PALATE . . .

Don't give in to the urge for sweet and mushy foods which old people have traditionally liked because of the deterioration of tastebuds and teeth. There's no need for either to deteriorate if you've taken good care of yourself, and we know several eighty-year-olds (in America, admittedly) who have wonderful sets of their own teeth and can still chomp their way through huge steaks and corn on the cob. If you've kept your palate stimulated with fresh foods and your teeth exercised with crunchy ones (and brushed and flossed properly) you should be able to eat well, if sensibly and moderately, at this age.

. . . AND YOUR MIND

If you've kept your brain stimulated, its neurons will still be capable of making new connections, so that even if the number of nerve cells has decreased you can achieve an ever increasing network and retain high levels of function (see Chapter Ten). Look at how Barbara Cartland has churned out novels into her nineties, and Simone Veil has remained active in European politics.

FIND THE RIGHT BALANCE

So what do our experts recommend to achieve such a happy state? 'Balance is very important at this age and beyond,

The one and only 'Cat Woman', Eartha Kitt claims to enjoy performing now even more than when she was younger. This proves that continuing to stretch yourself can bring rich rewards.

and keeping up a moderate exercise programme has been shown to prevent falls and give better balance when walking, as the reflexes are maintained in a better state,' says Professor Sharp. 'Even people taking up exercise for the first time at this age can markedly improve muscle tone and coordination. Exercise at this age also improves thermal control, helping active older people to resist hypothermia much better than sedentary ones.'

Mr Jordan adds that 'HRT for women of this age helps to keep the joints flexible, and it's very important for them to stay mobile and active so that they don't fall and fracture their hips.' Taking supplement hormones can also prevent the vagina from shrinking and the bladder from becoming inelastic, he says. Opponents of HRT should reconsider their mix of nutritional supplements to remain sprightly. Philip Kingsley recommends B Vitamins in abundance, particularly B6, to prevent hair from thinning as it so often can at this age.

USE IT OR LOSE IT

Anti-ageing experts stress that it's important to build up muscle tone and bone, possibly with injections of HGH if you want to go that route (and doses of other hormones designed to keep your metabolism at the levels of the aspirational thirty-something), but certainly with regular exercise. 'This is crucial if you're going to maintain independence in later life,' says Dr Perring. 'If your quads go, you can't even get out of a chair!' And many old people can't, judging from the number of advertisements in the back of Sunday supplements for ejector seats and devices to help people in and out of the bath and up and down the stairs in their homes.

The message for both body and mind at this age (as throughout life) is use it or you may lose it. It is crucial to keep your brain active to maintain independence, and if you are not constantly challenging it, you will not build up the new connections that keep it buzzing. If you don't have a job to provide the necessary stimulation, make sure you do quizzes and wordgames, watch *Mastermind* and *University Challenge* rather than *Blind Date* (although they've had some Third Age couples on that programme recently). Keep up with the news and, for the fun of it, write irate letters to newspapers or take part in TV or radio feedback programmes about current issues to keep your hand in. Or surf the net!

SPREAD YOUR WINGS

'In her seventies a woman can become a witch, which is a wonderful free thing to be, with powers of prophecy and mysticism, freed from the constraints of convention,' Dr Perring enthuses, having no doubt read Germaine Greer and Leslie Kenton. He has found that 'Many older women embrace mysticism as a substitute for sex and/or strong religious beliefs,' perpetuating the mythology of the witch or wise woman. Dr Weeks calls it the freedom to be eccentric. Whatever you call it, it's the setting aside of convention that is one of the most exciting hallmarks of later life for women.

NEW PASSIONS

If you yearn for family nearby and have none, why not adopt one? Some areas have 'adopt-a-gran' schemes or you could advertise locally for a family with children who need occasional babysitting and cuddles. Or pour your nurturing instincts into caring for animals or plants (as I do now that my children are getting too old for babysitting and, almost, for cuddles).

   This could be the time to take up painting or to try to write that novel that's been bursting out of you. It could be time for a change of residence. If you live in the country, might you be better moving to the city where public transport and facilities are better, food can be delivered to your door, and there are many activities to enjoy within a comparatively small radius? Many people dream of retiring to the country, but in so many ways the country is for the young and strong and city life is suited to older people with the time to enjoy cultural attractions – many of them free. But a small town may supply the support of a close-knit community. Decide what you want *before* you need to make such choices.

THE VISION THING

As vision, particularly night vision, may not be too good at this stage, driving can become difficult, which is why, in some countries like the UK, you will have to take another test in order to get your licence renewed when over seventy. Most of us will have some degree of cataracts by this age even if we don't realize it, and it seems safe to surmise that a generation which has been working on computers for

> ## UltraAge Prescription for the Seventies
>
> Grab life for what it is worth with your whole being. Resist becoming a passive observer in other people's lives and remain an active participant in your own. Keep as fit and free as possible while welcoming friendly help when needed, and offering it in return if you can.

so many years will have more than previous ones. But the latest operations to remove them are simple and highly successful, and we know several women in their seventies and eighties who have undergone the procedure with spectacular results, seeing better than they have in years and, thanks to the lens permanently inserted in their eye, without glasses! Having a good vision of what you'd like your future to be, and making comfortable provision for when you are frailer is very important now.

Eighties and Beyond: The Final Frontier

If you've reached this far, congratulations. You must be doing something – no, lots! – right.

KEEP WITH IT

Your main stresses probably come from the fight to keep your independence and your faculties, and to create a lifestyle you're comfortable with, even if all the choices aren't yours to make.

BUT LEARN TO LET GO

It's not surprising so many older people are backward-looking when looking ahead can be so frightening at this age. Reminiscing, and sharing those reminiscences with younger generations, can be pleasant and positive, but clinging obstinately on to the past, the sign of an old mind, is not healthy. Maybe it is time to shed the paraphernalia of your earlier life and pare down to essentials – both the practical and the pleasurable – eliminating clutter and chaos. Ensure you've made your preferences clear when the inevitable happens, whether it's preserving your head cryogenically in the hope of future resurrection, arranging to have the life-support system turned off if you're judged 'brain dead', becoming an organ donor, or leaving your whole body to science. 'Quality of choice is often important, and in many cases a lot of help can be given by medical specialists,' says Dr Weeks. A will can help make sure your posthumous wishes are carried out.

BODY AND SOLES

'Mobility and mental function are the main concerns of women of this age, followed by bladder function,' says Mr Jordan. So keep up the exercising, walking instead of running, of course, unless you're a compulsive runner like me who has to keep on going until you drop – and there have been some eighty-somethings in the London, New York and Boston marathons! Keep doing light resistance exercises, pelvic floor squeezes, and stretches or something such as yoga (we keep coming back to it because it's so good for you) for flexibility. There's no reason you can't stand on your head at eighty as yoga guru BKS Iyengar demonstrates.

Foot maintenance is also particularly important, as circulation will become worse and the reduced blood-flow to the extremities will make foot problems increasingly difficult to heal. Sometimes old people might not even notice foot problems if they have lost sensation in this area through neuropathy, and may not have the flexibility to see the bottoms of their feet, so that sores can fester and ulcerate. Foot and leg ulcers are one of the great banes of old women's existence. Britain's Queen Elizabeth the Queen Mother has been a very public sufferer from these.

An original Hollywood model for active, independent women, Katharine Hepburn has continued this trait in real life into advanced age. She willingly defied convention, and made men's fashions fashionable for women to boot!

Britain's beloved Queen Mother is a triumph of consistent personal style over decades of change. Is it her favourite tipple of gin and tonic, her interest in people, her love of sports like racing and salmon fishing, the closeness of her family, a belief in homoeopathy or simply her stolid Hanoverian genes that has kept her going for so long?

LOVE AMONG THE RUINS Love is still possible, desire still desirable at this age. Recent research by the Italian Professor Vincenzo Marigliano of La Sapienz University, Rome, seems to prove that a kiss and a cuddle a day keeps the doctor away, or at least that people who have affection in their lives in old age thrive better than those who don't, even if the latter group is technically in better health.

In his wonderful book *Love in Later Life* (Peter Owen, 1998) octogenarian gerontologist Dr Hamilton Gibson supports this theory, and shows how golden oldies have been finding that out for themselves, many enjoying richer and more rewarding sex lives than they did in their supposed prime. Fantasy (like the centenarian ceramicist Beatrice Wood's 'dream lover'), masturbation, and sensual relationships with the same sex are all options being joyfully explored. These forms of sexual satisfaction can be enjoyed well into the eighties and beyond, even when the vagina has shrivelled, as it may do, to a degree when conventional sex would be uncomfortable if not impossible. 'A satisfying sex life can continue throughout life if you remember there are other ways to obtain satisfaction than the traditional,' says Mr Jordan.

The late, great Marlene Dietrich, another sufferer, used to wrap her unsightly leg ulcers in layers of shimmering stockings. Not smoking would probably have helped more, however, since the cigarettes the sultry star was so often seen with may well have constricted the circulation to her legs later in life. Leg ulcers can be a very demoralizing problem, particularly for fastidious women like these, who take care of their appearance. Little can be done, however, about this horrible problem once it has occurred, which is possibly why so few health books mention it. All you can do is try to improve the circulation to the area through regular exercise and taking good care of the feet and legs, massaging dry, thin-skinned old legs regularly with emollient oils (or virgin olive oil) and being checked regularly by a chiropodist and doctor. Diabetics (see Chapter Three) are particularly at risk from complications.

STAY INVOLVED – WITH ALL AGES

'One of the greatest ageing factors is when old people are put together in homes,' says Dr Perring. 'The old tradition of "vertical families" is very important because there's so much in common between the very old and the very young,' particularly as you will have to come to terms with the loss of many of your contemporaries, a major stress factor at this age.

Professor Sharp emphasizes the 'social value of communal forms of gentle exercise such as yoga, t'ai chi or rambling, and the effect exercise has on enhancing the mood can be useful in countering the mild depression which age can induce'.

The importance of loving human relationships and physical contact should not be underestimated at this stage, as recent studies have shown them to be of prime importance to our wellbeing and longevity.

INDULGE – YOU ONLY LIVE ONCE!

Remember that, at this age, a little of what you fancy may certainly be doing you good if it hasn't harmed you yet, so you can indulge yourself a bit. Look at Queen Elizabeth the Queen Mother, reportedly knocking back the gin and tonics late into her nineties. At this age, nobody can tell you it's not good for you!

The Key Principles for All Ages

1 Don't smoke.
2 Don't sunbathe without a very strong sunscreen, and even then not for long.
3 Drink alcohol in moderation.
4 Exercise regularly, with resistance and bone-building exercises vital to the over forties, and modifying your regime according to your age and needs.
5 Don't worry – be happy, as the song says. A smile may not be your umbrella but it can offer a lot of protection to your immune system.
6 Plan ahead: don't be taken by surprise at the different stages of ageing. (But stay spontaneous and mentally flexible, too!)
7 Take care of your skin daily with cleansers and moisturizers morning and night; heavier duty products being necessary as you grow older.
8 Wear make-up – a good foundation and lipstick with UVA and B filters will protect your skin from photo-damage.
9 Eat a healthy and moderate diet of fresh foods, preferably organically grown, with a balance of protein, fruits, vegetables and legumes.
10 Pump the antioxidants that promise energy and a lessening of the degenerative processes of age.
11 Learn something new every day, and keep open to new ideas. This will exercise your brain, which, like your body, needs regular exercise to keep it going.
12 Laugh and love to the end!

3

Age Accelerators

'Old age seems the only disease;
all others run into this one.'

RALPH WALDO EMERSON (1803–82)

Warning: Dangers Ahead

We are all guilty in some ways of accelerating the ageing process, which can creep up on us slowly and insidiously as a cancer, gathering speed as it snowballs out of control. The young and super-fit don't care if you say 'stop smoking, cut down on the drinking, avoid junk food – they'll damage your body'. It's only when the wear and tear becomes *tangible* that the twinges of remorse set in and the realization dawns that we could have – *should have* – been kinder to ourselves.

Looking at ourselves in the mirror – and seeing no longer the vibrant person we felt ourselves to be somewhere deep inside (still screaming to get out) is what made us want to research the age-old condition of ageing.

What first made us aware of the age acceleration process? Our seemingly overnight 'blindness' (well, inability to read the newspaper any longer except at arm's length – a shock for me, who had always had excellent vision and, equally, for Victoria, who had always been shortsighted).

Chronic insomnia quickly followed for me together with other vexing precursors to the menopause (see Chapter Four). For Victoria it was the urge to sleep more than before. Both of us suddenly found it harder to leap out of bed with the birds or to stay up working until the wee hours and we were more keenly aware of any over-indulgence. We found we were no longer successfully juggling as much as we used to – and, even scarier, began to wonder why we *should*.

Then I started to experience digestive problems and food intolerances (previously dismissed as the domain of neurotics) and to notice sad, tired-looking lines on my face (see Chapter Ten). Victoria recognized that her skin wasn't what it use to be and started to use foundation and invest in expensive moisturizers with my chiding that she was locking the stable door after the horse had bolted! She gave up sugar (because of diabetes in the family) and started exercising with more determination while I cut down on obsessive running and began pumping iron as well as antioxidants.

From our experiences and with the help of experts, we have developed a list of what we consider to be prime 'Age Accelerators'. You might want to dive immediately into our A to Z guide – which, you'll be glad to know, provides a suggested 'UltraAge Antidote' to each

problem – or just dip into it as and if you need it. If you feel you don't, and that you are not an age accelerator but an 'age defier' or UltraAger, as we call you – all power to you.

Becoming an UltraAger

We all know people who look a good decade younger than their age. We call these age defiers UltraAgers. The chances are that they share certain characteristics. They are usually fit and active, have work or hobbies they enjoy, and a positive frame of mind. They also tend to have taken good care of their bodies and avoided what we call age accelerators, those attributes or habits which accelerate ageing or give you the appearance of being older than you are.

A merry widow we know of sixty could pass for forty and has a busy dating life with younger men. A frequently used phrase, as she refuses second helpings and extra glasses of wine at dinner parties, is 'Thank you but I've had sufficient.' We joke about it, but clearly her abstemiousness in indulging in some of life's pleasures has left her more able to enjoy others.

Bad habits like smoking are known to accelerate the ageing process, with smokers measurably more wrinkly than their non-smoking contemporaries.

One doctor says he judges people's age by the way they walk into his office: do they bounce on the balls of their feet, or do they drag themselves along even if they don't hobble or limp? Walking badly, either because of wearing silly shoes or because of bunions, corns or other pressure points caused by poor foot management, is a huge age accelerator which can lead on to others, stopping you from being active, causing you to avoid walking and therefore decreasing your general fitness. It also gives you the appearance and physical abilities of an older person.

Bad habits like smoking are known to accelerate the ageing process, with smokers measurably more wrinkly than their non-smoking contemporaries. Note that all of the traditional seven deadly sins are age accelerators, as has been known since ancient times, hence 'deadly'. Sloth, greed, envy, pride, anger, gluttony, and lust for the wrong types of pleasures (although not a healthy sexual appetite) all feature in our list although they come in different guises.

IT'S UP TO YOU

Your health is in your own hands. Throughout this book you will learn many ways to kick bad habits and ideas for improving how you feel through the food that you eat and the energy, and fun, that you will get from exercise. But your health care is also up to you. If your doctor is being obtuse, not giving you full explanations, answering all your questions or arranging tests as quickly as you want them, get bolshie. If you can't get the advice that you want from your doctor (e.g. about alternative treatments for conditions), you've got to find it somewhere else. Ask friends, write to health columnists on good newspapers, try some of the resources listed at the back of this book.

If the treatments you want aren't covered by your health insurance policy or a national health service, be prepared to pay for them or change the system. I was let down by traditional medicine while pregnant with my two daughters. The best gynaecologists and ear, nose and throat (ENT) specialists couldn't relieve symptoms that prevented me from breathing and sleeping. My sinuses were so swollen, and drugs were out of the question. I sought alternative help through an ayurvedic doctor who, with weekly cranial massages, homoeopathic potions and acupunture, could relieve my symptoms. I insisted that the 'recognized' doctors write to my insurance company agreeing that the ayurvedic approach did work. As a result, the insurance company paid for a full year of treatment, twice.

The A–Z of Age Accelerators

Our simple guide is of age accelerators you can do something about. It will tell you how to thwart these thieves of time which can steal your prime from you and even take years off your life.

AGE SPOTS

Also known as liver spots, these are the brown splodges that can crop up any time from the forties onward, most noticeably on the hand but also on other parts of the body which have been exposed to the sun such as the chest, neck and face. The skin is prone to all types of discol-

oration and changes in pigment as it gets older. Some changes, like liver spots, are just a fact of ageing; others may be rodent ulcers or skin cancers which need urgent medical attention (see 'Warts, Whiskers and All').

Once You've Spotted the Problem

Age spots on the face can be camouflaged with cosmetics, but those on the hand are more difficult to deal with. A bleaching cream such as hydroquinone may be prescribed. This doesn't actually bleach but appears to have that effect by reducing melanin production in the area. It is, however, a suspected carcinogen. Selenium (see Chapter Nine) is said to help and also to do away with the unseen age spots that apparently are echoed inside us on ageing organs. The best way to avoid the visible ones is through good skin care and staying out of the sun when without a high factor sunblock. Curiously, cold weather may make them worse once you have them. Ayurvedic practitioners may recommend massage with saffron oil. Like nail ridges, which tend to arise after menopause and are linked to lowered oestrogen levels, these are a way of assessing age as the rings on a tree are.

UltraAge Antidote
High factor sunscreens and antioxidants.

ALCOHOL

In excess, alcohol is ageing and, indeed, toxic, but the latest school of thought states that it is healthier to drink – wine and beer at least – in moderation than not to drink at all. Red wine is thought to have positive health benefits. A glass of red wine before each meal was part of the recipe for longevity, together with positive thinking and a good sense of humour, so set out by the world's oldest woman, Jeanne Calment, on her one hundred and twenty-first birthday in 1996.

Alcohol is only an age accelerator when intake becomes too regular, creating a dependency. Studies have shown that a drink a day, for women, may actually prevent heart disease. But second only to nicotine in terms of addiction, alcohol abuse not only shortens your life but can make it miserable for you and everyone around you.

One study which differentiated between pleasure drinkers and those who drank to drown their sorrows found that the death rate of the former was lower than the death rates of teetotallers whereas the death rate of the others was predictably higher.

If you answer yes to more than five of the following questions, you may have a drink problem:

1. Do your partner, parents, or children worry or complain about your drinking?
2. Do you ever drink in the morning?
3. Have you called in sick to work after a heavy drinking session more than twice a year?
4. Do you get into arguments, or, worse, fighting, when you have been drinking?
5. Have you lost friends because of your drinking?
6. Do you find it hard to stop easily after one or two drinks?
7. Do you drink every day?
8. Have you ever driven while over the legal limit?
9. Have you ever had a 'lost weekend' or other missing chunks of time?
10. Have you been embarrassed about something you have done while drinking (or suspect you would be if you could remember)?

Still, the potency of alcohol abuse is there for everyone to see with ageing, pallid skin, a weakened frame and visible nervous twitching or shaking. As Rosa Della Tolla, a recovering alcoholic turned counsellor, says, 'I can always tell if a woman's been drinking: her face will be puffy; her eyes will be jaundiced and bloodshot; there will be circles or bags under the eyes; and she will have an enlarged abdomen due to liver damage. The dehydration that alcohol causes makes the skin look dry and wrinkly.' She feels it is important to distinguish between 'the circumstantial heavy drinker, the person who will drink heavily after a bereavement or during a particularly stressed time', and the alcoholic. The former can go back to drinking moderately after the problem has passed whereas with the latter, well, 'If you take a cucumber and pickle it you cannot reverse the process.' Della Tolla has not touched alcohol for more than twenty years, but recent studies show a worrying trend in alcohol dependency among working women.

The greatest worry is the damage going on inside:
✧ Your liver can literally rot (cirrhosis).
✧ The heart can be weakened, with blood pressure elevated.
✧ Depression may be triggered.
✧ Fertility can be lessened; libido depleted.
✧ The stomach lining may be eroded.
✧ The immune system is made more vulnerable to illness at least, cancer at worst.
✧ It aggravates diabetes.

So, what's the Damage?

As outlined above, the potential havoc that alcohol abuse can wreak on a person's system and, potentially, long-term health, is considerable. For starters it can cause metabolic damage to every cell in your body, and lowers the immune system. The liver can become chronically impaired, unable to absorb nutrients, proteins and vitamins. Because alcohol prevents the proper digestions of fats, the liver gets clogged with fat. Long term this condition causes inflammation and scarring of the liver which are preventable by stopping drinking but not reversible if allowed to develop.

Balance with Supplements

Nutritional supplements help to counteract the damage alcohol does to the system, but don't fool yourself into thinking that all you have to do is pop a few vitamins and keep on boozing, as no amount of supplements will prevent the inevitable liver damage.

Consider using the following vitamins and minerals if you are going through a detox programme and trying to wean yourself off alcohol for a while. They will make you feel better, as well as virtuous, into the bargain.

✧ B Vitamins – especially B complex and B12.
✧ Amino Acids – help to regenerate the liver.
✧ Vitamin C and Bioflavonoids – strengthen your weakened immune system.
✧ Calcium and Magnesium – alcohol depletes both of these minerals; plus, they have a calming effect.
✧ Good Multivitamins – because you need topping up with everything!
✧ Zinc – helps to minimize alcohol poisoning to the cells.

Know Your Limits

The guidelines for safe consumption of alcohol are fourteen units for women and twenty-one units for men. But we all know that everyone is affected differently by alcohol. Some women feel the first drink, others seem to be able to consume quite a few before showing any signs of being affected. Outward manifestations of alcohol are only one indication of your own healthy tolerance point. Without testing your blood pressure and blood to determine what, if any, liver damage has been caused, you are playing a game of roulette with your health.

A Healthy Habit

Because of the damaging effects of alcohol, many experts insist that the only healthy level of consumption is zero. Okay, that might be a bit drastic and reserved as only sensible for alcoholics who can't ever learn to handle the substance in moderation.

Luckier mortals keen on a long, healthy life are advised to have total-abstinence, detox phases during the year which will allow them to experience the wonderful feeling of being truly healthy and alert without alcohol. After a forced hiatus, it is much easier to limit consumption to special social events rather than allow drinking to become part of your daily routine. If you can limit yourself to a single glass of wine in the evening, then well done. But anyone who finds it difficult to put the bottle away after one glass and almost never stops unless half or indeed a whole bottle has been consumed needs to be conscious of the grip alcohol has on her life and health.

Because of the damaging effects of alcohol, many experts insist that the only healthy level of consumption is zero.

UltraAge Antidote
Water and moderation!

After speaking to countless health experts, we advise anyone who loves their drink but doesn't want it to become addictive to follow these simple rules:

✧ Restrict yourself to drinking three times a week with four alcohol-free days to allow your system to recover.
✧ For every drink you consume, match it with a glass of water.
✧ Eat before you drink to mitigate the impact on your system.
✧ Drink a large glass of water before bedtime and have one ready for the morning to help minimize dehydration.
✧ Never drink when taking medicines like antibiotics, tranquillizers, antihistamines or even cold remedies as these can form toxic, if not lethal, combinations with alcohol.

ANGER

Anger is one of the most ageing of all emotions. Look angry just for a moment and observe your face in the mirror. The chances are that ageing frown lines, very different from laughter lines, have appeared between your brows. Some cosmetic surgeons suggest cutting the tendons that enable their patients to frown at all for just that reason, but it seems more sensible to try to control anger instead, since anger has an ageing effect on other parts of the body we can't see, such as the heart, the blood pressure and the immune system. Anger summons up a rush of 'fight or flight' hormones which course through our system and have been shown to clog up the arteries if they are not required to help us fight or flee. Dr Malcolm Carruthers, a Harley Street stress and hormone specialist, calls artery-clogging cholesterols 'the fatty fuels of fury', and likens anger to a car engine being gunned while the driver's other foot is still on the brake – not good for the car or the cardio-vascular system.

Learn to Let Go

Anger is by its very essence backward-looking. Learn to let go of past disappointments and instead of looking back in anger look ahead in anticipation and you'll be a much more youthful, forward-looking person.

Learn to laugh things off more because laughter has been shown to have a positive effect on the appearance and on the immune system. Blood pressure is lowered when we laugh and levels of cortisol, a substance released in times of stress or distress, are measurably lower when we are happy. Other positive enzymes and endorphins, the body's natural opiates, are demonstrably raised even by a short period of laughter. Students shown comic films had higher levels of positive substances (such as immunoglobin-A, which protects against respiratory infections) and lower levels of negative ones in their blood when they were tested immediately afterwards. Laughter can actually lower the blood pressure, as well as massaging the heart, lungs and abdomen. But whereas children can laugh several hundreds of times a day, in adults the number of laughs drops to around fifty if we're lucky.

In Britain laughter clinics have even been run on the National Health Service. These were the brainchild of Robert Holden who also holds workshops on laughter and happiness and the beneficial effect they can have on your life. Look at yourself in the mirror. Is your natural expres-

> *Learn to laugh things off more because laughter has been shown to have a positive effect on the appearance and on the immune system.*

sion a frown? If so, smile, and consciously try to smile more each day. As well as making you look younger, as your reflection will show, and exercising the face and neck muscles, the very act of smiling releases some endorphins and smiling more, even without any particular reason, will therefore make you healthier. Belly laughing is great exercise as well as bringing additional oxygen into the system. Bear in mind the sage advice of Marlene Dietrich: 'When you're young, never smile; it causes wrinkles. When you're old, smile all the time; it prevents them.'

> **UltraAge Antidote**
> Laughter, and learning to let go and look forward, not back.

BACK PAIN

You can't feel young with an aching, crumbling spine since it is your central support system. But chronic back pain, particularly in the lower back, is widespread even among the active, exercise-conscious Baby Boomer generation. Our largely sedentary lives are to blame (even those who exercise religiously for an hour a day spend most of the remaining twenty-three hours a day in chairs, beds and cars, at desks and tables). One leading chiropractor, Michael Durtnall, who runs the Sayer Clinics in London, reports seeing an increasing number of men with 'soft' pelvises like those of pregnant women, simply because they spend so much time sitting down.

Give Your Back the Back-up it Deserves

Invest in one of the specially designed 'back chairs' or kneeling stools that can save a lot on specialist treatment in the long run. Paying attention to the ergonomics of your home and work can also save a great deal of grief. Michael Durtnall runs a service that will go out to homes and offices and advise on steps to improve or, better still, prevent back pain, like making sure computer screens are at the correct height so you don't have to strain necks; phones and keyboards placed so you don't slump or stretch awkwardly; ironing boards and sinks at the correct height; car seats adjusted correctly, etc.

It is important to remember that back pain may be merely a symptom of a deeper problem such as fibroids, kidney or gall bladder problems. Victoria suffered lower back problems for years until she had

a large fibroid cyst removed from her pelvis, which, apparently, had been pressing her womb against her spine. That is one of the reasons that chiropractors usually insist on taking X-rays before they will manipulate patients with back pain. However, these X-rays may not show up problems in soft tissue, which require other types of scans, so be aware of the possibilities. Osteopaths, who may work on muscles and soft tissues as well as the spine, don't always work from X-rays. Treatments from both can be very effective as long as you find a reputable practitioner who works for you. Everyone's technique is slightly different and you may take to one but not to another.

Straight from the Hip

Back pain can be prevented by learning how to bend correctly – from the hip or squatting with a strong back – and by proper daily exercise. Strengthening the stomach muscles will take a lot of strain off the back, as will losing weight. Should your lower back go ping and you find yourself scarcely able to move, simply sucking in your stomach may make it possible for you to get yourself into a comfortable position where putting ice on the sore spot should ease the spasm. Too much heat, which people tend to apply to the back, can cause muscles around the spine to relax, making it easier for something to slip out if it has a tendency to. Beware sudden bends and twists while coming out of the jacuzzi or a hot shower.

> **UltraAge Antidote**
> Abdominal strengthening and other exercises for the stretching and mobility of the spine. Yoga is particularly good.

BUNIONS (SEE ALSO 'FEET')

Bunions are included as an 'age accelerator' not only because of the real suffering and retarded mobility that they can cause but also because of their association with 'old ladies'. Using bunions as an excuse not to enjoy life to the full does little to enhance your image as a swinger, but they are surprisingly common in women of 'a certain age'!

Some twenty per cent of women over the age of forty suffer from bunions, the painful outgrowth of bone matter on the inner side of the foot near the big toe. The awkward development of the bones,

near the big toe, causes painful swelling of the muscles and, in turn, fluid retention. Often bunions are inherited by women with a big toe that grows inwards rather than straight. The condition, of course, is exacerbated, if not caused, by wearing tight, ill-fitting shoes particularly when the foot is still developing. Lifelong corns and calluses can also be caused by pressure at such a formative time.

People who 'over pronate' when they walk, rolling the feet inwards, are likely candidates for bunions. The sad news is that often one bunion means two bunions. Hence, if your toe is quirky on one foot, it is likely for both feet to end up suffering.

Treatment

If you have a bunion or two that can be accommodated in comfortable shoes, then be smart and wear only appropriate styles. Natural materials like leather (inner and outer layers), canvas, or cotton allow excess fluid to evaporate. Choose these over man-made materials which can be more painful.

Some twenty per cent of women over the age of forty suffer from bunions.

Over pronating should be corrected as early as possible with specially moulded insoles – called orthotics – that prevent the rolling in and encourage 'pushing off' under the big toe rather than on the side of the foot. These can be obtained from podiatrists or chiropodists. A toe-straightening splint made from rubber that helps stretch the big toe away from the second toe, available from pharmacies, can also alleviate the strain.

If growth accelerates and the foot and bone structure become deformed, then an oseteotomy might be the only cure. This operation aims to straighten as best as possible the angle of the malformed joint to minimize swelling and pain. But sometimes operations on bunions can be unsuccessful. Carol, fifty, is sorry she's had one. 'I had the operation so I could wear attractive high-heeled shoes again,' she wails, 'and now I'm in more pain than I was before and have had to have several operations to get me back to where I was!' Far better to try to prevent bunions by wearing sensible shoes whenever possible than to have to treat them.

UltraAge Antidote
Love your tootsies and take good care of them!

CAFFEINE

Found in tea and cola drinks as well as coffee, caffeine is a diuretic and a mild stimulant. While good for a short 'kick' to stay awake while working or driving, in excess it can cause irritability and sleeplessness and can be addictive. When Victoria tried to wean herself off drinking ten to twelve cups of strong coffee a day she developed terrible headaches for two weeks. When they disappeared her head cleared and she felt better than ever before. Suffering headaches and drowsiness is common among those who suddenly stop taking caffeine. Because for many people caffeine-filled drinks replace water in the diet, and it has a diuretic effect, it can be very dehydrating to the tissues and therefore ageing. It also works against the absorption of water-soluble vitamins in the body and forces the kidneys to work harder without being flushed out. It blocks the effect of certain homoeopathic remedies and holistic doctors usually recommend avoiding it completely. But we can't give it up entirely!

> *Suffering headaches and drowsiness is common among those who suddenly stop taking caffeine.*

Don't Keep Going for the Buzz

As with most addictive substances, caffeine works less effectively as a stimulant in those who are accustomed to it, who keep drinking more, depleting their vitamin reserves, and dehydrating themselves still further. It can make you jittery and puts your whole system under stress. The odd cup of good coffee or tea is fine, and, indeed, may be better for you than some beverages that have been 'decaffeinated' by chemical means. Try to look for water-decaffeinated ones when you can. But try to intersperse your caffeine intake with herbal teas, and drink lots of water to keep your system lubricated and flush out the kidneys.

A 50 mg cup of tea in the UK contains 80 mg of caffeine while, curiously enough, a similar cup in the US contains only about 35 mg; a 150 mg cup of percolated coffee contains 100 mg of caffeine; a 150 mg cup of instant coffee contains 60 mg; and a 360 mg can of cola contains between 35 and 45 mg, depending on brand. Caffeine-free cola, coffee and tea are now available.

> **UltraAge Antidote**
> Water (again!) and enjoying the odd cup of coffee instead of drinking the whole pot.

CARING

For the 'sandwich generation' caught in the trap of having to care for teenaged or twenty-something children who haven't quite left home and ageing parents, caring can be a very ageing responsibility. The Carers Association offers support and helpful suggestions to those who feel trapped in the carer's role. It says that this situation will become all the more common in the millennium as old people live longer and young ones find it harder to leave home because of the difficulty in getting jobs and affording accommodation. The Baby Boom generation may find itself squeezed as never before.

Make Sure You Care for Yourself, Too

If you can't care for yourself, you won't be in a fit state to take care of anybody else. Don't feel you're the only person who can possibly do what you're doing for others. Make sure you take holidays from your caring responsibilities, making use of residential accommodation made available for the purpose by some local authorities and health trusts or by persuading friends or other relatives to take charge for a brief while to give you a break. The Carers Association will advise on grants and services that may make this process easier. But most importantly, don't feel guilty when you do take a break. No one can or should guarantee to be around all the time for someone else and all parties may benefit from a bit of a refresher.

One wonderful new idea that surfaced in 1998 is the Granny Crèche, as it is being called. A few forward-thinking companies such as Peugeot are offering employees the opportunity to bring their elderly parents into a supervised environment. Here they can theoretically, at the moment, enjoy having their hair done and taking tea with others of their generation while their carers are at work.

> **UltraAge Antidote**
> Take care of yourself.

CELLULITE

Many doctors insist it doesn't exist but most women would know that it does. These puckery pockets of fat can pop up even on sylph-like thighs, giving the skin an unpleasant orange-peel appearance. Few media reports offended the late Diana, Princess of Wales, as much as the ones suggesting that she suffered from cellulite. The princess, who

didn't deign to answer many graver accusations, issued a firm denial on that one. It was the pattern from her car seat, from a stool at her healthclub, anything but those cottage cheesy clusters of dimples which even supermodels like Cindy Crawford confess to suffering. Crawford says she rubs coffee grounds into her thighs to prevent it.

Although rare before your thirties it becomes increasingly common after that, and, since it seems linked to bad circulation, will get worse with age. The French take it more seriously than most nationalities, with many of the companies marketing anti-cellulite products based in France. While most consider it harmless, if aesthetically unpleasing, some say it's a symptom of bad lymphatic drainage and of circulatory sluggishness.

Breaking it Up is Hard to Do

However, you can try by drinking plenty of water, eating a healthy diet of fresh fruit and vegetables, avoiding alcohol, caffeine, nicotine and spicy or fatty food, and getting plenty of exercise. Massage may also be effective. Fiona Harrold, founder of the London College of Massage which has a Cellulite Clinic, believes, 'There's a cellulite personality: stressed, exhausted, living on coffee, sweets, cigarettes, and alcohol.'

She found cellulite sufferers often had a low self-image. The wide range of anti-cellulite creams have not been proven to be effective, although they are usually combined with a massaging action which may be. For further reading: Liz Hodgkinson's *How to Banish Cellulite For Ever.*

> ***UltraAge Antidote***
> Raw food, lots of water, and keep it moving through exercise and massage.

CHOLESTEROL

Cholesterol is vital for many body functions and, indeed, the human body produces its own supplies which, in turn, break down to form vital links in the steroid chain, helping to create many of the substances which anti-ageing doctors prescribe. But it also clogs the arteries, and high levels are associated with coronary heart disease and strokes. There is a great deal of confusion about cholesterol, which is now generally considered to exist in two types, the 'bad' low-density lipoproteins (LDL) and the 'good' high-density lipoproteins (HDL) which can actually, it is now thought, prevent heart disease. But high levels of LDLs in the

blood stream can cause arteriosclerosis, a build-up on the inside of the arteries, like plaque build-up on the teeth, which leads to the condition known as hardening of the arteries, and causes many of the conditions associated with senile dementia. Some experts feel that the way to lower the levels in your blood is to consume as little of it as possible, hence the popularity in the United States for omelettes and scrambled eggs made entirely of eggwhites. Others, such as the late and great American health food guru Adele Davies, argue that the body produces its own cholesterol, and it is only when it ingests cholesterol from outside that it produces enzymes which break it down successfully, where the body's own cholesterol levels would otherwise proliferate unchecked. The latest thinking is that avoiding saturated animal fats is better for controlling cholesterol than not eating the cholesterol that comes in eggs and shellfish.

Cholesterol Check

Have your levels tested. Most doctors and even some chemists offer simple cholesterol checks. Healthy levels are up to 6 mmol/litre. Certain foods such as shellfish, healthy in many other ways and low in calories, can contain high levels of cholesterol whereas other types of fish, the oily ones like mackerel, for example, have been shown to have a beneficial effect on cholesterol levels, helping the body to produce more HDL chlolesterol and less LDL.

> ***UltraAge Antidote***
> Oily fish (not the batter-fried variety!) and a diet low in saturated fats.

CIRCULATION

One of the things that shows your age more unpleasantly than grey hairs is swollen ankles and feet which ooze over the tops of your shoes. This is a symptom displayed only by women over a certain age with sluggish circulation and what is known as 'gravitational oedema'.

Swollen ankles can be a symptom of heart disease or lymphatic problems and should be checked out by a doctor. Numbness in fingers and toes can be caused by diabetes (see below) as well as by poor circulation to the extremities from vascular deficiency. Varicose veins are caused by and also cause poor circulation as the blood struggles to return against the force of gravity to the heart through plaque-clogged vessels.

Getting Back Into Circulation

First of all, get yourself checked by a doctor so that you know the reason for your problems. In extreme cases surgery can revascularize legs, taking healthier arteries from the groin and grafting them where they are needed. Synthetic arteries will soon be available. But there is a lot you can do yourself to prevent this condition, most notably by exercising regularly. Even when you are sitting down, as you may have to be for hours at a time if you have a desk job, rotate your ankles, flap your feet up and down, and change position as much as possible. But don't cross your legs! A stool under your feet will help to raise your thighs off the edge of the chair and improve circulation, a valuable tip for anyone travelling by aeroplane, which tends to worsen circulatory problems. If you're flying, good support or even surgical stockings can be a help, in addition to keeping your thighs off the chair edge and wriggling them about regularly, taking time to go for walks and stretches in the aisles.

> *There is a lot you can do yourself to prevent oedema, most notably by exercising regularly.*

If you have to stand for much of the day, a good pair of support stockings should help. These days they are imperceptible and very comfortable. If the problem is to do with veinous return, you should sit with your legs high for some time every day, or sleep with them raised at night. However, be careful: if your arteries aren't good, this will make it more difficult for the blood to reach the feet. If in doubt, keep your legs straight out. Evening Primrose Oil may be helpful and, if you can afford it, sessions with a reflexologist or a masseuse who is experienced in lymphatic drainage should stimulate the circulation.

UltraAge Antidote
Exercise and avoiding constrictions.

DEMENTIA

This is not an unavoidable accessory to old age and UltraAgers don't usually fall victim to it. Although no one knows quite what causes it, and there may be genetic or other triggers beyond our control, it can be caused at least in part by a lack of oxygen getting to the brain from clogged arteries (see above). One of the best things you can do to prevent it is to eat a diet low in saturated fat, take plenty of exercise, and 'feed your brain'. Once dementia has set in, brain exercises are not that effective. Prevention is the key. The 'A-Team' antioxidants and supplements should keep the

UltraAge Antidote
Antioxidants, brain exercise and brain 'feeding' (see Chapters Nine and Ten).

arteries leading to the brain elastic and prevent the likelihood of dementia. Brain nourishers such as Q10 and PS might help (see Chapters Nine and Ten).

DEPRESSION

The causes of depression are myriad, some purely chemical, others emotional. Many women and men as they reach mid-life and beyond naturally reflect on their achievements which sometimes have fallen well short of youthful goals and ambitions. A traumatic event, stress, allergies, illness, or even a chemical imbalance in the brain can set off depression. Symptoms include fatigue, insomnia, or excessive sleep, changes in appetite, irritability, digestive difficulties, and loss of interest in friends or hobbies.

Hormonal changes can cause fluctuating spirits but so too can bad nutrition and lack of exercise. Chronic depression is different from being temporarily depressed with good reason, such as because your boyfriend has left you or you have lost your job. If it is an unhappy life event that has caused you to become depressed, counselling can help you cope or, better still, change your perspective on the problem or help you take action to improve the situation. With long-term depression that defies help, anti-depressant drugs may be necessary.

Mood swings and feeling out of sorts are not necessarily symptoms of chronic or clinical depression, but any persistent downward spiral of the spirit, accompanied by increasing physical maladies, requires the advice of a physician for proper diagnosis and treatment.

Eliminate Junk Foods if Mood Swings Plague You

Consider adding some 'power nutrition' to get you back on an even keel. Oily fish, fresh and naturally green, yellow and orange vegetables together with fresh fruit should help instead of foods containing

artificial colourings. Try also reducing or eliminating dairy and wheat products if you suspect any relationship between food and your moods. Also reduce caffeine and alcohol. Better still, try to cut out both for a month and you may feel much more positive and peaceful.

Antioxidants and nutritional supplements can be very effective in mitigating the symptoms of depression. Vitamin C can actually prevent minor depression while B-complex helps to restore normal functioning of the brain and nervous systems. Calcium and magnesium have a calming effect. Depressed people often show deficiencies in zinc and folic acid which are worth restoring with supplements.

Light Up Your Life

If you feel your depression is worse in the winter months, you possibly suffer from Seasonally Affective Disorder (SAD). Consider using overhead lights or light boxes with full-spectrum light which stimulates the production of serotonin in the pineal gland, making us feel brighter and more alert. A daily dose of a couple of hours of this light has been a real booster to dispirited, if not depressed, people during the winter.

UltraAge Antidote
Get help. Don't suffer in silence!

DIABETES

'Late onset' diabetes, as its name implies, is an affliction of age and an ageing affliction. Evidence suggests that, unlike the more severe and always insulin-dependent diabetes which affects younger people, it can be avoided or its effects minimized by the right kind of diet. It seems to be a disease of affluent Western society, a disease of over-indulgence. It targets the overweight and sedentary. As it means that the pancreas can no longer produce adequate insulin to process the sugar in the system it is logical to infer that the pancreas may have been 'worn out' by having to process too many rushes of refined sugar in the past.

That spoonful of sugar may have made the medicine necessary.

That spoonful of sugar may have made the medicine necessary: late-onset diabetes can often be controlled by a diet that avoids sugar and only contains unrefined carbohydrates which metabolize more slowly

than refined ones such as white bread. Exercise also helps but diabetics have to be careful to match energy output with input and more severe cases require oral medication or injections of insulin as well. Diabetes, unless controlled with extraordinary discipline, can contribute to a debilitating range of side-effects. Diabetic retinopathy is the destruction of the retina that leads to blindness; diabetic neuropathy the destruction of the nerves in the extremities. One of the most horrific problems can be ulcerous sores on the legs or feet which will not heal because of the sugar in the blood and can lead to gangrene and amputation. What is more, diabetes seems to remove any natural protection pre-menopausal women have against heart disease and puts them on a par with men, who are more prone to cardiovascular disease. Post menopause they are in even greater danger than non-diabetic post-menopausal women.

Far better than controlling diabetes with diet and exercise, try to see if with careful diet and regular exercise you can manage not to succumb to it at all. You know you are susceptible if you have a family history, experience blood sugar 'highs' and 'lows' and crave sugar. Don't wait until you have the symptoms of the full blown disease itself, which include a raging thirst, blurry vision and recurrent thrush.

Diabetes Fighters

Chromium tablets, particularly in the glucose tolerance formula (GTF), are one possible preventative measure. Avoiding 'sugar rush' from excessive intake of sweet foods is another logical move. Garlic and onions are also supposed to be helpful for diabetics, as is nettle, which can be taken in either tea or capsule form.

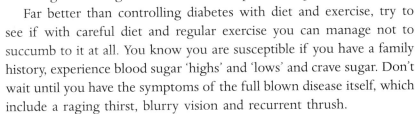

UltraAge Antidote
Chromium coupled with a low sugar diet and lots of exercise.

DRUGS

We'll assume you aren't mainlining heroin, your skinny arms tracked with needle marks, but many drugs can be addictive and have terrible side effects. Ecstasy, the fashionable drug among young people at the moment, has recently been shown to cause brain damage even if it doesn't kill you from dehydration or other adverse reactions at the time of taking it. And you can tell cocaine sniffers because their noses erode after a time. Even common or garden medicines such as antibiotics can mess up the delicate balance in the body, and can destroy vital micro-organisms needed for healthy digestion. We'd generally advise you to stay away from them, and even have our suspicions about some of the 'anti-ageing' (Chapter Twelve) and HRT (Chapter Four). Any drug can cause side effects. You shouldn't be taking painkillers: ideally you should be dealing with the source of the pain. You shouldn't be buying cold remedies – you shouldn't be getting colds!

About the only 'recreational' drug shown to have any positive effects on the body is marijuana (or cannabis), which is used by some doctors to ease the final days of cancer patients who are in a great deal of pain, and is said to have almost the opposite effect of cigarette smoking on the body since it is a relaxant. For that reason it can relieve the pressure in the eyes caused by glaucoma and is occasionally given to patients for that reason. Bill Clinton was the first US President to admit to trying it, but he claimed he 'didn't inhale'. The Body Shop brought out a range of beauty products made from the hemp (marijuana) plant to considerable controversy, and campaigns to legalize it, backed by respectable sources such as the *Independent on Sunday* newspaper in England, have continued. Apparently, some cigarette companies have already reportedly patented names for reefers.

> **UltraAge Antidote**
> 'Getting high on life', as some of us used to say in the '60s.

EATING DISORDERS

Women often develop eating disorders such as anorexia and bulimia because they are concerned about their appearance and fear they are too fat. But then the eating disorder itself becomes the greatest threat to their appearance and even, in extreme cases, to their lives. You can recognize bulimics by their chipmunk cheeks and often by their distended abdomens. They will, if the habit of vomiting food is long term, have the teeth of a much older person, as the corrosive stomach acids will have worn away the enamel. The same acids can cause stomach and mouth ulcers. The teeth, nails and hair of both anorexics and bulimics will suffer as they are not receiving adequate nutrients to sustain them. Their skin will be dry and often prematurely wrinkled. The late Diana, Princess of Wales, was lucky to get away with looking so good after her history of eating problems, but then she had conquered them by her early thirties. Many women don't, and develop a downward spiral of ill-health, self-loathing and diminished beauty.

Although these eating disorders are most associated with teenaged, twenty- and thirty-something women, they also affect men in increasing numbers and women well into old age. Dr David Weeks, consultant psychologist at the Edinburgh Royal Infirmary, says, 'I often see women of sixty with eating disorders.' Don't forget the 'social X-rays' that Tom Wolfe refers to in his *Bonfire of the Vanities*. You can see the society stick insects in all the best places, designer gowns drooping off their desiccated shoulders. But for some older women being anorexic is not, as with the Duchess of Windsor, a fashion statement that you can 'never be too thin'. Doctors have been advised to be aware that anorexia may be a consequence of the death of a spouse. Bereavement is apparently a very common precipitating factor among older women, as reported in the medical journal *Hospital Medicine* in 1998. Don't forget also that 'binge eating', leading to obesity, and chronic overeating are also eating disorders.

Even women of sixty can have eating disorders.

Forming Better Habits

There are now doctors and clinics in most countries who specialize in the treatment of eating disorders, such as Dr Dee Dawson and her Rhodes Farm clinic for teenagers and Deanne Jade at the National Centre for Eating Disorders. People with eating disorders usually need professional help, and it is worth going to a specialist who deals regularly with the problem. Perhaps your GP can refer you. Eating disorders which seem cured may recur in future times of stress. Often eating disorders are rooted in an unhappy childhood and poor self-image or are a way of avoiding facing the real problems in life. A professional psychotherapist can help perceptions to change and true problems to be tackled. Deanne Jade, who is one, says, 'People with eating disorders are often *avoiders*. When we tackle the issues in their lives that need addressing, the eating problem goes.'

UltraAge Antidote
Develop positive self-image – from inside and out.

FEAR – FEAR OF FLYING, FEAR OF TRYING

Fear is an extremely ageing emotion. Not only does it age you through the stress of worry, it does so by giving you an aged mindset. Someone

who is unwilling to try new things or to open themselves up to new experiences is, by definition, old no matter what their age or how youthful their body looks. Fear holds you back, fear makes you bury your head in the sand, fear prevents you from living life to the fullest.

Marjorie, a widow in her early fifties, had spent her whole life saying no to travelling anywhere that involved flying. Although she would pore over holiday brochures and dream of seeing exotic places, she always said no to such adventures, and her husband had humoured her phobia. After he died her children insisted she come with them on a trip to America. They filled her with gin and tonic (very bad idea – see 'Jetsetting' below) and plonked her on the plane between them, holding her hands. Marjorie loved the flight and has now been travelling the world, enjoying her new-found wings. On her last trip to Greece she met a young man she brought home to meet her children. Not quite a *Shirley Valentine* story, this one had a happy ending, because Marjorie didn't give up her home and family for him but just enjoyed having a fling. She realized that fear of flying and of trying all sorts of things had held her back for too long. Her children, not quite sure what to make of the young Greek while he was in her life, had to agree that she began to look, and act, younger and was much more fun to be with.

It is sad when fear of falling, or fear of being attacked, keeps older people indoors in front of the television when they should be out enjoying life. But if you keep working on your balance (through exercise) and have a balanced outlook on life, you won't be so likely to succumb to such fears. Franklin Delano Roosevelt memorably observed that 'The only thing we have to fear is fear itself.' That may not be completely true, but fear is certainly to be feared, and will rob you of as many years of happiness as the illnesses or accidents you fear.

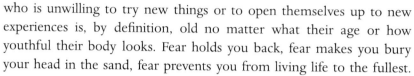

UltraAge Antidote
Try! You may like it.

FIBROIDS

Worried about your protruding abdomen and the way you seem to need to wear trousers that are longer from waist to crotch than you used to? Most women assume they've simply been putting on weight, and it's easy to confuse some of the symptoms of fibroids with middle-aged spread or menopause. Fibroids can also contribute to back pain

(see above) and can cause anaemia, heavy bleeding and severe pelvic pain. They are benign tumours which grow in or around the uterus, sometimes nestled deep into the lining, sometimes protruding on stalks. The peak period for fibroids is in women from their thirties to their early forties. Many will shrink spontaneously during menopause, so if your symptoms are mild and you fear surgery, you might be wise to wait and see what happens then.

Consider All the Options

Hysterectomy (see below) is still the most frequently offered option to women with large fibroids, but there are alternatives if you balk at that, and you should consider them and ask for a second opinion if you are not keen on losing your womb or if you would like to have more children. There are myomectomies, in which only the fibroid is cut out of the womb, but there is a high risk of haemorrhaging as there is with the more recently introduced option of myolysis, a laser treatment for fibroids, and with trying to remove just the womb lining. Arterial embolization, a new treatment at the time of writing, kills off the blood supply to the fibroid. A technique that can be carried out under a local anaesthetic, via a catheter through the groin artery, it holds exciting promise but can, like the other treatments aimed at conserving the womb, carry a risk of haemorrhaging.

> **UltraAge Antidote**
> Don't let unknown bulges fester: seek advice, it may be a fibroid.

FEET (SEE ALSO 'BUNIONS', ABOVE)

Nothing is more dispiriting than spending a day wearing the wrong shoes. When your feet are sore it's not that they alone suffer, your whole body aches and your mood turns as nasty as the feeling inside those shoes.

In addition to bunions a variety of foot problems from corns and calluses to athlete's foot and in-growing toenails can cause serious problems in later life when the circulation to the extremities will inevitably be less good and foot ulcers can form that may not heal and can lead to nasty problems (see 'Diabetes', above). All foot infections take longer to heal when you're older, and painful feet are huge age accelerators because they stop you from being as active as you want to be and should be.

Toeing the Line

You might think chiropodists are for old people but it's never too early to go to one to have your feet examined and kept in tip-top condition. Athlete's foot untreated can lead to severe fungal nail problems, corns can dig into the bone making it painful to walk, and ingrown toenails can give rise to serious pain and even infections. Regular appointments to have these treated by a professional should lead to good foot hygiene and health when you are older and regular trips to the chiropodist should be *de rigueur* for the over-sixties.

High heels shorten the Achilles tendons which can make normal walking actually painful.

But good shoes are the first line of defence: no struggling into or sliding around in something for fashion's sake. Nobody looks good tottering or hobbling in a pair of uncomfortable fancy shoes. Consider the fact that each day the average person clocks up about 10,000 steps. Now look at the equipment with which you attempt this amazing feat (no pun intended). Little strips of leather, or worse plastic, sometimes with your toes dangling out front ready for all sorts of bashings and encounters and often balancing your whole body perilously on a thin stick of a 'heel'. No wonder our feet scream back at us.

High heels shorten the Achilles tendons which then can make normal walking, like plodding around the house barefoot, actually painful. As we age, our feet become broader and longer yet we often still buy the same size shoes we always wore. Tight shoes then give us bunions, blisters, corns and calluses, making our ageing feet not only painful but ugly.

As we get older, feet also lose their youthful padding which makes good support and structure to our shoes even more essential. The skin gets drier, making them itchy, and poor circulation can lead to chilblains, especially in the cold weather.

Develop a Foot Fetish

By mid-life it is time you stopped ignoring your feet and gave them some extra and regular care to help them last the duration. Few things put you off living life to the full more than miserable feet.

Be supportive! As the soles of your feet wear down, support them by adding cushy inner soles to your shoes. If your feet have developed more quirks, consult your podiatrist or chiropodist for orthotics (shoe supports) tailored for your needs. It is most important to choose sane shoe designs for daytime, evening and any sporting activity.

By mid-life it is time you stopped ignoring your feet and gave them some extra and regular care to help them last the duration.

Warm up and cool down. If you suffer from circulation problems or cold feet in the morning, pop a hot water bottle into your bed while you have your first cup of tea for fifteen minutes to get the blood flowing. You will jump out of bed ready for action. In the evening, swollen feet plague many people, young and old. Raise your feet and nestle them on an ice pack or a bag of frozen peas, but don't place your bare skin directly on the packet in order to prevent 'freezer burn'. 'Cool it' for twenty minutes. Get up and busy yourself for another twenty minutes then 'cool it' again and the swelling should all be gone.

Corns and calluses mean your shoes don't fit. If you develop them and want to treat them yourself, try filing the dead skin with a good emery board or pumice stone when dry, then moisturize well with Vaseline after they have been softened from a shower or bath. Stubborn corns are best dealt with by a chiropodist.

In-grown toenails only rival bunions on the Richter scale of pain in the feet. To prevent them, again, your shoes need to allow the toes to move freely when you walk. If yours are chronic, and you also suffer from fluid retention, make sure you only buy your shoes late in the day, when your feet are at their fullest size. Cut your toenails straight across to prevent the nail from growing inwards. Don't 'dig out' painful in-grown nails but seek the help of a specialist podiatrist or chiropodist.

Smelly feet can indicate a fungal problem. If you notice spongey skin growing underneath the nails, you have a nail fungus. It might not hurt but will be both smelly and ugly. Some fungi can be treated topically with sprays whilst more persistent conditions need a systemic prescription to rid you of the problem.

The same anti-perspirant spray you use on your underarms can be effective in preventing your feet from getting damp and stinky. Wear only socks and hosiery made from natural fibres and ensure your shoes allow room for the feet to 'breathe' and expand. Rotate shoes so they, too, have time to 'breathe'.

UltraAge Antidote
Keep yourself sweet by caring for your feet.

FREE RADICALS

Free radicals are not political activists but destructive chemicals that our bodies produce as by-products of various processes. However, they

> *Free radicals are not political activists but destructive chemicals that our bodies produce as by-products of various processes.*

are like terrorists, waging a guerrilla campaign of destruction against the rest of the body's processes. They come from the combustion of oxygen that is necessary in order to keep us going. They are molecules that are one electron short and keep trying to make up this lack by scavenging on other molecules in our bodies. Jean Carper, author of *Stop Ageing Now*, calls them 'molecular terrorists'. If unchecked by a strong immune system or fed, as they seem to be, by fatty junk foods, and increased by cigarette smoke, breathing polluted air and other age accelerators, they cause damage and many of the diseases associated with ageing. They contribute to a wide range of conditions from arthritis to strokes, cataracts and cancer. The 'free radical theory of ageing' first suggested by Dr Denham Harman in America in 1954 is that ageing only occurs because our cells are continuously subject to attack by these scavengers, and that if we can keep them at bay, our cells will last much longer and we will age much more slowly.

Free Radical Fighters

Consumed in quantity, these can neutralize the free radicals by releasing one of their own spare electrons. They include the 'power foods' we describe in Chapter Nine, as well as the antioxidant vitamins A, C and E, antioxidant minerals such as copper, selenium and zinc, and antioxidant hormones such as melatonin. Substances called bioflavonoids, found in some Vitamin C tablets as well as naturally in fruit, red wine, green tea and certain spices and herbs, are also free radical fighters. Since free radicals are formed by the process of oxidation of fats, or

> **UltraAge Antidote**
> Radical revision of diet to avoid free radicals, and plenty of antioxidants to mop them up.

through, say, cooking meats at high temperatures, substances that neutralize this process are beneficial. Avoiding the process by not eating such things is even better. But since we can't avoid free radicals totally it is wise to be on guard against their insidious attack.

GALLSTONES

A peculiarly female affliction, found in 20 per cent of women but fewer than 10 per cent of men. The likelihood of having them increases with age and mothers seem more susceptible than childless women. This is often a disease of 'fat white women' like the one in Frances Cornford's poem 'To a Fat Lady Seen From the Train': 'O fat white woman whom nobody loves . . .'. Eating fat should cause the gallbladder to produce bile which is necessary to digest it. Gallstones prevent this process, and because they occur more frequently in women, who have a higher fat percentage than men – and fat women, who not only have more fat but probably eat more, too – it may, like the relationship of diabetes to sugar intake, have something to do with having worn out the gall-bladder since it has had to cope with too much fat. The stones are made of cholesterol, solidified from the bile fluid. Gallstones can go undiagnosed for years, and the symptoms confused with simple indigestion. If you have gallstones, the indigestion is more likely to occur after a fatty meal, and you may feel some tenderness under your right rib. Severe gallbladder disease can cause jaundice, fever and vomiting.

What's the Answer?

Surgery, and keep the stones in a jar to marvel at afterwards. The whole gallbladder will have to be removed, though, not just the stones, and you will have to avoid fatty foods for the rest of your life. Better still, avoid them to begin with. Since a low fat diet is prescribed to those with gallstones, why not start it before you get them and be generally health-ier anyway, while avoiding the problem? Look what a low fat diet did for Rosemary Conley: it was while condemned to one because of gallstones that she discovered the wonderful effect eating less fat had on her hips and thighs. You know the rest. Her bestselling *Hip and Thigh Diet* spawned a multi-million-pound inter-national industry with very fat profits and hundreds of imitators, the sincerest form of flattery.

> **UltraAge Antidote**
> A low fat diet helps prevent gallstones.

GLUTTONY

Gluttony is one of the seven deadly sins for good reason. All the latest research indicates that a moderate, if not a severely restricted, diet is

UltraAge Antidote
Learn to be a gourmet, and really enjoy your food, rather than a gourmand, who just gluttonously scoffs it down.

a predictor of longevity (see Chapter Twelve). Gluttony simply wears out our system and puts strains on our kidneys, liver, intestines and heart as well as causing obvious strain from the extra weight it makes us carry. The more fat we consume, the more free radicals we are likely to ingest, and excess fat consumption has also been implicated in many types of cancers, particularly breast and bowel, and in heart disease.

GREY HAIR

There is no such thing, according to trichologist Philip Kingsley, only white hair that mixes in with your normal hair and makes it appear grey. Your hair seems genetically programmed to start turning white at a certain stage, often around the same time as your mother's did. For some women this may be thirty-five, for others fifty. Victoria's grandmother died at seventy-eight with magnificent long brown hair that she coiled on top of her head in an Edwardian-style knot every day, and her mother didn't start going grey until very late in life. But it's a rare woman who doesn't have some white hairs by the age of forty. It is a myth that hair will turn white almost overnight due to shock, although, as we have seen, the actress Julie Walters has insisted that hers did when her daughter Maisie was diagnosed with leukaemia. But it has been suggested that pigmented hair is less firmly rooted than white hair and therefore falls out more easily after a shock, leaving proportionately more white. It's another myth that if you pluck a grey hair, two will grow in its place, says Philip Kingsley, although we all seem to have experienced that phenomenon. It is also a myth that grey hair is thicker than the rest of your hair: in fact it is probably thinner, as hair thins with age, but it may be drier and therefore appear coarser. Professor John Yudkin, professor of medicine at University College, London, has said that premature grey hair can be a predictor of ill health, and that those who go grey very early may be more likely to develop auto-immune disease of the thyroid gland or other auto-immune diseases later in life. But this is debatable.

Your hair seems genetically programmed to start turning white at a certain stage, often around the same time as your mother's did.

Colour Me Youthful

Hair can, of course, be dyed back to its natural colour or to a lighter colour than you are used to, since your colouring will change with age to suit a lighter colour. (For advice on the shade possibilities see my *Makeover Manual*.) Lighter dyes are generally safer, since the health scare about the tar-based ingredients was primarily to do with darker dyes. Grey hair can, of course, look sexy and attractive if it is bright rather than yellowy grey and if it is appropriately styled and not curled into a tight old-lady perm. One young fashion editor for a leading glossy magazine who moved on to become a fashion PR was envied for her striking grey hair, and Christian LaCroix had a grey haired model as his muse. Since some women go grey in their twenties and make it a style statement, grey hair need not be a badge of age. Finally, there is some evidence that the B Vitamins and Vitamin D, the sunshine vitamin, may go some way towards preventing premature greying.

UltraAge Antidote
Dyeing, vitamins or cultivating grey hair as a style statement.

GRUMPINESS

Grumpiness is one of the greatest age accelerators, far worse than grey hair. As the feminist novelist Fay Weldon once said, 'By a certain age you get the face, the health and the children you deserve;' and grumpy people certainly get a face that proclaims their nature to the world, with thin, down-turned lips that grow thinner with age anyway, frown furrows and a generally discontented expression that makes it hard to make friends and influence people.

Cheer Up!

Remember you're only hurting yourself. Practise laughing things off (see 'Anger', above). Look in the mirror and smile. Do some volunteer work in hospitals or for people worse off than yourself. Count your blessings.

UltraAge Antidote
Smile.

HAEMORRHOIDS

Varicose veins of the rectum, these can flare up during childbirth or from straining to pass stools. Not only are they painful, itchy and irri-

tating, they can be downright embarrassing, particularly if you are trying to maintain an active sex life.

Don't Sit On It

If they're bad, have surgery. This can in itself be painful and take weeks to recover from as Paula discovered when she decided to get hers operated on shortly after finding a new lover in her fifties. Although the operation was undertaken with a view to improving her sex life – 'It looks so ugly,' she worried – she was in considerable pain for six weeks afterwards and the fledgling relationship couldn't stand the strain either.

> **UltraAge Antidote**
> High fibre diet stops them piling up.

Much better to try to prevent or improve them by not straining when you're on the loo and eating a high fibre diet that will create softer stools that are easier to pass. Drinking a lot of water and taking regular exercise should help, too.

HEADACHES

There are all kinds of headaches, from the kind you use as an excuse for anything you want to get out of to the migraines that can feel as if they're splitting your head in two. There can be just a vague feeling of discomfort, a thudding in the temples or waves of intense pain. Whatever the cause, which can range from eye or neck strain to incipient strokes or brain tumours, they make you wrinkle up your face in pain, which can't be good.

> *Never ignore a strange new type of headache, or one that is persistent and painful.*

Migraines are actually caused by a spasm of the blood vessels supplying the brain and are a different breed of headache. They can be treated with some success if treated at the first inkling with some of the new anti-migraine drugs. But all types of headaches except for the occasional 'morning after' type should be checked out. Princess Margaret reported having headaches before her stroke in 1998, as did the publisher Robert McCrum, who has written movingly about his experiences. Never ignore a strange new type of headache, or one that is persistent and painful.

How to Get Rid of Them

In order to discover what may spark them off try keeping a headache diary, noting times, places, the foods you've recently eaten and what

circumstances seem to bring them on. See if you can change your diet or habits to avoid them. Do they come after you've been using the computer or reading a book? Have your eyes tested, too.

Consult your doctor, who will probably test your blood pressure, prescribe painkillers or anti-migraine drugs or suggest you go for an eye test. All types of complementary medicine can help with headaches. Chiropractic treatment seemed to cure the migraines of Polly Havers, wife of the actor Nigel Havers. Her chiropractor Michael Durtnall found they came from tension in the neck. Hypnotherapy did the trick for polo player Sandra Cronan, reiki (a Japanese form of spiritual healing) for actress Lori Fox. Acupuncture, osteopathy, homoeopathy and even general massage may help.

Consider your lifestyle. Are you sitting for too long each day at a computer? Not getting enough exercise? Working in bad light with too few or too many fluorescent striplights? Or are you just too vain to wear glasses?

Find a more stimulating sexual partner to whom you won't want to say you've got a headache, or learn to avoid people and situations which seem to spark them off.

> **UltraAge Antidote**
> Work on the cause, not the symptom.

HEARING LOSS

The Boomer generation, the first to go regularly to rock concerts and use personal stereos, looks like being the first to start suffering significant hearing loss in its forties. President Clinton led the way by leaving his medical examination in 1997 with hearing aids as he was losing higher frequency sounds and could no longer clearly make out conversations in crowded rooms. Although some hearing deterioration is inevitable with time, this is one area in which oldies can score over the younger generation these days. Hearing researchers at one British university were forced to turn to older people for their control groups when they discovered that too many twenty-somethings had already lost considerable acuity through, it was theorized, too great an exposure to loud music.

The fashion for having personal stereos constantly thumping close to the ear drum has been partly blamed for hearing loss.

Talking About My Generation?

The fashion for having personal stereos constantly thumping close to the ear drum has been partly blamed for hearing loss, together with the high decibels of sound at rock concerts in recent years. Usually it is the higher sounds that we have difficulty in hearing first, and it can become difficult to distinguish words when someone is talking to you in a crowded noisy room. Tinnitus can create a background cacophony you carry around with you. Many rock musicians suffer from this, with several such as Pete Townshend of The Who, Barbra Streisand and Sting talking frankly about their hearing problems. Few things are as ageing, and isolating, as not being able to hear, for who wants to be relegated to doddery old grandma status and be shouted at or excluded from conversations because it's too much trouble to explain things to us?

Can Anybody Hear` – or Help?

Hearing aids often only exacerbate the problem because they can heighten the background noise as well as the more precise sounds we want to hear. There is, at the time of writing, no successful solution to hearing problems brought on with age, despite the development of cochlear implants to allow the deaf some sensation of sound. The secret is to try to protect your hearing from damage. That means avoiding loud sudden noises like shooting or continual ones like drilling (wear ear plugs if you have to participate in these activities) and not walking around with ear phones all the time. If going to clubs, discos and concerts is part of your youthful persona – and all power to you – you might be well advised to wear ear plugs that will protect you from the worst of the noise. (You can't hear what people are saying anyway in such situations, so they won't notice the difference.) There are centres, such as the Tomatis centres in France and England, which claim to have some success with tinnitus through retraining the brain to ignore it, but conventional hearing experts are not convinced.

UltraAge Antidote
'Turn it down!'

HEART PROBLEMS

The heart is at the heart of life itself, and should be taken care of. Don't think that heart attacks are a male preserve. Although much less publicity has been given to coronary heart disease (CHD) in women,

it has been the main killer of women over fifty-five and still kills more women than anything else. Twice as many women die from heart disease as from all forms of cancer, and women recover less well from heart attacks than men do, possibly due to their smaller hearts and arteries. The National Forum for Coronary Heart Disease Prevention in Britain produced a report a few years ago that showed that the symptoms of CHD were less likely to be recognized and properly diagnosed in women, who were therefore referred to specialist help later than men.

Oestrogen offers some protection against heart disease to women who have not undergone menopause, but women in their thirties have been known to have heart attacks and these are much less likely to be accurately diagnosed and therefore treated in women before menopause. The only way to find a silent problem is to have an EKG while under a stress test (treadmill). This test is worth paying for if there is a family history of heart disease.

To HRT or not HRT seems to be the question. There is conflicting evidence over whether artificial oestrogen offers the same protection as a woman's natural stores, although HRT is often cited as an antidote to heart disease. Long-term oestrogen replacement therapy has been shown to enhance blood supply to the hearts of women with CHD, but if you are worried about this (see Chapter Four) what you can definitely do is stop smoking immediately, engage in regular aerobic exercise, keep your weight and blood pressure down, avoid oral contraceptives late in life, eat a low fat, high fibre diet, not drink heavily and not develop diabetes (see above), as diabetes turns pre-menopausal women into men when it comes to heart attack protection, and female diabetics have a risk that is up to five times as great as other women.

> **UltraAge Antidote**
> Take heart – check it out and treat it well.

HIGH BLOOD PRESSURE (HYPERTENSION)

Chronic high blood pressure means that your heart is having to work harder than it should. Arteries become constricted and eventually damaged which can lead to coronary artery disease and stroke. Often it is symptomless – silent and deadly. But headaches (see above) can herald it, as can dizziness. Ringing in the ears is another tell-tale sign.

Blood pressure normally gets higher with age and it is not unto-ward to have the upper figure (diastolic) be 100 plus your age, although the fitter you are the lower it will be. The bottom figure (systolic) should never be higher than 90 (70 or 80 would be better) and should not rise dramatically with age. A fit sixty-year-old might well have a blood pressure of 140 over 70 although it would not necessarily be worrying until the pressure was over 160 over 90.

Regular churchgoers also have lower blood pressure.

Take the Pressure Off

If you want to avoid blood-pressure lowering drugs and their potential side effects, try meditation, auto-genic training (a quick form of meditation suited to busy Western types) or another of the many stress relief techniques. Certain exercises may be particularly beneficial. Studies have shown that a programme of yoga and meditation allowed at least a quarter of those on it to come off their medication for high blood pressure. Regular churchgoers also have lower blood pressure. Cutting down on saturated fats, salt and red meats is also thought to help, as is bulking up on fibre foods including oats and oatbran, onions and garlic. Eat lots of fatty fishes providing Omega 3 fatty acids. Joan's husband was diagnosed as having high blood pressure but she didn't want him to go on beta blockers which could render him impotent. So in the week before he went for his second doctor's visit to discuss the subject she took him off his usual meat and pota-toes diet and put him on sardines and watercress, low fat, low salt meals. By the following week his blood pressure was at a safe level. Vitamin E and other antioxidants can also come in handy, keeping the blood vessels flexible and free from plaque that builds up and constricts the vessel, raising the pressure.

UltraAge Antidote
Diet low in fat but high in Omega 3 fatty acids; keep your weight down.

Keeping your weight down is also important as the blood has to pump much harder to cover a larger area. That is why it is often the overweight who suffer from this condition.

HYPOCHONDRIA

If you've actually got all the problems in this chapter you're not a hypochondriac, you're a very sick person. If you just think you have, or fear you might, then that's a problem in itself: you're a hypochon-

driac, and not someone people want at their parties giving 'organ recitals'. Remember that 'He who fears death dies a thousand times before his death' so you can save yourself a lot of agony (and your friends a lot of annoyance) by learning not to assume that every headache is a brain tumour, every spot skin cancer.

Worry creates stress, and stress (see below) is horribly ageing and more likely to kill you than your imagined ailments. And don't, on any account, watch any television soap operas or films

> **UltraAge Antidote**
> Take a reality check!

involving doctors, hospitals or coroners. Alternatively, develop a real fatal illness. Then everybody who told you to shut up and stop imagining things will be sorry. Won't they? (Only joking . . .)

HYSTERECTOMY

Today, hysterectomies are performed for many reasons. Some would say too many reasons, women's wombs being whipped out sometimes without their full awareness of what this entails. Hysterectomies are recommended for everything from fibroids (see above) to heavy periods, and sometimes this 'cure' can be worse than the problem, so carefully consider the alternatives. Early hysterectomy will lead to an earlier menopause than you were due to have, even if the ovaries are left intact. And that, of course, is ageing, as you will lose several years of your own natural oestrogen protection. The womb, gynaecologists may reluctantly confirm if you press them, also seems to be involved in the female orgasm, at least in enhancing its quality. Those with hysterectomies, particularly if they've had a total hysterectomy, involving the removal of the cervix (the neck of the womb) as well, may

Too many women's wombs are being whipped out, sometimes without their full awareness of what this entails.

find that the quality of their orgasm changes. And, since orgasms are supposed to help keep us youthful, releasing endorphins and human growth hormone (HGH), this in itself can be ageing. Studies have also found that some women suffer psychologically from losing their wombs, and feel somehow less feminine, which can inhibit sexual response.

Don't Rush Into a Hysterectomy

Unless you are in a life-or-death situation where you have no choice, such as with cancer of the womb, or are in horrible pain from endometriosis, consider the alternatives. Ask for a second opinion if you have any doubts about what your doctor advises. If there is no alternative to hysterectomy for your problem then consider the types of hysterectomy possible. Joseph Jordan, our consultant gynaecologist (see Chapter Two), would recommend a sub-total hysterectomy if there is a choice, performed through small incisions just above the pubic bone. 'A woman can be home in three days after this procedure,' he says. The cervix can be left in place, which should not interfere with the quality of a woman's sexual experience. A vaginal hysterectomy, which, again, produces no scarring, does not allow the option of leaving the cervix in place. Most hysterectomies performed for non-urgent reasons can be done through a 'bikini cut' just above the pubic bone and needn't be disfiguring. But if you are having one, make sure you've worked out before the operation what, if any, hormone replacement programme you will need afterwards, as you might be in less of a state to think clearly about it then.

UltraAge Antidote
Consider the alternatives.

INDIGESTION

This can come from many sources, some trivial, some serious (see 'Gallstones'). If you regularly eat a healthy, fresh, high fibre diet then you are less likely to experience indigestion when you suddenly eat something gaseous that your system is not accustomed to. It could have to do with a hiatus hernia, stomach ulcers, irritable bowel syndrome, diverticulitis or even colon cancer, so you need to be checked out before you start popping the proprietory remedies. In some cases heart problems can be mistaken for indigestion, as all hypochondriacs know. If you are stressed while eating or digesting, that may play a part. Try to eat slowly and calmly rather than grabbing things on the hop. Avoid late-night curries and fry-ups.

UltraAge Antidote
Calm and healthy mealtimes.

INFLEXIBILITY

Everything seems to become less flexible as you age – if you let it: your joints, your skin, your arteries, your mind. Mental inflexibility is one of the most ageing characteristics you can have, and it may be generated in part by a hardening of arteries to the brain because they are clogged with cholesterol (see above). Flexibility and spontaneity are characteristics of youth that you must continue to cultivate, even if it gets harder with time.

Stay loose in all ways! Just as taking regular yoga classes can keep your body flexible well into old age, so can making a great mental effort to keep open to new ideas at work and at home (see Chapter Eight) and exercising your brain regularly to keep it flexing (see Chapter Ten). Be receptive to change: don't condemn it out of hand. Be receptive to new styles: don't get stuck in a time warp. Be receptive to new ideas. For physical flexibility keep exercising, but not just jogging or cycling or aerobics classes. For flexibility, a method like yoga or t'ai chi is ideal, and can be enjoyed by all ages and all levels of confidence.

UltraAge Antidote
Loosen up!

IRON DEFICIENCY

If you have too much iron or too little, you are in trouble. Found in greatest quantities in the blood, iron is essential to the production of haemoglobin and myoglobin and hence the vital oxygenation of red blood cells.

Beware of taking iron if you have an infection as it will spread the bacteria more widely throughout your body.

Signs of Iron Deficiency

These include anaemia, brittle hair and/or hair loss; difficulty swallowing; dizziness; fatigue; fragile bones; brittle nails with discernible ridges; obesity; slow reaction time.

A deficiency in iron can come from not eating enough iron-rich foods or from consuming too many 'iron-depleting foods', like soft drinks containing phosphorus, or too much tea or coffee as caffeine robs the system of iron. Additionally, excessive menstrual bleeding can also contribute to iron loss. This is why any woman with chronically heavy periods must not endure them. Rather than just taking supplements, have a blood test which will confirm what's required. Exercise fanatics also run the risk of being iron-deficient as strenuous workouts and heavy perspiration dry up your iron stocks.

If you have too much iron or too little, you are in trouble.

Oversupply of Iron

Oversupply of iron can cause diabetes, cirrhosis of the liver, heart complaints, and a rare skin pigmentation called hemochromatosis, as well as cancer. There is a real danger of having too much iron after the menopause, which thickens the blood and seems to lead to an almost literal 'rusting' of the arteries due to oxidation, which leads to heart disease. Patrick Holford says, 'There is a clear association between high levels of ferritin – the way the body stores iron – in the blood and cardiovascular disease, and women's ferritin levels go up dramatically post menopausally. Too much iron can cause oxidation or damage to fats in the body. Another detriment of too much iron is that it's a zinc antagonist, leeching zinc from the body.' If you think you might have too much, try to drink tea without milk, which leeches iron from the system particularly well.

Foods Rich in Iron

These include eggs, fish, red meat, organs like liver, poultry, leafy green vegetables, whole grain breads and many enriched breakfast cereals. Other iron-rich foods are almonds, avocados, beets, beans, brewer's yeast (Marmite), dates, pumpkin, and other squashes, lentils, prunes, raisins, rice, soya beans, and watercress.

> ***UltraAge Antidote***
> Iron: pump it or eat iron-rich foods; supplement only on doctor's advice.

Absorption Tips

Iron is tricky as it needs enough hydrocholoric acid in the stomach in order to be absorbed. Vitamins A, B Complex, C and folic acid help to increase absorption. Too much zinc or Vitamin E can hinder it.

IRRITABLE BOWEL SYNDROME (IBS)

It may be comforting to know that an irritable bowel is cited as being as common as the common cold. To me it is about as 'popular' as having adult acne! Often referred to as a 'spastic colon', the condition is one of the most embarrassing and debilitating for the young as well as the old. The symptoms cover the spectrum of what can go wrong down there from constipation to diarrhoea to cramps, nausea and bloating.

I was devastated by IBS in my twenties while doing a graduate degree and eating only one daily meal during my shift working in a pub at night. Midnight would come and I would virtually explode. Obviously, my lifestyle and poor diet were causing the troubles, but the good news is that you can grow out of it as I did once I began living a more balanced existence.

How to Cope

Calm down as stress is a major cause of IBS. If you are literally in a vicious syndrome of hype and 'blow-up' then you have got to take yourself in hand before the condition worsens into something more sinister. Don't eat any meals on the run, dine, eat more slowly. You will be relaxed in the process and stand a chance of digesting things better.

> **UltraAge Antidote**
> Make friends with your colon: feed it well, stroke it kindly, and you will be great pals for life.

Cut out sweeteners, as well as sugar, which exacerbate a troublesome colon. Plus, monitor which foods seem to trigger the trouble and avoid them like the plague. Try herbal teas, especially peppermint, to aid digestion.

Massage helps when bloating starts or you feel cramped after a meal. Lie down and massage your bowels (from the outside, okay!). Calmly and gently massage the troubled region and you will shut down the trap door between the small and large intestine which often goes haywire, emitting some nasty enzymes that cause the cramps. Regular massage, say in a warm bath, helps to keep a jumpy colon calm.

JETSETTING

Frequent travel by aeroplane is indisputably ageing, but something Boomers and subsequent generations have done as never before. It puts considerable strain on the system, to judge by all the books which have appeared in recent years on how to prevent the adverse effects of flying For just two examples, try Farrol Kahn's *Arrive in Better Shape* or *Jetlag and How to Beat It* by Dr David O'Connell.

Research shows that frequent flying can lead to considerable health risks.

The air you breathe in planes is recycled, the atmosphere dries out the nasal passages, eyes and skin, having an ageing, desiccating effect.

The lack of oxygen in a plane leads to a measurable decline in bodily performance, similar to that you might experience if you had aged twenty years! You are also exposed to some degree of radiation each time you fly, which could be why frequent flyers have been found to be more prone to brain cancer, malignant melanoma and leukaemia, according to Dr David O'Connell, who runs a jetlag clinic in London. Curiously, however, he found their risk of contracting other kinds of cancer may be lessened, although a recent study of stewardesses suggested they may be more prone to breast cancer.

So Why Do Famous Jetsetting Celebrities Always Look So Great?

They follow certain procedures on which successful frequent flyers all agree. First of all, they usually fly first class, where the air is fresher and they can stretch out. If this is not an option on your budget, try at least to request a seat as far forwards in economy class as possible, as the air should be fresher there. Opt also for an aisle seat if possible, so that you can get up and walk up and down, as keeping active prevents circulatory problems such as swollen ankles. If you can't walk up and down the aisles, do stretches in your seat and wiggle your feet about regularly. Dr O'Connell advises choosing a Boeing 747, if possible, where the cabin is pressurized at a much kinder level than it is on many other types of plane, and the problems associated with hypoxia, lack of oxygen, are fewer.

Frequent flyers usually avoid the free drinks offered on the flight.

Frequent flyers usually avoid the free drinks offered on the flight. They know that alcohol is still further dehydrating at altitude and that they are better off to drink water until they get to their destination, when they can indulge. They know when it's more prudent (on night flights West to East) to pass up the meal and sleep through a whole journey instead, to arrive rested and refreshed. They know how to fool their systems into resisting jetlag by setting their clocks and adjusting their mindset to the new time zone, taking a sleeping pill or staying awake, as necessary, on arrival to fit in with the new time. One of the best pieces of advice is to always try to fly East to West if you have a choice, rather than the other way around, which has been shown to be much more debilitating. Make sure you always take a bottle of still mineral water with you (the fizzy may contribute to the gas extension problems that occur anyway at altitude) and ask the stewardess to keep filling it up so you don't have to be dependent on those teensy little plastic cups they offer.

Bring lots of moisturizing face cream with you to slather on your face at regular intervals, or just a good barrier to stop moisture being lost, like Vaseline. Artificial Tears, available from most chemists, can help prevent your eyes from going bloodshot. Otherwise opt for the celebrity dark glasses look.

To prevent varicose veins, swollen legs and the possibility of deep vein thrombosis, make sure you sit with your legs raised as much as possible. If your chair doesn't recline, at least place your legs on a footrest or on some luggage in front of you, high enough to raise your thighs off the seat. Rather than wearing tight shoes and kicking them off only to discover you can't fit into them again, wear loose and comfortable footgear. The real pros wear comfortable clothes like tracksuits or leggings on the plane – some airlines like Virgin even provide 'sleepsuits' for first class travellers – and then change back into their suits for an impressive arrival.

> **UltraAge Antidote**
> Drink as much water as you can, moisturize your skin and avoid alcohol.

JUNK FOOD

You are what you eat, and if you eat junk, you will, frankly, look like it. Would you put cheap petrol in your expensive new car and risk clogging up its engine and ruining its performance? Of course not. Would you put a fizzy drink in your baby's bottle and expect it to grow up healthy? Of course not. Yet many people in Western society consistently stuff themselves with poor, artery-clogging, indigestion-making, cholesterol- and blood-pressure-raising junk food. Generally people who eat a lot of junk food are malnourished, because they are so busy scoffing empty calories they don't have time to take in the essential vitamins and minerals they need. Spotty skin, lacklustre hair, allergies due to colourants are common among the first junk food generations to reach maturity.

You are what you eat, and if you eat junk, you will, frankly, look like it.

Junk food is usually more expensive than natural food (isn't a carrot cheaper than a bar of chocolate?), and high in sugar, salt and fat, which

may accelerate diabetes, high blood pressure and obesity. Worst of all, it is probably high in 'free radicals', particularly if it is fried (and if the oil is slightly rancid) as so many junk foods are, which as we know can wreak havoc in our bodies. Sure, we may all like, or just have to have, a burger or veggieburger from a fast food chain now and again. But try to have that salad with it or afterwards. And don't live on the same type of junk food day in and day out as the toxins can build up in your system. The definition of 'junk' food is debatable but ours is anything that comes in a packet, or fried, or contains lots of sugar, salt, fat, colourings, nitrates, flavourings and artificial or 'mechanically recovered' ingredients. You'll have to make your own definition according to how you feel.

Maybe It Was Okay When You Were Younger

It might have been okay to live on hotdogs and doughnuts when you were young and your body was more forgiving, but the longer you've gone on looking at food as a quick fix, the worse the damage your vitamin-deficient diet has done to your system. Freezing, microwaving, fast cooking all destroy vital nutrients in our food. We all have to eat 'junk' sometime, but we must intersperse it with good, fresh food. Make sure you drink water and not just sugary fizzy drinks which do not cleanse the system and may put strain on the kidneys.

> **UltraAge Antidote**
> Fresh food, as much as possible, a varied diet, and water (again).

KIDS

Kids keep you young, they say. Or do they? It all depends on your experience of parenthood. We're assuming you're past the baby stage, the sleepless nights, the post-natal depression, the arguments over who does the 4 a.m. feed. We hope you've enjoyed, or are enjoying, the pleasant childhood stages in between that and the teenage years. But then the worries about drugs, sex, and life choices start and the arguments with teenage children as they try to spread their wings can be very wearing if you let them be. Ambivalent feelings as children become more independent and flee the nest are a major cause of depression among middle-aged women. Knowing when, and how much, to let go is hard. Or maybe you're dying to let go but they don't want to leave home and keep leaving you with their dirty laundry and unpaid bills.

Be Interested in their World but Don't Try to Be Part of It

Undoubtedly if you keep communicating with your children, and let them know they don't have to be afraid to talk to you about the things that are important to them, that you're there to be helpful, not judgemental (easier said than done, we know), then children can be a rejuvenating experience. They keep you young if you're interested in their emerging world, if you keep up with their music and interests, and if you accept that you can learn from them as much as they can learn from you.

Mother love, not smother love, is best for you both. Know when to let go and your children will want to come back to you as adults, with their children. Try to cling to the past and you'll alienate them and be backward looking in an ageing way for yourself. Remember the sentiments of Kalil Gibran's *The Prophet* that your children are of you but not yours, and you are the bow from which they, the arrows, are launched in trajectories you cannot follow.

The actress Jane Lapotaire, a single parent, movingly recalled how she cried when her son Rowan left home for Oxford, and used to keep one of his dirty shirts to sniff like a comfort blanket. 'I imploded. I couldn't walk, talk or do anything and ended up in hospital for three weeks.' But eventually she learned to enjoy her new freedom. 'One of the joys of not being a mother, in the day to day sense, is learning to put yourself back at the centre of your life and having the luxury of being able to listen to your own body. I have learned the wonderful joy of having days and days when I don't answer the phone. I put on my walking boots and drive out into the Cotswolds with a picnic in my rucksack. I come back home, have a long hot bath, go to bed at eight-thirty and read for three hours. I couldn't have done that five years ago!'

> **UltraAge Antidote**
> Have your own life, before your kids tell you to get one.

LETHARGY

Lethargy is the opposite of energy, which is what all UltraAgers have in abundance. Therefore it is one of the ultimate age accelerators, living down in that twilight world close to death, and is also known as one of the seven deadly sins under one of its other names, sloth. Call it

lethargy, sloth or laziness, it is a lack of enthusiasm for life, a lack of curiosity, of interest, of everything that makes life worth living. Lethargy is often a side effect of depression and a harbinger of many serious diseases such as cancer and diabetes.

Causes of Lethargy

Make sure there is no organic reason for it by going to your doctor and explaining when you first began to feel lethargic, and how long you have been in that stultifying state. Take a good look at your diet and make sure it includes many of the 'power foods' mentioned in Chapter Nine. Are you getting enough exercise? Force yourself to even if you don't feel like it at first. As your lethargy gradually disappears, which it will if you exercise regularly, you will feel so much more energetic. Keep up an active interest in life.

UltraAge Antidote
Interest in life!

LONG IN THE TOOTH

A sure way of giving away your age is by smiling broadly and showing the world how 'long in the tooth' you are. Gums can recede with wear and tear as well as age. Cavities are more often a threat to the young, while gum disease (periodontal disease) which can show up in poorly cared for young mouths can also be insidious and creep up painlessly in older age.

Perio (around) dontal (tooth) disease is the most common bacterial disease known to mankind. It is also almost preventable with attention to diet, general health and oral hygiene. Partly due to the increased consumption of refined sugars in our foods and drinks, combined with poor oral hygiene, dentists report a worrying trend of an increasing incidence of periodontal disease in young people. Even brushing incorrectly can contribute to the loss of healthy gum tissue and it is vital to take professional advice both from your dentist and dental hygienist who will spend time advising you about the correct types of brush, toothpaste, mouthwashes, floss and tape for your particular situation. Every person has a slightly different requirement.

Periodontal disease attacks the tiny ligaments which surround your tooth roots and secure your teeth to the underlying jaw bone. Plaque bacteria attached near the neck of the tooth at the gum margin causes

Taking Care

Sure, you've been brushing your teeth for years, but have you been doing it correctly? Here are some tips from one of London's top dental surgeons, Dr Neil Lawson Baker, who marries the best of American and European wisdom with total commitment to providing dental hygiene teaching and treatment. If you pay attention, you can keep your own teeth all your life.

✧ Use a soft, child-sized toothbrush to enable you to work all the nooks and crannies around your teeth and gums. A hard brush can wear away gums.

✧ Change your brush monthly. They wear out!

✧ Use a fluoride toothpaste. A smooth and creamy one is better than an abrasive one.

✧ An electric toothbrush applies the right motion with consistent power. Try one. You'll be surprised how long two minutes can seem but it's a snap with a battery-operated machine taking all the strain. Sometimes a flashing light tells you when it is time to stop.

✧ Brush at least three times a day and after your main meals. If you can't always manage brushing after eating, try to rinse your mouth out with water to neutralize the acids and remove food debris.

✧ Brush your tongue gently to banish bad breath because, along with infected gums and tummy acids, a gungy tongue can be the cause of halitosis (smelly breath).

✧ A plaque-loosening mouthwash before tooth brushing can also help your oral hygiene. Ask your dentist or hygienist which type is best for you.

✧ Floss or dental tape your teeth nightly. Keep a pack next to your toothbrushes as well as in your office bathroom. Brushing does not do the whole job. You can even sit in the bath or on the loo flossing your teeth!

✧ Avoid junk, sugary foods.

✧ Vitamins C, E and Q have proven benefits for the teeth and gums. Dentists vary in their opinions so ask their advice or read up about them, especially about Vitamin Q10.

inflammation and bleeding, and eventually a shallow pocket between the gum and tooth may open up allowing the bacteria to penetrate down to the ligaments. If this problem is not halted quickly by accurate and effective cleaning then the ligaments will become chronically

(long term) inflamed and the infected tooth may eventually begin to loosen. This disease process can take place throughout your mouth and affect all your teeth, leading to extractions and the inevitability of dentures.

Besides good oral hygiene there are also many modern techniques which can help to save a badly damaged mouth. These include certain types of periodontal corrective surgery; the possible use of a Gor-Tex membrane to regenerate bone support and healthier gum tissue; bone grafting; and, of course, tooth replacements and bridgework supported by surgically placed titanium implants.

UltraAge Antidote
Don't brush over tooth care!

LOSS

Loss in itself is not necessarily an age accelerator. It's how you deal with it that makes the difference. Dr Weeks's 'Superyoung' tend to grieve and then get over their grievances and get on with life, wasting little time in finding a new partner. Raine Spencer, stepmother of Diana, Princess of Wales, was an example of that. There is little doubt that she was genuinely close and caring to her husband Earl Spencer and mourned not only his death but the loss of her stately home and status.

Loss in itself is not necessarily an age accelerator. It's how you deal with it that makes the difference.

But within months she was married again (albeit abortively) to a French nobleman quite a few years her junior.

Of course it seems easier for someone who travels in exalted social circles to grab a new partner on life's roundabout. Women who have spent the majority of their married lives stuck at home with young children can feel themselves incredibly isolated at such a time and not know where to turn.

But life continues and eventually you have to go with it, however great your grief, and move on. We can't all live in a social whirl like wealthy merry widows do, but we can make the effort not to close ourselves off to new opportunities, to sign on for evening classes in something we've always wanted to do, to work on friendships.

Where to Get Help

Charities such as CRUSE, the Samaritans and even Relate will counsel those who have lost a partner. Often the loss will be tinged with anger

if there was unfinished business with the deceased, and it can be particularly difficult to come to terms with if mistresses, love children or secret lives are posthumously revealed. Carrie found Relate, formerly the Marriage Guidance Counsel in Britain, very helpful in working through her unresolved anger about her husband's affair that she had only discovered during the last few months when he was dying of cancer. His mistress had turned up at the hospital but Carrie's husband had been too sick for her to confront him with all the questions and accusations that sprang to mind. She was therefore angry as well as sad when he died, and counselling helped her to work through her anger, enabling her to appreciate the times they'd had together and grieve in a healthy way.

Life Goes On and Being Part of it Isn't Wrong

Sally lost a husband in his early forties to a particularly virulent and nasty form of cancer. They had been childhood sweethearts with a long and happy marriage and she couldn't conceive of life without him. She refused all offers of friends to take her out or suggestions that she move house and start afresh as she wanted to stay in her house of memories. From a lively and beautiful woman she turned into a haunted and haggard looking one. But she is still young and will, we hope, make an effort to survive.

It helps to remember that life will go on and that you are meant to be a part of it.

Older people suffering loss, like the actor Mark MacManus, known for his portrayal of the tough Scottish detective Taggart on TV, or the American actor Jimmy Stewart, can more easily allow themselves to slip away from a broken heart. Both these men were devastated by the loss of the woman they loved and both died shortly after their partners, literally seeming to pine away. 'Dying of a broken heart' is not simply the stuff of fairy tales. Scientifically it is believed that the immune systems of those who suffer a severe loss are weakened, which is why the death of a spouse or child tops the league table of stressful life events, or they lose the will to live which is, after all, what keeps us going.

It helps to remember that life will go on and that you are meant to be a part of it. You're either with it or against it and it doesn't do to be 'anti-life'. Some find it helpful, as Britain's royal family clearly do, to cope with loss by sticking to tried and tested routines that they find comforting. Many people thought that taking Diana's sons to church on the morning of her death was a callous act on the part of their father and his family. But the boys might well have derived comfort from the familiar routine which would have helped to give some structure to their shattered world. Other people prefer to make a clean break with the past and, like Dominick Dunne, the Hollywood film producer who lost his daughter to a killer in California, move thousands of miles away to a new home (in New York), new career (as a writer) and new perspectives. There's no right or wrong, just what works for you.

Loss can mean not just the loss of a loved one to death but of a job, a way or a time of life. Women can experience a poignant sense of loss as piercing as losing a loved one when they lose a breast to mastectomy, a womb to hysterectomy, a child to university, or the monthly periods that have for so long measured out their lives. Divorce is loss, redundancy is loss, losing your hair to chemotherapy or son to another woman is loss. Probably the worst loss of all is that of a child, whether to death or drugs, to a bizarre religious cult or a partner you deem unsuitable. Don't expect not to mourn such losses. They must be grieved over in order to be properly laid to rest. Keep a quiet corner of your heart for them by all means. But don't let them engulf your life for ever. You owe it to yourself, and those who love you, to survive.

Ageing means loss of all kinds, although this book aims to show you how to minimize the sense of loss as much as possible. We lose all sorts of things when we get older, from our glasses (see Chapter Ten) to our youthful looks. All of these losses can be traumas if we let them be. It is particularly important, when adjusting to loss, to use and develop the skills that have brought you pleasure all your life. So it is important to continue with social or work activities you enjoy, and even when you are married or in a steady relationship to make time for the friends and fun things that you may need to sustain you in the future. Pat Chambers, an academic at Stockport College of Further and Higher Education in England, has done some interesting research into the state of widowhood. She felt the picture didn't need to be one of ill health, loneliness and grief but one of growth and development.

UltraAge Antidote
Continuing activities, friendships and pleasures help overcome loss.

Interviewing widows well after their period of bereavement she found that 'there was a richness to their lives which seemed contrary to the picture portrayed in the literature on older widows. But that was for those who had worked on it and had possibly even planned for it.

MEMORY LOSS

Memory loss is sometimes due to not having exercised your brain enough (see Chapter Ten), and we hope to help show you how to avoid this. 'It is a man's own fault, it is from want of use, if his mind goes torpid in old age,' said Boswell in his *Life of Johnson*, and it holds as true for women. Often it's stress (see below) and sometimes simply laziness that stops us from using our minds to their full potential. Memory lapses can occur at any age but are feared most in mid- to later life primarily due to the poor memory recall being associated with symptoms of dementia or Alzheimer's disease.

But occasional lapses of recall are natural at every age, particularly as we all try to process ever more information daily via the endless means of communication integral to office and home life, and memory loss is not integral to ageing. Stress creates memory loss, preventing us from prioritizing the information we need, when we need it. Lapses also have a lot to do with the loss of vital nutrients to the brain as we get on rather than loss of mental capacity. Free radicals, another nasty age accelerator, are notorious for causing memory problems as we age; deficiencies of the B vitamins and Vitamin Q10 can cause the brain to short-circuit and blank out. So

> **UltraAge Antidote**
> Feed your brain – use it or lose it!

feed the brain with good food and supplements, keep it motivated with good exercises and you can minimize those embarrassing lapses in recall which may popularly identify you as elderly.

MIDDLE-AGED SPREAD

This is an almost inevitable part of ageing for most of us, although a few lucky ones, like England's Margaret Read – featured in a newspaper as a phenomenon because of this – can still wear the same shorts at fifty-five as they did at twelve. To some degree it may be necessary, Mother Nature's way of giving us a little more fat to produce oestrogen when our ovaries pack in. But beware of putting on too much weight around your middle, as this is a risk sign for heart disease. Women who put on extra weight around their bottoms, thighs, upper arms and other peripheral bits are not nearly at as much risk as those who put on fat in a 'masculine' way around the middle.

Fight the spread with low fat spreads, a low fat diet generally, and plenty of waist-whittling exercises. Arnold Schwarzenegger swears by sideways stretches (one arm up at the side of the ear, the other sliding down the leg towards the angle) for keeping his formidable figure from spreading any further, and this exercise, with light weights added as you get better at it, also works well for women.

> **UltraAge Antidote**
> Waist-whittling ways.

NEGATIVITY

This is one of the most destructive mindsets, and encompasses emotions such as fear, worry, anger, envy. Negativity also means saying 'I can't' when you should be saying 'I can' and 'I will'. How many people are held back from activities they would enjoy, from life changes that would benefit them, and from loves or careers that would enrich their lives because they are too mired in negativity to embark on them?

Developing a positive mindset is vital, we feel, for successful ageing, although we're not always able to manage it in all circumstances ourselves. But over and over in this book you will see that we stress the importance of this, which is borne out by all the UltraAgers we have spoken to. In different chapters we look at different ways to obtain it, from practising positive visualization to developing the right kind of attitude to work and pleasure and to enriching your life with physical exercise and positive thoughts. Negativity is useless ballast that will drag you down. Don't let it!

> **UltraAge Antidote**
> Think positively! You can do it!

OSTEOARTHRITIS

Unlike rheumatoid arthritis, which can affect the young, this is a disease of ageing. People with injured joints, who are overweight, or who have an inherited disposition to it will be most affected. Most common in the hips and knees, it can also affect the spine and neck, leading to pain that radiates outwards. Heberden's arthritis is arthritis of the last little joint in the fingers, and mainly strikes women. Osteoarthritis can be chronically painful and debilitating.

Cure or Just Coping?

There are all kinds of supposed arthritis 'cures' you can try, from wearing a copper bracelet to drinking cider vinegar and eating New Zealand green-lipped mussels. Some people believe in avoiding aubergines, tomatoes and fungi. Or you can take the painkillers and anti-inflammatory drugs your doctor will prescribe, from aspirin to non-steroidal anti-inflammatories. A hot water bottle or icepack may give some relief, and losing weight if necessary could make a big difference. Codliver oil in high doses promises to keep joints supple and may help to prevent the advent of osteoarthritis. Surgery is a last option, hip replacement being the simplest, knee replacement more complicated. However, techniques are improving all the time and better 'bionic bits' being crafted.

> **UltraAge Antidote**
> Keep flexible, keep moving!

OSTEOPOROSIS

Osteoporosis is the softening and weakening of the bones due to lack of calcium that occurs in approximately one in five women after the menopause when oestrogen is no longer in plentiful supply to help calcium to be absorbed into the bone tissue. But osteoporosis can also be suffered by some men and by younger women, particularly those in intensive sports training. It is a known hazard for sportswomen who train hard enough to interfere with their periods. But ironically it's exercise, weight-bearing exercise, that will keep it at bay as we get older. It's a question of keeping the balance right, as in all things. Although it usually comes on with age it is not a natural consequence but a disorder of ageing, and leads to the fractures of the hip for which one in four elderly women are hospitalized and which is a major cause of death as complications set in, most usually lung or blood problems because of the immobilization. See Chapter Four for more links with the menopause.

Bone Up On How to Prevent It

Every woman should have a bone density test before she is peri-menopausal, so that she has a baseline figure to guide her. Subsequent tests will show whether there has been any loss of bone density. Hormone replacement therapy for at least a year has been shown to

be able to stop the progress of osteoporosis and restrengthen the skeleton, but not if taken for less time. And HRT cannot undo damage that has been done, it can only prevent more. Calcium and Vitamin D supplements can both be helpful, but it is important to take them as part of a balanced healthy diet that will improve absorption. Calcium is best absorbed in the presence of some fat in the diet, so women worried about osteoporosis but also worried about putting on weight might be wise to go for 98 or 99 per cent fat free milk rather than totally skimmed milk. Calcium can also be obtained from soya and other milks, as well as all dairy and soya products, sardines, salmon, sunflower seeds, dried beans and green vegetables.

UltraAge Antidote
Calcium and weight-bearing exercises.

PARTNER PROBLEMS

Your partner in life should be your soul- and helpmate, a source of love and mutual support. But all too often they can be the major source of stress in your life. Dr David Weeks noticed that his Superyoung subjects were, for the most part, quite brutal at shedding partners who were not enhancing their lives, and moving on to someone else whom they felt would. Cancer prevention expert Dr Jan de Winter observed that women in unhappy marriages were more prone to breast cancer than those in happy marriages. Since it is well documented that happiness leads to health and unhappiness can be demonstrated to weaken the immune system, an unhappy relationship with the person supposed to be the closest in your life can leave you very vulnerable. What happens with your 'other half' of course will profoundly influence you. But women tend to feel more undermined by partner problems than men, who are more absorbed in external issues like work or sport, despite the fact that women seem to thrive better without a partner than men do!

What To Do About Them

Communicate the problem. Don't let things stagnate and escalate. Organizations such as Relate and other counsellors are there to help. If you are trapped in an abusive relationship – mentally or physically – or one which consistently makes you feel bad about yourself, and if you are experiencing health problems, you might be wise to consider quickly what changes you could make. But realize that there have to be compromises. As the leading lady says in Alan Ayckbourn's play *Things We Do For Love,* 'You either live alone or you compromise.'

UltraAge Antidote
Work to make it work.

PROLAPSE

Prolapses are associated with old women and signal that a woman is not having an active sex life and may not be able to again, although some surprisingly young women suffer from them. In prolapses the womb literally drops down and bulges out of the neck of the cervix, causing considerable discomfort. This comes from not having a strong, well-exercised pelvic floor.

Not being afraid of being alone is important and an indicator of mental health.

Prolapse Prevention

There are numerous exercises a woman can do to strengthen her pelvic floor that will also enhance sexual pleasure. The most basic one is to squeeze and tighten your vagina periodically – anywhere, while waiting for a bus or in the bath. Can you stop a flow of urine in mid-stream by powerfully contracting the pelvic floor muscles? Practise, but don't do this too often: it's better to squeeze them when you're not weeing. There are more advanced pelvic floor exercises that can be regarded as a pleasure in themselves rather than simply a preparation for sex with a partner. In his excellent book *Sexual Exercises for Women* Dr Anthony Harris suggests many. He notes that 'Most women experience pleasure in the pit of their tummy after a few squats' when the pelvic floor muscles are being contracted, and says that 'Waves of relaxation will go up the inside of your legs and up from your crotch to your breasts.'

UltraAge Antidote
Pelvic floor exercises.

QUIET

A quiet life is not all it's cracked up to be. As one of the characters in Tom Stoppard's play *Rosencrantz and Guildenstern are Dead* wonders, 'is life in a box better than no life at all?' Solitude (the title of an reflective book by Oxford academician Anthony Storr) can be soothing, calming and nourishing to the soul. But human contact is vital for long-

term health. A recent Italian study showed that loving human contact, and feeling closely and lovingly involved with another human being, was a major factor in longevity. Yet another survey showed that over 80 per cent of over-seventy-fives said they were very happy not seeing other people.

Build Networks

Not being afraid of being alone is important and an indicator of mental health. Wanting to be alone all the time is unhealthy. We all need a good balance. Some prefer to be 'far from the madding crowd' while others thrive on the buzz of the big city. But 'a change is as good as a rest' and 'variety's the spice of life', as the sayings go. If you work with people all day long, some solitude can be pleasant. One of the saddest things about old age, though, is loneliness and the lack of warm, sensual, loving, humorous human contact.

Build up your networks of friends. Cultivate them. Cherish them. In the end they may be there for you when your husband's dumped you for a bimbo and your children have run off with unsuitable part-

> ***UltraAge Antidote***
> Don't be afraid of being alone, but don't be lonely.

ners. If they're good friends they'll respect your need for quiet times and offer you support when you need it, if you do the same for them. Quiet can be creative. Writers and artists need great quantities of it. But quiet can also be desolate. 'The grave's a fine and private place but none, I think, do there embrace' said Andrew Marvell to his 'Coy Mistress'. Embrace while you can. Embrace people and embrace life.

ROSACEA

This embarrassing skin condition – the appearance of a permanent blush with dilated blood vessels, inflammation, swelling and sometimes pustules – is a condition suffered primarily by middle-aged women.

What Can Be Done About It?

Not much, according to dermatologist Professor Ronald Marks. It's far better to try to prevent it from occurring in the first place. It is thought that heat may precipitate and aggravate rosacea, and that people who have been exposed to sources of direct heat either in their work, say,

as a cook, or in the home, by spending too much time in the kitchen or sitting close to an open fire, are more likely to get it, says Professor Marks. 'It comes from climactic exposure, genetic constitution and undue focal heat,' he explains. Don't let your doctor prescribe a steroid cream for it, he says, as that would only thin the skin and make it worse. Avoid hot and spicy foods and exposure to extremes of temperature because even chilling and chapping can exacerbate the problem.

> ***UltraAge Antidote***
> Keep cool!

SMOKING

This is probably the ultimate age accelerator as far as bad habits go. Unlike alcohol, on which the evidence is somewhat ambivalent and which may actually do some good in small quantities, nobody has a good word to say about smoking. Women smokers face extra risks. They are more likely to have an early menopause than non-smokers; they are five times more likely than non-smoking women to contract lung cancer and are up to twenty times more susceptible to heart attacks if they are heavy smokers. The combination of smoking and oral contraceptives is particularly bad. Smoking is also antisocial, as the evidence accumulates that passive smoking can kill, and more restaurants and public places are declared non-smoking zones.

> ✧ Smoking causes 120,000 deaths annually in Britain alone.
> ✧ Lifelong smokers are said to have a fifteen times greater risk of disease than non-smokers.
> ✧ Smoking doubles your risk of dying before sixty-five.
> ✧ Smoking increases the risk of a range of cancers, of heart attacks, cataracts and bone thinning.

But aside from these future fears there are the wrinkles forming now, the nicotine-yellowed skin, the bloodshot eyes, and the scrunched-up expressions that smoking causes, not to mention smelling like an old ashtray! So why do so many women continue to do it? Because they worry about their weight. They think smoking will help them to stay thinner, because when they've got a cigarette in their mouths they won't be stuffing them with anything else, and because nicotine speeds up the metabolism. Teenaged girls are notoriously unimpressed by the posthumous pictures of smokers' lungs sent to schools by various health-minded organizations such as the Health Education Authority and Action on Smoking and Health (ASH).

But who wants to be the thinnest, most hyped-up wrinkly around or in the cemetery? When Victoria stopped smoking over twenty years ago she took up swimming instead, and discovered the joy of feeling fitter, and that it wasn't normal to wake up every morning with a hacking cough. She's never looked back, and recommends the same approach to others. Taking up something new, something that it would be difficult to do while smoking, whether it's swimming or knitting, abseiling or flower arranging, is helpful when trying to stop. And just think of all the money you'll save with the price of cigarettes today!

'Yoga is the breath of life, smoking the breath of death.'

But How to Quit?

Some people find some of the nicotine chewing gums or nicotine patches helpful. Others have sought out hypnotists, who have proved very successful in stopping smoking. You can even buy tapes that claim to be able to help you to stop – the health food shops are full of them, together with herbal cigarettes and other healthier substitutes.

Organizations such as the **Promis Recovery Centre** specialize in all kinds of addiction, and will happily help smokers, pointing out that 'if you're a smoker you're an addict'. While anyone can quit for Non-smoking Day, or even for a few days, the trick is devising a strategy to help you stay away from the evil weed for good. That is what the numerous anti-smoking clinics and helplines around the world are designed to do. **Quitline** was founded by the Health Education Authority, and receives nearly half a million calls a year for its practical advice and just to talk about the problem. You can ring up whenever you feel your resolve weakening.

Other aids to quitting are a Nicorette inhaler that squirts nicotine, in vapour form, into your mouth (around £20 for a week's 'hits' from chemists); Nicorette patches for slower release nicotine doses (about £16 for two months' worth); acupuncture; hypnotherapy; and yoga.

Henry Dent-Brocklehurst, heir to Sudeley Castle in England, tells how yoga helped him to give up smoking several years ago. 'The deep breathing in yoga makes you not want to smoke,' he says. 'Yoga is the breath of life, smoking the breath of death.'

Don't make excuses. We have only three things to say about smoking: give it up, give it up, give it up. There are many ways to try but you have to want to for all the reasons listed above. You are worth it. You will eventually feel better, eat better, sleep better and look better.

> **UltraAge Antidote**
> Positive thinking: you can live without smoking. In fact, your life depends on it.

SNORING

Snoring is an age accelerator for both the snorer and the person they sleep with. Snoring is more than a nuisance, it also means that you are not sleeping well and possibly not getting the oxygen you need to your brain. Overweight people with difficulty breathing often snore, and it is a problem. They might even be suffering from sleep apnoea which wakes them up many times in the night without them realizing it, leaving them dazed and dozy and below par during the day. Snoring also means that perhaps not enough blood is getting to the brain. So snorers should be checked out by a doctor to eliminate possible pathological causes and effects of this disturbing habit.

Then they could try some of the many new aids on the market, such as elastic strips you put on your nose at bedtime to widen the nasal passage. You'll see many sportspeople using them during games simply to enhance their breathing.

> **UltraAge Antidote**
> Lose weight, get fitter, and treat your partner to a pack of wax ear plugs.

STRESS

Stress in its sustained, chronic form may actually kill off brain cells as well as taking its toll on our health – and looks – in many other ways. Stress can literally deprive the brain of oxygen, killing off the vital nerve cells that require high amounts of it to run efficiently. In *Why Zebras Don't Get Ulcers* Professor Robert Sapolsky, professor of neuroscience at Stanford University in California, asked, 'How many hippos worry about whether Social Security is going to last as long as they will, or even what they are going to say on a first date?' Let alone worrying about how they're going to pay their credit card bills, whether their teenage child is on drugs, whether their partner is in love with someone

else, whether they are going to be made redundant from their job, etc. etc. We all have to face stressful situations every day and can usually rise to each occasion. It is when the stressful situation doesn't go away and our body stays in a stressed-out state of readiness day in and day out that the long-term damage is done. The adrenal glands are pumping out the stress hormones needed for a fight or flight situation which does not arise. The body is confused, the mind out of control. Indeed, the sense of having lost control is almost a prerequisite for negative stress.

Take Control of Your Life

The surest way you can unstress yourself is to try to give yourself back at least the illusion of control. If you are feeling stressed because you fear you might lose your job, don't wait like a lamb in the slaughter-house until the axe falls. Take action and start looking around for alternatives. If you are stressed because of financial problems, take control of them. Rather than hiding from creditors and robbing Peter to pay Paul, why not take the bull by the horns and go to your bank manager or an independent financial adviser and discuss ways out of the hole you've got yourself into. There's sure to be one. Two invaluable tips on handling stress which we have heard from many sources and which became the title of a book on handling stress are: don't sweat the small stuff, and remember that it's all small stuff.

The surest way you can unstress yourself is to try to get back a measure of control.

Put your problems in perspective. Is it really life and death if you don't catch the 8:11 train? No. But it could be life and death if you crash your car rushing on the way there, or clog up your arteries by perennially leaving the house too late so you have to rush. Often just changing your perception of a situation is enough to make it seem less stressful. Sometimes you may have to change your habits, like making sure you leave the house ten minutes earlier every day so that you don't stress yourself out rushing for the train. Remember that stress is cumulative and that we can all take some in our stride. But it may be the last straw that breaks the camel's back, so don't turn molehills into mental mountains that your mind can't move.

The third tip is don't worry. Worrying is always stressful and hardly ever constructive. Think about your problems by all means and see if you can work out a solution to them, but don't just worry. Ever heard

the expression 'worried to death'? It's not surprising it got coined! If you worry when your teenage daughter is out late at night, make a plan for coping with it. Ask her to telephone you to tell you where she is at a specific time. Tell her if she doesn't you will a) call her friend X, b) call her friend Y, c) call the police – or whatever. Make a plan and stick to it. Don't just vaguely worry.

Put your problems in perspective. Is it really life and death if you don't catch the 8:11 train?

Stress Types

We have all experienced at least two types of stress. Think of them as positive and negative. Positive stress might be the stress you feel when called upon to make a speech, your heart thumping as you rise to the occasion, or to meet another kind of challenge or deadline. It is usually short term and can cause you to feel temporarily buoyed up by the adrenalin rush it provokes.

Negative stress is what you feel when 'shit happens', as the saying goes, and you feel powerlessly enveloped by it, totally out of control. This is the stress of money, job and relationship worries that seem to weigh you down and to which there seems no end in sight. The release of stress hormones is so continual that the immune system is depleted and the adrenal glands can be worn out, resulting in the condition known as burnout. The so-called 'hardy personality' is one that thrives on stress, and has learned how to regard as challenges what other people see as threats – to turn negative stress into positive stress. They are survivors. Hardy personalities cultivate the three cs: commitment, challenge and control. They also readily accept change.

You've heard of time-urgent Type A personalities, who speak, eat and act fast, do six things at once and even finish other people's sentences for them, and the more laid-back Type Bs who can stress Type As to death with their methodical plodding? Well, whereas Type B behaviour is undoubtedly healthier in the long run, those with the least chance of long-term survival are what is now known as Type H personalities, H for hurried and hostile. These are the opposite of hardy personalities and generally wear their immune system to a frazzle or go 'pop' with a heart attack or stroke.

How to Become a Hardy Personality

If you're not born that way and it doesn't come naturally to you, you either have to change the circumstances that stress you or change your perspective on those circumstances. So if it's your (younger) boss's patronizing attitude that gets you, either discuss it with him or her and explain what annoys you, prepare to move jobs, or learn to laugh it off. Don't sit and stew!

UltraAge Antidote
Control, and learning to see threats as challenges.

If you're constantly irritated by your elderly mother's criticisms (she's irritated you since childhood but now that she's living with you again it's unbearable), either tell her they can't go on or she'll have to make alternative arrangements or learn to laugh it off. Don't sit and stew.

THE SUN

Through this book we cite the prime cause of premature ageing to the skin as being regular, over exposure to the sun. Many women who could 'tolerate' the sun unprotected when young are discovering later in life that short exposure then means wrinkled and leathery skin now.

Like all things, sun exposure needs to be in moderation.

By now we should all know that the earth's atmosphere ain't what it used to be and that the ozone layer protecting us from the harmful rays of the sun is getting thinner and thinner. In many parts of the world, like South Africa, Australia and New Zealand, scientists confirm actual 'holes' in the ozone which means that people can 'burn up' without total protection of high-powered sunscreens or clothing.

For those of us who suffer from sun deprivation by living in the bleak, grey climates of Northern Europe, for example, it is so hard to resist the wonderful warmth of the sun's rays whenever they shine. A bright day elevates the moods and also brings a welcome dose of Vitamin D. Like all things, exposure needs to be in moderation. There is a huge difference to taking a long walk on a bright afternoon in the autumn or spring when the sun isn't so strong to basking on a white sandy beach, mid-summer, on an island near the equator, for hours.

UltraAge Antidote
Minimal exposure and maximum protection.

For full details of how to protect yourself from the sun see Chapter Five on beauty. If the sun has already taken its toll and you want to get rid of its ravages see Chapter Six on the latest laser techniques.

'TATT' – TIRED ALL THE TIME

Wanting to sleep too much could mean you have 'TATT' – doctors' name for 'tired all the time' syndrome, which can come about for a variety of reasons, ranging from auto-immune diseases such as ME to depression. It is often experienced by the newly retired who suddenly lack a sense of purpose in their lives, and can be a way of avoiding problems you don't want to face, or unhappy realities in your waking life. It can also be a symptom masking a more serious illness, so make sure your doctor eliminates all organic causes. Like all types of sleep problems from insomnia to snoring, TATT can be debilitating, disorientating and, ultimately, ageing.

Get the Right Fuel

If you're TATT, exercise and a healthy diet full of power foods is particularly important. If you're an insomniac, avoid caffeine, spices and dairy foods just before bedtime. In both cases consult your doctor. Restful sleep (see 'ZZZ' below) is important for many reasons: because of the mental refreshment it provides; because it 'knits up the ravelled sleeve of care', as Shakespeare said; because it stretches your spine (you can be up to an inch taller in the morning!); because it encourages the production of HGH and other hormones which help to keep us looking and feeling young. Disturbed or depleted hormone levels may be implicated in the condition, so it can be a vicious circle.

UltraAge Antidote
Refuel your energy stores.

URINARY PROBLEMS

Although there is a range of bladder and kidney disorders that one can succumb to, when it comes to ageing perhaps the most common problem is with leakage. All women need to practise pelvic floor exercises to keep the dribbles at bay. These exercises build strength and improve the endurance of the bladder.

A good way to get a grip (figuratively) of your pelvic floor is to hold your urine mid-stream for as long as you can. In doing this you are using the relevant muscles. Once you have found where they are and how to use them, however, practise this exercise when you are not urinating. You can practise clenching your pelvic floor muscles almost

anywhere (thrilling in the knowledge that no one will realize!) but continuing to try to stop your urine flow can result in a build-up of toxins in the urethra which can cause infection (urothritis), cystitis or other problems. At other times you can try to contract these same muscles for three or five seconds, increasing to fifteen seconds. Practise a few times each day, perhaps at the same time as doing something else, like brushing your teeth. Then every time you brush your teeth you are reminded to do your pelvic floor exercises.

Don't expect overnight results from these exercises. These muscles are deep and take time to strengthen. Allow a few weeks to see an improvement in stamina as well as your sex life (see also 'Prolapse').

Keep your bladder on the move, too, by urinating as frequently as possible and drinking plenty of water. If worried about holding your load, say, during a long meeting or while travelling, remember to empty yourself at the last possible opportunity and only drink water, avoiding alcohol or caffeine which will cause pressure on the bladder.

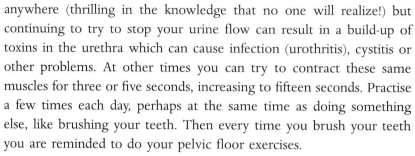

UltraAge Antidote
Exercise that pelvic floor and drink copious amounts of water and some cranberry juice. Avoid artificial sweeteners, 'feminine hygiene' sprays and wearing pantyhose/tights daily.

Some regular urinary problems like cystitis can be treated effectively with over the counter remedies or by drinking cranberry juice. But if you have more than two infections in six months or more than three a year, you should be seen by a specialist to make sure that nothing sinister is developing. If you find blood in the urine, develop chills or back pain, you need medical advice quickly.

THE VISION THING

Not having 'the vision thing' any more is a shock to Boomers. Reading glasses are an outward sign of age. You'll probably feel the need for them sometime around your fortieth birthday, when you discover your arms cannot hold your reading material far enough away for you to focus on any more. To those who have never worn glasses it can be a real shock. To those who have been shortsighted there can be a blissful period when you seem to see better than before, and then you discover you need bifocals. This happens because the eye, like the rest of the body, is becoming less elastic, and less able to change its focus quickly. When the focal distance becomes greater than the length of your arms you have presbyopia or old people's vision. There seems to be no way of preventing it, although Vitamin A seems to be beneficial for all eye functions, and other vitamins and supplements designed to enhance the body's lubrication and elasticity (See Chapter Nine) may hold back the symptoms a little.

Not having 'the vision thing' any more is a shock to Boomers.

Get Tested!

Other vision problems associated with age are glaucoma, which tends to run in families and begin in the forties, so those with a family history of the disease should be regularly checked. In glaucoma the pressure in the eye increases and destroys the peripheral vision first.

Macular degeneration will destroy central vision, as it affects the centre of the retina. There is a genetic tendency towards it which may be exacerbated by arteriosclerosis in the blood vessels that supply the eye so that a healthy diet may have some effect there. Glaucoma, which should be caught in time if you have the simple test for it every six months when you have your eyes examined, can be controlled with eye drops or through surgery.

Seeing More Clearly Again

For presbyopia, bifocal glasses and contact lenses are available. It is now possible, thanks to Boomer pressure, to get 'varifocals' without visible lines dividing the top and bottom of the lens, which was always an outward sign of age. Eye exercises may help prevent the problem at least to some degree. Your doctor or optometrist may be able to recommend someone who will teach them or you can learn from a book such as *Better Sight Without Glasses* by Harry Benjamin, which was first published in 1929 and was in its sixth edition in 1992. Mr Benjamin, a naturopath, improved his failing eyesight through the 'Bates Method' of exercises devised by a Dr WH Bates in New York in the twenties. They involve a series of simple focal distance changes, 'swaying', 'palming' and stretching the neck. Wonderful things are claimed of them and, logically, they should help, although many optometrists pooh-pooh them.

The Bates Method was developed in the early part of the twentieth century by New York ophthalmologist WH Bates. His system was popularized in Britain in 1929 by Harry Benjamin, who became a naturopathic practitioner specializing in 'natural methods of eye treatment'. He claims that, through a combination of a 'sensible naturopathic diet' – fruit, salads, etc. – and exercises, he was able to give up his very strong glasses. Eyes can be relaxed by 'palming' (covering with a cupped palm) and 'swinging' (swaying) and various exercises for the neck are recommended. For a patient with presbyopia, 'old sight', he recommended fifteen minutes' palming twice a day, and then eye muscle exercises, followed by reading a newspaper as near as possible without straining.

The eye muscle exercises include holding up the index finger of the right hand about eight inches in front of the eyes, then looking from the finger to any large object ten or more feet away. Look from one to the other ten times, then rest for a second and repeat the ten glances two or three times in rapid succession. This is said to improve 'accommodation' of the eye to focus close up.

If it is caught early enough, macular degeneration can be treated with laser beam therapy. Test yourself every day by looking at a vertical line first with one eye and then with the other. If there is a blank spot in it or it seems shaky, make an appointment to have your eyes checked immediately.

Until now there has been little hope for sufferers from macular degeneration, one of the leading causes of blindness, but new research shows help may be at hand in the early years of the new millennium to change this. Purlytin, being tested now by Miravant Medical Technologies, is a light activated drug which can be injected into the arm, and then made to function in the eye by the use of a cool red laser. Once activated it will seek out and destroy abnormal blood vessels which cause the leakage of blood responsible for the destruction of the retina which leads to blindness. This is envisaged eventually as a routine outpatient treatment at eye hospitals and clinics but the treatment may have to be repeated every three or six months. Further information can be obtained from the Macular Disease Society (see Useful Organizations below for details).

Cataracts

All of us would, apparently, develop cataracts if we lived long enough. A cataract is the progressive clouding of the gelatinous lens of the eye, although it is not always visible. The increasing opacity prevents light from passing to the retina and the vision becomes blurred. Most forty-somethings will find that they need brighter light to read in than they did when they were younger; and we of the computer generation may find cataracts come earlier to us than they did to our parents or grand-parents. Just as they are always shown in science fiction films to be a consequence of post-nuclear radiation, they do seem to be connected with radiation, whether from bombs or the screens at which so many of us now spend our days.

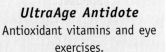

UltraAge Antidote
Antioxidant vitamins and eye exercises.

Fortunately cataract operations are now routine in the West and routinely successful. The clouded lens is removed and a clear synthetic replacement implanted. Sufferers may suddenly see more clearly than they have for years, and may no longer have to use glasses at all because their vision is so good, thanks to the implanted lens.

WARTS, WHISKERS AND ALL

'You should be women, yet your beards forbid me to interpret that you are so,' said Macbeth to the Three Witches. Shakespeare knew that whiskers were a sign of age in a woman, which is why witches are so often portrayed with them, and with giant warts on their faces. Whiskers can appear in more mature women because their oestrogen levels are too low to keep such secondary male sexual characteristics at bay. Warts, however, are more difficult to explain. Ian Thomas, a dermatologist at St Thomas's Hospital in London, explains that the warts and skin tags and other growths that are a normal part of the ageing process are not the viral warts we get in our youth, which can come and go, but permanent new additions to our skin. Most are harmless, but can be irritating if they appear on your nose, under your eyes, or in other areas where they are noticeable or catch on something like glasses.

To Remove or Not To Remove?

Professor Marks advises having every new growth checked out. His philosophy is, 'When in doubt check it out and if still in doubt chop it out.' That tends to be the American philosophy but not generally the British and European. But as Professor Marks puts it, 'Although

these don't normally develop into cancer, we can only be 80 per cent certain with some of them and it's better to be safe than sorry. There's little difficulty in removing a spot, or a seborrhoeic wart, or milia, which are tiny little cysts that form in the skin, but if we make a mistake and don't take them off it can be bad.'

Whiskers will have to be removed by tweezers, electrolysis or special depilatory creams that are safe for the face. Warts and all you'll have to live with unless you are so unhappy with them that you opt for laser surgery or to have them frozen off. Skin tags can be tied off with a piece of sterile cotton. Any growth, however, that is darker than skin colour, particularly if it is ragged in shape, itchy, or bleeds, should be seen by a doctor in case it is a skin cancer.

UltraAge Antidote
Unsightly bits needn't be.

WRINKLES

Many of our grandmothers and great-grandmothers never had a line on their faces until they hit their sixties. So why do many thirty-somethings and virtually all over-forties have to contend with vexing 'etching' on their faces?

The skin is the largest organ in the body, comprised of a thin outer layer, the epidermis, and a thicker layer underneath, the dermis. The epidermis is strong and has an outer layer of dead cells. The dermis contains nerves, blood vessels and living cells. As we get older, cell renewal slows down. Having taken 28 days, it now takes 40.

If you love and worship the sun, no doubt your skin has suffered and shows it.

The Causes

Causes are varied but the main one is the sun. If you love and worship it, no doubt your skin has suffered and shows it. Smoking is the second major cause as it reduces the blood flow to the skin, preventing the cells' ability to repair themselves. The constant puckering to inhale on a cigarette creates lip creases. Smokers also squint more to avoid the irritation of smoke in their eyes, so causing 'crows' feet'. A recent study at St Thomas's Hospital in London on identical twins found that the twin who smokes had substantially older-looking skin than the one who does not, with the smoker's skin being up to 40 per cent thinner!

At menopause, the skin worsens as its moisture and oil content lessens, resulting in collagen retraction, which is why women's skin seems older than men's. Without collagen support, the skin drops and wrinkles form. Dr Marion Froschle, in research and development at La Prairie International, says, 'The older we get the more cell renewal certainly does slow down. In older skin fewer renewed cells reach the surface while dead cells clog together and elasticity is lost.'

Other lines form on our face from the expression we make repetitively when communicating. When some of us listen we frown, an outward manifestation of concentration. Frown lines can be horizontal across the forehead or in two deep vertical lines between the brows. Other people can't convey the simplest of messages without employing almost every facial muscle. Even the way you sleep can contribute to wrinkles. If you are most comfortable face-down into the pillow, you probably have more sleep-induced lines than others.

It is essential to use moisturizing creams daily to protect the skin from outside pollutants.

Damage Limitation

Cosmetic surgeon Jan Stanek says that the key weapon against ageing skin is sunscreen, at least 25 SPF, which should be worn year round. Apply before you moisturize to ensure that your skin is totally covered and protected. Allow it to be absorbed before applying make-up. Don't take comfort in the SPFs added to many foundations. They aren't enough to protect the skin, particularly on bright days.

Sometimes regular sunscreens can irritate the tissue around the eyes. If you can't protect the eyes by wearing filtered sunglasses, then try using a waxy lip balm or stick with a high SPF. This won't run or 'bleed' into the eyes, causing irritation.

Repair Techniques

It is essential to use moisturizing creams daily to protect the skin from outside pollutants. Older skin benefits from applying moisturizer while the skin is damp. It will appear plumper and less lined with the extra moisture. A daily cream should be rich enough so that the skin doesn't feel dry and it is also not greasy so helps make-up last throughout the day. A richer night cream is recommended to boost nutrients and extra oil to the skin daily.

A dermatologist can prescribe Retin-A (retionoic acid), a derivative of Vitamin A, which is very effective in smoothing fine lines. Developed originally for acne sufferers, Retin-A can even out skin texture and colouring, minimize lines, and generally make the skin look fresher. Beware of 'over the counter' products using a similar name and implying similar results as the winning effects are only possible in high concentration creams. Users of Retin-A must protect their skin with a strong sunblock as the treated skin is far more susceptible to sun damage.

Aid natural sloughing-off of dead skin cells with an alpha-hydroxy acid (AHA) cleanser or cream in preference to an 'exfoliant' which can be very damaging to older skin as it removes too many cells, leaving the skin vulnerable to broken veins and irritation. AHAs are natural acids derived from fruit such as apples and lemons, sugar cane, milk and even wine. AHAs might not produce the same dramatic results as Retin-A but the latter can be very irritating and is not recommended for all women. AHAs are available without prescription and are now quite inexpensive compared to when they first appeared a decade ago. Don't sniff at good-value AHA creams with supermarket labels. You can save yourself a packet while repairing your skin.

Chemical peels are less frightening than they sound but must be administered by a dermatologist or cosmetic surgeon in one shot or via a series of treatments. The latest peels employ a mild acid (trichloracetic acid) that minimizes the previous problems with depigmentation (i.e. bleaching of the natural skin tone) and also shortens recovery time to a matter of days rather than weeks.

Dermabrasion is a method of line removal, originally developed for treating severe acne, by using a fine sander to work off the outer layers of the skin. Healing requires diligent care to prevent scarring. The face develops a scab that takes up to two weeks to heal. Patients are also warned to avoid sun or risk patchy pigmentation.

Laser treatments use beams of light which vaporize very thin layers of the face. Most cosmetic surgeons now recommend lasers as part of any face-lift procedure as they are very accurate and safe. The skill involves getting the intensity of the laser right as well as knowing how many times to go over an area to produce the desired elimination of lines and wrinkles. An added benefit is that the procedure stimulates the production of collagen in the skin which makes the texture

UltraAge Antidote
Stay out of the sun, drink plenty of water, and eat more fresh fruit and vegetables to keep the wrinkles at bay.

appear both plumper and smoother. Recovery takes seven to ten days, after which make-up can cover the skin while it heals completely.

X-CESS

X-cess anything can lead to problems, particularly since moderation seems to be the byword when it comes to successful ageing. A little alcohol is fine; too much is damaging to the system. A little of what you fancy does you good but too much can make you fat, lazy and less likely to live as long as you might. As Shakespeare observed, 'If all the year were playing holidays, to sport would be as tedious as to work.' While it is good for your body to have occasional treats, and regular holidays, it also needs a sensible routine of moderation.

> *UltraAge Antidote*
> Moderation and small pleasures.

X-HAUSTION!

We are both guilty of this, driving ourselves too hard, expecting too much of our beleaguered bodies, so that we need to collapse in a heap on occasion. We shouldn't get to that point, and our bodies will rebel and eventually break down if we keep driving them to it. Know your limitations and keep within sensible ones. Know you can't burn the candle at both ends any more and get away with it as you did in the first flush of youth. Look at your daily schedule and ask if you've built in any time for relaxation and restoration. Don't think you can stay on that treadmill without breaks. When we are exhausted our immune systems crack under the strain, and we are suddenly susceptible to colds, flus, skin rashes and 'the thousand natural ills that flesh is heir to'. When our bodies are rested we can resist such threats.

> *UltraAge Antidote*
> Sensible scheduling of rest, relaxation and refreshment breaks.

YOUTH OBSESSION

Curiously, obsession with staying young can be very ageing. Yes, it's great to keep a youthful mindset and to stay interested in what younger

people are interested in (see 'Kids'). In Chapter Eight we advise you to stay tuned to the wavelength of younger colleagues at work. In 'Kids' we say it's important to be interested in your children's world and be willing to let them teach you. In the rest of the book we show you ways to slow down the ageing process through outlook, exercise, diet and other means. But there's a difference between that and being fruitlessly obsessed with staying young. 'The oldest swinger in town' is a figure of fun, so is 'mutton dressed as lamb'. Any obsession is unhealthy. Looking backwards is extremely ageing, as is envy. Focus on more enduring aspects of your own life instead!

> **UltraAge Antidote**
> Enjoy your own life. Don't envy others.

YO-YO DIETING

This is one of the most ageing types of dieting there is, worse than the egg or grapefruit diet, very low calorie diets, or any other eating plan. If you don't know what yo-yo dieting is then hopefully your weight hasn't gone up and down like a yo-yo as so many women's does. This puts incredible strain on the system, the metabolism having to adjust not to steady weight loss or gain but to wild ups and downs as you binge and starve. It puts a strain on the heart which cannot be seen, but also on the skin, which can. Yo-yo dieters usually have terrible skin tone, having lost elasticity from all the times their skins have been stretched then expected to bounce back into shape. Leading cosmetic surgeon Gerald Imber in New York tells prospective patients right away if they've been yo-yo dieters: 'I can see it in your face,' he says. 'Losing and gaining weight is one of the most ageing things you can do.' Far better for your appearance and your health is to stay slightly plump if dieting is only going to begin a yo-yo effect. Research has shown that yo-yo dieting can actually take years off your life as well as putting years on your looks.

> **UltraAge Antidote**
> Sensible eating (see Chapter Nine).

ZZZ

Either being unable to sleep or wanting to sleep all the time is not at all good for you. Inability to sleep and fatigue problems are estimated to be experienced by about half of all people between the ages of forty and ninety. We should need less sleep as we get older – from ten hours as growing children to eight hours as young adults to six hours or less in our dotage – but no two people's needs or patterns are precisely the same. Some, like Margaret Thatcher, can thrive on five hours' sleep a night. Others, like Bill Clinton, like to spend more time in bed, though not necessarily asleep.

It is not uncommon to wake up earlier and earlier as you get older, partly because your ageing bladder is giving you urgent signals or perhaps because your arthritic hip is twinging. We feel that waking up early is great as it gives you a headstart on the day, extra hours to write or read that wonderful book, catch up on the news or get a degree from the Open University. But if you disagree, try going to bed later to counteract this effect.

> **UltraAge Antidote**
> Restful sleep that restores
> the body and soul.

Find Out What's Keeping You Awake

Ask yourself what stresses you have in your life that may be keeping you awake. Deal with them and sleep will probably follow. Try relaxing drinks such as camomile tea before bedtime. Avoid late-night coffee, curries, chocolate and cheese. Health food shops abound in natural herbal supplements that should be a safer substitute to sleeping pills.

4

Menopause is More than Hormones

'Nothing in life is to be feared.
It is only to be understood.'

MARIE CURIE 1867–1934

Menopause in the New Millennium

As Baby Boomers hit their forties and fifties, there are millions of demanding women wanting to know the ins and outs of what lies ahead for them. Where a 'new market' with specific, targetable needs was forming, soon an industry would follow. Drug companies; homoeopathic and vitamin suppliers; specialist hair, beauty and health products; fitness and diet advisers and programmes; even clothing lines targeted the ageing, fashion-conscious female who now wanted both style and comfort at any price.

Urging us to embrace the inevitable are leading feminists like Betty Friedan, Gloria Steinem, Germaine Greer, Erica Jong who all shared how it was for them and urged their sisters to celebrate the onset of becoming a 'crone', 'shaman' or even 'witch'. Gail Sheehy, Leslie Kenton and Germaine Greer guided us through the research and literature only to leave us more confused as we became informed. To HRT or to not HRT was only one of the questions. Others included whether we should or shouldn't colour our hair, bother wearing make-up, ignore fashion, sex or our former selves. No, the new-age crones advocated that we become different, empowered, challenging in our new-found wisdom because we would surface from the post-childbearing age richer and fuller; however, definitely not youthful or beautiful.

To balance the harridans are the actresses and beauty queens who go to great lengths to espouse personal fitness, diet and beauty routines to assure their contemporaries that they could be as desirable after the change of life as they were before it. Toyboys are paraded as proof (Joan Collins, Kate O'Mara, Francesca Annis, Linda Gray, Cher) that as long as you popped your hormones your hair would be glossy, your skin dewy, your figure a taut hourglass and your sex life orgasmic. We have steamy fiction with menopausal heroines to enhance our fantasies about what lies ahead. Television sitcoms like *Cybill* and *Veronica's Closet* joke about hot flushes and mood swings following that ground-breaking international hit about being post-menopausal, *The Golden Girls*. Hollywood films such as *The First Wives Club* made us cheer with the girls about impending battles with men once youth and beauty were on the wane. As long as we have Goldie Hawn, Jane Fonda, Lauren Hutton and Tina Turner to assure us that the menopause needn't mean whiskers, elasticated waistlines or short-changed careers, we can live in hope.

A Personal Journey

My own approach towards the menopause sharpened my senses and interest to learn more about this inevitable stage when a woman's menstrual cycle ends and her reproductive capabilities are well and truly over. But as with all who have found the need to report on their own menopausal experience, the quest to learn comes not so much from the simple cessation of a biological function, complicated and integral to a woman's femininity as it is. The menopause means real physical, emotional, psychological and spiritual changes – brand new experiences for every woman. And coming from a generation that has an inexhaustible need to know all as well as to 'do it differently' than previous generations, I wanted to delve into the thick of it, to learn everything there was and more, not soldier on or 'take it on the chin'.

The menopause means real physical, emotional, psychological and spiritual changes – brand new experiences for every woman.

I was prepared to take any and all pre-emptive strikes, including hormonal replacements, to keep any conceivable physical or emotional change at bay. Having run a female-dominated, international business for fifteen years meant that I had much experience of dealing with women 'going through it'. I would seethe with frustration when any consultant, enduring obvious emotional stress, would give the game away by bursting into tears or visibly burn up with a hot flush. Staff would gingerly advise a softer approach or tackle a partner instead when thorny issues needed confronting and the menopausal consultant or colleague was unlikely to cope with the standard, business-like approach. I swore I would never let it happen to me. I didn't want others tiptoeing around my 'change', unable to approach with the forthright candour I so valued.

Many women, like some of our mothers and grandmothers along with their forebears through the ages, have been conditioned to 'just muddle through' it. 'The less you think about it the quicker it goes,' explained my grandmother when I asked her why my own mother's moods became so erratic in her later forties. I would have none of it. For the last decade or so I was made to believe that I would inevitably catch the 'menopausal disease' and was convinced that there had to be a solution. What I was to find is that the solution isn't straightforward nor is it just a matter of getting your hormones back in kilter.

Just a Game of Roulette?

Even clinics designed exclusively for treating the menopause can be inconsistent in the way they dole out HRT drugs. When I first approached a London clinic specializing in the treatment (both HRT and alternative) of the menopause I was given a full series of tests to determine if I was, indeed, perimenopausal or not. At forty-three, right-fully, they questioned whether my symptoms were other than hormon-ally driven. I was training hard for a marathon at the time, clocking fifty-plus miles a week. Indeed, my levels were fine and I was sent away. Three years on, with night sweats now added to my symptoms, which were not debilitating or too upsetting up until the sweating began, I was given no tests to check my levels, just a prescription. And I was off.

At every six-monthly check-up, I would report my success or new 'symptoms' while on HRT, for example, bloating, weight gain, mood swings, headaches. Rather than being tested to determine what my hormonal levels were, I would be given a new formulation and told to see how that worked! After trying four different HRT prescriptions over eighteen months, each bringing new side effects not intrinsic to my nature or to previous monthly cycles, I asked for a test to see what was going on. Was I getting too much of one hormone and not enough of the other? Did I need oestrogen at all? Could I manage with natural progesterone cream and try to treat the other menopausal symptoms homoeopathically or nutritionally? When I spoke to one proponent of minimal oestrogen and natural progesterone, she was dismayed that at forty-seven and still having regular periods, I was on an HRT formu-lation strong enough for women who had had complete hysterectomies!

We would have hoped that a menopausal clinic would have been more proactive, directional and methodical with its patients. But like any woman who trots along to her GP, who is much less on top of the latest research and not inclined to offer non-medical, alternative ther-apies to treat the patient holistically, I felt my hormonal chemistry was just a game of roulette. Pop some new pills and see if you get lucky!

Up until the '80s, a woman entered her menopausal years bereft of any useful advice aside from her own experiences of other women who had been through it and the variable wisdom of her GP or gynaecol-ogist. There was a dearth of public information and popular self-help guides about the menopause, what it is and how to manage it, enjoy

and survive it. In the late '80s and '90s came the flood – books, articles, web-sites, helplines all to advise this burgeoning cohort of the population: women between the ages of forty and sixty.

The redefinition of the menopause began in the '60s when an American doctor, Robert A. Wilson, published *Forever Young*, asserting that the menopause was a destructive, debilitating experience. He reported that hitherto lucid, attractive, balanced women became dull, argumentative parodies, withered witch archetypes. 'The transformation is one of the saddest of human spectacles,' concluded Wilson. He sold 100,000 copies of his book in a few months. Hot flushes were hot? Menopause was seen as an epidemic and remedies had to be found to eliminate the disease from spreading!

Menopause was seen as an epidemic and remedies had to be found to eliminate the disease from spreading!

London's Dr Stuart Campbell wrote that women should be alarmed at the abandon with which oestrogen was being doled out in America. In 1976 he warned that what was required was 'deep understanding of the psychological, hormonal and other pathophysical changes in the perimenopause' which the international medical community were a long way from despite the pervasiveness and willingness to prescribe oestrogen replacement therapy.

So What Is It?

The menopause means 'the end of menstruation', hence a 'change' in the monthly course of living as women grow to know it. The average age for this to occur is fifty-one. It can happen as early as the late thirties but starting in the late forties to early fifties is the norm. Studies conflict over the correlation between the early onset of periods and an early menopause.

The menopause is a transition from the productive childbearing years and is referred to as the climacteric. These transitional years are divided into the perimenopausal, menopausal and postmenopausal. How long each lasts, how a woman feels and what she experiences is a totally individual experience that has something to do with her hormones and genes (e.g. how was it for Mum) but also lots to do with her own lifestyle – nutrition, amount of exercise, general happiness and self-

esteem along with other factors. The process is not uniform or predictable and involves more than fluctuations in the ovaries. The whole body is involved during menopause, with signals being disrupted between the hypothalamus part of the brain, the pituitary gland and the ovaries.

It Starts At Thirty!

Women are classified as being 'perimenopausal' five years before their last, natural period. This is the time when most symptoms start and when they seem to be most acute. But long before the mid-forties the hormones begin fluctuating at thirty, dropping in the late thirties when women experience changes in their cycles, perhaps with worse pre-menstrual tension (PMT). PMT has been studied and debated for the last decade with the medical establishment still unable to agree. Doctors do concur that it is a 'psychoneuroendocrine' condition that involves both the body and its biological functions as well as the mind, hence the psychological side to the debate.

When they know it's time for the horror to begin, women keen to avoid drug therapy to control PMT are advised as follows:

Exercise regularly. Working out will influence depression and mood swings as well as help with fluid retention. The more you sweat the better balanced your bodily fluids, plus the rush of endorphins, those slap-happy hormones, will help you ignore any symptoms that might get you down. If you work out three to four times a week starting this month you will definitely feel better before your next period.

Treat yourself to carbos. If PMT really haunts you, forget other diet prescriptions and eat plenty of complex (the good-guy) carbos: vegetables, fruit, pasta, grains. Avoid 'dead' or simple-carbohydrates found in junk food. They will jolt you up fast enough but the crash will cause an unpleasant mood swing.

Working out will influence depression and mood swings as well as help with fluid retention.

Lastly, watch the salt. If fluid retention is part of your greatest problem, cut it out of your diet. There is plenty of salt hidden in foods, particularly in ready meals or restaurant cooking, so don't add any. Also, drink plenty of water and you will actually retain less fluid because you will be forcing it through your system more efficiently.

The Perimenopause

Sounds cute, doesn't it, the peri-meni, but don't be fooled. This five to ten years pre-shutdown is when you can feel most loopy. But you think, 'Hey! I'm not menopausal. I am still a vibrant, young woman. Don't talk hormones with me. I'll see you in ten years.' Okay. So you won't initially have hot sweats or a dry vagina. But you might have crying fits, mood swings and a real drop in energy and be blaming it on a bunch of other things, which might, admittedly, be valid, rather than your hormones doing the high jumps.

Perimenopausal symptoms listed below occur when the ovaries are in their greatest hormonal flux before they cease functioning, producing varying and variable amounts of oestrogen and progesterone. The medical establishment still does not understand conclusively the best way to respond to the upset to our reproductive systems during the menopause nor how to treat the woman holistically when her body starts suffering such upheaval internally and externally.

Signs of being perimenopausal include:

⬦ Irritability, memory lapses, lack of concentration.

⬦ Painful sex due to the drying up of the vaginal fluids, resulting from falling oestrogen levels.

⬦ Headaches and insomnia, the latter possibly leading to depression if it becomes chronic.

⬦ General fatigue though studies conflict as to whether this is due to the actual physical process of the menopause or other lifestyle causes.

⬦ Hot flushes. Often brought on by stress or emotional upset, these are exaggerated by the visible red flushing in the neck and face and profusion of sweating. Between 50 and 70 per cent of menopausal women experience hot flushes regularly.

⬦ Night sweats. Similar to but different from hot flushes, in that women are awoken by sodden nightclothes and bedding, caused by an uncontrollable surge of sweating. 70 per cent of women experience these at some point during the perimenopausal years.

It's no wonder that one of the fastest growing users of anti-depressants, like the ubiquitous Prozac, are women in their late thirties and forties.

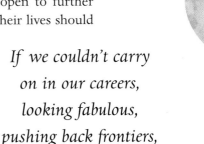

Something Must Be Done!

When alarmed by this pervasive 'disease' now rampant among modern Western society, it was agreed that if it could be prevented then it must. Doctors concurred that many of their female patients could benefit from alternatives to tranquillizers, heretofore the only prescriptive palliative used to 'treat' menopausal women. Women, themselves now politically, sexually and more economically liberated and open to further education via the popular media about how fulfilling their lives should be, were convinced that the menopause had to be avoided at all costs. If we couldn't carry on in our careers, looking fabulous, pushing back frontiers, we would be doomed.

> *If we couldn't carry on in our careers, looking fabulous, pushing back frontiers, we would be doomed.*

HRT's original proponent, Robert Wilson, reported that the mental and physical anguish that women were suffering could be quite unbearable and possibly lead to suicide! 'I have seen untreated women who had shrivelled into caricatures of their former selves . . . Though the physical symptoms can be truly dreadful, what impresses me most tragically is the destruction of personality. Some women . . . subside into a stupor of indifference.'

Harnessing the Hormones

During the *climacteric* a woman's ovaries decrease the natural production of oestrogen and progesterone. Her cycles become irregular because ovulation is erratic or not even taking place. When there is no ovulation occurring, a woman's progesterone levels are depleted. It is now thought that this hormonal imbalance has more to do with the upset in a woman's physical and emotional state than the fluctuations in her oestrogen levels. Yet originally the focus was on oestrogen replacement exclusively.

Hormonal replacement therapy first became available in the '60s and was hailed as not only the panacea to menopausal symptoms but also as the elixir of youth. Most major pharmaceutical firms jumped on the bandwagon, eager to continue selling to a generation of women now used to paying daily for birth control. If they were clever, the drug companies could take hundreds of dollars annually from most women

from their teens into their sixties. Even back-of-the-envelope arithmetic convinced many leading firms that the investment in HRT research, development and marketing would make them richer than they had dreamed possible.

The wonders of HRT were heralded in the eighties and nineties as the only sane choice for modern women facing the menopause. Opt out and you would transform into a sad, wrinkled crone. Life, as you had grown to know it, sister, would be over. Menopausal women bought the HRT elixir in droves, 75 per cent of American, 50 per cent of Australian and 30 per cent of British believing it to be the correct choice.

HRT: THE EVIDENCE

✧ 'Confirmed: HRT really does stop wrinkles.' Dr Laura Dunn at the University of California tested almost 4000 post-menopausal women aged forty to seventy-four. Those that were using HRT had fewer wrinkles and less dry skin!

✧ 'HRT keeps your voice feminine.' Doctors testing the effects of oestrogen (via HRT) on women's voices found that those not on HRT had voices that were weaker and more hoarse than those that took HRT. Those on HRT could avoid 'elderly voices'.

✧ 'Get an hourglass figure with HRT.' Italian gynaecologist and sexologist, Dr Alessandra Graziotti, says that HRT helps to improve a woman's appearance, figure (trimming the waist!) and sex life as oestrogen keeps the vagina moist.

✧ 'Oestrogen improves your brain power.' Dr Frederick Naftolin at Yale University insists 'There is not a cell in the brain that is not directly oestrogen-sensitive.' Author Gail Sheehy adds, 'Oestrogen may act as an antioxidant and anti-inflammatory agent that can inhibit age-related deterioration of brain cells, elevates mood, and may protect against depressive illnesses.' Hallelujah!

✧ 'HRT prevents heart disease' because oestrogen makes blood vessels more flexible and lowers the levels of fats in the blood stream, although HRT combined with progestogen (synthetic progesterone) may mitigate these benefits.

WEIGH IT UP FOR YOURSELF

◇ 'Proven protection against osteoporosis.' *Although recent studies show that natural progesterone alone may protect against bone depletion and even help to increase bone mass.*

◇ 'Protects against heart disease by up to 50 per cent, falling off once a woman stops taking HRT.' (Note the PEPI postmenopausal oestrogen and progestin [the American term for progestogen] interventions study of 1994 looking at 900 women over three years raised it from 30 to 50 per cent.) *Although preventive measures against heart disease are possible without HRT via diet and nutritional adaptations, exercise and other drugs proven to be safe.*

◇ 'Possibly protects against cancer of the colon', according to an American study of nurses. *Equal protection and strengthening are possible via diet and nutritional supplement as well as exercises.*

◇ 'Possibly prevents Alzheimer's disease, with risks halved after long-term use.' *Further longitudinal studies are needed to verify this conclusively with more research about environmental, dietary and genetic influences needed to balance against the benefits of HRT.*

◇ 'Prevents strokes.' *Diligent diagnostic and preventative measures can have equal if not greater impact than HRT.*

◇ 'Improves the skin tone and hair texture.' *Many of these findings compare affluent women with healthier diets and lifestyles, who are more likely to be on HRT than their sisters who aren't as well off and are less likely to be able to afford quality grooming products and routines or HRT.*

◇ 'Improves muscle tone and strength.' *So too do weight-bearing exercises.*

◇ 'Improves moods and creates greater emotional balance.' *Arguable when some placebo studies also registered mood enhancement. Again, diet, exercise and lifestyle play a role as well.*

◇ 'Without it, you'll be dysfunctional for years.' The Amarant Trust warns, 'If a woman takes nothing at all she may have menopausal symptoms up to her sixties or seventies, not for just a few years.' *However, many women's lives are not disrupted by the menopause thanks to good nutrition, exercise and homoeopathic herbal elixirs.*

Worries Surface

The alarm bells about unwarranted and unmonitored oestrogen supplements began to surface when links between breast cancer and HRT usage became apparent. There are potential risks after being on HRT

for five or more years. There is an increased risk of ovarian cancer after being on HRT for ten years and if a woman has had fibroids or endometriosis, HRT could exacerbate either condition. It is said to increase the risk of breast cancer (indeed Tamoxifen, the anti-breast cancer drug, works by blocking oestrogen) but conflicting reports keep coming in. Mr Jordan points out in the *Lancet* in October 1997 that fifty-one studies on breast cancer showed that while there is an increase in the risk of breast cancer related to the duration of HRT use, this disappears within about five years of stopping the treatment. Also he notes that 'The type of breast cancer which women on HRT have seems to be less virulent, less likely to spread to the lymph nodes and to have a higher likelihood of cure.'

If you never take HRT your risk in contracting breast cancer is 45 in 1,000. This rises to 47 in 1,000 for those on HRT for five years, to 51 per 1,000 for those on HRT for ten years and to 57 per 1,000 after fifteen years' use.

If you are considering HRT, it is critical to assess your own medical history in the light of the likely benefits over the possible risks to your health. Any oestrogen supplement is risky if you have a personal or family history of breast cancer, uterine cancer or fibroids. It seems universally agreed now that oestrogen therapies without synthetic progestogen (UK)/progestin (US) or natural micronized progesterone do increase the risk of uterine cancer. Any woman on oestrogen exclusively must have an annual endometrial biopsy, a procedure carried out by your doctor. (Note, this is painful so you might want to take pain relief beforehand.)

If you suffer from liver or gall bladder disease, you should not consider HRT, as these organs need to be in prime condition to process the hormones. Overweight women are advised against HRT as they already retain excess oestrogen in their body fat and might increase their risk of certain cancers such as breast cancer in taking more.

Which Hormones Do We Really Need?

Until recently, the primary hormone that got all the attention when it came to the menopause debate was oestrogen, which women produce naturally in their adrenal glands, their ovaries, as well as in fat. According to nutritionist Patrick Holford, 'There isn't a problem in women producing enough oestrogen in their non-fertile (menopausal) phase, provided they don't have exhausted adrenal glands or aren't exceedingly skinny. The other factor which interferes with the ability to use oestrogen is blood sugar. With bad blood sugar control you produce more cortisol, an adrenal hormone, and that interferes with the ability to use oestrogen and progesterone.' Being stressed out and skinny means being terribly imbalanced, hormonally speaking, according to Holford.

If you are considering HRT, it is critical to assess your own medical history in the light of the likely benefits over the possible risks to your health.

The question to ask about oestrogen is, should we supplement it, and if so by how much and in what combination with progesterone to sail through the menopause unperturbed? But who can advise us without a vested interest? *The Menopausal Industry* by Australian Sandra Coney exposed the corporate interests involved in HRT while doctors and several journalists who refuse to accept the simplistic mass market approach to menopausal treatments provide compelling pressure to search further for improved understanding of the problems and possible, better solutions.

Lack of Sound Research

Despite the blaze of studies that appear regularly both for and against HRT there are problems with much of the research. Many 'conclusive' reports are anecdotal; some are biased, comparing women on HRT who are more affluent and health-conscious to begin with against non-users who aren't; and some research is of questionable validity due to being underwritten or provided by the drug companies who thrive from the growing usage of these drugs. But perhaps the most disconcerting are the double-blind trials of HRT, where neither patients nor doctors knew who was on the drug and who was not. Menopausal women on the placebos reported great improvement in their symptoms!

The British Medical Research Council is set to remedy such erratic research by commissioning the largest study of its kind over the next twenty years. It will monitor 18,000 menopausal women on HRT and placebos and measure the impact of both in terms of all the factors from breast cancer, heart disease and osteoporosis to the impact on

their emotional states and general appearance. Initial findings will offer compelling indications by 2007. A similar longitudinal study is also underway at the US National Institute of Health.

Is Natural 'Unnatural'?

It can be the synthetic progestogens/progestins in HRT that are not easily broken down by the body when taken orally that wreak possible havoc. The metabolic changes caused by progestogens in the liver can result in an increased incidence of high blood pressure, fluid retention and blood clots. 'Natural' progesterones used in some formulations (provided by mare's urine) can be problematic for obese women, smokers, women with high blood pressure or varicose veins.

... check the list of possible side effects provided with your HRT prescription to get a sense of the game of roulette you are playing with your health

There is a great debate over what are called 'natural' and what 'synthetic' hormones. Some doctors, like Michael Perring in England and Vincent Giampapa in the States, say that animal-derived hormones, for example from pigs' ovaries or, like Premarin, from mare's urine, are natural only to those animals, not to humans, despite many doctors' attempts to assuage our worries by calling these hormones natural. 'True natural hormones' are those that are man-made but identical (although synthetic) to what our bodies produce themselves. The most 'natural' replacement for our own oestrogen stores, the doctors feel, would be a synthesized combination of oestrone, oestradiol and oestriol in the quantities naturally produced by our pre-menopausal bodies. For progesterone the preferred approach for replacement would probably be micronized or synthesized progestogens or a natural progesterone cream. Whereas in the older preparations the progesterone component was taken in the second half of the cycle, causing a monthly bleed (which some women find reassuring) the newer combinations do away with the monthly period.

Any woman concerned about potential problems with HRT needs only check the list of possible side effects provided with her HRT prescription to get a sense of the game of roulette she is playing with her health, both in the short and long term.

HRT side effects can include:

- ✧ Migraine-like headaches.
- ✧ Sudden loss or change in vision.
- ✧ Shortness of breath.
- ✧ Sharp pains in the chest or calves.
- ✧ Yellowing of the skin or whites of the eyes.
- ✧ Pre-menstrual tension.
- ✧ Excessive vaginal bleeding.
- ✧ Breast tenderness, pain, enlargement and secretion.
- ✧ Nausea, abdominal discomfort, bloating.
- ✧ Rash, itchiness, change in hair growth.
- ✧ Nervousness.
- ✧ Change in weight.
- ✧ Aggravation of the metabolic disorder known as porphyria.
- ✧ Leg cramps.
- ✧ Changes in interest in sex.

The Progesterone Debate

Dr John Lee, a Californian proponent of natural hormonal products, as well as some other pioneers and the nutritionist Patrick Holford, recognized that the key problem could be progesterone. This is only produced by the ovaries when a woman is still fertile, and a tiny bit is produced by the adrenal glands. Our own progesterone can turn into oestrogen when our body needs it but not the other way. For years Lee worked with natural progesterone creams on those of his own patients who were unable to use HRT or oestrogen replacement, being deemed to be high risk, with histories of breast cancer or high blood pressure. He subsequently discovered the remarkable properties of progesterone on strengthening bones and minimizing the distressing symptoms of the menopausal experience (as he laid out in his book *Natural Progesterone: The Multiple Roles of a Remarkable Hormone*). Unfortunately, no one by the time of writing has yet undertaken a major scientific investigation into its effects, although Professor John Studd and colleagues are working on one in Britain. But Lee exposes why it is not in the interest of the pharmaceutical giants to focus on progesterone: because progesterone can't be patented as it was first synthesized in the thirties and is now in the public domain. A natural source for progesterone is wild yams, something easily and cheaply grown outdoors, not in expensive laboratories. Yams have been used by herbalists through the centuries as a treatment for both menstrual and menopausal problems. Rather than use a natural source for progesterone, the pharmaceutical companies

developed their own synthetic versions, progestogens, which could be patented. Lee claims that the synthetic stuff doesn't do the job the real stuff does.

Lee's small studies of his patients indicate that the progesterone produced from yams (just eating them is not enough!) is more like the hormone our bodies produce naturally and does all the positive effects that the synthetic formulations manufactured in HRT are supposed to have, like prevent osteoporosis. But, according to Lee, progesterone cream does even more: it improves bone density without any risk of breast, liver or endometrial cancer – although this is still open to debate and trial. Other doctors warn that the 'natural' tag on progesterone does not imply an innocuous formulation and that the synthetics might be more natural, both easier to absorb and more effective.

For years it has been accepted that menopausal women inevitably lack oestrogen, but John Lee says that this isn't the case. Some women lose more than others, but it does not drop to zero as progesterone does. Only when women are producing eggs do they produce progesterone. When we stop ovulation we are without this vital, protective, balancing hormone.

But the jury is still out on natural progesterone. The hype around this 'natural' panacea may turn out to be as fallacious as the original claims of oestrogen-exclusive therapy. According to the National Osteoporosis Society in Britain, these creams are 'unlicensed' products and there are to date no conclusive randomized, controlled trials to show the benefits that Dr Lee claims, although they are, we are pleased to note, underway.

Work in Progress

The British 'father of HRT', Professor John Studd, who had previously told patients that it was likely to be as effective as 'snake oil', is, at the time of writing, running such a trial at the Chelsea and Westminster Hospital in London. The National Osteoporosis Society called for some of the companies making money out of natural progesterone creams to help finance research as it could not afford to. But we feel that is the problem: that so much of the research in this area is financed by those who stand to gain from it. We would like to see more money made available by governments for independent, unbiased studies. The

plea was made during a debate on the value of natural progesterone at the Royal College of Physicians in Britain in 1998, where Dr John Lee argued its advantages; he was opposed by Professor David Purdie of the Centre for Metabolic Bone Disease at Hull Royal Infirmary and the British Menopause Society, who called for urgent scientific investigation of Dr Lee's claims. Dr Lee's data was confused, he argued, by the fact that some of his patients were also on supplementary oestrogen, others on vitamins and/or taking exercise, so the increase in bone-mass recorded after taking natural progesterone might have been due to a combination of factors. Dr Lee conceded this, but then he had stressed that osteoporosis is, indeed, a multi-factorial' condition.

It is strongly in its favour that so far no one seems to have found any negative side effects of natural progesterone. As Prof. Purdie observed, 'It's so weak it's unlikely to be capable of side effects,' which is why it is sold over the counter as a cosmetic rather than a medicine in the States. Yet several women spoke up about how they had benefited from natural progesterone creams, with one remarkably youthful-looking fifty-year-old asserting that natural progesterone prevented her from having a threatened hysterectomy because it controlled the incessant bleeding she had been having. However, there is still considerable confusion over progestogens and progesterones, with some negative effects of the former being used to frighten women off the latter.

So far no one seems to have found any negative side effects of natural progesterone.

At the moment, Dr Perring recommends a combination of Hormonin, which mimics the make-up of the natural oestrogens in our body. It consists of 0.27 mg of oestriol, 1.3 mg oestrone and 0.6 mg of oestradial, the most powerful natural oestrogen in our body. Crinone, a new natural progesterone gel, can be used, ideally rubbed into the vagina, for the last twelve days of your cycle. Perring explains, 'You use four per cent Crinone and it should avoid the side effects of bloating and weight gain which can come from taking progesterone tablets and it mimics exactly what your natural cycle should be.' But this may not prevent cancer of the uterus.

Most experts seem to agree that oestrogen in HRT does have a positive impact on heart disease in post-menopausal women. And while death from heart disease among Western women is four times that of breast and endrometrial cancers, oestrogen will have many champions.

But until studies compare women on HRT with those who aren't, and accurately analyse the effects of alternatives such as exercise, dietary and nutritional regimes, we are panicked into choosing the drug, just in case.

Know the Score

The key is for women to know what their hormonal levels are in order to have them treated accordingly, and this is not easy, considering the deficiency of baseline data. Indeed, if a woman were very low in oestrogen it would be recommended to take a supplement. Any woman who has had her womb removed produces no oestrogen and needs replacement along with progesterone. But for any woman whose level is just lower than it was previously, but who is still producing all the oestrogen she needs to combat perhaps the most worrying result of the menopause, osteoporosis, the best solution might be to use a natural progesterone cream.

The side effects of synthetic progestogens make some women nauseous, with other nasty side effects including menopausal acne, bloating, backache and depression.

Progesterone can be taken orally in pill form but this isn't the ideal option, as explained above, because of difficulties in breaking it down. Mr Jordan says, 'Most problems we see with HRT stem from the oral progestogen supplements.' If you don't feel well on them you might have a problem with absorption and would do better on a cream. Some women who have menopausal problems with periods that seem to have gone haywire, sometimes coming twice a month, sometimes continuously bleeding, may simply require a progesterone implant directly into the lining of the womb, rather like an intra-uterine device. This puts the progesterone just where it's needed, without problems with absorption or side effects elsewhere, Mr Jordan explains. The side effects of synthetic progestogens make some women nauseous, with other nasty side effects including menopausal acne, bloating, backache and depression. However, a natural progesterone cream can be rubbed into the skin and is claimed to be easily absorbed into the blood. In America, progesterone creams like Progest are available over the counter but in Europe they require a prescription.

Maggie Tuttle, director of the Menopause Helpline (for advice or for numbers of other menopause helplines worldwide), actually goes so far as to claim that 'Women are being killed by hormone replacement therapy.' Yet nearly a third of post-menopausal British women are on HRT and, unlike Tuttle, the author Shirley Conran, the actress Patricia Hodge and others who have tried it and given it up, they must find it beneficial.

At the time of writing, the Menopause Helpline charity, founded in 1996, was planning a chain of menopause clinics to offer bone density and hormone level tests and advice on alternatives to conventional HRT such as food supplements and plant oestrogens. Tuttle, fifty-four, who says she suffered all sorts of complications after having been on HRT for fifteen years since her thirties, is a keen advocate of coral calcium granules which she gets from Sweden. She insists these actually reversed the osteoporosis she had been suffering, incredible as that claim seems.

Hope on the Horizon?

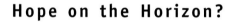

There is one exciting new hope on the horizon for menopausal women, that those in the know are referring to as HRT Replacement Therapy [sic]. After twenty years of research and tests, it became available early in 1998 in the States and late in 1998 in Britain and could revolutionize menopause management.

SERMS, as it is known, stands for 'Selective Estrogen Receptor Modulators', explains Professor David Purdie, chairman of the British Menopause Society, who has helped to test these new 'selective' hormone substitutes at the Hull Royal Infirmary where he practises and runs the metabolic bone disease unit, specializing in treating osteoporosis.

A cousin of the anti-breast cancer drug Tamoxifen, which acts by blocking oestrogen receptors in the breast, Raloxifine, the first of the SERMS to be licensed, has been developed to have a positive effect on the bones and possibly on the heart, with none of the bad effects on the breasts or uterus associated with traditional oestrogen replacement therapies. (Even Tamoxifen carries with it a heightened risk of uterine cancer.) Raloxifine 'locks on' to the same receptors as natural oestrodial does. 'Tamoxifen, an anti-oestrogen, was found to protect the

skeleton which was astonishing,' says Prof. Purdie. 'How could an anti-oestrogen do what an oestrogen was supposed to do? Then it began to dawn on the scientific community that it could be an anti-oestrogen at certain places like the breast but not at others like the bone.'

Although SERMS will not treat the immediate symptoms of the menopause such as hot flushes and distraction, they will work on the long-term consequences, which is what most women worry about. So Prof. Purdie, who challenges Dr Lee's assertion that natural progesterone offers protection to the bones, would recommend going on a short course of conventional HRT if you have problems. This would not be long enough to seriously increase the risk of breast and uterine cancer but would get you through the worst of the symptoms and then you could move on to SERMS post menopausally. 'If you've had an early menopause or a hysterectomy, have a bone scan done to see what your risk is. You may not need it, of course,' he advises. Despite three years of SERMS in human trials, at Hull, and in London, Edinburgh and Sheffield as well as in the States, Prof. Purdie warns that 'It's early days yet – caution, caution. But we have hungered for this for a long time!'

Maybe SERMS are the way forward.

Although there is some evidence that SERMS will be protective against heart attacks and strokes, it is not yet known whether they will offer the supposed reduction of the risk of Alzheimer's disease that conventional HRT is said to. 'We're now honing it down,' says Prof. Purdie. 'If we look forward twenty years we will have an even more selective oestrogen, and there might be a whole range of SERMS, each one dedicated to a particular area where oestrogen is needed.' In the meantime he is recommending line dancing to patients who want a side-effect-free method of strengthening bones.

So, You Want Medical Advice, Do You?

Sadly, the pursuit of information about what is happening to our bodies as they start to change during the perimenopause is so variable and incomplete as to be worthy of the charge of medical negligence. In the United Kingdom, if a woman goes to her GP and she is about the right age and shares the symptoms that conveniently fall within the scope of the menopausal meanies, out comes the pen and prescription pad and off she trots to her pharmacy for her first jolt of artificial hormones. Generally, the GP is professional enough to add, 'If you don't like these come back and we will try some others.'

The varying strengths and hormonal mixes of HRT prescriptions now number into the hundreds and it is unlikely that your GP, gynaecologist or even specialist menopausal clinician will be able to pin-point even your three best options. To complicate things, some HRT prescriptions are for three weeks with the last week in the month off, while others continue unbroken for the full cycle. Some involve oestrogen for two weeks then progestogen for the remaining two or oestrogen for three, progestogen for one or an oestrogen and progestogen combination for two with oestrogen only for two weeks. The permutations go on and on. With oestrogen pills and a progesterone cream or gel, women need to be diligent in noting when to start and stop the latter in their cycles as they don't come in the handy monthly packs like other HRT formulations. If you aren't certain about pills you can consider a patch or implant, which again come in complex varieties.

The pursuit of information is so variable and incomplete as to be worthy of the charge of medical negligence.

The Story Varies from Woman to Woman

While American writer Gail Sheehy, British MP Teresa Gorman and actresses such as Jill Gascoigne, Jane Asher and Kate O'Mara sing the praises, no, virtually campaign for HRT, the anti-HRT lobby is equally well represented with Germaine Greer and Leslie Kenton as literary and beauty gurus respectively along with such impressive UltraAgers as Shirley Conran, Patricia Hodge, Nanette Newman and Katie Boyle, living proof that HRT is not always necessary.

Superwoman Shirley Conran ('Life is too short to stuff a mushroom') told us how she gained over 30 lbs on HRT and had a terrible reaction to the Premarin, feeling much better coming off it. British and European television presenter Katie Boyle (who looks fifty in her seventies!) says she too had a terrible reaction to HRT so she determined to sail through the menopause with only a positive frame of mind and a

beautiful Spanish fan to see her through the hot flushes. 'The fan was my only help,' she says. 'I acquired a whole collection of them!'

The actress Nanette Newman, best known for starring in her husband Bryan Forbes' famous film *The Stepford Wives*, though far from one herself, says, 'I went on HRT for a couple of years and it made me feel terribly ill. It just didn't suit me. It gave me terrible aches and pains, I don't know why, so I gave it up and never really had any problem with the menopause. I think the main thing is to keep active!' With two young children to keep her active, both born when she was in her forties, Patricia Hodge agrees. She switched from HRT to natural progesterone cream and found she felt much more energetic on it.

I feel that each woman needs to take control of her menopause and be proactive in finding the best solution for her.

After weighing all the pros and cons, suffering the symptoms, and consulting the experts, I feel that each woman needs to take control of her menopause and be proactive in finding the best solution for her. Ask for tests at appropriate times in your cycle to determine your hormonal levels. If you are fluctuating, what might be the most gentle and natural option for dealing with your symptoms? If your doctor's approach to the menopause doesn't jive with yours, find one that does. You might be at a point in your life where you simply have to function and can't struggle with diet and natural alternatives that might take time to work. And if your doctor's approach is at all offensive, it won't work. Guidance during these years must be empathetic and, for many, holistic. If your doctor doesn't probe to determine what other aspects of your life might be exacerbating the symptoms and seems rather blasé in whipping off yet another HRT concoction, shop around for someone else. Find other therapists to complement your gynaecologist's advice to see if you can alleviate stress, mood swings and depression in other ways before possibly turning to hormones that might be more disruptive to your system. In the end I came off HRT and feel terrific on the natural progesterone cream aided by a fistful of daily antioxidants and minerals.

You might consider the nutritional supplements opposite and the 'herbal helpers' on the following page to help manage specific problems associated with the menopause, whether or not you are on HRT.

Nutritional Alternatives to HRT

PROBLEM	SUPPLEMENT	DOSAGE
Hot flushes	Evening primrose	500–1,000 mg daily
	Vitamin E	400–1,600 IUs daily
	Multivitamins with potassium	As directed
	Siberian ginseng	400–1,200 mg
Mood swings and irritability	Calcium and magnesium B-Complex	1,000 IU Complex in formulation. Check pack recommendation
Bloating and Water retention	B6	50 mg 3 × daily
Vaginal dryness	Vitamin E	Insert vaginally nightly for a month then use as needed
Hormonal imbalance	Selenium	200 mcg daily
Bone loss	Calcium and magnesium	1,000 IU
	Multivitamin and Vitamin D	5–15 minutes of sunshine daily
	Zinc	100 mg from all supplements
Dry skin	Selenium	100 micrograms
	Evening primrose oil	500–1,000 mg

In addition to the above, every menopausal woman should take Vitamin C (1,000 to 3,000 IUs) daily in conjunction with bioflavonoids which enhance the absorption of Vitamin C which strengthens your entire immune system.

(Sources: James F. Balch, MD, and Phyllis A. Balch, MD, *Prescription for Nutritional Healing*; Marilyn Glenville, *Natural Alternatives To HRT*; Jean Carves, *Stop Ageing Now*)

Herbal Helpers

FOR	TRY
Vaginal dryness	Aloe vera gel applied directly into vagina. Comfrey cream can also be applied internally and externally. 'Astro-glide' gel developed by NASA.
Insomnia	Camomile tea before bed. Also, leave a cooled cup by your bed and sip through the night. Melatonin 15 to 30 mg (not on sale in UK).
Hot flushes	Black cohosh, yarrow, motherwort, dong quai (angelica). (In pill or tea form.)
Bloating	Parsley, dandelion and fennel.

Homeopathic and herbal remedies sound so lovely but when self administered can result in some sinister effects. It is best to read a thorough guide book (such as *Natural Alternatives to HRT* by Marilyn Glenville or *Menopause the Natural Way* by Sada Greenwood), or better still to consult a qualified homoeopathic physician. See Useful Organizations at the end for details.

Natural Oestrogen Foods

Many foods are rich in natural chemical compounds called phyto-estrogens. Dr Ronald Klatz of the American Academy of Anti-Ageing Medicine, believes that soya beans rich in phytoestrogens hold the secret to successful menopause. In his book, *7 Anti-Aging Secrets*, Klatz and co-author Dr Robert Goldman note that 'Japanese women suffer hardly any menopausal symptoms and Asian women in general are only about one third as likely to suffer from menopausal symptoms such as night sweats and hot flashes . . . Recent clinical studies found that when women were fed 45 grams of soya flour per day, menopausal symptoms were reduced by approximately 40%.' This is believed to be due to the isoflavones, the plant oestrogens, contained in soya beans which, it is thought, may bind up the oestrogen receptors in the body, blocking other types of oestrogen. Eating soya beans and soya proteins may also help to strengthen the bones as they also contain calcium.

The Burgen Loaf, a 'foodaceutical', or 'neutraceutical' (a developing breed of foods which act like drugs), is made of soya flour originating in Austria and claims to reduce hot flushes and other menopausal symptoms. But the phytoestrogens in soya, while possibly effective for women, can have unhelpful effects on men as some studies have found that soya products reduce sperm counts. So you might be advised to have 'his' and 'her' toast for breakfast!

Lifestyle Changes Required

When you are feeling the most upheaval during the menopause you might consider the following advice, culled from an array of nutritionists, therapists, and women who have discovered direct links between certain foods or drinks and the onset of a symptom.

Your spice and sangria days are over. Note if your moods seem more chaotic after a spicy meal or eating at a certain time (late for example) and make changes. Hot flushes seem more frequent and worse for women drinking too much, eating curry, drinking lots of caffeine, or pigging out on something very sweet.

Treat yourself to a daily walk in nature. Every major city has some beautiful parks. The exercise will be good for you (weight-bearing and weight reduction!) and the fresh air will calm your nerves. When you return, you'll be too relaxed to get into a sweat.

Hot flushes seem more frequent and worse for women who drink too much, eat curry, drink lots of caffeine, and pig out on something very sweet.

Drink water constantly. Have a bottle with you at all times, by your bed, at your desk, in the car. It helps to minimize water retention, keeps your dry skin moist and mitigates hot flushes.

Sleep alone on nights when the sweats are particularly disturbing. Why turn a bother into a crisis!

Substitute garlic and onion for salt in cooking. Salt depletes your calcium supply and contributes to water retention.

Reduce dairy and animal fat products which contribute to hot flushes. Animal foods are acidic and deplete needed calcium resources.

Add natural calcium foods to your diet for added calcium: watercress, dandelion greens, kelp, seaweed, tofu and soya products plus oily fish, especially ones where you eat the bones, like sardines.

Treat yourself once a week. The menopause can make you miserable so, pamper yourself to remind yourself how lovely you are despite the occasional emotional and physical havoc. Set aside an hour to give yourself a proper manicure; have a wash and blow-dry at your favourite salon; walk in at the spur of the moment and get a free make-up at a beauty counter; ask nicely (in return for a later curfew?) for a head massage from your son or daughter or partner; take a bubble bath in the afternoon; try a cooling eye mask before bed; suggest a rub-down in your favourite oil by your partner and see what other treats might be in store!

Take the Tests

With the many physical changes occurring around the menopause, women are advised to be both diligent and demanding in getting the appropriate and necessary diagnostic test to help guide both her and her physician as to the best steps for getting her into optimum condition. Dr Giampapa takes hormonal measurements from simple saliva tests, which can even be posted for testing! With these you can see what needs balancing to keep you feeling in optimal health. Useful tests also include:

BLOOD TESTS

Important readings to check include: full blood count for anaemia; thyroid; liver; lipid (cholesterol) profile; and thrombotic risk profile.

HORMONAL LEVELS

If you are experiencing any menopausal symptoms, or when your periods start being erratic or changing at all (with a lighter or heavier flow, mid-month spotting, new and different PMS), then it is worth finding out your oestrogen, progesterone and testosterone levels. Your follicular stimulating hormones (FHS) and Luteal Hormones (LH) will be measured and found to be in the non-menopausal, perimenopausal, menopausal or post-menopausal range. However, hormonal levels are measured in different ways in different countries and can vary from person to person.

CERVICAL SMEAR

A smear is required every three years and can be administered by your GP, Well Woman Clinic, your gynaecologist or by a menopausal clinic. If you have any history of irregular smears or have had cervical displasia, your doctor may advise more regular smear tests to determine if there is any indication of precancerous cells in the cervix or uterus. Sometimes your doctor may recommend an endometrial biopsy to ensure the lining of the womb is in a healthy state.

BONE DENSITY SCAN

One doctor we consulted considers a bone density scan critical to monitoring a woman's health as mammograms or cervical smears. She says that it is essential to know the state of your bones before or at the onset of menopause to find out what measures might be required to help strengthen them. With this information you can learn if your bones show worrying signs of weakness. If not, in five years you can have another test to determine if there has been any change indicating the onset of osteoporosis. Women with small bones or a light bone structure or coming from a family with members who have suffered bone loss are advised to be the most proactive and diligent in learning about their own bone density.

Leslie Kenton's book on natural approaches to dealing with the menopause, *Passage to Power*, recommends an inexpensive way to determine if your bones are in trouble. As you once did when a child, measure your height, noting the time of day, and make a point on the wall. Do this yearly. When you notice a change of three centimetres or more you might be in trouble and need an X-ray. Follow nutritional and exercise solutions to help build up those bones.

PELVIC ULTRASOUND

An abnormal swelling of the abdomen in the ovaries or womb can sometimes be felt by the woman herself but is often detected by a doctor conducting an internal examination. An ultrasound may be recommended, as it will determine if the enlargement is due to a cyst or possibly fibroids. Women with fibroids, endometriosis and other growths of tissue in the pelvic area may be advised to avoid HRT which

encourages such problems. Further examination may be required by magnetic resonance imaging (MRI), a scan or a laparoscopy. In this way a doctor can get a closer look at the area and extract tissue samples for lab testing to determine if the growth is cancerous or benign.

MAMMOGRAM

With the increasing incidence of breast cancer occurring in menopausal and post-menopausal women it may be advisable for any woman with a history of breast cysts or a family with breast cancer to undergo a breast X-ray or mammogram. While diligent, monthly personal breast examination can prove very helpful in determining lumps or changes in the breast, deeper or developing growths are only detectable from an X-ray.

Artificial Menopause: Hysterectomy

Hysterectomies are performed for many reasons today (see Chapters Two and Three). Too many, some would say. By the age of sixty-five, 20 per cent of British women and 40 per cent of American women will have had their wombs surgically removed. In Europe, the figures are considerably lower. Even within countries, doctors differ markedly as to the costs and benefits to women. The operation involves the removal of the uterus, the cervix and often the ovaries.

Sadly, even though only one organ may be the source of the problem, most doctors pursue the 'total plumbing job' as an insurance policy against cancer striking later on, even though the risk is not high. Fibroids, for example, plague about 25 per cent of pre-menopausal women. These are benign growths, which can change in shape with the monthly cycle, and can be quite uncomfortable. Sometimes they enlarge for unexplained often benign reasons. If doctors become alarmed at the size of the fibroid, they may order its removal along with the womb and ovaries if childbearing is no longer an issue. After menopause, when the hormone levels drop, fibroids tend to shrink on their own, so you may want to play a waiting game, with your doctor's approval, and have regular examinations.

Whenever cancer is detected in the cervix, ovaries, or uterus, a hysterectomy is usually recommended. Endometriosis, a disease in which the womb deteriorates, breaks up and migrates out of place, is the reason for one in six hysterectomies. Sometimes hormonal treatments or special laser procedures can provide an alternative. After fibroids and cancer, really miserable periods are the most common reason for a hysterectomy.

Early hysterectomy will certainly lead to an earlier menopause than you were due to have, even if the ovaries are left intact. And that, of course, is ageing, as you will lose several years of your own hormone protection. Some women who have hysterectomies and don't allow themselves ample time to recover develop adhesions or scars in the area. The actress Gayle Hunnicutt talked movingly of the problems she had with adhesions from, she believed, going back to work too soon after her operation. Adhesions can also be inherited, but only become apparent later in life. The acute pain resulting from adhesions can be misdiagnosed as irritable bowel syndrome or other such maladies. If caused by an operation or other gynaecological infection, doctors prefer to treat adhesions with laparoscopy (keyhole surgery) rather than another abdominal operation which can potentially cause more adhesions.

... most doctors pursue the 'total plumbing job' as an insurance policy against cancer striking later on, even though the risk is not high.

Even without a womb and no longer menstruating, women can still experience a 'monthly cycle' as the cycle is not just hormonally influenced but, as explained earlier, also involves the brain and pituitary gland. These are still sending monthly signals to each other. If the ovaries have been removed, the body will not be producing oestrogen or progesterone. Hence, hormone replacement therapy becomes the most viable option to keep your system on an even keel. However, 40 per cent of women having had hysterectomies, go free-fall into the menopause and beyond without HRT.

Osteoporosis

One disease definitely associated with the menopause is osteoporosis or bone thinning. It affects one in three women, resulting in a raft of complaints from aching joints to hip and other fractures that can lead to premature death.

You are a high risk candidate for osteoporosis if you:

✧ have relatives with osteoporosis – granny or the aunties might not have developed the dowager's hump but if they shrank beyond recognition later in life, they had it. This is a major factor in appreciating if you will also fall victim to this debilitating disease.

✧ have a small or thin frame.

✧ are Caucasian or Asian.

✧ have had a hysterectomy.

✧ have had an early, premature menopause.

✧ have had to take cortisone drugs for asthma, arthritis or cancer.

✧ have been on thyroid treatments.

✧ have had a diet devoid of calcium-rich products for many years or as a child and through the teenage years.

✧ avoid regular weight-bearing exercise, for example walking, lifting weights.

✧ are a heavy smoker as smokers reduce their bone mass by 25 per cent.

✧ consume excessive amounts of alcohol and caffeine which are acidic and deplete calcium available for bone cell regeneration. (See 'Age Accelerators', Chapter Three)

PREVENTATIVE MEASURES

Calcium

The key mineral for supporting and recreating your bone mass is calcium. But before you grab the supplements, appreciate that you need to purge your diet of calcium-depleting foods (processed, junk and animal fats) and drinks (alcohol, soft drinks containing phosphates, caffeine). To have the best stock of calcium we need to eat calcium rich foods and take the right supplements in conjunction with others.

The proposed milligram content on the supplement is only one consideration. Select one with the highest amount of elemental calcium as in calcium carbonate. You must also consider how well it will be absorbed. Take your own tablets and pop one into a cup of vinegar, stirring for a few minutes. If it doesn't dissolve completely in thirty minutes forget it: it won't either in your own stomach.

To improve your bone density, take a calcium (1,500–2,000 mg) and magnesium supplement (1,000 mg) in conjunction with other essential anti-ageing antioxidants like Vitamin C and E and a multivitamin

containing Vitamin D and beta-carotene. Specific nutritional 'bone-builder' supplements that contain these nutrients are another alternative. Those with kidney disease or any other serious illness should check with their doctors about any supplements they wish to take as they might interfere with your own medication or, in the case of calcium supplements, can contribute to kidney stones.

Add the following calcium-rich foods to your diet:

- dairy products.
- oily fish.
- fish with bones as well as shell fish.
- green leafy vegetables.
- brewer's yeast (Marmite).
- almonds.
- broccoli.
- cabbage.
- carob.
- figs.
- kelp.
- oats.
- prunes.
- seeds.
- soya products.
- watercress.
- yoghurt.

Exercise

Equal in importance to a high calcium diet for strengthening the bones is exercise. To be effective in building bones the exercises must be 'weight-bearing'. This means that you either use weights or resistance in working out, for example in the gym on equipment, or your skeletal frame needs to 'bear your own weight' while being active, for example with brisk walking, jogging, rowing or dancing.

Start slowly if you are unfit. Once stronger and more capable, keep pushing rather than taking it gently. Schedule at least three (five is ideal) sessions of forty-five to sixty minutes when you are working out. You will not only feel fitter and be stronger but you will also look terrific and have more energy.

Fertility

The loss of fertility can be one of the most demoralizing aspects of ageing to women who feel 'defeminized' by the menopause. Gail Sheehy talks in *New Passages* of 'the women who turn up at infertility centers in Southern California' who 'look like the most enviable specimens of their age group, virtual Wonder Women' and wonder why they can't get pregnant. 'They can pay the fees for fancy health clubs or PTs [personal trainers] and go to spas and stay in great shape,' says Sheehy,

but they can't turn back the clock on their fertility, and that hurts. However great the outside can look thanks to diet, exercise and surgery, the inner biological clock cannot be reset. At least not yet. But post-menopausal wombs can be prepped to receive donor eggs, so should a time come when egg-freezing techniques are perfected, women may be able to carry their *own* babies in their fit fifties and sixties.

The Menopause is a State of Mind as Well as Body

We believe that the modern, menopausal woman, and all those following closely on her heels, wants to strike a balance between the feminists, too eager to write obituaries to beauty and vitality, and the women who struggle to remain ageless sex symbols. The feminists are right to scream at the inconsistencies in the medical advice, accepted as popular wisdom, along with the notion that the menopause is a disease. We should join them and refuse to be guinea pigs until safe allopathic treatments are offered in conjunction with the alternatives to improve the quality of our health and wellbeing during this vexing change of life. At the same time, let's cheer Goldie Hawn's beauty along with her honesty when she admits that, of course, she is 'cosmetically enhanced'. There are plenty of surgical and non-surgical beauty and fashion choices for the woman who still prides herself in looking wonderful, interesting, vital and beautiful although not necessarily young (see Chapter Six). The two positions, at present seemingly diametrically opposed, need merging to create a positive spectrum of choice for all women to embrace as they enter their menopause.

We don't want the menopause to mean that careers need to change because we can't stand the heat. There are many of us who love our work or who don't have the choice to go off into the sunset at fifty and take up more genteel or fulfilling pursuits more in keeping with the changed nature and vitality of the menopausal woman. We deserve to remain at the centre at the very least, if not to rise to the top, as we sail on through mid-life to prove that our experience, our knowledge and wisdom is key to shaping future perspectives for the good of women and men, the young and the ageing.

Whatever it takes to help sustain us, without harming us, needs embracing and advancement. If many women are exhausted and want

to get off the merry-go-round at the menopause, they should be encouraged to do so while being shown exciting, meaningful choices for spending the next stage of their lives. Perhaps the feverish pursuit of a wonder drug to help menopausal women stemmed from the fact that previous generations having given so totally of themselves to family and community during their healthy, productive years had few choices for fulfilment when their nests were empty or their partners gone. Who wouldn't feel suicidal without any helping hands or role models to offer them an alternative to loneliness and social invisibility?

It is today's menopausal millennium women who will rewrite the script on surviving and thriving despite having to endure a hormonal change mid-life. They may opt for missing out on it completely or to postpone it until later in their sixties or seventies. Best of all, they should have at their disposal improved, safer hormonal replacements. If we will be able to extend our lives as healthy, active women (see Chapter Twelve), then today's menopausal woman will become tomorrow's UltraAger, vigorously firing on all cylinders, grappling with the exciting choices about how she lives the next hundred years. We find that prospect both exhausting and thrilling!

5

Beauty: A New Perspective

'As a white candle in a holy place, so
is the beauty of an aged face.'

JOSEPH CAMPBELL, *The Old Woman* (1881–1944)

New Know-how Needed

Mid-life and beyond requires a rethink of your entire beauty routine. Favoured skin care products and techniques that have worked fine so far might not only be ineffective now but could be causing premature ageing or even damage. The fuzzy line you might have drawn between caring for your face and caring for your body by sharing creams, or worse, exfoliants, now requires definition. If you haven't learned the correlation between what you eat and drink (or smoke) and the state of your skin, it's now time you did. And it's essential that you develop your own prescription, your own beauty routine and no longer follow ones dictated by self-proclaimed beauty specialists with vested interests in your 'addiction' to their products.

> *Beautiful skin is not synonymous with being wrinkle-free. Every line conveys character, personality – a life.*

Then there is your make-up. Few things date a woman quicker than the colours and how she wears her make-up. Baby blue eyeshadow might come round again in fashion, but when worn by an older woman it looks dated, not current. Any look that you have been through once needs refining to be worn again, fifteen or twenty years later. The same applies to clothes.

In this chapter, you will learn what is happening to your skin, your nails and your teeth and discover the remedies, low or no cost, as well as the high-tech investments that can reverse or mitigate the ravages of time. You will need a bin bag at the end of the chapter as any new beauty regime begins with a purge of nasties lurking in the bathroom cupboard or dressing table that have been letting you down or causing you harm. You may find your new, UltraAge routine is simpler than your present one. But the 'soap and water' babes will need to take a deep breath because you are going to be chided into investing a bit more time and, possibly, money to keep yourselves beautiful.

The good news is that some damage can be reversed with the latest creams, some of which require prescription, while many signs of ageing can be prevented or slowed to a snail's pace just with some judicious know-how and perseverance. With the advancements in anti-ageing proceeding at such a hectic pace, pressured by demanding Baby Boomers, the technology to banish wrinkles, bags and sags is surely just around the corner. But beautiful skin is not synonymous with being wrinkle-free. Every line conveys character, personality – a life. The goal

is not to despair at the damage already done, just to take measures to prevent any further damage and to learn how to enhance your many lovely features.

Beauty Tips from Timeless Beauties

There is no single recipe for timeless beauty. You have to find what works for you. But we can share the sometimes contradictory advice of those who seem to have found the right combination of maintenance and damage prevention. The ageless Sophia Loren says that France is the best country for appreciating mature beauty. 'A Frenchman once told me something that I have never forgotten,' she recalled in her book *Women and Beauty*. 'Between the ages of thirty-five and forty-five women are old. Then after the age of forty-five the devil takes over some women and they become beautiful, warm, splendid.'

Ms Loren says her secrets of successful beauty include finding 'a completely individual look' that will stand the test of time, learning that 'You can no longer stay up very late and arise with a fresh face,' and that 'You have to work a little harder to keep your figure in shape.' But she says, 'If you put on a little weight, find that you need glasses, get twinges of pain in your knee and notice that a few dark brown spots are showing on your hands, don't despair. There is a fountain of youth: it is your mind, your talents, the creativity you bring to your life and the lives of the people you love.'

The pneumatic Raquel Welch says in her *Total Beauty and Fitness Program* that beauty routines, like exercise, shouldn't be about being able to 'fade away into the sunset looking like nineteen from the rear end', but about making yourself feel and look better for yourself and your own self-esteem.

The actress Nanette Newman uses Johnson's Baby Oil to clean her face or sometimes the almost equally inexpensive Oil of Ulay cleanser. 'I never use soap on my face, never have done.' She thinks 'We're all too hung up on labels, and think something's good because there's an exciting brand name, but the contents are often as good in something less expensive. The prices of some products have become ludicrous and I wouldn't pay a fortune for them because nothing is worth it. I was in Montreal once and found a skin cream costing over £100. Ridiculous! I think the beauty world plays on women's insecurity.'

Broadcaster Katie Boyle's beauty secret is never to put moisturizer on her face at night. 'You have to let the skin breathe at night,' she believes. 'But I always put a herbal lotion from the medical herbalist Claire Swann on my neck and face while I'm in the bath and it soaks in wonderfully. Then I put half a phial of Coup d'Eclat on to my face, and the rest I mix with my foundation, and it doesn't let the make-up sink in, so you are protected all day. I love learning new make-up tricks. It's terribly ageing to say, "I haven't changed my make-up in years."'

The English actress, novelist, TV presenter, cake queen, and, of course, one-time girlfriend of Paul McCartney, Jane Asher, defies her years, looking about thirty, despite having 'challenging' delicate porcelain skin that generally ages most quickly. 'I'm an absolute sucker for anything that says "look twenty-two again in ten minutes" and you see a picture of a nineteen-year-old model and think, "if it can do that . . . !" I fall for all the advertising and I love fancy packaging.' Being a redhead, Jane, who generally goes for Clinique products and their system of cleansing, toning and moisturizing, went against the trend of her generation and stayed out of the sun so that mid-life she looks so good.

Shere Hite, the feminist sexologist and author of *The Hite Report* on male and female sexuality, the family, etc., also attributes her incredibly youthful-looking skin in her mid-fifties to staying out of the sun more than to any beauty routine. A nocturnal creature, she likes to work deep into the night, and has never enjoyed sunning herself on beaches. Her complexion is phenomenal as is her lithe figure and handspan waist, partly due to not eating sugar for many years.

Face Facts

Deterioration begins in your twenties when the skin starts slowing down its former rapid cell regeneration and natural, protective oil production, but often isn't noticeable until the thirties. From a young age all women are acutely aware of the havoc the monthly oestrogen and progesterone hormones wreak on the condition of the skin. The particular problems occur in the latter half of the cycle when the progesterone kicks in and the sebaceous glands go into overdrive, producing zits, blackheads and other horrors.

The skin is a marvellous organ. The largest, it not only holds us together, it also breathes, both 'inhaling' oxygen as well as expelling

Grey Can Be Great!

Anne is a grandmother and an award-winning image consultant with Color
Me Beautiful. She fibbed about her age when applying to train with CMB,
fearing that a 53-year-old would be written off. 'My heart was set on this
career and I really felt I would be discriminated against if you knew my real
age', Anne confesses. Some 8 years later she's still with us, proving that her
energy, enthusiasm and maturity were just what the job required. In fact, some
of our top consultants are 50-plus.

Here's Anne at 53 and at 60. We encouraged her to let the grey come through
as she is blessed with beautiful 'salt 'n' pepper' hair, and is a wonderful
example of how to make the change from brunette to grey successfully. 'I
know from my work that it is much easier for blondes,' admits Anne. 'When
white hair comes through it looks like highlights. For we brunettes, it is a
more obvious – and painful – transition.'

Crossing the line to grey hair meant that Anne switched her Color Me
Beautiful 'season' (colour range) from Autumn to Spring – still featuring warm
colours, but clear versions rather than sludgy ones. 'It was strange
to follow my own advice! And doing a complete wardrobe
switch has taken some time,' she confides, 'but I'm getting
there.' We'd argue that Anne's already arrived!

body toxins. It is only via the skin that we can absorb Vitamin D from the sun and at the same time prevent millions of bacteria from entering our systems. The surface is comprised of cells that are dead or dying off. Hence, it is essential to regularly remove this layer not only for the health of newly generating cells but also to look healthy. A grey, life-less pallor often results from negligent cleansing and exfoliating rather than from ill health. But, as you will learn, sloughing off dead cells requires a much more gentle routine as you get older.

It is essential to be diligent with sunscreens, year round, to prevent further damage to increasingly weak, thin skin.

The outer layer of the skin, the epidermis (stratum corneum), absorbs most of the atmos-pheric substances as well as UV rays. Cell regener-ation slows considerably with age from every two weeks in a twenty-year-old to every month or slower from mid-life onwards. The epidermis becomes more uneven in appearance with varying pigmen-tation occurring depending upon dormant, deep damage to the dermis caused over the years by excessive sun or pollution exposure. It's no wonder that foundations are second only in popularity to lipstick in women over thirty-five; they can cover or even out a multitude of sins. It is essential to be diligent with sunscreens, year round, to prevent further damage to increasingly weak, thin skin.

In between the epidermis and the dermis lies the basal layer which provides oxygen and nutrients to cells in the regeneration process. With ageing and the accumulation of free radicals (see Chapter Three) the basal layer becomes less effective in supporting the cells as they struggle to recreate themselves.

Collagen and elastin, two hot properties essential to beautiful skin, are stored in the dermis along with hair follicles, their attendant seba-ceous glands and blood cells. Both are protein fibres that bind the skin and ensure its resilience. Collagen and elastin weaken with age. Lowered hormone levels post menopause are thought to be implicated in this process and, interestingly, the skin and bone seem to thin together, with particularly 'thin-skinned' women more likely to have osteoporosis, according to Professor John Studd of the Chelsea and Westminster Hospital. Both are associated with lowered collagen levels. Imagine a bouncy, 'trampoline' layer beneath the surface of the skin. Well, collagen is bouncy in youth then gets flaccid later on; hence the ability of the skin to shape and retain wrinkles and bags. Think of it like a pair of

old leggings that eventually forms wrinkles and sags at the knees and the bottom where it has been subjected to the most wear!

The propensity to wrinkle can be genetic but is more down to lifestyle.

The propensity to wrinkle can be genetic but is more down to lifestyle. My grandmother had few wrinkles, even in her nineties, but then she never sunbathed or did regular aerobics classes, let alone run marathons.

The subterranean layer of the skin even deeper below holds the subcutaneous tissue. Here we start off with a protective, fatty layer that makes our skin plump as well as resilient. With the drop in hormones mid-life, even before full-blown menopause, this layer becomes thinner and less capable of providing a cushion to all the upper layers. It is the progressive thinning of each layer of the skin with age that makes it more vulnerable to both internal toxins as well as the sun and pollutants from outside. The sooner you take action to protect and nourish each layer the longer you will retain healthy, vibrant skin.

With the skin on the lips and eyes being the thinnest, it also makes them the most vulnerable. The first signs of ageing occur here from squinting or certain expressions, with fine lines taking shape in the late twenties. This is why the eyes and lips require special protection early and consistently. Remember, if you think that you are beyond any remedial help with skin care, there are surgical options outlined in Chapter Six for you to consider.

Enemy Number 1: Mr Sun

Remaining oblivious to the perils of the sun's harsh rays leaves you vulnerable to premature 'photo-ageing' as well as skin cancer. If found and treated early, most melanomas are not fatal. But sadly, too many are increasing as our environment's natural ozone barrier protection to filter UVA and UVB rays is destroyed.

The sad fact is that the damage caused by over exposure to the sun is cumulative. Being a beach bunny as a teenager means you will pay big time mid-life. Indeed, most damage is done by our twenties which is why parents should be charged with negligence (if not abuse!) if they don't protect as well as educate their young children about the sun's potentially harmful effects.

The catalogue of damage by the sun follows:

✧ Weakens collagen causing premature sagging.

✧ Interferes with melanin production, the skin's natural protective mechanism, which later will generate age spots (see Chapter Three) in vulnerable, damaged areas.

✧ Toughens the epidermis causing a leathery, taut and uneven texture to the surface of the skin.

✧ Aggravates moles or beauty spots to change in texture and become potentially precancerous or full-blown melanomas.

✧ By weakening the dermis layer, it interferes with blood production and causes burst capillaries or spider-veins.

✧ Tanning beds and booths are worst of all, with UVA emission being 100 times stronger than natural sunlight. No wonder you only need to be blasted for a few minutes to get the equivalent of a full day's exposure! Avoid them. Your life may depend on it.

Enough of the bad news. Although you can't put back the clock and reverse the harm that has been done, you can help strengthen new cells as they regenerate each layer by protecting the skin completely from UV rays with a high SPF sunscreen, using a minimum of factor 15, with 25 or 30 preferable.

A Skin Care Regime: What's Right For Me

The right skin care routine for you might not be the one you could be given if you consulted a dermatologist or anti-ageing guru. The right one depends on your objectives and your attitude towards your ageing face. Answer the quiz on the following page with true or false to determine the best regime for you.

What's the Right Regime for Me?

1. My attitude towards ageing is that it is mad to try to defy nature. Best to 'go gracefully'. *True/False*

2. The wrinkles on my face remind me of pleasant experiences and rarely depress me. *True/False*

3. If I knew that drinking too much or smoking contributed to premature ageing, I would be unlikely to change these habits for this reason alone. *True/False*

4. I would never spend more than £10 on a face cream. *True/False*

5. Cleansing isn't necessary in the morning as your face is still clean from the night before. *True/False*

6. Tissues are just as handy for taking off make-up as cotton wool. *True/False*

7. My skin hasn't changed for twenty years. There's no need to change my routine to something different. *True/False*

8. I have a lovely body lotion that I use all over and add just a bit extra to my face most days. *True/False*

9. There's not much more you can do for an ageing neck apart from wearing high collars and scarves. *True/False*

10. Vaseline is just as good for moisturizing the skin as those expensive creams. *True/False*

11. Foundation is a waste of time. All you need is a bit of blush to brighten up the face, or powder to take away the shine. *True/False*

12. Your fingers are just as effective applying eye shadow as brushes. *True/False*

13. Moisturizing creams are really only needed when your skin feels dry and itchy *True/False*

14. As long as you rinse your face well a toner is unnecessary. *True/False*

15. After a late night, leaving cleansing until morning can cause no real harm. *True/False*

16. Giving your skin a rest from skin care and make-up does it good. *True/False*

17. Night creams are a marketing gimmick. Your skin doesn't know what time it is. *True/False*

18. Expensive, high-tech creams and potions aren't worth their price tags. *True/False*

19. A nice hot flannel or steam really cleans out the pores. *True/False*

20. Borrowing my daughter's facial mask is economical. *True/False*

ANSWERS

1 to 5 True Responses

You are a high maintenance, high-tech woman prepared to do everything possible to improve the health and appearance of your skin. When it comes to your skin and probably your image, you are prepared to devote time daily, at least twice, to taking care of your skin. You won't need convincing of the benefits of a monthly session with a beauty therapist for a specialist facial massage, cleansing and rehydrating. Nor will you quibble over investing in products that deliver promised results. You may have been less diligent in your youth but with the clock ticking, you are prepared to do all to keep the ravages at bay. You've probably already read Chapter Six and have earmarked a few surgical options for consideration.

6 to 12 True Responses

You are the 'Shocked So Show-Me' woman who only recently took a good look in a magnifying mirror and realized what was really happening to your skin. You care about your appearance but remain unconvinced about the investments required to look your best. You might be willing to turn over more of your hectic schedule to take care of your skin but will prefer less expensive, yet effective, alternatives to the high-tech products. No doubt you will be willing to work on your skin from the inside out and will jump to Chapter Nine on healthy ageing to see what you might cook tonight to glow more tomorrow. You've got the right attitude, you just need re-orientation.

13 to 20 True Responses

You are a 'Wrinkled and Wayward' woman who needs to read this chapter, no, this book, cover to cover. You have neglected yourself not necessarily willingly nor consciously and no doubt because you have been giving of your 'all' to others instead. You need another look in the mirror. This time, focus first on your lovely eyes. Your cheeks and mouth may also be beautiful. If you don't think so now, stick with us and try some of the skin care suggestions plus the many make-up tricks to bring all your features back to life. Remember: you can improve what you've got. The show ain't over: it may only be about to begin!

CLEANSING

Take no short cuts and cleanse twice a day. In the morning, your face is covered in dead cells and in the evening you are wearing the world on your face – dirt and pollution on top of your make-up. After a late night on the town, resist the urge to flop into your warm bed. Your make-up, plus pollutants including smoke, will clog up your pores and ensure that deep-seated problems like blackheads and pimples take root.

H$_2$O

Sorry, but not any old water does the job. There are degrees in perfection if you care to learn them. First off, avoid very hot or very cold water. You might think that hot, steamy water will *really, really* clean your face but it will only serve to strip the needed natural oils away and potentially cause burst capillaries. A splash of cold water that granny always recommended will indeed snap you to your senses first thing in the morning but, again, is too severe on thinner, older skin and will also cause spider veins. OK, Paul Newman looks great despite supposedly dousing his face in a bucket of icy water every day, but for most of us the best temperature for cleansing is lukewarm.

Skin care specialist Helen Sher, founder of the Sher system skincare range, goes one step further, insisting that you must get the Ph balance of the water correct. She makes a crystallized compound and recommends a capful into a sink of water before washing to ensure that the water doesn't strip the skin's natural acid mantle. Sher, along with countless other skin care gurus, recommends splashing or rinsing off your cleanser up to thirty times using the water in a basin to rehydrate the skin as part of the cleansing process.

THE RIGHT STUFF

Cleansers come in countless forms from 'soap' bars to foams, gels, mousses and creams. Regular bath soaps are too alkaline for the skin and leave a drying residue on the surface. Other 'moisturizing soaps', while richer than normal soap, still leave a film residue on the skin. Clear glycerine soaps like Neutrogena are fine on younger, oily skin but can be drying and harsh on older skin.

Cleansers, in lotion or foam, that wash off with water are a combination of cleanser and moisturizer. Many women don't feel clean unless they involve water in the process so these are fine. If you rinse your face many times, you will eventually clean off all the cleanser and not really require a toner. Other cleansers that need no water but wipe off absolutely require a toner to follow to ensure that no residue is left.

HANDS AND CLOTHS BEST

Now for some fundamentals: use your fingers to massage the cleanser around the surface of the skin. For a fully made-up face, be prepared to wash twice: the first go to remove all the make-up you've applied and the second wash to ensure the surface is completely clean.

Use circular motions with your finger tips, avoiding the eye area (see below). The action will stimulate the muscles and blood, encouraging cell regeneration, help to lift the make-up and grime off for easier removal and feel like a real treat.

Even though tissues are often used in demonstrations or even recommended for removing cleanser, they derive from wood pulp and are very harsh on older, thinner skin. Best to use a flannel or even a thick piece of gauze, while nappies cut up into squares are terrific. The slightly rough, natural surface will have a gentle exfoliating effect which is all that is needed to slough off dead skin.

Best to use a flannel or even a thick piece of gauze, while nappies cut up into squares are terrific.

TONERS

Toners or fresheners should be alcohol-free if used at all. Toners are best if you use a cleansing bar or wipe-off cleansers to ensure that all traces of make-up and cleanser are removed.

MOISTURIZERS

Don't think for a minute that you can do without moisturizing your face, twice daily, as this is key to maintaining buoyant, plump (well, as much as you can) skin. Using the right kind of moisturizers, particularly those containing antioxidant vitamins such as A, C and E, has now been scientifically shown to be able to thicken the skin, as well as effecting some repair of damage. Expect a whole new generation of moisturizers to capitalize on these findings!

However, maintaining moisture inside the skin is the primary point of this product. When the skin becomes dehydrated from excess loss of water (through not drinking enough or not maintaining it with a moisturizer) the skin dries out and becomes red and irritated, with damage to the epidermis and dermis setting in rapidly.

Finding the best formulation is a matter of trial and error. During the year, your skin changes depending on the amount of time you spend indoors and outdoors, in centrally heated air-conditioned atmospheres, in the warm or cold, sweating through exercise, and that's before you consider your diet. A moisturizer that makes your skin feel great and provides an easy ungreasy base for make-up might be fine for many months then you notice or feel a difference. So it is time to switch for a while to something lighter, for example more water than oil based, or something richer like an oil-based cream.

You might opt to put your 'serious' money into your daytime moisturizer then use an effective, richer cream at nighttime when you can add needed oil and moisture to the skin without worrying about make-up going greasy on you. Some women skimp on their daytime moisturizer, as many inexpensive products do a terrific job, and invest in luxurious night creams. I use the former approach as I am very fussy about how my make-up looks and lasts and swear by the un-sexy, but effective, E45 at night.

NIGHT CREAMS

Despite many manufacturers' claims about what some of these creams can achieve as we sleep, the way you should think of night creams is

as nutrients. Avoid the old-fashioned cold creams that are heavy and greasy as they don't penetrate the skin and are just theatrical in making you feel as if there is some great performance underway. Better are the light, modern creams, gels and oils that are readily absorbed and do help to enrich the skin after a hard day's work surviving under make-up and in our polluted world.

Don't think for a minute that you can do without moisturizing your face, twice daily.

As with your daytime moisturizer, it is wise to let the cream settle into the face for five minutes. Any excess can be blotted away with a tissue – yes, tissues are fine for blotting, not for wiping! Try not to choose a cream that is so thick it needs to be applied in such a way as to drag the skin when you rub it in.

As you will find when we get to body care, oils and creams are more readily absorbed on warm, moist skin. So, apply your night cream after an evening bath (which will also help you sleep) or after cleansing, leaving a warm flannel on your face for thirty seconds to ready it for its enrichment.

EXFOLIATE OR BE DAMNED!

Another precept drummed into women is that we must scrub our faces weekly with coarse grains or gritty pastes to dead-head the redundant cells. We also tend to 'go for it' with these gritty potions and scrub so vigorously that we damage the skin, particularly as we age and it gets thinner.

Using an alpha hydroxy acid (AHA) cleanser or moisturizer has an exfoliating effect without the harmful abrasiveness of exfoliant scrubs which, it has to be said, are terrific for younger combination or oil-prone complexions. Also, by using a cotton flannel or muslin wash cloth when you wipe or wash off make-up you are actually exfoliating.

THE EYES WILL HAVE NONE OF IT

The eyes, our special 'jewels', are housed in the most delicate part of our face. Hence, you need to treat the eye area very specially when it comes to cleansing and moisturizing (more tips on special eye treatment in the make-up section below).

Clean off all eye make-up using a non-oily eye make-up remover. These can be inexpensive so you can save your pennies for other products. Wet a cotton wool pad then add remover lotion. Press, don't rub the pad on to the eye lid, to remove eyeshadow. Place a cotton wool pad under the lashes and with a cotton bud soaked in remover, stroke the lashes downwards on to the pad to remove mascara. These are the most gentle techniques for cleansing the eye area. Most women are far too frantic with cleansing the eyes and only end up damaging this delicate tissue, causing bags and wrinkles.

Avoid any other face products – cleansers, toners, moisturizing creams, foundations on the eyes – unless specifically formulated eye creams or gels – as they will make the eyes puffy. The regular formulations are far too heavy for the eye area tissue.

The Latest and the Greatest

Enough of the basics; it's time for the high-tech advancements for serious age-defiers.

RETIN-A

Retin-A or the generic drug Tretinoin has been used by dermatologists for years in the treatment of acne but only in the last decade for the treatment of wrinkles. Based on a Vitamin A derivative, retinoic acid, this formulation penetrates the layers of the skin and works to increase cell generation by speeding up the natural production of collagen and elastin. The outer surface of the skin becomes smoother after usage, with blemishes disappearing and fine lines diminished. Consistent use of Retin-A also helps in minimizing age spots caused by sun-damage, with one study showing that it can even prevent damage from the sun. By using Retin-A before exposure, the cream can control the enzymes that would normally break down collagen and elastin, a remarkable claim: too bad it was reported by the manufacturers of Retin-A and not by an independent research body. So, perhaps we should hold fire in rushing to Retin-A as the panacea for all ills until more conclusive, independent studies are conducted. But getting the US Federal Drug Administration's (FDA) approval means that many of the claims are valid and that, under proper direction, it shouldn't harm us.

Still, Retin-A takes some time to get used to, and should not be used without first consulting a doctor or dermatologist. I, like many women, had a wicked initial reaction with terrible irritation, redness and peeling. Naturally, as I do little in moderation, I was using too much. However, with proper use it can deliver. You should be monitored closely by a dermatologist or cosmetic surgeon to ensure that the right strength cream is delivering the desired results. The nub is that once you stop, so do the effects. So, Retin-A is a long-term and pricey commitment.

When using Retin-A, sunscreen is no longer just advisable, it's essential. Your skin will be raw and vulnerable even though it looks rosy and smooth, and will require extra protection even in grey old London, with a daily thirty SPF sunscreen.

ALPHA HYDROXY ACIDS

AHAs offer a great bridge between basic moisturizers and the heavy duty Retin-A. Formulated from natural sources like sugarcane and fruit such as apples, lemons, grapes and even milk, AHAs encourage natural exfoliation or skin sloughing as you wear them. No, your face doesn't drop off during the day, your cells just break up rather than clump together, with the newer cells released and the skin appearing smoother and plumper.

Think twice about sharing your AHAs with your kids – they are not inexpensive.

As with Retin-A, AHA creams come in a variety of concentrations, with creams containing up to 10 per cent generally considered safe. Higher concentrations of 30 to 70 per cent have a peeling effect and are best used only in conjunction with a dermatologist.

Color Me Beautiful added AHAs to its basic, aromatherapy skin care line two years ago and women said that they – and their husbands – loved the effect. AHAs work on 'improving the appearance' of fine lines. Note, they do not remove the lines, but they do fade age spots. When you use AHA creams be sure to smear any excess on to the backs of your hands which, no doubt, harbour more than a few different shades of flesh. Even teenagers' skins benefit from AHA creams as they alleviate blackheads and white-heads. But think twice about sharing yours with your kids – they are not inexpensive.

LIPIDS, MICROSPHERES, CERAMIDES, AND LIPOSOMES

These and other new treatments will offer all sorts of time-released therapies or 'binding effects' or suck 'moisture from the atmosphere' to penetrate deep into the layers of the skin. The consumer is wise to remain sceptical but should be open to real *developments* that work for some women. I, like thousands of women, jumped on to a new 'active anti-ageing tissue defence' cream called Servital that was tested by a reputable, independent hospital with amazing results. At £75 for a 50 ml tube it promised results and results it delivers. I use it sparingly and it lasts for six months. I've given up other things like the occasional facial to be able to use it. But, I am a high-tech, high maintenance kind'a girl to Victoria's occasional horror.

DO PICK 'N' CHOOSE

Every company will swear by this enduring principle: you must use compatible products together, like cleanser, toner, moisturizer, night cream, eye cream, etc., or your skin care regime won't work. Worse, you could harm your skin! Nonsense. Put your own routine together and invest as you see fit, not according to some sales pack. You don't

need an expensive array of skin care to look terrific as you age. But if you aren't blessed with good genes or harbour plenty of sun damage on your face, think of other things you can skimp on to treat your skin to restorative, nourishing products.

BE PATIENT, NOT A SUCKER

You can't expect overnight results from a new skin care regime. Combining a good, twice-daily regime with night cream along with drinking as much water daily as your kidneys can stand, and eating more fresh vegetables and fruit, you should have glowing results in three to four weeks. If not, maybe you should consult an expert. Start with a good beauty therapist by recommendation. Beauty therapists are lousy sales people. They are drawn to the profession because they love beautifying women, bless them. Most will bend over backwards to assess you and share as much as they know. Consider their suggestions but, again, hold back on making an extensive, across-the-board, investment into a whole line.

If your skin is really getting you down, maybe it's time to talk to a dermatologist. A course on Retin-A might help to clarify the skin and provide a better base for beginning a new, basic skin care regime. Again, you don't need to commit to Retin-A for the duration but can use it as a preparation, a launch-pad for beginning your work.

Kathy is a stunning model, still busy at the age of 43. She attributes her beautiful skin to being unfortunate enough in her childhood not to be taken on sunny summer holidays but spending them in the cool, grey of the north-west of England. But she's thankful today, blessed with great skin as a result of being kept away from those rays.

PS: YOU KNOW WHAT ABOUT SUNSCREEN

Sunscreen is essential every morning. Apply a high SPF of at least 15 under your moisturizer. Most dermatologists recommend an SPF of 30 to minimize wrinkling. Select a sunscreen that can work with make-up and is made for the face. I use one made for the sensitive skin of babies with an SPF of 45. Body sunscreens are too thick and often too greasy for use on the face. Also, body sunscreens can be very irritating to the eyes. Some new moisturizers have been formulated and approved by the American Food and Drug Administration to contain sunscreens of SPF 15+ that work effectively.

Sunscreen is essential every morning.

For women still keen on that bronzed look in the summertime, try bronzing powders for the face or one of the many terrific new fake-tanning creams that have improved considerably over the last few years. The key to success with tanning creams is to exfoliate before usage and to apply as evenly as possible. Also, remember to wash your hands thoroughly after use or you end up with orange palms.

By the way, as we've said before, don't be fooled by the claims that sunbeds are 'safe'. The latest generation of sunbeds rarely 'burns' anyone, but with a higher density of UVA rays they may accelerate the ageing process faster via wrinkles rather than if you sun yourself gently outdoors. You have been warned.

Neck Care

Perhaps the most visible sign of ageing occurs on the neck. It takes many of us years to figure out that if we only extended our skin care regime below the face we could look even younger. As the skin of the neck is thinner it is most vulnerable to dryness and a crêpey appearance. With fewer nerve endings here, however, we don't feel the dryness as acutely as we would on our faces and tend to ignore it. Besides, who wants oily streaks on their collars?

There are many new products exclusively for the neck which make a range of claims from moisturizing to firming, toning and lifting! No cream will firm or lift the neck, but you can improve the appearance of the skin by moisturizing it daily. You can use any facial moisturizer or night cream on the neck and should do so in preference to a body

cream which will be too heavy for this delicate area. By virtue of just bothering with the neck, by cleansing, massaging and moisturizing, you can see improvements quite quickly. Many women swear by specialist neck creams but you might want to save your money by getting one product to do the job of face, neck and décolletage.

Body Care

Back to the super job that our skin does for us by 'breathing' in oxygen and 'exhaling' toxins. We need to help it along by keeping the pores both clear and fed in order to do their jobs.

When I first read Leslie Kenton's *UltraHealth* in the early '80s and learned about skin brushing I was shocked at the idea of brushing dry skin to slough off dead cells. Until now, I had thought that the occasional waxing of the legs and a body loofah was all that was needed. But body brushing does work wonders in keeping the skin soft and helping work against toxin build-up that can contribute to cellulite formation.

If your skin is dry, it is a sign of dehydration. Up your water intake and you will notice a real difference in as little as a week. As with facial creams, you might need a couple of different ones to help, depending on the time of year, how exposed the body is to fresh air or how sealed up in hosiery and trousers.

You can spend a lot of money on beautifully smelling, luxurious creams which are a treat if you can afford them. I always ask for these as presents as I can't quite bring myself to spend the money on them. No, I discovered the best body treatment in a Swiss sauna which I shared with an Italian woman. After her sauna and shower, she rubbed pure virgin olive oil on to her skin, using a flannel. She had the softest skin I ever felt aside from a baby's bottom, and she was forty-two. Yes, she insisted I have a feel, and then proceeded to 'do me' head to toe to the bemusement of a self-conscious American couple from Kansas City! I followed her advice and can confirm (or my husband will) that regular 'oiling' after a bath or shower will produce beautiful skin. Don't worry about smelling like a salad: as long as you use pure virgin oil there is no smell.

Virgin olive oil can give you skin as soft as a baby's bottom.

Neck care: use a specialist neck cream, or those for your face in lieu of any old body cream, to preserve this delicate skin.

SALTY SCRUBS

Exfoliation is as beneficial for the body as it is for the face. And there are some lovely products to do the job. Again, if you want a cheap yet effective alternative to them, try sea salt. After a warm shower, stop the water and rub yourself all over, or get help from a friend, using chunky sea salt. Once done, blast yourself for as long as you can stand it under a cold shower. All the dead body skin will be washed away and your skin will glow.

CELLULITE

You know what it is without an elaborate description or picture and no doubt sport a bit on the thighs and bottom. As the beautiful Sharon Stone has quipped, 'Never trust a woman without cellulite.' She proves that even the most beautiful stars suffer from the condition.

Dr Elizabeth Dancey, author of *The Cellulite Solution*, proclaims that cellulite is a natural female condition related to our oestrogen production. As we age and our surface skin becomes thinner, Dancey says our hormonal induced fat sacs are more visible. In women with sluggish lymphatic systems, resulting from yo-yo dieting, lack of exercise, or eating and drinking the wrong things, cellulite is more noticeable and more difficult to shift. No matter how much Jane Fonda screamed to 'Go for the burn', for some women even 'spot', or focused, exercises don't budge the stuff.

How Do You Get Rid of Cellulite?

Indeed, you can really reduce the blobs, although ridding yourself of cellulite might call for liposuction and even then it is never foolproof or 100 per cent effective (see Chapter Six). Start with exercise and diet.

Aerobic exercise of any kind (see Chapter Nine) will help burn fat, build muscle and stimulate the lymphatic system to work off toxins. Body brushing, mentioned earlier, really does help. Use circular upward movements of the brush but don't do it for so long or so roughly that you draw blood.

When it comes to cellulite creams, a market worth $20 million in the States alone, they promise to be the panacea to the dreaded lumps and bumps but are not effective, according to Professor Marks. This view has been confirmed by the prestigious Johns Hopkins University in the States, which tested thirty-two international brands and concluded that none of them worked. Still, they keep selling.

If you want to spend some money, an AHA cream will help to dissolve the surface dead cells to help eliminate the toxins from inside. This does not mean that fat will evaporate, it just means that if you are eating well, drinking lots of water and exercising, you will see beneficial results. But body brushing and any old cream massaged well into the target area will probably achieve the same.

Hand Care

The hands are an indicator of age as well as the life you have led. While we may have been diligent about protecting our faces and our bodies, it is often the hands that get short-changed. Essential to communication, hands convey much about a woman. The most beautiful hands are not necessarily those that have a weekly session at the manicurist or flash a number of blinding gems. No, beautiful hands are used by a woman to express herself and in doing so convey some care and attention for all to appreciate. Often you meet a very average-looking woman with the most stunning hands, so stunning that you watch them more

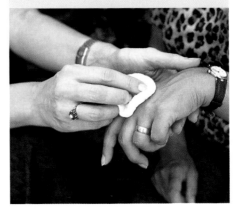

Hands deserve as much attention as the rest of your body. Olive oil is a great natural moisturizer.

than her. They announce themselves as her pride and joy and demand our compliments.

The basics of good hand care are known to all – avoid contact with very hot or cold water, detergents, and protect them from the sunshine and cold weather. But, for most busy women these caveats are wishful thinking as the rubber gloves are never where you left them and that puppy's or kid's mess needs sorting out immediately. Then there are those of us who work with our hands and will always put our tasks before our beauty – potters, gardeners, painters, cooks, craftswomen. We wear our toil and despair at the ravages on view when in the company of women with beautifully tended talons. When you have crummy nails you also tend to use your hands as tools, for example, in lieu of a screwdriver or staple-remover among other things. Remember how Scarlett O'Hara failed to convince Rhett Butler she'd been leading the life of a lady when he looked at her hands? Beautiful hands will be 'gone with the wind' if you abuse them!

Lovely hands result from a combination of genetics, diet and lifestyle. While not being able to influence the first, we can all do something about the others. Good nutrition is evident in the strength and colour of the nails. White flecks under the nails indicate a deficiency in zinc whilst dryness and ridges can mean not enough B vitamins. Healthy nails should be pink, proving a healthy blood supply working beneath. Weak nails can be genetic but also stem from inadequate calcium, so adding a supplement or eating more calcium-rich foods is recommended. Lots of water plus carrot juice, rich in calcium and phosphorus, will help as well. Royal jelly and evening primrose claim results for the nails as well as premenstrual tension among other things.

Lovely hands result from a combination of genetics, diet and lifestyle.

Many homoeopaths and ayurvedic practitioners can read a range of worrying conditions from the nails, from a propensity towards arthritis or bad circulation to kidney and liver disease. Nail ridges may start to appear when you reach your forties. Like the rings on a tree, and the rings around your neck, if you're unlucky, they are a sure way of dating you and show up injuries, ill health and the general wear and tear of your life.

Some home-made solutions can be as helpful in strengthening nails as expensive paints and creams now luring us at every turn in the pharmacy and supermarket. Soaking your fingertips in warm olive oil enriches the nails while softening the cuticles for easy shaping. I have

friends who swear by cider vinegar for soaking their talons, which they insist strengthens them.

A final word about the cost of nail polish. The stuff in the jar, regardless of the label, costs a few pennies to the manufacturer. Unless the colour is to 'die-for', you are wasting money on very expensive brands as all nail polishes chip at about the same rate. Better to invest in a good cuticle cream like Jessica's and buy inexpensive polishes.

TOP TIPS FOR TANTALIZING TALONS

✧ Soak your hands and fingertips before a manicure.

✧ Don't cut cuticles or pull hangnails unless you want both chronic problems and weak, ugly nails.

✧ Use a basecoat – yes, it isn't a gimmick and helps nail colour remain true.

✧ A top coat does prevent chipping, making the effort last longer.

✧ Use artificial nails only for very special occasions like a wedding, as they can weaken your own nails no matter what claims are made to the contrary. You may not only damage your own nails from them but absorb chemicals via the cuticle and leave yourself vulnerable to fungus infections. If you must, acrylic tips that don't choke the cuticle are a better alternative.

✧ Short nails are more manageable for the accident-prone and can look cute polished. Better to cover them with colour than to expose them with a clear or French polish.

✧ Avoid sawing back and forth with your emery board. File nails in one direction to prevent them from splitting.

Make-up Rethink

As with your skin care, it is essential that you rethink your whole approach to make-up. Techniques that you use along with the product and colour selections that worked well years ago are probably announcing your age before you even speak.

In this section you will learn guidelines for changing your approach to make-up. But first you need to clear out the clutter and see what, if any, new tools might be required to help you look your best.

COLOUR CHECK

Get out all your make-up and line up the array of colours. First, discard anything over a year old as it will be contaminated with bacteria. Next step, take out colours (eyeshadows, lipsticks, blushes, pencils, etc.) that you know have not worked and are unlikely to now, and toss them out. You are left with some marginal colours that you wear sometimes along with your daily favourites.

You may know what colours suit you or you could be rather confused. If you think that you can wear both blue and brown eyeshadows or either plum or salmon lipstick you are definitely confused. I believe that you will always look your best if you wear colours harmonious with your natural colouring. Okay, you may be playing around with Mother Nature by colouring your hair to something quite unlike its natural state. If you look fine with that hair colour without make-up, then it is probably a terrific choice. If, however, you wouldn't be seen dead without the help of make-up, then maybe you have made the wrong choice.

Indeed, you can wear any hair, make-up and clothes colours that you want. The snag comes with how much time you are prepared to put in to effect the look.

My advice is to have fun with your colouring within reason. In my book *The Makeover Manual* there is lots of advice on how to assess your colouring, with suggestions for changing it if you want to. You can discover what wardrobe and make-up adaptations will be required when you colour your hair. So, if you are game for a total new look, read that book. Here you will get some general guidelines and tips on colour.

To update your make-up look, why not ask your granddaughter for some tips? Then modify them to make them appropriate for you.

Many women begin to reassess their hair colour in their thirties either when the white hairs start sprouting or when they feel that the colours they used when younger are beginning to look jaded.

Carolyn started with highlights in her twenties, evolving before long into the full peroxide job. By her mid-thirties she wanted a new look, but was fearful of what a drastic change might entail. As a CMB image consultant, she knew that if she complimented her skin tone and eye colour with warm tones then she wouldn't need to toss out her entire wardrobe. As

a blonde, Carolyn was a Soft Autumn; going auburn made her a Warm Autumn, perfect for her natural colouring yet giving her an exciting new look.

With the array of colouring techniques available today, from mousses and wash-ins to permanent and semi-permanent, all women can have fun livening up their own hair colour. Covering grey couldn't be more simple, and it's well within everyone's budget. If in doubt about your best possibilities, see an image consultant or good colourist (on recommendation).

Colour: Losing Your Way

As we age, our colouring can change in many ways. Of course, grey hair can profoundly change our looks. If you opt to let it come in naturally, you know that it can be different from other women; some grey hair is beautiful, some isn't. That is not to say that the latter should definitely be coloured as many women don't want that expense or commitment. But grey hair does require new colours in make-up and clothing to look both harmonious and exciting.

Our skin also changes. With age it can become more sallow and dull. Then there is the discoloration that can become more pronounced as we get older, for example in age spots, burst capillaries, sallow patches,

etc. This starts in the thirties and can be very pronounced as early as your fifties. The seasons can also ring havoc with the skin and its appearance, requiring different colours and approaches. All of this means a reappraisal of your make-up shades as well as the type of products you use.

GETTING STARTED

A good make-up takes a few, say ten, minutes to give you a beautiful, long-lasting effect. For best results work facing natural daylight.

The babes you see in the perfumery departments who look like mannequins themselves are not the standard you require to look wonderful. They spend a good thirty to sixty minutes applying their whole range of products and surely require a pneumatic drill to get the stuff off their faces at night. Manic measures which we all employ for that dash out to the shops are fine if you know you won't be bumping into any chums or folks who need influencing. But for a finish that will sustain you the whole day, or evening, consider the following steps.

Step 1: Doing the Face

Foundation
Choose light-diffusing formulations, as these deflect the attention and light away from the skin so that lines aren't as noticeable. Remember to also select brands that promise a sun-protection factor in case you forget your trusty layer of sun cream first. The colour should match your jawline to ensure easy and natural blending with the neck. Your blush, eyes and lips add all the colour you need to hold attention.

The colour should match your jawline to ensure easy and natural blending with the neck.

If you are an out-doorsie sort of gal, and notice a change in colour to your complexion during the year, prepare to have two different colours that you can use, blending them together for those 'in-between' months.

Facial hair needs dealing with if you want to present your lovely features in the best light possible. If your hormones have activated the fuzz production, consider if just a bit of judicious plucking or bleaching is all that is required to 'negate' the effect of an unsightly shadow. If

facial hair is more troublesome there are two alternatives: electrolysis or waxing. The former method can be painful and expensive but does work. If you're sensitive, you might want to consider taking a painkiller before treatment. Waxing might seem drastic but is very effective. It lasts six to eight weeks and the hair does not re-grow coarser but is actually softer as a result.

Apply foundation assured that your moisturizer has been absorbed. If the surface of the skin feels creamy, blot off the excess cream. When it comes to foundation, less is best. Squirt some on to the back of your hand and use a cosmetic sponge to apply thinly and evenly all over the face. If you apply foundation directly from the container with your fingers you will, no doubt, use more than you need.

Use downward strokes to prevent your facial fuzz from becoming prominent.

Concealer

Please don't think you can do without this key product or step because as we age and those shadows and discolorations occur we need extra help to balance out our canvas before adding colour. If you don't minimize the dark bits they will compete with the eyes and the lips. The colour should be lighter than your foundation in order to negate the dark areas. However, avoid concealers that are so light as to appear chalky and unnatural.

Concealers come in a variety of forms from creams and liquids to sticks. The latter are dangerous to apply as they will 'drag' the skin and stretch out areas you need to keep as taut as possible for as long as possible. So, as with everything you do to the face, you want to choose the most gentle formulations, allowing you to apply them easily and effectively.

If using a liquid, avoid the applicator provided in favour of the tip of your ring finger which will be better for tapping the concealer accurately into position. As with a cream formulation, you can also use a light 'concealer' brush, probably the best choice for accurate as well as gentle application.

Powder

Translucent powder is essential to help the foundation last all day and to give you a light matte finish. Be choosy about the formulation you choose. Again, the 'light-diffusing' products never look clogged and cakey.

To lift the face, use upward strokes when applying blusher. For best effect, use a lighter colour on the cheekbone and a slightly deeper colour underneath.

Use a big puff dusted in the powder. Press the powder into place, never wiping it, which only disturbs the lovely base underneath. It doesn't matter if it initially looks a bit dusty as it will be absorbed during the time you spend completing the rest of your make-up. Any excess can be brushed away then.

Blusher

Blusher can be applied now if you intend just to dab on some lipstick and mascara and head for the door. If you are into a complete make-up, wait until your eyes are done to get the correct balance with your blusher.

Blending two blusher colours, not together, but in conjunction with each other, can be very flattering and modern. If you were a contour queen in the past, time to retire your dull brown blusher used lower on the face which will now look very ageing.

Avoid, no, throw out, the brush or applicator which comes with the blusher in your compact. These only result in stubborn blotches of blusher and are hopeless for blending. Every dressing table, if not handbag, should be equipped with a proper blusher brush. Use the lighter blusher colour high, near the outer edge of the eye brushed upwards into the temple and hairline. Blended beneath is a deeper (albeit not dark) blusher that highlights the outside of the apple of the cheek, brushed upwards into the hairline merging with the lighter blusher. You do not want to discern two separate colours.

Dust the brush across your blusher colour and tap off any excess against your wrist before applying. Where you place the brush tip first is where most of the powder is. If you ever 'over-do' it with the blusher, soften the effect by pressing in more translucent powder.

If your face seems to absorb blusher, i.e. you despair that it doesn't last, try applying a cream blusher *before* your powder then apply a powder blusher on top. This will help the blusher last for hours.

Eyes: Dos and Don'ts

Left eye – shiny, iridescent shades, even if the vogue, accentuate crepey skin. Heavy liquid eyeliner is also less effective than a light line of kohl pencil dusted with a little shadow. Right eye – matte shades and lighter tones lift the eye. Use use upward strokes when applying eye shadow, and be careful not to drag the colour outside the corner.

Sponge applicators that come with eyeshadow compacts should be thrown away; they drag the skin causing lines and wrinkles.

Avoid pulling the skin when applying eyeliner.

Brushes are much more gentle on the delicate eye skin

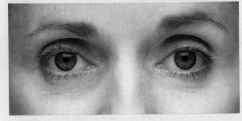

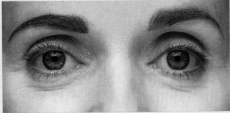

The art of make-up is principally to take away distractions. Before applying colour be sure to eliminate all shadows and natural discolouration with a good concealer. Apply this lightly with the tip of your ring finger, or a concealer brush. Left – unaltered eye; Right – light touch of concealer.

EYEBROWS: Left: The Joan Crawford Effect – very ageing. Right: Instead, fill in the thin bits with soft shadow, lighter than your natural brow colour.

Step 2: Doing the Eyes

The approach you have towards doing your eyes depends on the effect you desire. If you just want to 'finish them off', you can get away with a soft base of a light peach all over the eye with a soft contour shade, for example cocoa or grey and some mascara. But I find missing out on eyeliner disappointing as the older eye will look more defined and special with that extra definition.

As with everything so far, the best effects will result from using a few key tools. As crêpey skin needs shadow to be 'placed' and softly blended, it is important to use good brushes instead of your fingers, foam applicators or cotton buds.

As with everything so far, the best effects will result from using a few key tools.

'Place' the shadow on to the eye without rubbing. Once there, the shadow can be merged together. Your eyeshadow will be less likely to 'crease' or 'bleed' if it is applied on to dry skin or over an eye base. Use upward strokes and pressing motions to help 'lift' the eye. A lighter colour on the inner eye, which should have a light base of concealer, and a dot on the outer eye will create the effect of a wider eye. Don't stretch the skin when you are applying shadow as when the skin folds back into its normal position the shadow won't be where you want it. Leave the skin where it is and dab on your colours where you want them then blend softly together, using upward strokes.

Avoid using eyeliner all around the eye as it will make it look smaller. You can use it only along the top lid, or a good approach is to line the outer half or third of the eye only. Always 'set' the eyeliner with shadow applied using a small, stubby tipped brush for best effect. Kohl pencils are good as you don't want a harsh line. If you find a particular eye pencil too hard to apply, 'warm or soften it up' with a few strokes on to the back of the hand. Liquid liners can get wedged into folds and never look soft.

The softest option on the skin is to paint on a gentle line using a water soluble eyeshadow and brush. The key is not to see a definitive line, only to gain more depth and definition to the eyes. Be adventurous in using different coloured shadows over your basic eye pencils to create interesting effects. Eyeliner colours are best if mid-tone to deep, although black is too dark. Light or bright liners look silly.

The brows shouldn't be forgotten as they frame the eyes. Often they will thin or lighten with age so experiment with soft grey, taupe, and

cocoa colours for filling in. If you use a pencil, sharpen the tip and use short strokes rather than drawing a long line (very Joan Crawford!). Shadow can be softer and equally effective for filling in bald patches. Brush the brows outward and upward and consider using a tiny bit of gel to secure the most recalcitrant hairs into place.

Mascara is the last, final step to beautiful eyes. Better to apply a few, thin coats rather than one thick one. The goal is thicker lashes not gloppy ones. Black mascara will be fine on women with deep colouring but softer shades of navy, brown, grey or plum can be more effective on women with lighter colouring.

Consider curling the lashes before applying mascara to 'open up and lift' the eyes. Another trick is to apply mascara only to the outer half or third of the lashes to 'widen' the eyes.

Step 3: Doing the Lips

If you want to look older, don't wear any lip colour. The lips fade, thin and crevice with age so they need help with both conditioning and make-up to look terrific. I love beeswax formulations to treat dry lips as they feel better immediately and seem to improve within a day. A bit of Vaseline overnight can also work wonders.

The formulations for lipsticks become more extensive every year with the beauty industry now providing such an array that it is confusing trying to choose the best one. Long-lasting formulations can be drying whilst moisturizing lipsticks slide away within an hour of application. Pearlized lipsticks and glosses make lips look thicker but can also identify fine lines more readily. Lip-fix products can provide a perfect base for lipstick or be worn over lipstick to seal it into place. However, if you are a lip-licker or plan to eat or drink, I *Finally, never apply your lipstick directly from the stick but with a lipbrush for a light, even effect.* advise against these products as they start to 'undo' and require a back-to-base repair job that can be quite labour-intensive and challenging.

After years of experimentation, I come out in favour of using a moisturizing lip base in conjunction with a lip-liner then lipstick. This is a fool-proof and comfortable way to long-lasting lipstick. The lip-liner should be sharpened to a fine point. For thinning lips, be bold and go along the natural, outer edge of the lips. Always 'lift' the line at the corners of the lower lip to make you appear upbeat, not sad and literally down in the mouth. Remember not only to line the lips but to fill

Lips: Dos and Don'ts

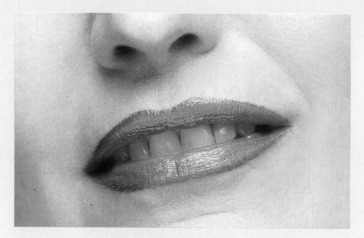

Baywatch Babe lips are contrived and ageing.

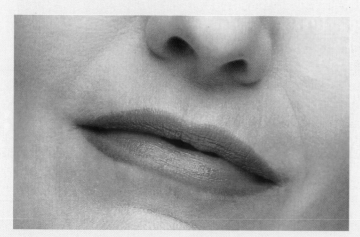

If you're fearful of wearing bright lipsticks apply just a thin coating over natural lip pencil, instead of the colour directly from the tube.

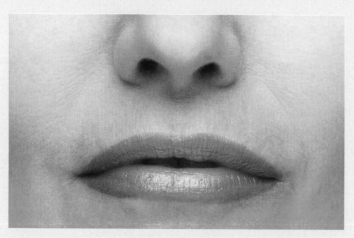

As we age our lips get thinner. To make them look fuller use a natural lip pencil to outline the lips as well as fill them in. Then use sheer, lighter colours over the top.

them in with the liner. Finally, never apply your lipstick directly from the stick but with a lipbrush for a light, even effect. Unlike the eyes, you will need to smile wide and stretch the lips to ensure total coverage. Another tip for thinning lips is to use lighter shades, not pastels necessarily, just lighter than you normally wear. Conversely, darker tones make full lips appear less so.

The goal is to see you first, your beauty – not the make-up you're wearing.

General Make-up Colour Principles

✧ Use lighter colours to balance dark areas and softer, mid-tone shades to blend lighter areas.

✧ Soften dark eyeliners like black or navy with a lighter eyeshadow like taupe, grey or jade.

✧ Avoid brown blushes in favour of lighter pink if your colouring is cool, deep salmon/peach if your colouring is warm. These will look fresher than brown which can be both dull and ageing.

✧ Vibrant blushes like fuchsia or red will compete with your eyes and lips and look unnatural on caucasian women.

✧ Define eyebrows with an eyepencil or shadow that is always lighter than your own brows. This will blend better and look more natural.

✧ Use soft coloured or 'natural' lip pencils to define the lips as deeper shades will only make the lips look their age.

✧ Ivory or champagne shades are more flattering than white.

✧ Very warm shades like gold, moss green or rust on the eyes are only wearable by women warming up their natural hair colour, for example, those with red, henna or auburn shades.

✧ With brown and hazel eyes, brown shadows that are soft like pewter, cocoa or taupe are more flattering as a contour than deeper shades.

✧ Blue or soft grey eyes are wise to avoid brown shadows in favour of grey. Soften by blending in blue, jade or plum for best effect.

✧ Avoid colour under the eye like eyeliner or mascara as it will only accentuate the lines, wrinkles or bags.

✧ Dusting a pale pink or peach all over the eyelid provides a healthier looking base for defining the eyes with contouring colours and eyeliners.

✧ Bright, warm lipstick colours like coral, ginger or orange make ageing teeth look more yellow!

FINAL CHECKS

Step back after all your work. Do the lashes need a combing? Could a bit more powder make you look more polished? Or would a spritz of mineral water give a more youthful, dewy look? Have the eyebrows drooped in the process of putting on your top and do they need a quick comb back up into place? Perhaps a dash of lipgloss in the centre of the upper and lower lips would ensure a smacker later on from Mr Wonderful!

Helen Gurley Brown went so far as to camouflage her receding hairline and thinning eyebrows with tattoos, as she recounts in her book about ageing, *The Late Show*. Her philosophy is that 'You can take the world seriously, do whatever you can to make it better and fit in exfoliation and lip gloss.'

PS: Zzz . . .

Beauty sleep is not a myth. Researchers have discovered that overeating and lowered immunity leaves you vulnerable to disease and both are linked to disturbed sleep (see Chapter Three). Avoid stimulants in the evening like caffeine and alcohol. Try not to eat too late, and to allow at least four hours between it and bedtime. Along with a good diet and regular exercise, effective sleep is the key to remaining your beautiful self. So take measures to reset your clock if it is out of synch. It is essential to your health as well as to your beauty.

6

Cosmetic Cuts and Shortcuts

'Youth's a stuff will not endure.'
SHAKESPEARE, *Twelfth Night*

'We have the technology. We can rebuild you,' claimed the 'futuristic' doctors in the '70s hit television series *The Six Million Dollar Man*. Today, that's exactly what some people want and are doing. The technology is within all of our grasps, even if not all of our bank accounts will stretch to it.

Once upon a time, we had to accept our looks, and those with cleft palates, clubfeet, big noses and other imperfections had to put up with society's scorn. Now even children are going in for cosmetic surgery, with men increasingly electing to enhance their own bits from pectorals to penises.

Aesthetic plastic surgery, as it is correctly known, should, ideally, be carried out by an aesthetic plastic surgeon recognized by the Royal College of Surgeons in Britain or the American Society of Plastic and Reconstructive Surgeons. No longer the preserve of just the very wealthy and the incredibly vain, it is being viewed by the mildly discontented as a worthwhile expense, say, in lieu of a holiday. Some have taken advantage of the cheap cosmetic surgery on offer in Russia and other former Soviet bloc countries or have combined a vacation with surgery in a country with a favourable exchange rate like South Africa. One British woman enthused that her ten-day stay in Moscow with a full facelift performed at the department of Cosmetic Correction linked to the Academy of Sciences cost less than £1,000 inclusive.

Before You Plunge: Think, Research, Beware

The catalogue of horror stories associated with cosmetic surgery is too numerous to list here. Any surgical procedure has risks from as little as slight nerve damage to things ending up lop-sided, to death. That's why you will have to sign a consent form before surgery absolving the surgeon of any responsibility, although many surgeons who were really 'unqualified butchers' have been successfully sued and struck off medical registers. But the damage to many unlucky women is irreversible.

While no surgery is failsafe you can minimize risks by doing your homework. Consulting registers of bona fide consultant surgeons and specialists in plastic, reconstructive and cosmetic surgery in your country is just a starting point. The next step is to interview at least three surgeons and to get the names of some of their patients who

would be willing to speak to you about the experience. You may have to pay, usually a nominal charge for each consultation, but it will be worth it.

The best surgeons really want to know about your reasons for choosing cosmetic surgery and will advise against procedures if your reasons aren't valid. For example, if you are depressed, a new bustline will not lift it. If your husband has left you for a younger woman, a facelift won't turn back the clock in that respect. You need to be healthy physically and mentally before considering cosmetic surgery.

You will want to go to a consultation with a list of questions ranging from the options to achieve the desired results – some may be surgical, others non-surgical – to the options for local or general anaesthesia; recovery time; how long before you see the desired results; how to prepare yourself for surgery; and aftercare.

I had a facelift and an eyelid job, which cost me £5,000, and I don't regret a penny of it.

As you will discover in the section about my own experiences with cosmetic surgery, all surgeons have their own aesthetic sense about beauty. Some are willing to work with you and others are more dictatorial about what you need. You only need to look at the results on someone like socialite Jocelyn Wildenstein (the tabloids' 'Bride of Wildenstein') to appreciate that certain approaches are less than desirable.

In this chapter we cover a range of surgical and non-surgical procedures available today along with an array of potions and gadgets for you to be aware of. By providing this information we are not saying 'give it a go' as we wouldn't try many of them ourselves. It is up to you to read about possibilities and to explore them further if one or two seem to suggest a solution to something that is bugging you.

It Takes a Trigger

The most common triggers for rejuvenating cosmetic surgery for women are loss of a partner through divorce or death, a new partner, job loss, and a new job. A milestone birthday can also be a spur. One woman said, 'I was fifty-two when my husband died and I'd looked after him for years and thought, sod it, I'm going to do something for me. I had a facelift and an eyelid job, which cost me £5,000, and I don't regret a penny of it. I've had several much younger boyfriends since

then and I'm enjoying my life tremendously. Before, I felt like an old hag widow!'

For another it was when the youngest of her four children asked, 'Why have you got all those lines?' At forty-eight she felt she looked older than many of her contemporaries, and 'being in the fashion business I've always been very aware of how I look. Appearance is important in my industry,' she said. 'I've had two laser treatments around the eyes and mouth and I feel fabulous. My ten-year-old says I look wonderful and I've been told I look like my thirty-year-old daughter now. But the treatment was really for myself, and I think any treatment should be done for your own sense of self-worth, not for a man or a career, but for how you feel about yourself from within.'

We agree. It is important to remember that a more youthful brow or jawline won't necessarily change your life and those who think it will cannot help but be disappointed. Women who have cosmetic surgery in desperation because their husband is attracted to someone younger will, inevitably, lose said husband anyway. But if they have it after he's left to give themselves confidence in the job or dating market, it's a different matter. Ivana Trump sported a dramatically different look after her marriage to tycoon Donald Trump, but it proved the face that launched a new life.

Feminist and femme fatale Gloria Steinem told Victoria a few years ago, 'I couldn't do it. I'd be afraid,' adding, 'It's not the thing itself but the motive for choosing it: if you think your husband will leave, or that the breasts are more important than brains, you'd be fine without it. I find it very sad that Jane Fonda has [resorted to cosmetic surgery]. I don't pretend to know how she feels inside, but from the outside it seems to me as if she's still trying to gain the approval of a cold and distant father.' Steinem suggested the idea of 'confidence clinics' instead, to enhance women's confidence in what they have. When someone commented that she didn't look like fifty, it was she who proudly said, 'This is what fifty looks like!' But only time will tell whether she changes her views if her beautiful face, which has successfully weathered more than six decades, begins to change beyond recognition.

Joan Collins gives herself room to manoeuvre in her best-selling *My Secrets*: 'I'm not an advocate of plastic surgery because I've seen too many mistakes and disasters . . . However, for the future I shall reserve the right to have plastic surgery should I feel the need arise.' She recommends instead, as most doctors now do, drinking plenty of water to

keep the skin moist, avoiding overzealous exercise, because 'every time you step or jump the breasts, buttocks and chin, which are not supported, are hurled downward, creating loose chins, sagging breasts and saggy bottoms.'

Nips and Tucks Through the Ages

Cosmetic surgery is generally reported to have been performed since the nineteenth century, with the first nose job – the focal point of the earliest procedures – supposedly performed in Berlin in the mid-1800s. An otoplasty to fix protruding ears was undertaken in Manhattan in 1895 and the first breast enlargement and tummy tuck tried about the same time. Eyelid treatments and facelifts followed. But earlier cosmetic surgery was apparently carried out by an Italian plastic surgeon of the sixteenth century, Tagliocezzi, who reportedly said of his profession, 'We restore, repair and make whole those parts which nature has given but which fortune, or time, has taken away, not so much that they may delight the eye but that they may buoy up the spirit and help the mind of the afflicted.' According to leading cosmetic surgeon Dr Vincent Giampapa, 'nose jobs' were known thousands of years ago in the East. The mind boggles at how they were done, though!

Early facelifts had to be repeated to be effective, with Marlene Dietrich in her later days reported to have stuck hat pins into her scalp beneath her wig to prevent sagging! Eleanor Lambert, the ninety-something compiler of the *International Best Dressed List*, has admitted to having 'a few nips and tucks'. She told Victoria, 'I think cosmetic surgery is a very important weapon in a woman's arsenal, but only up to the age of sixty-five. After that age you should avoid having unnecessary anaesthetic. The important thing is to keep your marbles! A lot of women are so keen to keep the face going that their minds go. The Duchess of Windsor had a facelift at eighty-two and was never the same afterwards,' claims Lambert, whose own mind remained razor-sharp.

My Triggers, My Results

One of the motivations to write *UltraAge* came from the fact that I was becoming increasingly aware of my own ageing, from experiencing the

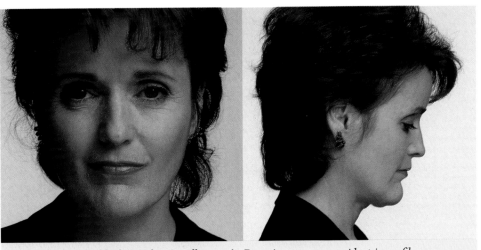

Not awful, but tired-looking when I really wasn't. Drooping was more evident in profile.

menopause to real sadness whenever I spent more than a few minutes in front of the mirror in the morning. Sure, after walking the dogs, slapping on some make-up, and putting on my 'face the world' mug I looked better; but, in my eyes, not much better.

The realization that you are looking older is both insidious and swift. The first shock often comes from seeing yourself in photos, those happy snaps taken off-guard, unposed. You think, yikes, is that me? I must have been feeling pretty bad that day. And, of course, the lighting is so uncomplimentary. Then comes the breath-snatcher when you are using the magnifying side of your mirror for shaping your brows and you inadvertently explore further afield and see the wrinkles and crevices taking shape – definite ageing that you can no longer dismiss as bad lighting.

Facing the Music

At forty-seven, my skin looked its age if not older. Like many of my generation, I was a late convert to the benefits of skin care and spent many a summer slathered in baby oil to develop the teak-coloured glow so desirable in the sixties and seventies. It probably wasn't until my late twenties or early thirties that I can honestly say that I bothered with a twice daily ritual of cleansing, toning and moisturizing.

I still abused my skin through my thirties. At every chance the sun shone, I was out in it unprotected, dismissing the ultraviolet rays in

Britain as not worth the bother. At least once a year for the past fifteen we have escaped the bleak greyness of Blighty for the Caribbean, the Far East or Africa – anywhere just to see some sun! I would 'prepare' my skin for the sun with a half dozen blasts on a tanning bed to enable me to stay in the sun longer on holiday without worrying about burning. Ha! What mad rationalizations we can invent. I might not have been burning my skin but I was certainly accelerating its ageing through my sun worship.

As the forties took their grip, so too did other changes to my face, changes that not so much announced my age, which I honestly don't give a hoot about, but rather, made me look glum. The most distressing to me was the appearance of fine lines around my mouth which I would learn were the result of both too much sun and having a very animated face. Also, for years I have whistled for my dogs, which has developed lines equivalent to being a three-pack-a-day smoker!

In Search of a Panacea

In my early forties, I was often told by complete strangers to cheer up as I was walking down the street. My brow had dropped, creating serious furrows, and the corners of my mouth were definitely droopy, giving the impression of constant disapproval.

In my early forties, I was often told by complete strangers to cheer up as I was walking down the street.

I recently learned that my lifelong devotion to distance running had probably accelerated the ageing of my face. My daily training sessions and marathon goals had kept me fit but had taken a toll on my face by breaking down the elasticity of my facial muscles. But this wasn't reason enough for me to stop running. I just had to find a solution to 'make it better'.

In the late '80s, the craze was to teach your face exercises to look younger as advocated by Eva Fraser, author of *The Facial Workout*. I booked an introductory session to try out her facial exercises. If Eva in her early sixties could look so fresh, virtually line and bag free, then surely I, twenty years her junior, could manage some improvements? Was the Fraser routine all I needed?

On closer inspection, Eva is blessed with the most beautiful bone structure. You know the kind of cheekbones that we would all die for, high, defined and pronounced. Skin of any age would be supported majestically by them. Eva's Mediterranean genes mean she also has stronger, thicker skin than we of Celtic or Anglo-Saxon extraction.

I don't accept the syllogism that what is beautiful is good and that most people equate beauty with youth.

I worked with Eva for a few months and indeed, started to feel that my face was in better shape than before. I couldn't tell if it was lifted, necessarily, it just felt more 'together'. But I noticed when working with Eva that she hardly moved her face when speaking. She could be telling me a funny story or something rather tragic and her eyes and face retained the same, slightly frozen expression. Indeed, Eva advocated limited facial movement when not performing the exercise rituals to inhibit potential lines and sagging as we aged. But for me, this would be quite impossible without a personality transplant. I make faces constantly and can't express myself without doing so. As with my running, there would be no changing the way I spoke despite the lines and bags forming at an alarming rate.

I persevered with Eva's routine and felt it did produce results, just not dramatic and long lasting enough for me. The lines still developed, the mouth drooped and I was increasingly dismayed at looking so tired. No amount of daily facial callisthenics seemed to help.

It's Not About Looking Younger

Maybe some women choose a facelift in the hope of looking years younger, as a way to compete with their contemporaries in the youth-obsessed beauty stakes. I have always looked younger than my years mainly because I am small and also because I have an excess of energy and dash around quite inelegantly, certainly unbecoming for a woman my age.

I don't accept the syllogism that what is beautiful is good and that most people equate beauty with youth. Therefore, we must not accept that what is young is good and, conversely, what is old isn't, as suggested by the American feminist author Letty Pogrebin in *Getting Over Getting Older*. Many of us know of countless over-40 beauties like Catherine Deneuve, Tina Turner, The Duchess of Kent, Shirley Bassey, Liv Ullman, Joanna Lumley. Such trite assumptions are too simplistic and not fair.

But I do agree with Pogrebin that the more a woman relies on her looks when she is young the tougher it is for her to accept ageing than the rest of us average lookers. We'll never know how two of the twentieth century's greatest beauties, Marilyn Monroe and Diana, Princess of Wales, would have coped with seeing their beauty erode with age, but Greta Garbo wanted to be alone and became a virtual recluse.

Comments from others, that I looked younger than my years, honestly never registered. I readily give my age in interviews and have done so with even more determination in my forties, feeling a responsibility to stand up and show what being a certain age looks, sounds and feels like.

No. I just wanted to look better, fresher and more spirited as I still felt inside, not to win unnecessary compliments about looking ten years younger. I keep bothering so that I don't bother about what I look like. By virture of the fact that my bags and wrinkles are bugging me I am more bothered, conscious and aware of how I look than I was years ago. I would prefer not to linger at the mirror and to make do with a quick glance instead.

It's All Image

As an image consultant, of course, my appearance is always under inspection. I spout the importance of personal image, dress, grooming, behaviour, fitness, voice and communication, and need to reflect the values that I preach. But I am not a paragon of perfection like some image consultants. Frankly, I cannot be bothered. I am too busy with school-aged children, dogs to walk, and a garden I would prefer to pamper than myself.

I use my image as a tool to be aspirational for other busy people.

I use my image as a tool to be aspirational for other busy people. I am no beauty, have a quirky figure and am almost fifty. I need to look the part of an image consultant, like a dynamic player in business and politics, yet want to convey the importance of expressing individuality through personal image. What I don't need is to look more haggard than I feel and, therefore, have to spend more time on make-up and grooming just to look on top of things.

My staff will attest to how crazy I can look, from the odd-ball get-ups I throw together to walk to and from the office each day to how

I screw up my hair and make-up after a long planning meeting or drafting session. Thank God I have a team of troopers who pointedly whisper 'Powder, lipstick and brush, you nutcase!' just in the nick of time, all the time.

I work with all age groups and enjoy the awkwardness of teenagers, sparring sessions with new MBAs as well as leading challenging discussions with senior managers. I also facilitate motivational sessions on image for retirees that can be as wild and unpredictable as with any group of school kids. I want to look fresh and appropriate for each audience and increasingly felt that my younger clients might be dismissing me as a 'mother figure' because my face was, well, looking mumsy!

First Plunge: the Brow Lift

At forty-four, I decided to test the waters with cosmetic surgery with a limited procedure designed to smooth forehead furrows and 'open up' the eyes. A New York friend was singing the praises of her recent brow lift. 'You will just look more awake, less like death warmed up,' she enthused. I found Jan Stanek FRCS in London through a recommendation and felt confident in the fact that he not only used the latest technology but also promised that this endoscopic procedure would be effective and natural. It seemed simple enough and was so effective that unless I told someone I had had a brow lift they didn't even notice the change. The results were confirmed by the compliments: 'You look well. Have you been away?' Not: 'What happened to you?'

Stanek advocates women start surgical remedies in their forties when the skin is still elastic enough to respond well. I also liked the idea of sorting out problems as they developed rather than waiting until everything was lined and dreary and the after effect such a shock on everyone. No, subtlety is what I wanted – and more women today do.

More Help Required

As I approached forty-eight, the brow remained unlined but the rest of the face was definitely dropping and the bags and lines were out of control – although Victoria disagreed. As business was taking me to Los Angeles and New York within months I booked to see a few of

the leading cosmetic surgeons to compare techniques and costs on both sides of the Atlantic.

In Los Angeles, the home of cosmetic surgery, few families can mention some member who hasn't had some help from a plastic surgeon, beginning with the teenagers upset with their noses (remember the film *Clueless?*) to the aspiring models and actresses in search of implants to present the requisite, formulaic figure of the moment, to Dad's eye job and Mom's facelift, then granny's biennial liposuction on her tummy to allow her to eat how she likes without bothering to exercise or diet! I even found women in restaurants inspecting each other's scars over lunch.

One doctor coolly suggested that it was never too late to 'correct your genes'!

The Californian approach to cosmetic surgery, from my experience, aims to make up for where Mother Nature left off. Surgeons tell you where your 'facial imbalances' and imperfections are and offer a panoply of techniques and measures to recreate your face. 'But then I wouldn't be me,' I would exclaim. One doctor coolly suggested that it was never too late to 'correct your genes'!

'You don't want to stop with your face, do you?' asked another surgeon to the stars. 'Your hands are worse than your face. What do you do for a living?' Ha! Unlike any of his pampered clients, I have always worked with my hands. As a child growing up in a large family, I was the superwhiz cleaner of bathrooms, the kitchen floor, even the cars. My hands lived in buckets of harsh detergents. With my own family, though blessed not to have to do all the domestic chores myself now, I still scrub and polish quite unconsciously and never use rubber gloves. But the worst havoc on my hands has been caused by years of gardening. I love nothing more than digging deep into the soil using my hands. I am proud of the work, the activity that is etched on their surface. My hands proclaim I am not a lady of leisure and, indeed, cast my age as probably older than I am. No, it's the sad face that bugs me, nothing else.

I had seen the effects of Californian philosophy and techniques too often in the famous. Remember how beautiful Faye Dunaway was in her early career? Now she seems sadly blander to me, no matter how technically perfect her face might appear.

In New York, unless pushed, surgeons offer less radical suggestions. But the ones I spoke to suggested a scarless facelift. Rather than show the scar in front of the ear, they rebuild the front of your ears with excess facial tissue so no one is any the wiser. The only problem with the new ears was that it would mean never wearing earrings or exposing your ears again. The lumpy new nubs I found worse than a small scar in front of the ear.

In the end, I opted for the European approach offered by Mr Stanek in London who recommended the full facelift (rhytidectomy), an eyelid operation (blepharoplasty) and some laser resurfacing of the skin to rid my mouth of the fine lines firmly etched from making faces all my life. None of his patients ended up looking bizarre or noticeably 'done', which was just what I wanted.

Three procedures at once took some consideration in terms of time lost, the recovery (how ghastly it would be) and the cost. If laser treatment were to be included, it would be better to have the operation during the winter with as little potential exposure to the sun as possible. By now, of course too late for my own skin, I had sworn off the sun and begun wearing sunscreen year round.

I told Stanek that I needed to be functional within two weeks as I simply couldn't be out of action any longer. He assured me that I would be. 'The key is to rest for three days afterwards and not to pursue any vigorous activities for a few weeks,' he said. In other words, retire the trainers for a month at least or your ear will end up in your neck (just joking).

'The key is to rest for three days afterwards and not to pursue any vigorous activities for a few weeks'

Trying to imagine the pain and recovery was less simple. Stanek's post-operative notes were clear and functional but devoid of gory details. Other clients I spoke to reported such varied experiences that I dismissed them, assuming an investigative, open attitude to go through and report it all myself.

The third hurdle, after sorting out time lost and the likely agony of my new and improved face, was, of course, cost. Jan Stanek is one of London's finest, and although other cosmetic surgery clinics offered 'deals' and payment plans I opted to pay Stanek's fee of £7,000 to get the best expertise.

We scheduled the operation for early January, just after the Christmas holidays, while I was completing the manuscript for *UltraAge*, prior to a four-day conference that I had to conduct at the end of the month.

Preparation

I wanted to prepare myself as best as I could for the surgery weeks in advance to ensure that my recovery would be swift, effective and provide encouragement for others. The first step was to get advice on anti-oxidants and other supplements to aid healing.

Helen Bransford's terrific little primer *Welcome to your Facelift* provided a lot of helpful advice from her own facelift along with advice from many leading cosmetic surgeons. Combining her advice along with Dr Stanek's, I prepared my system for the onslaught and recommend that anyone planning similar procedures takes note. Two weeks before and after the operation eliminate alcohol, caffeine and smoking to enhance the body's ability to absorb nutrients essential to healing.

I wanted to prepare myself as best as I could for the surgery, weeks in advance.

Alcohol is also dangerous to combine with painkillers. Increase water consumption and fibre via fresh fruit and vegetables to help flush toxins through the system prior to and after the anaesthetic. At the same time, drink herbal teas and cranberry juice to stimulate the kidney and bladder functions often affected by anaesthetic.

To strengthen the blood, two weeks before and after surgery take Arginine and Ornithine (see Chapter Twelve) and other amino acids, B12, B Complex, folic acid and eat as many fresh green veggies as possible. Take Lysine before and Zorivax for 1 week after to prevent cold sores to which lasered skin is especially vulnerable. Your surgeon will provide a prescription. Stop Vitamin E and Selenium, which affect blood clotting, two weeks before and two weeks after surgery. Also avoid all aspirin, Ibuprofen and other anti-inflammatory tablets in favour of paracetamol for the same reasons. Stock up on Vitamin C (3,000 mg taken in 500 mg doses six times daily) to help strengthen the immune system and minimize bruising two weeks before and two weeks after.

From surgery up to 4 weeks after take Acidophilus in tablet form or better still via live yoghurt to restore bacteria eliminated by antibiotics post surgery, essential to maintaining a healthy gut. For minimal bruising take four arnica tablets three times daily prior to, on surgery day, and for three days afterwards, and apply arnica cream topically to any bruises that might appear.

Diary of My Facelift

SURGERY DAY

I was scheduled to arrive at the hospital at midday, so had a morning of interviews to keep my mind off the impending surgery. Discussed the future of the Tory party with the BBC, gave *Homes and Gardens* a list of helpful gadgets for maintaining your wardrobe and identified the top footballers with winning images for a sports magazine.

Just call me Pumpkin Head. I seem to have swollen up beyond recognition.

Sadly, the pre-op hours dragged on and after a final word of assurance from Dr Stanek and a few of the horrid 'before' pictures, I was taken down for slicing and frying at 5 p.m. I feared that Dr Stanek would be tired after a long day and out of puff for my dear old face. He told me not to worry and that by me being the last patient he could take all the time needed to make me beautiful.

The three procedures, blepharoplasty (an eyelid op), rhytidectomy (facelift) and laser resurfacing to smooth away lines from the mouth and eyes, took three-and-a-half hours. I had an uneventful but disturbed first night with attentive nurses checking ice and face packs every half-hour. Pain was minimal but discomfort not insignificant. I had to sleep for the next week sitting up at a 45-degree angle to minimize swelling. Movement and shifting were anything but subtle, requiring the full body to work in sync whenever I needed to move.

DAY ONE: RECOVERY

Just call me Pumpkin Head. I seem to have swollen up beyond recognition. Dr Stanek is at my bedside at 7.15 a.m. and spares me the gruesome specifics of the operation itself but insists that I rest for the next several days to achieve the best results.

On my second shuftie into the loo I catch a glimpse of myself in the mirror and see two Martian-like bobbles, filled with blood, on the top of my head. These are obviously reservoirs, draining blood from somewhere. In my groggy state I try and think where the blood could be coming from. Back in bed, I start to examine my head and neck very gingerly to discover two drain lines running in my scalp down inside my neck behind each ear. I touch them and nearly pass out. Now

every time I think of the drains I want to vomit. As I am checking out of the hospital at noon I only have to suffer the sensation another few hours.

A nurse returns later to remove the drains and to show me how to manage the 'second skin' masks that I will need to change three times a day for the next five days. All seems too skilled for both my fingers and brain but I am packed off with instruction sheets and my DIY face repair kit for home. Wrapped up with my mummy mask, I put on a chic headscarf and 'Jackie O' sunglasses and pose in front of the clinic for a pic. Who wouldn't want to remember today?

DAY TWO

Masked up into my 'second skin' I only have a peephole for my mouth so am limited to drinking and eating with a straw. Only water is palatable through a plastic straw. Even though I am dying for a cup of tea on this second morning, I give up after one suck. By now, I am starving, not having eaten for forty-eight hours. Mouth movement is severely limited so decide to try some oatmeal. Remove the mask for long enough to savour a bowlful and, feel so satiated, I sleep soundly for the first time since the operation.

Masked up into my 'second skin' I only have a peephole for my mouth so am limited to drinking and eating with a straw.

Although I have a pack of painkillers, I avoid taking them as the pain isn't so bad and I prefer to keep lucid to mumble pathetic nothings to my daughters, Anna, fifteen, and Lucy, twelve, who are now in full Florence Nightingale-mode, competing with each other for head nurse post.

After my morning nap, I convince myself that a slow shuffle around the park with my husband would do me the world of good. Wrap-up like Greta Garbo and hit the park on a brilliant Saturday morning. I feel his embarrassment as he senses the stares of passers-by. Oddly, the next morning my fifteen-year-old daughter would guide me about the park totally oblivious to the horror-struck strangers, remarking, 'If they don't like it, it's their problem.'

Seeing me in this limpid, unrecognizable state made my husband uncomfortable. He didn't have to say so but when he announced that he simply had to drive down to our country house that morning to clean out the garage and not return for a day or two I read between

the lines. He had to bolt as the sight of me was turning his stomach. But I was in good hands with my daughters Anna and Lucy now taking turns napping next to me in bed, applying ointment to my stitches, fetching ice packs from the freezer every hour and whipping up quite unimaginable treats in the blender.

Of the three procedures that I have had – facelift, eye job and laser resurfacing – it is the latter that is causing me all the grief. But Stanek insisted that without it the facelift would be less effective. My face is now throbbing, itching, oozing. I find the 'second skin' mask claustrophobic. I want to rip it off my face but know that its cooling sensation is better than the hot throbbing without. The staples in my head, running vertically along behind my ears, are getting itchy.

Because I have been vegging for almost three days I can't sleep for very long. This second night drags on endlessly and is only alleviated in its tedium by the BBC World Service. Have caught up on all the essential goings on in Azerbaijan, Mexico City and Algeria. Looking forward to not having to use eye potions tomorrow so that I can read and watch a bit of TV, having discovered that listening to television without seeing it has to be the most mindless of exercises. My heart goes out to any housebound blind person without access to a Braille lending library after this experience!

DAY THREE

Full of energy this morning and start the day at 5 a.m. keen for a walk. Venture out on my own (dumb) and do two miles. Return feeling a bit feeble and quite faint, realizing that if I had, indeed, fainted it would not have been good news. So, went back to bed and waited for one of the girls to escort me for another loop a few hours later.

Manage to load and unload the dishwasher, tidy (I think) the kitchen and make a few phone calls to friends using the speakerphone. The line of stitches in front and behind the ears makes nestling a handset uncomfortable. My mouth still won't expand beyond the width of a teaspoon, so managing on chicken soup and milk shakes that are nutritious and satisfying. Used Melatonin to help me sleep tonight.

DAY FOUR

Monday morning and everyone but me is off to school and the office. Walked the dogs at 6 a.m. with confidence and aplomb but scared the

Diary of My Facelift

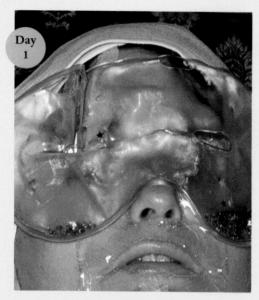

Day 1

Day 2

Tender and swollen. Only solution is the icepack for the eyes.

Back on my feet and ready to go!

The effects of laser more evident immediately than the facelift.

A neat job, with the stitching around the ear and sutures hidden in the hairline.

Day 3

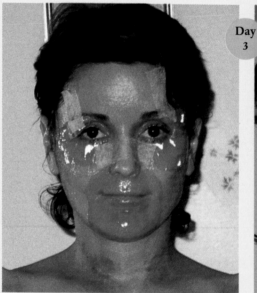

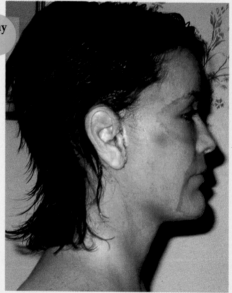

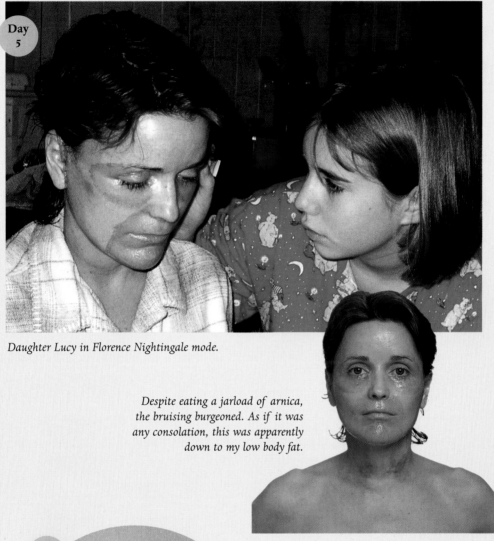

Day 5

Daughter Lucy in Florence Nightingale mode.

Despite eating a jarload of arnica, the bruising burgeoned. As if it was any consolation, this was apparently down to my low body fat.

Day 14

Doing a photo shoot for Sainsbury's The Magazine I wore a thick layer of concealer/foundation, was still slightly swollen, and fashioned a slightly strange hairstyle to hide the stitches.

hell out of the porter when I returned forgetting I am still swathed in my mummy mask. Later stripped off the last layer and switched to lathering my skin for the next three days in Vaseline. Liberation!

Seeing perfectly fine today so hit the computer and telephone with vigour, although needed an hour-long nap midday to recover from all the activity. Photo session scheduled at teatime to coincide with visiting, gawking friends from the office. My husband returns from work and is so thrilled to see my normal, yet wrinkle-free, face returning invites me out to the movies!

Seeing perfectly fine today so hit the computer and telephone with vigour.

DAY SEVEN

Walked five miles to Stanek's office to have my staples and stitches removed and collect my pot of camouflage cream that works a treat at masking my pink, lasered skin. Working the cream as concealer, all I need to do is blend a bit of my own foundation and eureka, normal skin!

Stanek is a bit shocked at the whopping bruises on my neck. I blamed him but confessed that I'm a bit of a bruiser, despite eating a packet of arnica tablets.

The next night I would go out for drinks with friends and my camouflage make-up fooled everyone. Well, no one mentioned either my skin or my long-lost bags and wrinkles. I was very pleased.

PS

The lasered skin healed more quickly when I switched from lathering my face with Vaseline as recommended (a great protector but *not* a moisturizer) to washing and moisturizing my face with the wonderful and inexpensive E45 products. Within the first day of usage, my skin looked much improved and make-up went on more effectively. I would recommend it to anyone having laser. Dermablend camouflage cream and one-step powder foundation both worked well in concealing the red, lasered skin beneath. It would take five weeks before I could get away with my own foundation, never forgetting to use an SPF30 sunscreen first to ensure that my beautiful new skin stayed unlined for as long as possible.

After two weeks, I was doing television interviews, conducting seminars and going out to dinner without anyone being aware that I was recovering from such extensive cosmetic surgery. By week three, I spent a day training a group of consultants and only received compliments like, 'You look rested, Mary. Been away?' At a plenary session during our annual conference the next day, I announced the 'new me' and was besieged by gawping women wanting a closer inspection. I was delighted to oblige them and you, too, with pictures of me before, during and after.

Anything's Possible

Eventually, it's been predicted that, thanks to bioengineering and cloning possibilities, almost every organ system will be able to benefit from retoning, retuning or replacing. Already synthetic veins, bladders and heart valves are available, and skin can be grown or synthesized in a laboratory. The increasing sophistication of keyhole surgery, coupled with the use of lasers, means cosmetic surgery scars will become smaller and less visible. Some doctors are reportedly even doing breast implants through the navel to avoid scars at all and a total free transplant is on the cards. With the new techniques and better anaesthetics, recovery has become quicker and prices have been coming down thanks to less time needed for post-op care and drugs. A generation raised to be comfortable with technology is not afraid to shop around for a new nose or to remove an unsightly new bag. One young man in his thirties had six different cosmetic surgery procedures including liposuction on 'love handles', lip enhancement, jawline enhancement and pectoral implants. As he put it, 'I would be more obsessed with my looks if I kept having to look in the mirror every day and see things I didn't like. We have the technology to change what I don't like and then I can get on with my life.'

Some doctors are reportedly even doing breast implants through the navel to avoid any scars.

New technology also makes it possible – even at the hairdresser's, let alone the plastic surgeon's – to see what you'll look like with the change you desire before you take the plunge. Computer programmes similar to those used by the police for their photofit pictures of criminals allow you to see whether that retroussé nose and stronger chin would really suit you.

'Everybody's' Doing It

Around 3 million people a year have cosmetic surgery in the States and around 65,000 in Britain. Nine out of ten are, not surprisingly, women, but the percentage of male patients is going up quickly, particularly now that buttock, pectoral, calf and penile implants are available. I have advised many a corporate executive to rectify a hang-up like protruding ears or eye bags, with many willingly taking up the suggestion.

Breast enhancement is by and large the most popular type of cosmetic surgery.

With the introduction of resurfacing lasers and modified facelift techniques the 'full Monty' of the traditional facelift might be on the wane. Breast enhancement is by and large the most popular type of cosmetic surgery, generally among younger women, the facelift coming second. Even teenagers today are requesting cosmetic surgery to help them look like their idols. Britain's Jackie Randle made headlines at fourteen by saying she was saving up her £5 a week pocket money for cheek implants and liposuction to her thighs to help her turn her podgy schoolgirl looks into those of her heroines Claudia Schiffer or Julia Roberts. Reputable aesthetic plastic surgeons were aghast at the prospect but there's no doubt some would take her money.

The rumour machine has it that few Hollywood stars have not had something done by the time they've reached fifty and that age is dropping, however much they deny it. Melanie Griffiths reportedly had breast augmentation during a break in filming, claiming that the part called for a more voluptuous physique. Political wives such as Raisa Gorbachev, Nancy Reagan and Betty Ford have all benefited from facelifts. Some well-known people, like the sylphlike singer Cher for example, are more open about cosmetic surgery than others. Even Jane Fonda, who persistently claimed that exercise was enough, eventually succumbed to surgery in the pursuit of the perfect body.

The face that Julie Christie presents to the world in her Oscar-nominated performance as the frustrated wife in *Afterglow* looks beautiful, natural and worth more than every penny she must have paid to achieve it. She is a stunning woman who has worked hard to keep in shape, so what is wrong with her resorting to measures to keep her face as fit as her body? If anything, post-facelift Christie looks more 'herself' than the pre-facelift version.

Not all experiences for beautifying oneself or turning back the clock are happy, however, and many a woman has been scarred physically and emotionally for life. Former model and wife of Rod Stewart, Alana Hamilton, had her silicone breast implants removed, claiming, as hundreds more have, that they ruined her life, causing her to suffer from chronic fatigue syndrome and infections, although the jury is still out on this issue, some studies declaring them safe. So, the wise woman contemplating any surgical solution should learn as much as she can about the latest procedures and only choose a qualified surgeon who willingly gives you bona fide patients to speak to about their experiences.

Early Measures Best

When it comes to rejuvenating plastic surgery, the leading American plastic surgeon Dr Gerald Imber, author of *The Youth Corridor*, believes in early intervention. He has clients who come to him in their early thirties for procedures such as laser resurfacing incipient crow's feet and, a favourite with him, to have the corrugator muscles that create frown lines in the forehead divided. That prevents developing deepening furrows between the eyes that can be so ageing.

The new types of anti-ageing surgery go beyond standard cosmetic surgery techniques.

He favours the modified S-lift facelift, so named for the S-shaped incision just behind the hairline, and likes to perform it at a much earlier age than the traditional full facelift. 'It is designed for the earlier stages of facial loosening,' he explains. 'It tightens the skin and underlying muscle, effectively lifting everything as in a cradle from under the chin to the forehead ... [in] consistently younger patients who are unwilling to wait for things to get out of hand.' For younger women he might also recommend microsuction of the jawline, a sort of microscopic liposuction for the little bit of fat that can make the jaw look less youthful from about the age of thirty-five. As with many other cosmetic surgery procedures today, this can be done under local anaesthetic and sedation, while the patient is in a 'twilight' state, which does away with some of the dangers associated with deep anaesthetic.

Endoscopic treatments are performed through pinholes with a tiny endoscopic camera sending pictures back to guide the surgeon. These have minimized scarring in facelifts and browlifts and make possible deeper knitting together of tissues beneath the skin for better results.

Dr Vincent Giampapa, a leading American aesthetic plastic surgeon and in the forefront of the anti-ageing medicine field with his Longevity Institute International, says that the new types of 'anti-ageing surgery go beyond standard cosmetic surgery techniques'. Giampapa, who has perfected a fifty-minute necklift which doesn't require a general anaesthetic, says, 'In anti-ageing surgery we begin by evaluating photos of patients when they were at the peak of their physical appearance and try to bring them back to that state.' This might involve removing some of the cartilage at the end of the nose, which lengthens with time, and shortening the earlobes which also become longer as we age rather than simply giving them a standard brow- or facelift. Portions of fat may be repositioned or transplanted into certain areas of the face which have lost that underlying layer, but the idea is not to change the key features or personality. Dr Giampapa also believes in preparing his patients for surgery with strong vitamin and mineral supplements, high levels of antioxidants and even by augmenting hormonal levels if necessary.

Many procedures can simply be done under local anaesthetic.

A Shopping List of Surgical Solutions

ABDOMINOPLASTY

This tummy tuck is for looseness around the abdomen from pregnancy, weight gain and loss, or simply from the effect of the forces of gravity and bad posture. Some overweight women have an 'apron' effect of flesh on their front which will not disappear and can even become more pronounced if they lose weight later in life. A 'mini tuck' is for small amounts of excess flesh, with a 'full tuck' tackling more bulk. Some call this a 'Body Lift' with loose flesh cut away and belly buttons repositioned. Loose muscles can be tightened during liposuction. Scars are similar to those for hysterectomy and a special girdle will need to

be worn for up to a month after surgery. There can be numbness and considerable discomfort. Costs are from around £4,000.

BLEPHAROPLASTY

This involves removing excess skin on or around the eyelids and sucking out any pads of fat if necessary. Most commonly performed on people in their forties, it is one of the earliest popular cosmetic surgery procedures because of the delicate nature of the tissues around the eyes. Possible ways of avoiding the necessity for having this procedure include not rubbing your eyes, inserting and removing contact lenses with great care, and taking off eye make-up gently with a non-oily eye make-up remover instead of scrubbing with a facial cleanser. Also take care with applying eye make-up, using good brushes instead of foam applicators which drag the skin. Complications can include tear-production prob-lems after surgery, leading to 'dry eyes', or diffi-culty in closing the eyes if too much skin is removed. Costs range from £2,000 to £5,000.

In addition to liposuction, bottom implants can be carried out to create perkier rears.

For younger women with puffy lower eyelids but no loose skin, what is called a 'subconjunctival blepharoplasty' can be performed. No incision is necessary as this operation is undertaken through the inside of the lower eyelid. It costs about half as much as blepharoplasty.

BOTTOM LIFT

In addition to liposuction, see below, bottom implants can be carried out to create perkier bottoms, an operation which particularly appeals to gay men. British surgeons generally shy away from this but one Hollywood surgeon has perfected the technique of positioning the implant so that it is held snugly by interlaced muscles and not simply beneath the skin where it can slip and slide away. Costs upwards of £3,000.

BRACHIOPLASTY

Lifts and tightens upper arm skin which can be particularly trouble-some after weight loss over forty-five when it grows crêpier and saggier

with time. If you can't bear lifting weights maybe this is for you. A scar will result under your armpit. Costs from £2,000.

BREAST AUGMENTATION

This is an increasingly common operation among younger women which is supposed not to interfere with the ability to breast-feed. Silicone, saline or soya implants are inserted behind the breast, usually from the crease beneath the breast or sometimes from the armpit in order to hide the scars. Bruising may take over a month to disappear and patients can sometimes complain of numbness or hardness in the area after surgery. Infections may require antibiotics.

Silicone implants have been implicated in a wide range of auto-immune diseases although many doctors feel they are perfectly safe. Implants can burst with pressure on sudden impact. But whereas older implants made mammography-reading difficult, the newer soya and saline models are translucent. Implants cost from around £3,000.

BREAST REDUCTION

Breast reduction is a way of defeating gravity and making pendulous breasts perkier as well as smaller. The nipple will be removed and excess tissue taken from an incision beneath it before the nipple is replaced in a new, higher-up position and the breast stitched. Some scarring will be visible in this operation and, as with breast enlargement, some hard scar tissue may develop. The breasts will never feel the same again.

After all breast operations bras must be worn day and night for six weeks and breasts need to be massaged to prevent them from hardening. Breast reduction costs around £5,000.

BROWLIFT

An endoscopic browlift involves keyhole surgery with five tiny incisions an inch deep into the hairline. Small studs or staples are used to lift the skin and removed a week later. Beneath are the dissolving stitches which hold the newly lifted skin in position. Some bruising results around the eyes and creeps down the face over a week, but after seven days you are ready to see the world. This costs about £1,500.

CHIN AND CHEEK WORK

Double chins can often be corrected by liposuction or liposculpture alone, but sometimes the loose skin that is left needs to be tightened with facelift techniques (see below). Cheeks can either be hollowed and resculpted with liposuction, or wrinkles plumped out by injections of the patient's own fat, or from the new moulded hard tissue replacement (HTR) polymer implants which are beginning to replace silicone in popularity for girding up cheekbones and weak chins. This sort of work can cost anything from £1,500 to £5,000, depending on the complexity.

DERMABRASION

Dermabrasion or skin resurfacing is good for removing fine lines on the face such as those that can form around the lips, causing lipstick to 'bleed'. The operation can be performed by scraping with a fine brush or, more recently, with ultra-pulsed, carbon-dioxide lasers. The skin can become very red and sensitive in the areas treated, and may flake or crust, but within two weeks fresh new skin will appear. However, it could be two months or more before it blends in with the rest of the face so be prepared to have good quality concealing make-up on hand to blend everything in. Laser treatment is said to stimulate collagen production and tighten the skin, and causes less loss of pigmentation than other types of treatment. A similar effect can be had from facial peels with alpha hydroxy acids (AHAs, see Chapter Five) or fruit acids. Dermabrasion costs from about £500.

If you don't choose your surgeon well, the dreaded 'wind tunnel' effect, or look of permanent surprise, may result!

FACELIFT

This procedure lifts loosened skin on the face and neck, pulling it back and, where necessary, tightening the underlying muscles. Recovery time is usually about two weeks. Complications can include possible injury to a facial nerve, blood clots and, if you don't choose your surgeon well, the dreaded 'wind tunnel' effect or look of permanent surprise.

There are many different facelift techniques, some of them endoscopic, and it pays to shop around and compare carefully. Different

surgeons have their specialities, like Dr Imber's S-lift. At least women usually have plenty of hair under which to hide the scars which are about an inch long behind the ears. Facelifts cost from £4,000.

FAT TRANSPLANTS

These are suitable for small areas that need plumping up with subcutaneous fat, like worry or frown lines, hollow cheeks and even ageing hands. Fat is taken by liposuction (see below) from areas that can spare it, like the stomach or buttocks, then injected where it is needed. The problem is that fat can slip and be broken down and reabsorbed and is therefore not a permanent solution. The procedure may need to be repeated, as only some of the transplanted fat cells will survive. Fat transplants are the first breakthrough for ageing hands and can dramatically disguise the crêpey texture of older hands. They can also be used in the lips. Transplants cost from £200.

FROWN LINE PREVENTION

This entails cutting the expressive facial muscles called the corrugator muscle. It costs from £2,000. Botox injections also produce similar results. See non-surgical techniques.

LIP SERVICE

Chieloplasty, as this operation is technically known, means that lips which thin and wrinkle with age can be plumped out by some of the techniques such as collagen injections or Gore-Tex implants. Lips can be outlined with a more solid filler like Artecol and then infilled with collagen or Hylaform (see below).

LIPOSUCTION AND LIPOSCULPTURE

Liposuction is performed to remove excess fat from the bottom, thighs, stomach or waistline. It is only recommended when diet and exercise have failed. Some women can be very slim on top but suffer from 'saddlebag' thighs or fat on the inside of the knees, or even podgy ankles, which drives them crazy.

Liposuction can also break up areas of cellulite. Fat is liquefied by injecting enzymes or using ultrasound. It is then vacuum-pumped out of the body under local or general anaesthetic depending on the area. Pressurized bandages would usually be worn for a week afterwards full time and for up to a month part time. This procedure is less successful in people over forty-five who have less elastic skin and can lead to lumpiness or unevenness with a less skilled practitioner.

Ultrasonic liposuction emulsifies and sucks out fat with less likelihood of bruising and blood loss.

Ultrasonic liposuction emulsifies and sucks out fat with less likelihood of bruising and blood loss. Liposculpture on the other hand is usually performed with smaller syringes in a manner that is more precise than liposuction but only used on smaller areas such as face, ankles, calves or knees. Costs start around £1,000.

NECKLIFT

Not an easy area to help, the neck is one of the first to show signs of ageing with the loose, crêpey skin often making a woman appear older than she might be. By fifty, the platysma muscle divides so that two cords appear at the front of the neck. Dr Vincent Giampapa has developed a fifty-five-minute necklift called the suture suspension technique that can be done under sedation and local anaesthetic that seems, from photo displays in his office, to have amazing results on even the grossest 'turkey necks'. Suspending the neck muscles by two sutures, it requires only a small incision under the chin and one behind each ear and no general anaesthesia. Dr Giampapa says, 'There are no nerves to injure and very little lifting of the skin at all which limits the danger of haemotoma or blood collection.' This costs about £3,000.

VARICOSE VEIN REMOVAL

These unsightly blue badges of age and unhealthiness can be both surgically and non-surgically removed. 'Avulsion' means cutting the offending vein into several sections and removing them individually through tiny incisions which are hardly visible after a couple of months. 'Stripping' involves putting a wire down the varicose vein and trying to pull it out in one piece. This is an older technique performed under general

anaesthetic, whereas 'Avulsion' allows a quicker recovery time. But remember that varicose veins can return if circulation to the area is not improved. Varicose vein removal costs from about £500.

Thread veins, little spidery veins lying closer to the surface of the skin than varicose veins and often developing on the face, can be treated with injections to close them off (sclerotherapy) or with laser or electrolysis. This costs from £75.

Non-surgical Alternatives

BOTULIN TOXIN TREATMENT

Botox – a poisonous Botulin toxin – can be injected to paralyse the facial muscles (the corrugators) that cause certain wrinkles such as worry lines on the forehead. But the effect is temporary and the procedure would need to be regularly repeated about every three or four months at a cost of about £150 a treatment.

CACI

CACI, the first non-surgical facelift, has been reputedly favoured by many celebrities both male and female. It works by passing a micro-electric current through facial muscles to 're-educate and re-tone' them. CACI stands for computer aided cosmetology instrument and works rather like Slendertone and other muscle-twitching devices do on the body. It is supposed to be like taking your face to the gym. The initial treatment involves a dozen sections, starting with three a week and then one every six to eight weeks. It costs about £45 from salons.

CELLULOIPOLYSIS

A treatment to reduce the appearance of cellulite, this involves the insertion of eight pairs of fine needle electrodes into the affected areas. A current is turned on and slowly turned up. Over 50,000 European women are said to have tried this, perhaps because of its double benefits of making the skin look better as well as reducing the size of the thighs. The only side effect is bruising. Six sessions cost £1,000 but the results are said to last for years.

COLLAGEN INJECTIONS AND OTHER FILLERS

For plumping up the skin to get rid of wrinkles on the face and/or to make lips fuller and less lined. As collagen is a bovine version of what we all have in our skins, we should perhaps be cautious in this era of 'mad cow' concern, but it is commonly used and has not been implicated in any health scare that we know of at the time of writing, although some women can *reject* it. The skin is anaesthetized so the injections should be painless and the procedure usually doesn't take more than half an hour and is often done during people's lunch breaks.

The effects, which are immediate and often dramatically good, are, alas, only temporary as the collagen will always break down and disappear within about six months. Regular treatments are needed for this to be effective. Problems can include an allergy to collagen.

> *The effects, which are immediate and often dramatically good, are, alas, only temporary.*

Hylaform is a newer form of filler which is said to cause no allergic reaction. But it also only lasts up to about six months. Artecol is a combination of collagen and plastic cement particles which is good for deeper furrows such as the nasolabial lines that run from the nose to the corners of the mouth. Gore-Tex, the same fabric used in outdoor clothes, is effective for plumping up lips that have grown thinner with time. One thread or two can be used depending on the thickness desired. Gore-Tex is permanent, but can be removed – rather like pulling the drawstring out of a tracksuit hood.

CLEO II involves sticking little electronic sensors on your facial muscles or other muscles and letting them be electronically twitched. This could be seen as a home version of CACI.

COSMETIC DENTISTRY

One of the first things starlets and models are ordered to have done is their teeth if they look a bit wonky or discoloured. With the amazing array of gadgetry and treatments available today there is no excuse not to smile to your fullest because of bad teeth. Fake 'gum guards' can be worn over the teeth if you are looking a bit 'long in the tooth' and veneers can cover any crack or fill a space to give you a near perfect set of teeth. Some bleaching treatments (see the *Baywatch* babes) are still illegal in Europe but good hygienists can work wonders on

tea, red wine or caffeine stains. Costs vary dramatically so it pays to shop around.

FACIAL FLEX

Facial Flex is becoming the butt of television comedians as the American 'advertorials' are hilarious to watch. It is comprised of a metal and rubber band instrument of torture designed to workout the face when you compress it in your mouth. In only four minutes a day over two months your face muscles are claimed to be improved – firm and lifted. It costs about £50.

INTEGRAPLUS

Another home treatment machine, portable, and about the size of a mobile phone, Integraplus passes 'micro currents' through the skin, supposedly to speed up circulation and encourage collagen production. It costs about £200.

OXYGEN THERAPY

This is probably the hottest concept at the time of writing, with models such as Cindy Crawford and Christy Turlington going for it at New York's exclusive Bliss Day spa. It involves 'blasting' the skin with pure oxygen supplemented by 'oxygen-enhanced' creams. Some companies such as Karen Herzog offer oxygen facials with an increasing number of cosmetic companies launching oxygen products which should be more than a lot of hot air with price tags around £75 for either a therapy session or a bottle of cream.

REJUVANESSENCE

Rejuvanessence is a facial massage which claims to pump out the skin and leave it more elastic. A month's course of six treatments costs around £400.

SKIN REGENERATION

This is an outgrowth of CACI, using ultrasound vibrations to peel off the top layer of skin to improve the appearance and tone of the face. It is said to be more pleasant than chemical peeling in a salon, with high-concentration AHAs (alpha hydroxy acids) but works much the same way and leaves the skin firmer. Gel is put on the face and scraped off. It costs about £30 a session from salons.

ULTRA TONE FACIAL

This is a home unit with two probes to charge a current through the skin. You're supposed to use this daily to plump up the skin and to tone underlying muscles. It costs about £20.

Keeping Apace

Every week there seems to be some new cosmetic surgery development or break-through which promises to make us all look younger or sort out our most niggling body flaw. But resist the urge to be a guinea pig for the 'latest and the greatest', and rely more on valid research findings published in medical journals than what you might read in the tabloid press. If you see a reference to a new study in a magazine or newspaper, call and get a copy of the complete report to read the findings for yourself.

Many valid, safe and less expensive techniques become available each year. But as with any cosmetic surgery procedure, you must probe the specialists to establish what training and experience s/he has for doing the work. And finally, always get a second or third opinion.

7

Doing It In Style

'Age cannot wither her,
nor custom stale her infinite variety.'

SHAKESPEARE, *Antony and Cleopatra*

If you have the 'infinite variety' Shakespeare attributed to Cleopatra, then custom certainly can't 'stale' you even if age may eventually wither you. As an image consultant, I am interviewed regularly about how to dress in ways that don't give away your age. The whole subject of dress guidelines according to your age implies that at thirty-five or forty-five or sixty you can't do certain things and it leaves me a bit cold. Indeed, we have all sympathized with the poor dear who wears unflattering clothes geared more for a daughter or, worse, granddaughter. But maybe she feels terrific and the people she cares about love her that way. Then there are the characters that break all the rules in the book and look wonderful. Who are we to judge?

But judge we do because appearances do matter. We dress for both private and public pleasure and know that what others think can matter a lot to us. You might be at a point in your life where you don't give a hoot about what people think. But if you are still working or looking to influence others or to make new friends, you might be wise to consider some of the signals your clothes send out about you.

What Are You Trying to Project?

Don't be unconscious about your look, be definitive. The way you dress speaks volumes about the kind of woman you are at this point in your life. That's why wearing the same old gear that did the job fine a few years ago might be letting you down now when you want people to view you differently as someone capable of *new* things. But bear in mind that a new look does not mean a whole new wardrobe. Women hoard some amazing gems over the years and often require just a reshuffle, along with a few new accessories or simple bits to bring the look bang up to date.

The way you dress speaks volumes about the kind of woman you are at this point in your life.

In your head there is an image of yourself, not the one you sigh over when you feel down in the dumps – the one you dream about, that gets wonderful reactions from others. What do you look like? How do you behave that gets the people you want to respond how you want? It's time to make that dream a reality. No one is holding you back but yourself. Expect friends and family to resist changes in your image because they love you how you are, no

matter how you look. Explain that a new look is important to you and bring them along on the journey of discovery as you recreate yourself into the new woman you dream of being, and probably *need* to become, for the next phase of your life.

Ruts and Mistakes are Inevitable

None of us, even the experts, can say that we have never been in a style rut or made some pretty nasty mistakes. We tend to stick to tried and tested favourites in labels, in colours, in cuts without appreciating that our body, our colouring, our lifestyles have changed. To shed an old image is liberating. Both your body as well as your personality can shout 'Hallelujah!' as a result.

To see if your image is in a rut, answer the following questions with true or false:

1. As long as you are well groomed and wear expensive clothes you will always look smart. *True/False*

2. Pearls finish off an evening look better than anything. *True/False*

3. When in doubt, nude sheer hosiery does the job. *True/False*

4. You can't go wrong with a black or navy suit. They are always smart and can be brightened up with many different colours. *True/False*

5. Simple court shoes are your best investment for shoes as they work with skirts or trousers. *True/False*

6. If you have nice legs, stick to shorter skirts. *True/False*

7. Matching nail and lip colour is elegant. *True/False*

8. I have worn my hair pretty much the same way for ten years. *True/False*

9. A long sweater or jacket hides a multitude of sins. *True/False*

10. Pretty scarves can hide an ageing neck. *True/False*

ANSWERS

Fewer than 2 True Answers: 'Still aspirational'

You know what suits you but don't want to play it predictable or safe. Even though your legs might be shapely you know that if short skirts are out of fashion you will look your age by sticking to them. Your hosiery drawer offers a range of texture, colour and denier along with some funky, sporty socks. You know that while black and navy are sooooo flexible they can also be ageing colours. Your photo albums will attest to your experimentation over the years, which means you still want to be contemporary, regardless of your age.

3 to 6 True Answers: 'Struggling and confused'

You like the safety of knowing what's appropriate for an occasion and looking the part. Perhaps you aren't ready to stand out of the crowd, but you do want some guidance in breaking old habits that are, quite frankly, making you look and feel old as well. You love all the newer accessories but aren't sure how to select winners or wear them. And if you are still wearing matching lip and nail colour, be sure you turn to Chapter Five for ideas on how to break out of the 'elegant dowager' mode.

7 to 10 True Answers: 'Well and truly stuck in that rut'

Safety and camouflage are your guiding principles as you don't want others to realize that your figure, in particular, isn't what it used to be. Whose is? You aren't a bag lady, woman, so stop hiding away under shapeless sacks. There are plenty of clever ways to disguise broad hips other than big sloppy jumpers. And although your neck is showing its age, stuffing it under a prissy scarf is as good as announcing to the world how crêpey things are underneath. If your neck doesn't have the length or space for wearing scarves, you will look fatter as well as older. Who needs that? You will learn plenty of ideas for taking care of your neck and features in Chapter Five and getting your body into the best shape possible in Chapter Nine, but read on if you want to leave your rut behind.

Retiring last year at 60 meant that Jill could increase her tennis playing from twice to six times weekly. She's now got a figure to die for – and is a true UltraAger. 'But my wardrobe is really confused,' she confessed when she applied for a makeover.

'As a doctor's receptionist for 20 years, my dress code was jackets and skirts. Trousers just weren't acceptable – which was a real bore.' Now, Jill rarely puts on a dress or skirt! 'But my husband likes me to look more feminine, so I'm open to some suggestions.'

Like other women who finally give in to their grey hair, Jill is still wearing colours that were fine when hers was its naturally shade – in her case, warm and auburn. But dark browns and olives now make her look tired, and her pretty grey hair, well, pretty lifeless.

Jill has been going to the same hairdresser for 19 years. She does a lovely job, but isn't the hairdresser to give Jill a new look. So if, like Jill, you want a revamp, try elsewhere. You can return to your beloved stylist with your new look for them to copy. Tell them a white lie, that you had it done while travelling, if you don't want to hurt their feelings! We wanted to try a more relaxed look for Jill, which we knew would be fresher and more modern for her.

For clothes, Jill needs to move away from dark colours and golden tones to soft, cool colours like this pretty teal blue, more flattering to her hair and skin. In Color Me Beautiful 'speak', Jill is now a Soft Summer. The knit dress presents a feminine alternative to her trousers, but it's still comfortable – Jill's main priority.

We've 'broken up' Jill's hairstyle, and introduced her to some new products to help her recreate the look easily herself. A light styling mousse gives her more volume, and a top dressing of a light pomade or wax gives the hair more texture.

Lucy, a 43-year-old mother of two teenaged children, has found an enterprising way to work from home since her children were young. A nutritional consultant advising on everything from vitamin supplements to nourishing face creams, Lucy follows a strict beauty regime to keep her beautiful skin moist and supple.

'I cleanse, exfoliate, feed, firm and protect every morning and night, no matter how tired I am,' she explains. Because of her commitment to skin care, Lucy doesn't have to wear any

Having just turned 50, Christine admits that the anticipation of the milestone was worse than the arrival. 'I dreaded this birthday and was questioning so many things about my life. I felt that I had to re-evaluate my career, especially because the extensive travelling it has involved was really taking a toll on me, and no longer providing the enjoyment it once did.' Christine is a senior hotel inspector for the national tourist board. 'Sumptuous dinners and fully-cooked breakfasts on each trip also meant problems for my figure.'

Christine's husband Martin had also begun making more comments about her looking drab and frumpy. Perhaps her stunning looks and soft figure weren't necessarily complimented by the severe suits she used to wear for work.' But he's always looked 10 years younger than he is, and loves fashion, so keeping up with him has taken some effort. It's no fun

foundation on her flawless complexion. Her active schedule along with a weekly tennis session is all she needs to keep her petite frame trim. But she's as fanatical about her food as she is about her skin.

Lucy's interest in nutrition came about from a bout of chronic fatigue syndrome, combined with candida albicans when she was a young mother. But her present diet, together with nutritional supplements, keeps her fit and healthy.

Although a proponent of natural beauty and nutrition, Lucy was amenable to shedding her 'natural' colours for bolder ones when she learned that clear colours were more complimentary on her. To really make an impact in her presentations, we recommended royal blue for a jacket – a colour that's both confident and approachable. Lucy can also team it with many other colours for variety year round, so it's a great investment.

living with Peter Pan!' she says half-jokingly.

Without a line on her face, Christine is a champion of good skin care, and could certainly pass for someone much younger. Her striking colouring means that make-up can be minimal, particularly with such glowing skin. All Christine needed was a new hairstyle. Wearing long hair up in a new way can actually make women look younger – fear of the opposite effect is a misconception arising from probably not doing it right! A scraped-back bun will do little for anyone over 25, but a twist secured with an attractive clip and polished with a glossy wax is both simple (only three minutes!) and stunning.

We suggested Christine abandons her tailored jackets and suits and switches to knits and jersey combinations instead. 'My husband was convinced that this was an expensive designer outfit. He couldn't possibly believe it came from my favourite chain store (the same place as all those boring suits had come from!).' Not only do softer fabrics and tailoring travel more easily; they are also more flattering on a curvy figure.

Christine's philosophy for staying young is to mix with younger people – 'Tonight I'm having supper with five friends, all in their 30s.' She also goes on new adventures and keeps learning new things. 'Last year I tried canoeing, this year we are off pony-trekking. I am also learning to ring church bells – very good for toning up the bust!'

What it Takes

My strategy to guide a woman somewhere new, better, with her look is to help her forget what she used to be when she was younger, perhaps slimmer or what she considers to have been a previous prime time. A rethink must start from zero then proceed from there with the new dream. It's not a total reinvention of the wheel because you have learned so much and have developed an affinity for many aspects of your own style. These can and should be woven back into the new look but shouldn't be the basis from where you start. That is, if you really are game for a new image.

If you are ready for a quantum leap, what adjectives would describe the new look? Out of the following list, circle the top five you want to describe your style: modern, elegant, chic, expensive, colourful, relaxed, continental, ethnic, classic, feminine, eclectic, streamlined, sexy, simple, country, powerful, creative, dramatic, individual, casual, romantic, approachable, vibrant, understated, comfortable, international, sporty, futuristic, professional, fun.

How compatible are the values on your list? If you have some diametrically opposed images, for example, classic and eclectic, then you need to ask yourself a) if you are feeling a bit schizophrenic today; or b) have you been one thing for a while, for example, classic, but really now dream of being more creative, individual and eclectic? Work to develop a concept that will describe the dream. For example, a woman who wants to look romantic can also be modern, comfortable, individual, simple and country. 'Romantic' doesn't mean sexy necessarily; but if it does to you, girl, go for it!

Face Your Own Wardrobe

Lay out on your bed a few outfits that you normally wear. Pick daytime: perhaps a work ensemble, a casual look and a dressy outfit. Okay. Now look at the adjectives you want to describe your style. How compatible are they: your new values and your current clothes? Don't grab a bin liner yet – you might well be able to reshuffle your items to achieve your desired look later.

Do be ruthless in editing out anything that no longer fits, however. Be honest: it's unlikely ever to do so. Even if you get back to that size again, it's bound to look well past its sell-by date by the time you do.

Next, inspect things that you rummage by daily, weekly and monthly, consider for a moment but always put back, choosing something else instead. Why do you pass it up? Is it uncomfortable? Worn out? Unflattering? Or is it just a white elephant, bought when the hormones were doing high jumps, that refuses to coordinate with anything else? If you say yes to any of these questions as you edit through your wardrobe, put the item to one side to give to someone who will be thrilled with it: there's bound to be someone.

Now you are left with clothes that you like and others that you simply can't bear to part with yet. Your task now is to see how you can rework what you have into new, more exciting, more modern combinations to make you look and feel that dream.

Capsules Easiest to Swallow

Every season discipline yourself to clear away any and all superfluous items, limiting yourself to a core capsule of clothes that easily work together. Store perfectly good, perhaps dated (this season only?) gems out of sight as you know that you won't be choosing them and they are only cluttering up the wardrobe.

Unless you are desperate for space, hold on to all your 'antiques' as you never know when you or your children or grandchildren will be in need of a 'fancy-dress' costume. Avoid piling the lot into a bin liner and stuffing it away, unable to determine what's inside. Invest in some good storage boxes or zip bags (best with a see-through slot) and label the outside with the types of contents. I like to store stuff by season, for example, summer casual; beach things; Christmas possibilities; jackets; accessories, etc. Be sure that everything is clean prior to storage and include cedar or moth balls to ensure no unwelcome scavenger finds anything too tasty.

Better a wardrobe with plenty of spare capacity to see what you have than one jammed full of confusing possibilities. A well-thought-out capsule collection is all you need to live your life. You will also be more keenly aware when shopping of target investments that will enliven this season's capsule. Learning to wear fewer clothes during a season gives you the licence to spend more on anything you buy. You will get so much wear out of it you won't mind. The French always use this approach to shopping and lead the world in looking terrific, even on a meagre budget.

CLASSIC CAREER GEAR

Keeping up to date for work means updating classic essentials like a great (and comfy) shift dress or simple suit with modern (not mumsy) accessories. Choose a colour scheme for your wardrobe pieces that flatters you as well as working together. Use your own imagination to take these few bits even further with other elements – e.g. black trousers and skirts, simple T-shirts, twinsets, etc.

'NATURAL ROMANTIC' STYLE

Comfort might be the order of the day, but women still keen to be feminine take note: stretch waistbands shouldn't be bulky but sleek; lighter fabrics are your best bet rather than denim, corduroy or wool.

Fabrics that drape, like jersey and fine knits, and skim your silhouette, are flattering on all sizes and shapes. Choose a great neutral colour like charcoal (black can be too harsh), and build around it with more vibrant colours near your face. Avoid classic treasures in favour of fun, quirky jewellery to look more modern. And functional shoes needn't be frumpy: try sweet flats to go the distance, while still looking cute!

Put Your Money Where Your Life Is

Most of us don't have an unlimited budget nor want to spend all of our time shopping. So, we must get smart about what we do hunt for as well as possibly reconsider where we shop. Your money is most wisely invested in the clothes that you live in. I love holiday gear and could easily spend a fortune on swimming costumes and lounge wear. Then I do a reality check and say 'Whoa, girl. If you are lucky you will see two weeks this year by a beach or pool, and there is still life in those glam togs of five holidays back. So, dig 'em out.'

If you are short-changing your day-to-day look and spending money on clothes you get to wear only for the occasional night out or in the hopes of achieving a different life, you are short-changing your image.

To help you prioritize, think about the percentage of time you spend your waking hours over a season on:

✧ Work.

✧ At home with the family.

✧ Socializing with friends.

✧ Hobbies (sports, etc.).

✧ Travelling.

✧ Entertaining.

✧ Evenings out.

✧ Community activities.

How well does your current wardrobe meet the demands of your life? Where are the imbalances, the gaps? Is it time to reapportion your spending to reflect better how you live? If you formerly worked in a traditional office environment but have more flexibility these days in how you dress, does your wardrobe provide you with the right options for looking and feeling your best? Are you being as influential as you need to be or are others struggling to understand how you fit into this new organization?

Perhaps you have one side of your life pretty well sorted, for example, your work clothes or casual gear, but whenever a special opportunity arises for a night out on the town you have 'nothing to wear'. Of course you have stuff to wear but nothing that seems right for the occasion. If so, this is the wardrobe gap that needs filling as a priority.

Do your 'comfy clothes' let you down when you have an unexpected visitor? Maybe you could improve your relaxed look with any of the many new, hard-wearing and washable fabrics that are so much more

flattering than sweatsuits or jeans. Just ask yourself, 'When do I feel less than my best, regardless of the occasion or activity', and work to enhance that look so that your terrific style and personality are always packaged to do yourself justice.

Make Peace With Your Body Shape

I do hope that after reading Chapter Nine, along with the rest of this book, you are motivated to get yourself healthy and as a by-product of that get yourself in better shape than you have been for years. But even so, you will still have your basic proportions and body shape. So, if you are a short-waisted pear shape, you still will be when you weigh ten kilos less, if that is a goal, and are fitter. But any figure shape looks better when it is toned, so being perfect doesn't matter. All you need to know are the tricks to balance your body and to draw attention to where you want it to be drawn.

Most women don't need elaborate diagrams to figure out their own shape. We know it quite intimately, bumps and all. Proportions are a bit trickier. If you want more details, see my last book, *Makeover Manual*.

General guidelines to look slimmer:

✧ Tone colours head to toe.
✧ Don't clutter your fullest areas.
✧ Avoid details like pockets over breasts and hips.
✧ Avoid gathered or overly elasticated waistbands on skirts and trousers.
✧ Wear clothes that fall straight when you stand still although they might 'move' when you do.
✧ Opt for interesting fabrics rather than busy patterns.
✧ Matte fabrics are more slimming than shiny.

✧ Work to bring the attention with colour and necklines towards your face. If it is nicely made-up and framed with a flattering hairstyle we won't notice your figure.
✧ A slightly higher heel adds elegance to the heftiest or shortest legs.
✧ Avoid jackets and tops 'ending' at your widest point.
✧ Open up the neck area if it is short or wide.
✧ Shorter haircuts and styles that frame the face and lift from the side and back are also slimming.

THE DRESS!

When the wardrobe requires a total overhaul, try rebuilding yours by starting with a great dress. A bias cut with simple lines in jersey can take you to a picnic, the office or out to dinner, depending on what you put with it. Always buy the jacket or top that matches to give you more flexibility in pulling the look together. Then select a few key pieces to help adapt the dress to your needs, making it casual, classic, and when necessary, dressy . . . like our classic jacket, sweet cardigan, comfy pullover, matching top and some scarves. Such a dress can work with heels, sneakers, sandals or boots. Ghost – not the gods – designed this particular winner dress.

C

D

B

E

A

F

EVENING COVER-UPS

The majority of women over 40 hate their upper arms and will go to any lengths to hide them. But you don't want wreck your look – or sex appeal! – by covering up in heavy, matronly jackets.

Great options include: A) The colourful plain or embroidered shawl. B) The 'Shrug' – a sheer, cropped cardigan that only covers the arms leaving the décolleté on view – thank God for Donna Karan! C) An evening jacket should never see the light of day. This classic stunner succeeds with trousers, short skirts or over long dresses.
D) Alternatively, treat yourself to an elegant cardigan for the evening, in lieu of a jacket.
E) Sexy tops and bodies are now widely available with semi-transparent sleeves.
F) Sheer, colourful jackets over simple camisoles or strapless tops can be fun and distinctive, as well as drop-dead gorgeous.

Pulling a Look Together

In addition to making the most of your figure, with the goal for most of us wanting to appear taller and slimmer, you also want to check how aware you are of your total look. Often we concentrate on one item, a new blouse or trousers, but lose the impact because what we combine with it negates its freshness and style. Here are some simple guidelines on colour coordination and accessorizing that will help you ensure that all that you wear is complementary – to each other and especially to you.

COLOUR COORDINATION

A good starting point towards pulling a look together begins with colour coordination. Ask yourself if the colours flatter you. Do you look drained, as if you need more make-up? Does the outfit 'fight' with your hair colour – for example, a moss green sweater against grey hair or fuchsia worn against red or golden blonde hair? If so, the colour near your face might need changing.

Does your make-up relate to your outfit? If your outfit is blue based (i.e. a cool tone), avoid brown-based make-up. If you are wearing warm colours, avoid cool, pink make-up. When wearing reds or pinks, tone your lipstick to the outfit; otherwise, don't fuss too much about 'matching' your clothing colour to your make-up. If you are wearing a strong, high-contrast colour combination, your make-up will require more definition in the eye shadow and lipstick. Conversely, beware of wearing too strong or too bright make-up with a soft, neutral outfit or with light, pastel colours.

ACCESSORIZING

The most simple dress or casual outfit can look more expensive and interesting when you use accessories effectively. Fashions change but some guiding principles remain the same. Don't worry about getting it right or wrong. Just ask yourself what will be better, more interesting or more appropriate. But don't stick to the same old combinations. Surprise yourself and your chums by looking different each time.

Hopefully, you will have saved a lifetime of accessories from belts, gloves and hats to scarves, necklaces, earrings and brooches. We all have a mixture of timeless gems and fun junk and only need to remind

ourselves of their potential and recycle them from time to time. Why not edit out the rubbish from your accessories drawers like the single earrings or peeling belts and toss them away to see what potential really exists? Any bits requiring repair should be done now or they remain useless clutter. Good costume jewellery is worth repairing as well as the real stuff.

Be sure your hosiery is both appropriate and up to date. As we age, we tend to treat hosiery as a foundation rather than a fashion item. After shoes, inappropriate or dated hosiery wrecks an outfit faster than anything. Be sure your hosiery is right for the time of year (for example, no thick denier in spring or summer or 'suntan' legs in mid-winter. Ensure your look is complementary, for example, woolly tights with a short skirt and flat shoes in winter are appropriate, comfortable and timeless.

Scarves, necklaces, and brooches should add value to the look and not be an obvious attempt to liven things up at the last minute. Is the item effective or does it clutter things? A scarf over a fussy neckline is redundant. Does the item complement the look? A pearl brooch looks odd against a bold colour or geometric pattern. A dainty necklace is ineffective with a plunging neckline. Aim for balance and for every-thing to enhance each other.

YOU FIRST, OUTFIT SECOND

Step back and view yourself in a full-length mirror. Does anything stand out first – the belt buckle, the shoes, your tights? You want the look to be interesting but for everything to be in harmony, especially with you. Coco Chanel once said, 'When a woman is badly dressed you notice the clothes. When she is well dressed, you notice her.' Remember this every time you put yourself together. It isn't about showing off your clothes, let the kids do that. We want to see you first, with the clothes and accessories complementing who you are.

UNDERPINNING

Your underwear is increasingly important as you get older, as bits start to sag and bulge due to gravity. So underpinning your whole wardrobe it is vital to have a good selection of bras, pants and all-in-ones that do the business. Otherwise whatever you put on top won't look good.

New colours can make you look years younger. Do yours make the most of your natural beauty?

Developing a new look

Are you open to new ideas for changing your image? If so, explore some fresh possibilities for looking and feeling different.

An image consultant should never dictate a certain style or range of 'right' colours. You are what's important – your dream, not anyone else's notion of who you should be or look like. A good consultant can tell you how well your current image makes the most of your colouring, figure and lifestyle, and discuss ideas for making even more of yourself.

Try visualization. Imagine how you like others to react when you enter a room. And then work to achieve that. Experiment with new ideas, worrying less about your imperfections and concentrating more on your possibilities to make that dream a reality.

A new look should be fun and needn't cost a fortune. Maybe it's time to book a make-up, colour or style workshop with your friends. You may learn even more about each other than you do about yourselves!

None of us are objective about ourselves. We concentrate on our flaws and imperfections while others mostly see our assets.

With an image consultant or sales assistant, get advice on ways to get the most out of your clothes. If you can't wear something more than half a dozen ways it might be a useless purchase.

Learn the fine points of making an outfit look twice what you paid for it!

As we age, an elegant fit with a bit of drape and movement is more sexy than figure-hugging numbers.

When in doubt, do a reality check. How does it work from front, side and rear?

Does it do cartwheels? Whatever your test, make sure the outfit moves with you. At our age, comfort reigns.

The importance of a well-fitting bra can't be overemphasized, and most stores now offer a fitting service for these. An estimated 80 per cent of women are walking around in the wrong size or shape of bra, according to one survey by fitters. Just because you've always been a 36B doesn't mean you are still one. When was the last time you checked? It's amazing what having children, breast-feeding, exercising, gaining and losing weight and just plain ageing can do to the bustline. There are few more unattractive sights than flesh bulging out awkwardly around an ill-fitting bra, or a bra strap that rides up to the shoulder-blades because of the weight of the breasts pulling it down. Choose a bra that gives you a youthful outline, and keeps your bosom where it should be, midway between your shoulders and elbows.

If you're a bit flabby around the middle, it's best to consider one of the new, light, all-in-ones, not a floppy silk 'teddy', please, but one with Lycra that holds you in and creates a clean, smooth line. These can be worn year round and get rid of midriff bulge and visible panty lines.

Make sure you have different underwear combinations for different looks – a well-supporting strapless or backless bra for evening wear, an all-in-one for wearing under clingy knitwear, a short, slimming panty-slip combination for revealing clothes, waist- and full-length slips for when they're appropriate, etc. 'Bikini' pants are all very well, but not if they cause a bulge under trousers. You might want some higher, fuller panties for certain occasions.

Think Trends Not Fads

Keeping up with fashion can be both exhausting and expensive. If you have 'been there, done that' and have countless T-shirts to prove it, you can feel fed-up with fashion. You feel beyond worrying about the latest label, handbag or look but still want to project your best when it matters to you.

Fads that are hyped each month as 'must-haves' this season are best completely avoided. An investment in a fad item will never give you the wear you want without it looking dated and sad. Even though mid-life, third-agers are less concerned about fashion in a 'life and death' sense than a twenty-something is, it is still important to us.

A fashion trend is different. This is when fashion is changing to reflect the times, society, what's happening.

Trends last for several seasons and can look fresh for up to five years, even if worn differently every year. Things to notice are:

- ❖ How structured and tailored are today's designs?
- ❖ Are neutral tones more modern than brighter shades or vice versa?
- ❖ Are accessories piled on or pared down?
- ❖ Do shorter skirts look fresher? Are longer ones more current? Does it matter now?
- ❖ Are dresses worn on their own or as a base to an outfit?
- ❖ Is drape more important than tailoring?
- ❖ Are shawls ageing or elegant?
- ❖ Should hemlines swing or be neat?
- ❖ How fuzzy or defined is the line between day and evening wear?
- ❖ What kind of trainers are acceptable with casual gear?
- ❖ Is hosiery an issue or a non-event?
- ❖ Are boots best with skirts or trousers or both?
- ❖ Are jackets fine for smart and casual?
- ❖ Should the make-up be subtle or more defined?
- ❖ Is elegance matronly or chic?
- ❖ If you clash textures and fabrics, will you look current or like a bag lady?
- ❖ Are accessories delicate or defined?
- ❖ Are colours monochromatic or blocked?
- ❖ Are trousers fresher than skirts?
- ❖ Is evening wear theatrical or subtle?

Trends that we all remember include the early '90s, Armani destructured jackets and suits. Mainstream manufacturers not only copied his tailoring but also his muted colour schemes. Then there were the comfy bodysuits, perfected in colour, construction and fabrics, and made available for women of every size. We wore them for years instead of blouses. We also had leggings with jumpers or big blouses, or with neat T-shirts for those with the figures, a trend that the fashion industry despaired of and couldn't understand surviving so long. Boot-legged trousers were honed to make every woman's legs look longer. Donna Karan's wrap skirts and Diana Von Furstenberg's recycled seventies wrap-dresses are also examples of lasting, much copied design. Functional yet stylish walking shoes replaced trainers with our suits to and from the office. Bright scarves were worn over jackets and coats. Shopper handbags proved winners from morning to night with colourful, interesting bags replacing staid, black clutches for special occasions: all durable fashion trends, all well worth our money. So, going

Bridging the generation gap: casual style tips to suit each and every age

Molly

Approaching her landmark sixtieth birthday, Molly is a very stylish headmistress. She loves clothes, and has built up an enviable wardrobe through judicious choices. Her classic black, grey and brown suits have lasted her years; designer investments have paid off with good returns. She chooses only well-priced more colourful, fashionable items, wearing them to death then banishing them when they have served their usefulness for the season.

Jeanne

This busy American mother and former model is in enviable shape in her early forties. But mixing with many younger friends, Jeanne is now questioning what is 'right' for her age. 'I don't want to dress like a "woman" yet,' she confesses, implying a fear that once you hit forty you can't have fun with fashion. But that's nonsense, as Jeanne herself demonstrates.

Shazia

Like many impoverished graduates lumbered with debts and pursuing their first big career break, Shazia has learnt many short cuts to looking good – and being adult without ageing herself!

Molly

Molly's 10-year-old trousers are given an airing every once in a while when the fashions might call for classic grey. She knows to update them with accessories, and loved the suggestion of a fun cardigan to ring the changes.

Molly's make-up benefited from a professional update. We used a much lighter eye shadow to brighten her deep-set eyes, and suggested a more translucent, moisturizing lipstick for daytime, instead of her usual matte red.

Jeanne

When a forty-something women keeps herself as fit as Jeanne it is a pity for those results to be hidden under shapeless, bulky clothes. We applaud her 'show-off' trousers and pretty twinset – far preferable to mumsy skirts and starchy blouses. Modern classics need not be ageing. Note how her jewellery makes these simple basics quite funky. Although Jeanne's younger pals might be still sporting crop tops, she's called a halt to them for herself, particularly as her own teenaged daughter now wears them with such aplomb. All mothers are wise to assess the viability of the styles they choose when they see how they look compared to their daughters!

Shazia

Shoes need to be functional when running around so most students opt for either trainers or boots. But twentysomethings need to keep theirs in good condition for grown-up 'cool'. Shazia has a 'natural' style personality so is best in simple, unfussy styles like these great combat trousers and ethnic T-shirt. Anything more tailored or classic would inhibit her personality.

forward, try to spot the trends and spend your money there. No doubt you will be both comfortable and 'with it' as a result.

Adapt and Update

Mindful of trends, you can adapt your look as well as your new image and bring yourself into the modern mainstream without, necessarily, having to buy new things all the time. You may not have any flirty skirts in your wardrobe and if they are a definite fashion trend, your alternative to buying one might be to wear the comparable look in trousers. Flirty skirts essentially mean a more feminine look, so simply soften what you would wear with your trousers, e.g. try a ruffle blouse, and you can still look the part. Consider how a simple dress can be worn differently to look newer. A long, shirt-dress can be worn with or without a belt (depending on your waist), with court shoes, sneakers or boots or even as a 'duster-coat' over a simple shift dress or tank top and trousers. Jeans (not conventional 'work-wear') can look sweet with a pretty twin-set or be worn to the office with a smart shirt and blazer.

If you are happy with your clothes, they fit well and are classic enough, ask yourself how your hair and make-up can be revised to keep that classic look fresh and not boring. Magazines aren't a good guideline for new hairstyles as too often they over-do the effect. Watch for changes in trends on television, not with the news presenters who play it safe and smart, but the morning programmes whose presenters often set trends with a style which is more approachable and realistic than the magazines. American TV programmes are also good for trend-setting, but not British or Australian soaps!

Help at Hand

Each season it pays to carry your wardrobe editing further. So far, you have reconsidered your wardrobe in terms of your new, redefined style along with the current fashion trends. If you are still confused with a mountain of stuff in a jumbled heap, not sure of how to put your dream image together or how to select what's best from fashion, why not get some personal advice? Reading magazines and the dictates of fashion editors who are generally around thirty, living quite a different

life to yours, won't help you. It is so hard to be objective about ourselves, with most women more negative than they need be about their possibilities. Some friends may be very talented in putting things together, but remember that is *their* style, their personality at work, not yours. That's why every time you buy something that a friend does it never looks as good on you as it does on her!

A reputable image consultant's only objective is to make you look and feel great about yourself. There are also many talented personal shoppers in department stores who don't pressurize you into shopping. However, they do work on commission and have sales targets to meet. Hence, you might not get the time you need to learn about yourself and to discover your many possibilities without feeling obliged to purchase something.

Of course, an image consultant will charge you for their time. You will receive advice and take home lots of notes that are relevant and long lasting. A session will cover everything from a great palette of colours to help you look healthy and also coordinate together (colour analysis). Explaining your body shape, proportions and scale and how to make the most of your figure will be covered in style analysis. Key to a style consultation are specific ideas on how to update your look with the latest trends. Advice on possible hairstyles and colouring is essential, along with a new make-up look teaching you techniques to try yourself. You leave reinforced on many things that you are doing well along with a laundry list of new possibilities to try.

Expect to be prodded out of your old ways but not dictated to. If you are, demand your money back!

A good consultant should be open either to taking you shopping (not to purchase, unless you want to, but to look at the suggestions) or to referring you to a range of sources within your budget to help you achieve your goals. Expect to be prodded out of your old ways but not dictated to. If you are, demand your money back! An image consultant is just that – a consultant. Sure, they know a lot, but must work with you and not attempt to turn you into someone you don't want to be. If you absolutely hate some suggestions, say so. If you dislike the colours that they recommend, ask what might be an alternative. Technically, the consultant may be right, but they should work with you, not against you, to create the look that you want. (See 'Useful Organizations' for image consultants.)

Bridging the generation gap: dressy style tips to suit each and every age

Molly

Like all women, Molly wants to look stylish (even downright sexy!) when that special occasion presents the opportunity. But like most of us over 40, Molly hates to expose her upper arms. This terrific, simple black number with sheer sleeves does both jobs beautifully. This dress actually cost a fraction of others in her wardrobe, but Molly has had a lot of mileage from it thanks to its versatility and timeless style.

Jeanne

When the occasion might call for more than her usual smart evening pants and jacket, Jeanne loves a dress, but usually short rather than long. Here, basic black is softened against her gentle colouring with sequins and an attractive V-neck, which mitigates the potentially overwhelming power of black when worn higher.

Shazia

Faced with the prospect of a seriously dressy occasion many young women on a limited budget can panic. We chose a fab, yet simple, black velvet dress from a market, then trimmed it with feathers to create a stunning look — for less that her taxi fare home from the ball! You can also save money and create a dash by stylizing basic evening bags with modern trimmings. Even inexpensive glittery hair clips help forgo the need for costly earrings.

Finally, a key tip for anyone on a limited budget, whatever their age: good grooming – sleek hair and complete make-up – always makes your overall look appear more expensive and accomplished, like designer rather than market gear.

Avoid a Second Adolescence

Many women can be so thrilled with a new look that their former good sense goes out of the window temporarily as they then stop at nothing. Feeling good and younger in a new look, they now pull out the stops and give everything a whirl.

Often with a landmark birthday looming women go on a diet and get fit for the big day to show off how they really don't look their age at all. Along with the new figure comes the bizarre outfit, showing a bit too much cleavage, leg or worse really designed for their daughters. This is not to say that many mums can't successfully trade some gear with their daughters, it's just when they try to copy the look from head to toe, from the hairstyle to stilettos, that it fails.

Forget trying to look younger and aim just to look your best. A wonderful image is timeless and doesn't date the woman as fast as trying too hard to deny your years. As you approach each new decade some definite items to retire, to ensure never being called 'mutton dressed as lamb', are listed below.

IN YOUR THIRTIES:

You can get away with just about anything provided you are fit (not flabby) and have the personality to carry it off.

IN YOUR FORTIES STOP WEARING:

- ✧ full, short skirts.
- ✧ crop tops.
- ✧ ankle socks.
- ✧ baby-doll anything.
- ✧ no bra.
- ✧ ankle bracelets.
- ✧ revealing lingerie (daytime).
- ✧ short shorts.
- ✧ trainers except for sports.
- ✧ G-string bikinis or undies.
- ✧ white leather.

IN YOUR FIFTIES RETIRE ANY:

- ✧ white shoes.
- ✧ Wonderbras.
- ✧ fishnet tights.
- ✧ metallic fabrics.
- ✧ puffed sleeves.
- ✧ halter-top T-shirts.
- ✧ cleavage during the daytime.
- ✧ aerobics gear anywhere but the gym.
- ✧ men's ties with suits.
- ✧ transparent skirts or trousers.

IN THE SIXTIES THE FOLLOWING HAVE HAD IT:

- ✧ transparent shirts.
- ✧ T-strap shoes.
- ✧ knee-high boots.
- ✧ black leather anything.
- ✧ high-heeled sandals.
- ✧ granny boots with short skirts.
- ✧ petticoat trims beneath skirts.
- ✧ skirts shorter than an inch above the knee.
- ✧ flashy belts.
- ✧ bustiers.

8

Keeping Pace at Work

'It is never too late to be what you might have been.'

GEORGE ELIOT (1819–1880)

Working Smarter

For many women a key motivation to appear younger than their years is the pressure to fit in and remain viable at work, whether you need to work well into your later years to top up the pension that will now have to support you for maybe thirty or forty years after the traditional retirement age, or whether you enjoy your work and simply want to continue doing it and not be pushed out to pasture. Since having enjoyable work, or even a sense of vocation about what you do, has been found to be a common factor among those who thrive in old age, we feel you should not be denied that opportunity. And, in the future, with a top-heavy population in age terms, employers will have to revise their often rigid views about the cut-off age for certain jobs. Otherwise there won't be enough workers to support the economy.

Today the choice for continuing in work beyond your middle years is all too often between shaping up and shipping out. But increasingly women are looking towards starting their own businesses where they set the standards. This is possibly why female self-employment increased by 78 per cent between 1981 and 1991 in Britain, as compared with only 45 per cent for men, and why such a high proportion of new businesses are started by women – and one third of all retail businesses, for example.

According to the Federation of Small Businesses, nearly one third of businesses worldwide are now owned by women, and the motivation for running those businesses has been, in many cases, combining work with motherhood or wanting to gear up at a time when employers expected them to gear down. And it might cheer you to know that in the *Guardian* survey of the fifty most powerful women in Britain in 1998, 80 per cent were over forty, a large proportion well, well over forty, and that of all businesses started during the last recession in Britain in the eighties, those started by women have survived the best!

Changing Attitudes with Attitude

Many of the women we know who have kept on working into their seventies, eighties and nineties work for themselves. Mevagh Horton is a healer, serene and lovely in her eighties, who also runs a small art gallery. Slim, fit and active she has retained much of the beauty captured

THE RISE OF THE FEMALE EMPLOYER – AND EMPLOYED – IN EUROPE:

International figures (from the Age Concern Institute of Gerontology) showing women as a percentage of the population in employment in different European countries show that in Belgium, Greece, Germany, Italy, Luxembourg, Spain and Portugal the percentage of women in employment actually goes UP for the over-65s (in Belgium from 24 to 32%; in Greece from 39 to 43%; in Germany from 31 to 33%; in Spain from 25 to 27% and in Portugal from 35 to 36%). The earlier figures are for women aged 50 to 64.

But in almost every country the percentage of female employers rises in the 65-plus bracket (in Belgium from 20 to 30%; France from 21 to 28%; Greece from 19 to 25%; Germany from 15 to 17%; Ireland from 10 to 12%; Luxembourg from 28 to 33%; The Netherlands from 11 to 12%; Spain from 21 to 26% and the United Kingdom from 21 to 26%). Italy remains stable at 20% while only Denmark and Portugal drop 2 percentage points each, from 11 to 9 and 38 to 36% respectively.

In 1996 there were 12.3 million women in the labour force. By 2006 female participation is predicted to rise by nearly 1 million to 13.2 million, with almost three-quarters of that increase aged between 35 and 59 years.

in an early sculpture of her and radiates the contentment that she helps her clients find in themselves. Liz Keeble is a yoga teacher who first stood on her head at seventy and continues to inspire those who flock to her classes. Victoria's mother has had her own public relations company in New York for fifty years and continues to run it in a hands-on way and to be active in the music business at an age she wouldn't thank us for mentioning. Even though now, due to diabetic complications, she has difficulty walking, her brain is as sharp as ever and if you saw her behind a desk or behind one of the restaurant tables at which she derives so much pleasure, you would think she was much younger than she is. Eleanor Lambert, the New York-based compiler of the *International Best Dressed List* and doyenne of fashion PRs, admits to being in her nineties yet jetsets all over the world to service her list of high-profile clients, arriving fresh and ready to give interviews or set up deals after long-haul flights that leave younger colleagues jaded and jetlagged.

Yet none of these women would probably be allowed to work if they were part of a bureaucratic corporate system with mandatory

retirement ages and equally inflexible views about human potential. (The hero pilot whose quick thinking saved the Leeds United soccer team from death in 1998 was sixty-one – six years over British Airways' mandatory retirement age for pilots and one year over Virgin Airlines'.) Changing demographics mean that business attitudes towards women and men of these ages have got to change, and they will and are changing, thanks to the attitude of these 'UltraAge' entrepreneurs.

Helen Sher, who runs the successful Sher system of facial products and routines from London's Bond Street with her daughter Glenda, likes to tell how she only started her internationally known beauty business after she was told she was too old to continue working in the beauty business. Although Sher, a petite dynamo with jet black hair and fabulous skin, looks to all intents and purposes like a forty-five-year-old at sixty-three, she was considered past it for working as a cosmetics executive dealing with department stores and with major companies in such an aspirational, youth-orientated field. 'I couldn't even get in to interviews and I'd written to about eighty companies,' she remembers indignantly. 'I think a woman of a certain age isn't even given the opportunity to present her credentials, yet to make a success of the business needs the experience and expertise a younger woman may not have.' But in the end her rejections turned out to be for the best. Her triumph, and her impressive list of famous clients, is testimony to the fact that putting beauty before age is foolish, and that the two are not mutually exclusive. But even in less looks-orientated fields, employers want their staff to be 'lively', 'enthusiastic' and have other qualities usually associated with youth.

German Ursula Bornstein was a history teacher until she was sixty-five but had no intention of retiring when she was forced to by a system which doesn't brook exceptions. So she started a worldwide translation service, WPIS, which grew to have 600 freelance translators she can call on to translate 'love letters, business documents – anything!' She is seventy-four at the time of writing, and business is booming so much that she scarcely had time to speak to us. A woman who moves briskly and is incredibly spry for her years, despite 'a bit of osteoporosis and arthritis', she has the commanding voice of someone twenty years younger and a beautiful head of hair that is only just beginning to go grey. 'I would never want to retire,' she told us. 'And when you work for yourself you don't have to.' Which is why so many women have

been starting their own business so they can, like Prime Minister Margaret Thatcher wanted to, go 'on and on'.

When the husband of American publisher Frances Lear left her for a younger woman after twenty-eight years of marriage she started the mould-breaking magazine bearing her name, which claimed to be 'for the woman who was not born yesterday' and boasted an average reader age of fifty-one, with models all in the forty-sixty age range, a growing industry. 'Older women of our generation have been described as depressed, sad, menopausal, decrepit, unproductive,' said Lear as she fought her way through what she called 'a maze of negative perceptions' and discovered, on the way, a huge waste of human potential. 'We must look in the mirror and smile,' said Lear at seventy, an easier promise to make than the other she made at the same time: 'I will remain sexually viable until I can no longer walk!' Alas, despite the admiration it attracted, her magazine did not remain viable, as few magazines for older women have, reinforcing advertisers' conviction that youth is the aspirational model for all. But as Baby Boomers mature, the media and advertisers are taking note that both real and older role models are tools for attracting sales. The Gap has led the way using hip figures of every shape, size and generation to make their collections accessible. Virgin Cola with its 'Cooler Longer' strap line has fun with sixty and seventy-somethings sporting lilac hair and 'street-cult' gear their grandchildren wear. New fashion and lifestyle magazines with their relevant advertising support, like *Frank* and *Red* in the UK, are consciously aiming to fill the gap, aware that mid-lifers are bored rigid with magazines obsessed with youth.

'I will remain sexually viable until I can no longer walk!'

Woman's Journal, under the direction of former 'Cosmo Girl' and *Cosmopolitan* editor Marcelle d'Argy Smith, is targeting 'Boomer' readership: women bored with the sex-obsessed glossies aimed at their daughters, less interested in child care theories and paraphernalia, but more into personal development – provided it is delivered with a generous dose of glamour and aspiration.

Harriet Close, a model who stopped getting work when she was considered too old, started her own model agency for more mature models at the age of forty-four. The Close Agency has models from thirty-five to sixty-two on its books and Harriet, who still keeps her hand in with a few choice jobs herself, says, 'I think we're going to see

a lot more agencies like this. People don't want to see a nineteen-year-old advertising wrinkle creams. They are fed up with ageism and, with women taking better care of themselves, they look better for longer so why shouldn't they continue modelling?'

Just like the modelling, publishing, education, beauty and advertising industries, big business will have to change its attitude to older workers as changing demographics mean that soon there won't be enough under-fifties to support our ageing population, particularly as the Baby Boomers approach traditional retirement ages but refuse to countenance a traditional retirement. Texas governor Anne Richards has been among those on both sides of the Atlantic spearheading the fight against age discrimination. And she has visibly practised what she preached, riding a Harley Davidson at over sixty, and getting up at six each morning to do a three-mile run before work, proving she was just as fit and with-it as any younger entrants in the political arena. We need more women with 'attitude' to change prevailing attitudes to age and work.

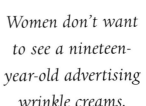

Women don't want to see a nineteen-year-old advertising wrinkle creams.

Refuse to be Another Statistic

A study by Age Concern in 1998 claims that nearly 8 million people, a third of Britain's workforce, have been discriminated against at some time on the basis of age. Job advertisements which can't specify race or sex still ask for candidates under the age of thirty-five, or for bright, young things to join enthusiastic young teams.

Yet anyone who has ever been a customer in a shop will know that it is often the young sales assistants who will be bleary-eyed, bored and disinclined to assist, whereas the older ones are interested and helpful. We know whom we'd prefer for selling and service, and some companies such as B&Q, the do-it-yourself chain of hardware and home supply stores in Britain, have been discovering the benefits of older employees with a specific over-fifty-fives hiring policy. Apparently customers appreciated the expertise, patience and empathy provided by the older salespeople, who understood the use of screws and skirting board, and the impact of dado rails and double-glazing much better than young colleagues would have.

Thank goodness British employment minister, Andrew Smith, aged forty-seven and a member of one of the most youthful cabinets the country has known, decided in the same week to announce a code of practice to end job advertisements that discriminate on the basis of age. What a pity that at the time of writing, it is only a code of practice, and will not make age discrimination illegal, as Age Concern argues it should be.

Women at Work: New Images

The Age Concern charity launched a poster to promote its case in February 1998, featuring an attractive, bosomy model wearing a sexy, low-cut black satin bra. 'The first thing some people notice is her age,' ran the caption, because the model, Pearl Reed, was a fifty-six-year-old woman. A furore ensued, with newspapers publishing photos of bosoms of all ages to see how they compared, and letters columns bristling with those protesting that fifty-six-year-old women were too old to be photographed in nothing but their bras – and others eager to do the same.

Jilly Pengilley says she was asked to pose for that controversial poster but declined, fearful of what her son, a barrister, and daughter, a teacher, would think. But other offers of work have been pouring in for Jilly, at sixty-two the oldest model on the Close Agency's books. In fact, Jilly enthuses, 'My sixties have been the happiest time of my life,' since she began modelling again after over a twenty-year gap in the career she loved. Jilly started out as a catwalk model at nineteen, and still boasts the same weight of 9½ stone and size 14 (US 10) figure as she had then. Her hair is blonde, bouncy and fashionably cut and her 36DD bust is full and firm.

When her children were born she made the switch from the glamour of the catwalk to being the 'girl next door' in ads for household products. Then her husband died and she went off to live by the sea, to bring up her children near relatives. 'I bought a hotel where I invested all my money and lost it,' she remembers ruefully. 'For ten years I fought a legal battle but then the year I turned sixty was an amazing one for me, like the phoenix rising from the ashes. Having spent ten years of stress, coping with legal battles and cancer – I lost a kidney

to a tumour, I'm sure it was from the stress I was going through – I was able to come back to London and get back to modelling as I'd dreamed of doing. Within a week I was working on a shoot for Saga Holidays [specialist holidays for the over-fifties] and now I'm more contented and happier than I've ever been, I think. I love the work I do. It really gives me a kick. It's like having a hobby I enjoy that I also get paid for, and it's so much easier to do now than when the children were little, although I do have five grandchildren now to see!'

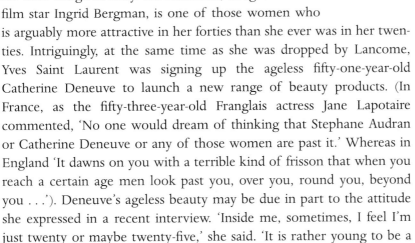

The year I turned sixty was an amazing one for me, like the phoenix rising from the ashes.

Only a couple of years before Oil of Ulay signed up Jilly to model in a special Mother's Day promotion of its products, the beautiful Isabella Rossellini was dropped from the advertisements of a major cosmetics company, Lancome, beause she was considered too old for their image at forty. Yet Rossellini, daughter of the film star Ingrid Bergman, is one of those women who is arguably more attractive in her forties than she ever was in her twenties. Intriguingly, at the same time as she was dropped by Lancome, Yves Saint Laurent was signing up the ageless fifty-one-year-old Catherine Deneuve to launch a new range of beauty products. (In France, as the fifty-three-year-old Franglais actress Jane Lapotaire commented, 'No one would dream of thinking that Stephane Audran or Catherine Deneuve or any of those women are past it.' Whereas in England 'It dawns on you with a terrible kind of frisson that when you reach a certain age men look past you, over you, round you, beyond you . . .'). Deneuve's ageless beauty may be due in part to the attitude she expressed in a recent interview. 'Inside me, sometimes, I feel I'm just twenty or maybe twenty-five,' she said. 'It is rather young to be a cultural monument . . .'

A number of companies have been using older models in recent years – some, like Vivienne Westwood, Gap and Levi jeans, probably more for shock value than anything else. Others, like Revlon, which signed a multi-year contract with supermodel Lauren Hutton, or Estée Lauder with forty-something Dayle Haddon, seemed to recognize the very special quality of more mature beauty.

Intriguingly, at the same time as it was running its poster of Pearl Reed and its campaign against ageism at work, Age Concern made headlines for forcibly retiring at seventy a woman who felt she still had a lot to give to the organization. Well, they said she could give it, as

a volunteer, she complained, but didn't want to pay her a salary for her skills and enthusiasm. What a shame!

It is 'the best of times and the worst of times' for women in their 'prime' on prime time television, with some actresses, like America's Cybill Shepherd and Britain's Maureen Lipman, complaining of age discrimination. Cybill was reported as saying her sitcom *Cybill*, ironically about a middle-aged actress who has trouble getting good roles, was threatened with losing its prime time slot because she was forty-eight and considered past her prime by television executives. But other actresses insist that forty-plus is prime time for them and that they've never had it better. There are strong roles for over-forty females in both British and American television these days, from *Veronica's Closet*, starring Kirstie Alley as an overweight divorcee suffering menopause and mid-life crises, to *The Ambassador* with the dignified fifty-nine-year-old Pauline Collins in a power role. And two of the nominees for the 'Best Actress' Oscar in 1998 were British actresses of a certain age – Judi Dench and Julie Christie – and Helen Mirren was voted 'Sexiest Woman on TV'.

'I wouldn't be twenty again if you paid me.'

Cybill's co-star Christine Baranski, forty-five, plays the acerbic divorcee Maryann in the series and says real-life divorcees follow her around in department stores and into the ladies' room in restaurants to ask her for advice on how to get even with their exes. She says her career has really taken off in her forties. 'I've never felt more empowered as an actress,' she told Victoria. 'I wouldn't be twenty again if you paid me. I feel that I've paid my dues and am out there working and being appreciated, and I've had a better career in my forties than I had before. I kinda went "boom". Since I've come into my forties my skin has been better than it was when I was younger and more stressed and kept comparing myself with other people and feeling insecure about my inadequacies, and my body's in better shape than ever before. I feel totally happy with my family life and secure in my profession.'

Prepare your Pension

The British government's half-hearted move in the right direction has a deeper, and far from altruistic, motive. It is to prevent older people from swelling the ranks of the unemployed at the age of fifty or sixty,

proving a greater burden on society and on overstretched pension funds that can't stand the strain of supporting people for nearly as long as they've paid into them. British women of forty-seven and under today have already been told they'll have to work until older than sixty – the age they were originally told they would have to work until when they started working – in order to draw a state pension, with the pension age due to even off with men at the age of sixty-five.

In America too looms the vexing, real dilemma of paying pensions due to the burgeoning ageing cohort in the US. Federal Reserve Chairman Alan Greenspan said in 1997 that there was increasing pressure to raise retirement age for everyone to seventy in order to avoid overburdening the Social Security system in the new millennium. The system is destined for bankruptcy when today's thirty-three-year-olds turn sixty-five if something radical is not done.

Many of America's policies on senior citizens, as they are called, rather than the more patronizing 'pensioners' with its implication of being pensioned off into oblivion, are due to the agitation of the American Association of Retired Persons (AARP) which was founded in the sixties and quickly developed considerable political clout.

A similar organization, the Association of Retired Persons over 50 (ARP), was set up in Britain in the eighties by an expatriate American couple, Robert and Jackie Rose, now retired. Predictably it walks more softly and carries a smaller stick, for British retired people haven't quite woken up to the potential of 'Grey Power' that the 'Grey Panthers' in the States have been exploiting.

Its chairman Eric Reid, sixty-nine, says Britain is much better off than many European countries, even though its pensions only yield 60 per cent of the average income compared with 80 per cent for Germany. 'Britain is the only country in which a wife can get a married woman's pension even if she hasn't contributed anything,' he says, 'bringing the total pension for a married couple to around £103 a week which is comparable with Germany. And, of course, you have to compare average earnings in the two countries. Some European countries are in terrible shape. In Italy the total pensions debt now exceeds the GNP and pensions are being cut, but in Britain before the middle of the next millennium (if National Insurance contributions aren't cut back) the pension fund should begin to go into surplus because we have been aware of the possibility of a pension squeeze for some time. Although the American pension is between 70 and 75 per cent of average income,

it is complicated by the fact that state pensions vary from state to state and, of course, you won't be able to draw them until you're seventy or maybe seventy-five.' But any surplus will come too late for all but those lucky Boomers who live to a very ripe old age, and pensioners relying on the state pension in Britain do not have a very easy time of things, despite their free bus passes. That is why we are being bombarded with exhortations to take out private pension policies.

Old Dogs Can Learn New Tricks!

Concerned employers have formed the Employers' Forum on Age with an eye to spreading the word that you *can* teach old dogs new tricks, to everyone's advantage.

Jo Cutmore and Mark Scott of Jamieson Scott and Prowess were just conventional headhunters until, coming into their forties, they realized the need to retrain redundant workers in their forties and fifties for the 'portfolio careers' long propounded by the management guru Charles Handy. Now they also spend considerable time helping stunned middle-aged managers to realize that they can cope with change, even the dramatic change of losing their jobs, and be retrained and given the confidence to act as external consultants, interim managers (managers hired on a very short, fixed-term contract for a finite purpose) and 'troubleshooters'. As they point out, 'You may have been the specialist in dealing with leaves on the line for a rail company which can no longer afford to hire someone for a whole year just to deal with that seasonal problem. You've got to consider how to market your skills year round to other companies, while hiring yourself back to the rail company as an external consultant or interim manager each autumn to deal with the problem of leaves on the line.'

Prepare yourself for a 'portfolio' existence in later life.

Their advice to anyone worried about losing a job is: Don't get into that situation without having prepared yourself for a 'portfolio' existence in later life. Prepare yourself by having something outside mainstream permanent employment before you're without it: be on the board of a charity or voluntary organization, for example. Remember that we no longer have life-long careers. We have jobs and not for life. We're in a new job culture that's task, not individual, orientated, so you need to develop transferable skills that are necessary to organizations.

They joke that 'in the future you'll come out of education at thirty, needing a PhD to sweep the streets', but it's not a joke that they feel 'you'll probably have a core in corporate life of about fifteen years, say from thirty to forty-five, before being forced to diversify'.

Sometimes adversity, which forces us to find new paths, can be a friend if we learn to perceive its threats as challenges in the way life's winners do. Treating threats as challenges is the hallmark of the so-called 'hardy personality' of survivors who can thrive on stress. Maintaining the capacity to learn into old age, and to be flexible and change course, is a huge advantage. Having to change our jobs, ways of working and even our perceptions of ourselves may be better for us in the long run than sticking to a single, well-worn routine, however comfortable we are with it. Although it did seem the height of heartless bureaucracy when the British Post Office refused to let a seventy-one-year-old postman complete his goal of fifty years of service, even though he protested 'It's my life', and that his daily ten-mile walks for the past forty-eight and a half years had kept him fit as a fiddle.

Still Sharp

Don't let anyone, least of all a potential employer, tell you that at forty, fifty, sixty or older you are too old to learn. Quote the following to them: The Carnegie Inquiry into the Third Age in the early nineties discovered that 'As older individuals can learn new tasks and improve performance with practice they are, therefore, equally likely to benefit from training.' However, they have different needs from younger workers when it comes to learning and training, which should be addressed by a new generation of, hopefully, more caring and flexible employers.

The Carnegie Inquiry found that 'A fast pace, for either presentation or recall, handicaps the older learner but, if allowed to work at their own chosen speed, their performance can equal that of younger individuals.' So a video might be preferable to a demonstration because it can be paused or rerun. 'Given appropriate pacing,' it was found, 'older workers do learn effectively, as has been shown for driver retraining ... use of a software package ... and training for word processing.'

Just using computers, in any capacity, can help older workers to stay 'with it'. Professor Jeffrey Goldstein, an American expert on toys and

play based at the University of Utrecht, has found that playing computer games at home or joining some of the computer clubs now available at job centres, libraries and 'cyber-cafés' 'enhances the ability of older people on so many levels, and gives them better reflexes and coordination. It's wonderful what can be accomplished in a comparatively short time,' he says.

Decline in Working Skills not Inevitable

In tasks that they have been well trained to do, older workers can often compensate in efficiency for what they lack in speed. A chart on the productivity of garment workers by age showed a rise in productivity in those in skill jobs but a marked decline after the age of sixty in those with speed jobs. The report concluded that as far as work performance goes, 'the stereotype that the older worker is less competent and productive persists though evidence of changed performance with age is at best "mixed" . . . there were studies showing improvement deterioration or no change with age.'

Sure, we may get a little slower as we get older, but older workers usually don't suffer as much as younger ones from 'mornings after the nights before' and are less likely to be missing days to deal with family emergencies, for social events or simply to malinger. According to Chris Trinder, who was director of the employment section of the Carnegie Inquiry study, 'Older people tend not to take odd days off sick. When they do it's often for longer periods which are easier to plan for. The stereotypes that employers have aren't based on fact, and older people often don't get the chance to show how they can fit the bill. Employers worry, for example, if they feel someone's only got a few more good years, but they may only get a year or two out of younger workers before they move on!'

The message is that there is no reason why healthy older workers should be a greater risk to employ than people half their age. They have also been found to have a good deal more patience and interpersonal skills, plus the benefit of experience, when it comes to dealing with people. Customers, apparently, like dealing with older staff. However, there can be a danger in 'ghettoizing' older workers when what is needed in most businesses is a mix of ages so that the younger workers can benefit from the experience of the older ones and the older from the ambition and drive of the younger.

According to the Carnegie Inquiry, the comparison of strengths in workers according to age is:

YOUNGER WORKERS	OLDER WORKERS
Ambition	Stability
Trainability	Reliability
Flexibility	Commitment
Health	Responsibility
Information Technology	Maturity
Qualifications	Management skills
Mobility	

But this doesn't mean that you still can't harbour ambition, be trainable, flexible, healthy, IT-literate, well qualified and mobile at any age, as we hope this book will show. Professor Patrick Rabbitt, a professor of age and cognitive performance at the University of Manchester, whose work was quoted heavily in the report and who used what he called 'a group of gallant geriatrics' to undergo all sorts of cognitive tests from playing computerized video games to memorizing lists of names, observed, 'From our work it's very clear that people who were in their fifties in 1982 were ageing very much less rapidly than previous generations due to better diet and health care, personal care and exercise and, very plausibly, heightened expectation and motivation.' We like to think that our readers will benefit from that heightened expectation and motivation, as well as the more tangible benefits of diet and exercise.

The Seven Ages of Skills

Who would make the safest choice for a job involving a lot of driving: a twenty-five-year-old or a sixty-year-old? If your plane suddenly has to make a crash landing, would you prefer your commercial airline pilot to be thirty or fifty? Should a surgeon be allowed to perform a delicate eye operation if he's nearing retirement age? Could a copy-typist of seventy-two be as fast, and even more accurate, than one of twenty, and would you hire her if she was?

Professor Malcolm Hodkinson, former professor of geriatric medicine at University College London and one of the authors of the Carnegie Inquiry into the Third Age's report on *Health: Abilities and Wellbeing in the Third Age*, notes that 'We experience a series of trade-offs as we get older: experience and skill can trade off against the deterioration in certain physical abilities.' He assessed the 'Seven Ages of Skills', subjectively, rather than scientifically, as follows:

TEENS–TWENTIES

Rock bands and other musicians technically, pure mathematicians, financial market traders and computer games salespeople, athletes, prodigy tennis players.

TWENTIES–THIRTIES

Soccer, cricket and tennis players, racing drivers, jockeys, dancers, mathematicians and scientists who apply the concepts to complicated problems in real life, such as statisticians.

THIRTIES–FORTIES

Inventors, middle managers, surgeons dealing with emergency operations, singers.

FORTIES–FIFTIES

Commercial pilots, senior managers, musicians (combining technical proficiency with interpretation), motivational trainers (integrating experience and perspective).

FIFTIES–SIXTIES

Surgeons dealing with complex routine operations, where experience counts; specialist doctors doing diagnosis, senior managers, drivers (it's the peak of the safest driving period, as actor Morgan Freeman demonstrated in *Driving Miss Daisy*, with accident rates falling with age until the late sixties and seventies).

SIXTIES–SEVENTIES

Judges, company chairmen, politicians (experience and contact related, with a sense of history beneficial); conductors, great musicians (interpretation eclipsing the need for precision).

SEVENTIES AND BEYOND

Artists and writers can keep amazing us at this age, we know, and judges and politicians can go on and on, but would you believe so can copy-typists or anyone with keyboard skills? In a 1984 study of typists ranging in age from nineteen to seventy-two, Timothy Salthouse found that 'although reaction time tests increased significantly with age, speed of copy-typing remained constant across age groups. Keeping up speed didn't sacrifice accuracy, as *older typists also made fewer errors!*' The emphasis is ours, the findings taken from the Carnegie Inquiry's Research Paper Number 9 on *Health: Abilities and Wellbeing in the Third Age*.

Whereas some skills can grow rusty with age, others improve. There may be more differences within individual age groups than between them, the Carnegie Inquiry found.

While this list is subjective rather than scientific, and 'all generalizations are wrong', as the generalization goes, all too often workers are being laid off for being 'too old' at ages well below those of the people who are running their companies, or running their country! And some of the greatest contributions to literature and the arts have been made by older people, from the composer Verdi and the playwright George Bernard Shaw to the artist Grandma Moses, a great late starter, and the writer PD James, another. A recent meeting of the Longevity Society in Britain discussed the particular longevity of conductors which may be, it was speculated, due to the exercise they get on the podium. Conductors are also known to have healthy libidos (and egoes)! Now there are more female ones.

Older typists make fewer errors!

It's Official: Life Begins at Forty-five

You might also be cheered to know that it's official: life doesn't begin until your mid-forties! A seven-year study funded by the Economic and Social Research Council recently found that women in their mid-forties enjoyed higher self-esteem, better family relationships and better jobs than younger women. The study tracked women from their late thirties into their sixties and found that the strongest change for the better in the forties was usually work related. It was the decade when many women were promoted to managers, began courses in higher education or started their own businesses, consolidating their success during the coming years.

For those looking farther ahead, Richard Schilling, eighty, and emeritus professor of occupational health at London University when he made this point in the *British Medical Journal*, noted that 'Women's superior longevity over men begins at retiring age and gradually increases.' Nearly 88 per cent of the over-one-hundred age group in England and Wales are women. The causes underlying this sex difference are complex. Cyril Clarke, an eminent physician and geneticist, suggests one reason why women live longer. [Because] 'There is no retirement for them, whereas many men, after gainful employment ceases, become less active both physically and mentally.' We mustn't give up this advantage, now that women's work encompasses what was once considered men's work as well as our seven-day-a-week, twenty-four-hour-a-day household responsibilities.

Fifties and Beyond: Prime Time

American management consultant Sydney Rice Harrild who runs The Coaching Company is fifty-seven and a believer that the years between fifty and seventy should be seen as 'prime time' for women. She says one of the most important things older women in the workplace can do is not buy into the conspiracy theory that says you're too old.

'Women often collude in being sidelined instead of standing up for their years of experience,' she warns her clients. 'A woman professor at Harvard came to me with three years left to go until her retirement and a contract up for negotiation and she was afraid they wouldn't re-hire her. All her friends said, "You're too old, and too expensive for them because you've been there too long. They could get someone younger for less." But I told her, "Go and tell the university what you can do for them that only you can do for them and that you can only do for three more years." That started her thinking about what she had to offer, and when she told them, they were happy to re-hire her, on a higher salary, and she had a wonderful run-up to retirement!'

Don't Let Work Stress You Out

Stress used to be considered an 'executive' affliction but the truth is that stress, the ultimate 'age accelerator' (see Chapter Two), is more likely to affect those struggling along in the middle of organizations than those at the top. The reason for this is that those at the top have

more control over their working lives. Sure, they may have to make megabuck decisions, but at least they get to make the decisions. It's far worse for the stress levels, as oodles of research in recent years by Professor Cooper and others has shown, to be lower down in the pecking order and have all your decisions made for you, or to feel in the dark about decisions affecting your job and your life.

How many people who feel powerless at work come home and take it out on their families by quarrelling with their spouses and shouting at their children? For older workers, many of whom may not have spouses or children, the stress is more likely to manifest itself in serious illness. Depression and feeling unable to cope are also symptoms of stress, not to mention all those furrowed brows and hangdog expressions which are so ageing.

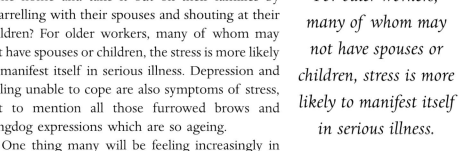

For older workers, many of whom may not have spouses or children, stress is more likely to manifest itself in serious illness.

One thing many will be feeling increasingly in the next millennium will be resentment within the work environment. There will be tension from older workers wanting to retire but who can't, from the younger workers having to pay more for the strained social security systems (especially in the States), from those who have planned for their retirements and those who haven't. The American social security system originated in the thirties to move out older workers and give opportunities to younger people. Now the system is trying to lure people back or keep them in as long as possible, not because they want people to stay in satisfying jobs but because they can't pay for them to retire.

Companies concerned about the growing scale of stress-related problems have hired stress counsellors and put in gymnasia so that staff can work off their frustrations, but more enlightened retirement policies could help. Changing pension law would enable people to phase out gradually, as Professor Sir Richard Doll (eighty-five) suggests, rather than being forced to work more than full time until retirement age in order to collect a decent pension, as the pension is assessed on the basis of that last year's income rather than on an accumulated average over the years.

COMMON CAUSES OF STRESS AT WORK

These include uncomfortable working position (computer screen too high / close / far away; unsuitable chair; worksurface that's too low, etc.),

unpleasant working environment ('sick' building without natural light, fresh air, pot plants; working with foul-smelling chemicals in improper ventilation; being subjected to noise, etc.), feeling over-pressured by work and feeling 'sidelined' and insecure about your job.

Job security has been a major stress factor over the past decade, with 'downsizing' and 'delayering' and all those fancy new words that mean firing being bandied about. Middle managers are either squeezed between the layer above and the layer below them or find themselves without those protective layers, doing the work of all three, as part of the new streamlining.

WAYS OF COMBATING STRESS AT WORK

Define your problem, to yourself, at least, and preferably to someone in authority if you have a reasonable complaint. Think of what needs changing in your working environment and see if you can change it without simply complaining about it. Bring in a book to raise your computer on if necessary, a back support for your chair, a pot plant to refresh the atmosphere around your desk. Join with other workers, if relevant, to protest against poor ventilation, chemicals, etc. If your company doesn't have a trendy stress counsellor, try to speak to your union representative or a 'health and safety executive' in confidence if you feel there is a serious safety issue.

Make sure you take plenty of exercise and have a healthy diet (see Chapter Nine) to combat the ill effects of your working environment.

Give yourself a game plan and a time scale to put it into action.

Always take a lunch break in which you try to get some fresh air and refuse to work consistently long hours that you feel are undermining your health. It's better if you don't just refuse, of course, but suggest a more constructive new working plan. If you bring your boss a problem, you're just dumping more stress on him or her which won't be appreciated. If you bring a solution, then you'll end up being more appreciated, and feeling less stressed.

To ensure you're not sidelined, apply some of the techniques we outline below, by keeping up with the office grapevine, relentless networking, and making yourself too valuable to get rid of.

All these simple measures will, most importantly, help you to take control of your working life, which should in itself alleviate much of the stress in it because stress comes from feeling out of control. Try

to change what you can, rather than just moaning about it, and if you feel change is unlikely then look for a way of getting out. Take a training course during your spare time. Look at opportunities in other departments. Give yourself a game plan and a time scale to put it into action. Don't just potter on until you're retired.

Image Matters

Partner to not thinking that you are past it is not looking past it. Image is key to remaining a viable member within a team if not holding on to your hard-earned management post. With age, some women become complacent and let their image slide from dynamo to mum to pensioner. While you don't need to exhaust yourself keeping apace with seasonal fashion fads you do need to look senior or equal to colleagues, whichever is appropriate. It is no wonder that older workers begin to get side-lined from crucial meetings and enjoying the visibility and influence they deserve because of how they present themselves. Perhaps one of the key things you do as you age and want or need to remain employable is to revamp your image.

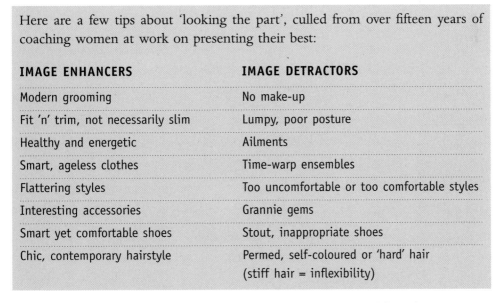

Here are a few tips about 'looking the part', culled from over fifteen years of coaching women at work on presenting their best:

IMAGE ENHANCERS	IMAGE DETRACTORS
Modern grooming	No make-up
Fit 'n' trim, not necessarily slim	Lumpy, poor posture
Healthy and energetic	Ailments
Smart, ageless clothes	Time-warp ensembles
Flattering styles	Too uncomfortable or too comfortable styles
Interesting accessories	Grannie gems
Smart yet comfortable shoes	Stout, inappropriate shoes
Chic, contemporary hairstyle	Permed, self-coloured or 'hard' hair (stiff hair = inflexibility)

One of Dr David Weeks's Superyoung women noted that although she had more than her fair share of wrinkles she looked younger than contemporaries, she felt, because she dressed in a more up-to-date way.

Along with looking the part is also acting the part. If some recent setbacks have dented your confidence, try not to convey your anxiety to others. Don't be brushed aside. If you get sidelined from important meetings, protest and ensure you are included next time rather than grumbling. Insist that your issues get on the agenda but rethink their presentation to keep them fresh. Your views should be sharp, focused and not too opinionated ('I think; I know; from where I sit, etc.'). Bite your tongue when new approaches are raised as your inclination to continue to do things 'as we've always done it' will make you appear older and set in your ways. Even though you might not agree, if consensus is to change then heartily add 'let's give it a go' for everyone to know that you will, indeed, be cooperative rather than co-opt their efforts.

WATCH YOUR BODY LANGUAGE

Don't hold back in introducing yourself when you are assembled with people you don't know, and the younger oafs don't have the manners to introduce you or want to imply that you aren't a key player, rather an observer. Speak up, clearly and confidently, with those you need to influence. Don't sneak tentatively into rooms. Instead walk tall, despite, or because of, the incipient shrinkage underway, and hold your head up high. Your facial muscles have probably dropped so go into 'perfor-mance puss', holding a positive smile and open eyes. Otherwise you will look like you are scowling. If taller, younger people try to intim-idate you by talking down to you both literally and figuratively, suggest that you both sit down, now eye to eye, to discuss things. Hold eye contact for effective periods, even though you might not be listening, to imply how captivated you are by what is being said, as younger colleagues are always desperate for an attentive audience and rarely get one!

Don't Let your Attitudes or your Arteries (or your Hairstyle) Harden

Along with fitting the image stereotype of being 'past it', beware of the ageist assumption about your skills or potential to learn new ones. It is often, perhaps widely, assumed that the older you are the less computer literate and able to adapt to changing circumstances you will be. Technophobia is just one more type of inflexibility against which UltraAgers have to guard. It is a problem you can work on more easily than getting rid of wrinkles and the results of your efforts will probably be more beneficial in the long term

Inflexibility can be a consequence of ageing on many levels. As our arteries, joints, bladders, eyeballs and other physical components become less flexible, so often does our mindset. This is something we must fight against if we want to age successfully, and a battle that we can win even if we can't win back peachy skin and perky breasts. Keep a nice soft hairstyle, since 'hard' hair implies an inflexible mindset, being set in your ways, a die-hard traditionalist, like the Queen. Sticking to the hairstyle you've had since your teen years can also be regarded as being inflexible, although it seems to have worked for fashion models Jerry Hall and Marie Helvin among others. With my image consultant hat on I've been dying to get my hands on Victoria's long locks which, with few exceptions, she's worn the same way since 1968. But she's inflexible on that point!

Inflexibility is something we must fight against if we want to age successfully.

The ability to be flexible is an important distinguishing feature in 'hardy' personalities, who can bend and twist around whatever life throws at them, or rise above it. Consider, for inspiration, hardy women of the past: The 'Flying Duchess' of Bedford took to the air at the age of sixty-one, when she was advised that the constant buzzing in her ears, a legacy of typhoid she had contracted as a girl in India, would be helped by flying, and at seventy-two, flying solo, disappeared into the sky in a grand exit. Or one of the great early women explorers such as Evelyn Lucy Cheesman who, unable to fulfil her ambition to become a veterinary surgeon, joined a scientific expedition travelling from the West Indies to the South Pacific when she was forty-three in 1924, and later made many lone expeditions. Or Rosita Forbes, who crossed the Libyan desert just after the First World War disguised as a Muslim and travelled from Kabul to Samarkand, India and South America, where she made a solo flight of 14,000 miles, in her late forties.

For every middle-aged woman who becomes more staid and set in her ways with age, there is another who thinks that life is 'an awfully big adventure' and continues to pursue it with vigour. We know which we would rather be.

Be an Adventuress if you Don't Want to be Left Behind

An 'old maid' mentality makes it impossible for some women (and men) to entertain the possibility of new ways of working, and makes them complain about change rather than embracing it as those with a more youthful mindset would do. These are the people who, to paraphrase the late Bobby Kennedy, see what is and ask why, usually querulously, rather than visualizing what might be and asking 'why not?' as more youthful and flexible minds would do. But even the notion of the 'old maid' is an anachronism in an era when being single is the lifestyle of choice for many young twenty and thirty-somethings who have the world at their feet, so get with it!

Mindsets, not chronological age, are what hold us back. We have all met, or worked with, 'old heads on young shoulders' or 'Young Fogies' who still believe that only a navy suit is acceptable for looking professional, and that letters should only be signed with a fountain pen. For every one of them there is a hip gran in Lycra who's a computer whizz and sends letters only via e-mail, and they should become more prevalent now that more senior citizens' clubs are introducing computer literacy courses and clubs and libraries are helping oldies to discover that on the net, at least, they can be ageless.

Nothing is more ageing than an inflexible mind, and it may be that rather than your staid skirts, sturdy shoes, stocky figure and stiffly set hair you need to zap up if you want to keep your place and even move ahead in the working world. So don't protest that you can't use the new computer system; do take advantage of any training opportunity offered by your company; if you still don't understand, do sign up for an evening or weekend course yourself; do learn from and share information with colleagues; don't underestimate the importance of office gossip, which is often where the really useful information is transmitted; and don't underestimate yourself and your potential!

Stay in the Mainstream if you Don't Want to be Sidelined

One complaint I often hear from people is that older workers increasingly use their age to isolate themselves. 'That's fine for you young things but at my age I would never try/do/learn/consider that.' When you start to become the 'office mum', then slide further into the 'office gran', you are limiting your potential and therefore become vulnerable to demotion or redundancy.

Older workers must keep up with the buzz, with what's happening. Rather than talk about your children and grandchildren all the time or, worse, your latest health problem, ask others' views on current events or new films or plays. Better still, organize the occasional evening out that would be a welcome change from their routine but still fun. Don't use every lunch hour to do the shopping or errands. Make a point of having a sandwich with some colleagues to catch up with the gossip. Rather than raising your eyebrows at the stories of last night's adventures, jest along with them. Try to interpret their lifestyle and views (ignoring some of the language!) and remember how you felt at their age. Their social madness is probably not far off what you used to get up to yourself. Ask their opinions and their advice so that you aren't always the one dishing it out.

Older workers must keep up with the buzz, with what's happening.

If younger colleagues do use you as a shoulder to cry on, or someone to come to for motherly advice, Professor Cary Cooper says you shouldn't feel insulted or threatened. 'Don't think of it as a granny role, think of it as a counsellor's role which is very important in an organization. Listen to people and spend time with them and they'll feel they were helped, and you will be invaluable. What keeps you young in the workplace is working happily alongside young people, people who are living in today rather than yesterday. Refresh your attitude, which can only happen when you're confronted by new ideas and new ways of working.'

Give yourself role models and find mentors to inspire you. They might be older – they might also be younger than you! Be on the lookout for them and for those you might mentor. 'When the pupil is ready the teacher appears.' It's a tough world out there for young and old, and we all need all the help we can get.

Different for the Boys

It is still easier for men to go on and on in high profile, front-line professions, whether they're ageing rockers like Mick Jagger, the Grateful Dead, Pink Floyd or the Eagles, ageing newscasters like Walter Cronkite

or Trevor MacDonald, celluloid sex symbols such as Clint Eastwood and Sean Connery, or ageing businessmen like Lords Hanson and Weidenfeld, Rupert Murdoch and Ted Turner. Women manage more easily to continue working if they work behind the scenes, like writers, artists or academics, with rare exceptions such as Tina Turner, former Irish President and now UN High Commission for Refugees Mary Robinson and America's veteran broadcaster Barbara Walters. But Boomers will even the odds, it is predicted, and with Barbra Streisand modelling for *Vogue* in her fifties and Cher for *Playboy*, the Duchess of Kent for *Tatler* in her sixties and models like Lauren Hutton and Jilly Pengilley setting the pace, perceptual barriers are being broken down every day.

Working it Out

Whether you can keep on working will ultimately boil down to your individual interests, skills and motivation. That's why it helps so much in keeping going if you love what you're doing. But all too many people don't. Why not see if there's something you can do about that right now? Make a list of what you like about your work, what you don't like, and what your ideal job or career would consist of. If the 'don't likes' far outnumber the 'likes' in your present line, why not see how you can move yourself closer to the ideal?

This might involve some compromises – a temporary period of hardship, perhaps, while you go on a course to acquire the necessary training or qualifications to move in the new direction. When one friend decided, in her fifties, to train as a psychotherapist after having been a psychology lecturer it took all her savings and the tolerance of her husband and family to see her through. But now she loves her work so much she hardly remembers the two years of scrimping, saving and uncertainty, and is making a far better living than she was. Better still, she is now in a job that doesn't carry any mandatory retirement age like her previous one, and where she feels part of a professional body that gives her support and social contact, yet is also self-employed and able to work from home and make her own hours. To her this is the best of all worlds.

Many colleges now offer opportunities and special assistance to women who are trying to make their mark in the workplace for the first time, and there is no reason why you can't take advantage of these for a change in career. These same colleges have careers advisers who may be able to help you. Courses for women 'returners', meant for women returning to work after raising their children, may help you to make a late-life career switch as so many women have, even if you don't have children! As Helen Sher, who managed one so successfully, advises, 'Go for your dream!'

Remember also for inspiration the many wonderful women writers of recent years who only began their careers in mid-life. Crime writers Minette Walters and P. D. James are just two.

Loving Your Work is Loving Yourself

Have you ever noticed how those who love what they're doing tend to look and feel younger while they're doing it? These people may appear to age quickly on enforced retirement. But those who are not happy in their work can be late bloomers when allowed to get on with hobbies and non-work interests they enjoy.

I remember how dreadful President Jimmy Carter looked during the stressful latter days of his presidency, when I worked on one of his more tenacious problems of immigration, then watched how he flowered into a distinguished elder-statesman afterwards.

Those who love their work tend to look and feel younger.

The opposite was true of British Prime Minister Margaret Thatcher, who aged terribly at first when she was unwillingly ousted from office. She seemed to wander around in a daze, and in a poignant interview told *Vanity Fair* magazine that when she had been so summarily 'bundled out' of No. 10 Downing Street, 'the pattern of my life was fractured. It is like throwing a pane of glass with a complicated map upon it on the floor and all the habits and thoughts and actions that went with it . . . you could not pick up those pieces.' Sometimes this great political mind could no longer remember what day it was, she lamented. But she managed to achieve a new equilibrium when she realized she could still be respected as an elder stateswoman, and be able to make a fortune on the international lecture circuit and run her own prestigious foundation.

As the famous naturalist the Honourable Miriam Rothschild observed at eighty-three, 'It is very important in old age to keep an

interest in one's work. If you're lucky enough to combine work and pleasure, as in my case what I call work is really pursuing my own interests, I see no reason why you shouldn't go on till you're a hundred!'

The nonagenarian best-selling novelist Barbara Cartland obviously agrees with that philosophy. As she has said on a number of occasions, 'The fatal thing is to stop and do nothing. People keep saying to me, "Why don't you retire?" It annoys me so much. If you retire your brain withers.'

But not everyone's brain 'withers' in retirement. For many, properly prepared, this period can be both rewarding and fulfilling and provide an invigorating new lease of life. However, those who don't choose retirement and are brushed aside because of age can lose their edge as well as their vitality.

> *The fatal thing is to stop and do nothing.*

It can be even harder if you're coping with a man who's lost his job at an age – anything over forty-five – when he's not easily likely to find another. As exercise expert Lizzie Webb, who started her own fitness studio for women after exercising her assets on morning television for ten years, observes, 'Several of the women I teach have husbands who are out of work for one reason or another, and the disintegration of those men can be painful for their wives to deal with.' This is because men tend to have fewer interests and friendships outside work than women do, and therefore go to pieces and age visibly on any retirement that's not a planned one they were looking forward to – and sometimes even if it was, when their lack of purpose and status can sink in.

Keep on Going to Keep Going Strong!

Some sort of vocation – work you love doing, whether it's paid or unpaid – is as vital for a healthy old age as loving companionship, a good diet and regular exercise. This is borne out by Pat York's memorable study of seventy-five over-seventy-fives who were still *Going Strong*. York asked her seventy-five respondents in their seventies, eighties and nineties the same questions, including 'Where do you get your creative force and energy?' and 'Do you have a personal formula you have followed?' While the answers were all fascinatingly varied, the majority boiled down, it seems, to the same thing: enjoying a continuous love affair with life; being curious, not complacent; looking forward with enthusiasm rather than back in anger or regret; and remaining intensely

involved with other people and in absorbing work, be it paid or voluntary, hobby or vocation.

Socialite and philanthropist Brooke Astor, high in her nineties, told York, 'My working day starts a little after 8 a.m. and goes on uninterruptedly from morning till night. Twice a week I do yoga . . . I go out every single night . . .'

Dilys Powell, the celebrated film critic, said at ninety, 'If I didn't have work I'd end up unfocused and unmotivated, and that would be absolutely appalling.' 'Late starter' Harriett Doerr, who published her first novel, the critically acclaimed *Stones for Ibarra*, when she was in her seventies, said at eighty-one, 'Use everything you have. Whatever your talent is – gardening, planting, painting, words, music – don't just shake your head. Try it at any age!'

Katherine Harris went back to college at the age of seventy-six, surrounded by students a quarter of her age, and went on, because of that, to write three short stories which were broadcast on the radio. She is currently writing a book on her childhood in East London. 'By the end of the first lesson I was accepted,' says Katherine at eighty-two. 'There's nothing older people can't do if they put their minds to it!'

The message that emerges is that it's never too late, but that it's important to remember that this life isn't a rehearsal, so seize every opportunity and make the most of it.

9

Healthy Body

'The body dies; the body's beauty lives.'
WALLACE STEVENS (1879–1955)

ALL AGEING IS NOT EQUAL

The recipe for successful ageing, barring accidents, unfortunate genes, or sheer bad luck, includes exercise (physical and mental), a healthy diet, a positive outlook, absorbing work or interests and plenty of love and laughter. The recipe is being dished out to you in, we hope, palatable form. In this chapter, we are focusing on the body, what shape you are in and what you can do to get it in tip-top form both inside and out.

Often you see a stunning woman – well groomed, well dressed, probably slim. You think, Wow! Doesn't she look terrific for her age? You don't know her actual age but think she looks mighty good. Then you might meet one of these gals on the way into the gym. She gets undressed and her image deflates as she exposes the real body underneath. The glamour-puss is transformed without her armour into a frail, vulnerable, older woman. You see the slight stoop heretofore unnoticeable under the well-tailored jacket. Then there are the varicose veins. The thighs and underarms are flabby. You might see her working out and wonder if the poor dear is really up to it! This woman clearly cared about appearances from the outside and was just going through the motions of exercise, but not very energetically or often. So, remember that even if you might be looking your years on the outside, you might be strong and vibrant internally and last much longer than younger lookers.

We age in different ways, not always coherently or, we may think, fairly. But the way we age can tell us a lot about ourselves. One woman we see in the gym has a body that would not look out of place on a twenty-one-year-old, no kidding, and yet her face beneath its tightly permed, iron grey hair, is that of a seventy-year-old. Her real age is somewhere in between – fifty-five, she says. She's had a tough life emotionally, has been through a messy divorce, but through it all kept exercising. It shows.

Genetics play an important part in ageing but so too will the body, mind and spirit that you have developed on your own. UltraAgers tend to keep their figures pretty much the same as they were in their youth within a pound or two. One spectacular example is Margaret Read, who at the age of fifty-five was still wearing the same pair of white shorts her mother bought her when she was twelve, and still looking fabulous in them. Margaret, mother of two daughters, remained a trim size 10 thanks to dancing classes and the fact that she was able to wear

shorts in 1984 to a fancy dress party, dressed as a holiday camp hostess, shows that she has a good sense of humour which has also no doubt helped to keep her so youthful looking. In the pictures published of her in the shorts, still white and crisp, in the *Daily Mail* she looked closer to thirty-five than fifty-five!

Some women, however, who have made remaining slim, as opposed to fit, their priority, can age badly. A thin woman will lose her skin elasticity more noticeably and quickly without decent muscle mass or extra body fat to plump it out and can look years older than a fuller figured gal. The important point is not to fret about size or the scales but to concentrate on a healthy body mass and finding the optimum weight to feel good about yourself. Once you're there, you'll know if you're gaining or losing weight by the way your waistbands fit, another important reason for avoiding elasticated ones as a rule. If you're hefty but firm and able to move well, fair enough. You are probably healthier than someone who's slimmer but flabby and frail. The old 'pinch an inch' guideline is probably fair enough. If you can pinch more than this from your waist or the back of your arm then you've got flab to lose, and flab never flattered, or improved the health of, anyone. It is dead weight: get rid of it!

Vitality and fitness are far more important than simply looking good at any age. Yes, this is an image guru speaking! I tell this to all my clients, male or female, of every generation that if you are fit you will be a magnet to others. Your clothes can be discount specials and they will look like designer gear if your body is toned, your posture positive and your pace energetic. Lethargy is one of the key age accelerators and results from not viewing your food as fuel for your system and not getting enough exercise of the right kind, duration and mix.

Exercise: Key to an Active, Painfree Life

SIMPLE LIVING, SIMPLE PLEASURES

It is already possible to live to be twice the biblically allotted span of three score and ten even without the help of the anti-ageing experts. The world's oldest man just before this book was published (well, it's always difficult to be sure, but his is one plausible claim) was Bir Narayan Chaudhari of Nepal, born in 1856. His key to longevity? 'Raw tobacco

and no alcohol', he said, puffing on his pipe, surrounded by his loving grandchildren, great grandchildren, great great grandchildren and even one great, great, great grand niece! His diet was always a sparse one, consisting of grapes, rice, vegetables and, occasionally, pork washed down with plenty of water in an area with little pollution, no processed foods and no high pressure deadlines.

'People who live simple lives, away from modern stresses, live longer,' explains Dr Mario Kyriasis of the Longevity Society. 'It's a healthy peasant lifestyle with plenty of exercise in the daily work. They also eat very small amounts of food – up to 30 per cent fewer calories than most people.' Supported by much recent evidence, the super-slim Dr Kyriasis believes that 'Over eating is the main reason why we don't tend to reach our maximum age in the West.' Nepal, Bir's homeland, has the world's biggest cohort of centenarians.

Fewer than 50% of women over 55 find walking at a normal pace possible!

Curiously, Bir had several heads of hair over the course of his life. He lost it and then it would suddenly sprout back, sometimes grey, sometimes black like a young man's. And every time his teeth fell out another set supposedly appeared. He was never in a hospital and must have been blessed by an amazing metabolism. While we might not possess Bir's wonder genes or his simple, stress-free lifestyle we can be doing more to make the most of our own potential lifespans both in terms of quality as well as breadth. It is encouraging to know that half of all seventy-five- to eighty-four-year-olds in our society, and more than a third of all eighty-five-year-olds, are healthy and require no special care or treatment.

AGEING ACHIEVERS AND UNDERACHIEVERS

Read this carefully: fewer than 50 per cent of women aged fifty-five to seventy-four find walking at a normal pace on ground level possible! That's in Britain, according to the Allied Dunbar's National Fitness Survey 1992. If it is that bad in the United Kingdom, one wonders what the results would be in the States. There, although there are many white-haired show-offs power-walking, pumping iron and running marathons, the vast majority of people of all ages rarely walk anywhere and are far more reliant on their cars for transportation than Europeans.

Yet, as exercise physiologist Professor Craig Sharp points out, 'The mean age of a recent Himalayan expedition was seventy, a golfer shot

At sixty-one South African fitness expert Sally Mills is living proof of the benefits of exercise. Told at the age of fifteen that she was destined to a life of pain and to be wheelchair-bound, Sally decided to take her destiny into her own hands by making herself strong and fit despite the experts' diagnosis.

As a bubbly child of eight, Sally had a passion for doing somersaults, not on the ground like most kids but in the air, in trees! So, unsurprisingly one day she fell out of a tree and earned herself an injury that eventually caused scoliosis (curvature of the spine) which went untreated until she was fifteen. Then the orthopaedic surgeons forbade this sports-mad teenager from pursuing any more exercise so that she didn't exacerbate her badly aligned vertebrae.

Sally ignored their advice and was determined to continue with sports that she loved – dance, tennis, hockey and swimming. With the help of her physical education teacher at school she developed an exercise routine to stretch and strengthen her back muscles. The programme was so successful that she continued her sporty life for many years.

With the difficult birth of her fourth child by Caesarean section, Sally was forced to rest. But the rest caused her back to seize up so badly that she became totally incapacitated. Sally again defied the gloomy prognosis of her doctors and used her common sense to sort herself out. She accepted medical help for her acute pain but worked up a 'remedial routine' of stretching to strengthen her back. 'If I stop exercising, the pain returns. It has become a way of life for me for thirty years,' she explains. From all her stretching, Sally is as supple as a teenager and remains free of back pain without drugs.

'Older people can develop back problems even if they have never felt a twinge of discomfort earlier,' according to Sally. She insists that exercise is the answer to a pain-free, active life. 'The connective tissue between the bones and the muscles thickens with age and cuts off the blood supply to the muscles. Without adequate circulation of blood in the muscle you develop aches and pains. So you've got to keep moving,' she says.

Sally now has a mission to teach older women and men how to remain supple and free of backache in their later years. Through her Health and Fitness Professional Association in South Africa she trains instructors in her proven techniques and is proud to have the endorsement of many medical practitioners. 'I want to convince everyone of any age that if you take responsibility for your own health and fitness you will remain energized and supple for as long as you want,' says Sally. Just seeing Sally in action, despite a twisted spine, is living proof of her conviction.

a hole in one at eighty-seven, another was still playing at a hundred and six and a cross-country skier died at a hundred and eleven.' So there is no excuse for such pathetic statistics. Particularly when, of the world's 40,000 centenarians only 22 per cent are men – married, not bachelors; although the largest portion of women who reached 100 were not married!

Today's mid-lifers will ensure that the streets are cluttered with geriatric joggers in the years ahead. We have grown up with fitness regimes from competitive school sports through to countless crazes like the aerobics boom of the seventies and eighties, belonging to health clubs and gyms and, for the really privileged few, acquiring a personal trainer. We have tried our hand (and body) at a host of active pursuits and, hopefully, have one or two that are integral to our lives. We know the benefits of achieving and maintaining fitness and want to sustain that as we age.

EXERCISE: IT'S GOT TO BE JOYFUL

If taking exercise is a chore, you haven't figured it out yet. Sure, you are doing what you should be doing, but without the enjoyment factor you won't sustain it or worse the workout will become stressful and actually be detrimental to your health. From the perspective of a couch potato it is difficult to envisage the wonders of fitness. It is harder even to contemplate moving if you are stiff, tired or in some pain due to arthritic joints, a bad back or other problem. But the more you do the more you will want to do as you start to experience the absolute joy of a fit body and new energy.

If you have been badgered into a new regime and hate it, stop. Seek an activity you can look forward to. The fun of exercise should not only be in the doing but also in the anticipation as well as in the aftermath when you feel satiated in the endorphins, your body's natural ones, pumping around your system. As a runner, I try to plan my runs the night before when, after checking my next day's schedule, I find a convenient spot to get out and run. I envisage the time of day and how I will feel as well as the course that I will take. Sometimes my plans go out of the window due to unforeseen interruptions or my body just saying 'not today, thank you'. It is important that you listen to these messages. But that never puts me off planning the next run and feeling even better knowing that the one day off will ensure an even stronger, faster pace.

You might be thinking, she's obsessed. Indeed I am as are all fit and active people. Exercise isn't whimsical to us, it is integral to our lives. Going without a workout is as disruptive as eating badly or having insomnia. It is part of our equilibrium both mentally and physically.

DON'T JUST TALK. WALK YOURSELF FITTER

If you are able bodied and can walk you can change your life today. You can have stronger bones, more energy and a better figure just by walking more every day. It is one of the best all-round exercises, aerobic as it works the cardiovascular system and increases your lung capacity but low impact, hence there is little chance of injury. Walking is also weight bearing and strengthens your bones without jarring your joints. If you really walk, rather than saunter, you stretch and tone the muscles which keep the whole body supple.

You can walk with a purpose, to the park, the shops, the office, or you can be aimless on your own or with a friend or dog, but you must walk briskly for the effort to have some benefit, with a mile taking you about fifteen minutes. Your goal should be to walk for at least thirty minutes at least three times a week. But once you start, you will no doubt start building it into your daily schedule. When walking becomes your favoured means of transport it is no longer just exercise but your method of getting about. Avoid carrying heavy bags, especially shoulder bags always worn over one shoulder, in preference to a back pack which distributes the weight evenly and is carried by the stronger back muscles. Use your back pack to carry your pretty shoes for wearing later because serious walkers only wear the right gear for getting about – well-supported shoes or boots or trainers.

If you are able bodied and can walk you can change your life today.

Your breathing should be heavier than normal when walking for effect but you should be able to hold a conversation. In fact, not being able to walk and converse is a sign of poor coordination and of someone more likely to fall, according to Dr Dawn Skelton, exercise expert.

MAKE IT SOCIAL

Many people feel more committed to exercise if they can do it with friends or find an activity that helps them meet new people. In every town, village or city in the Western world there are a panoply of exercise classes from yoga and keep fit to line dancing and karate. There

is something for everyone regardless of age or previous experience or ability to look good in Lycra.

When intrigued to get involved in something new, try to watch a session in action to get a feel for it. Speak to both the instructor as well as a few participants and ask about joining up and how it felt for them at first. Even the snazziest health clubs have a sense of camaraderie when it comes to new people joining in. We all remember what it felt like ourselves so there are bound to be several people to show you the ropes. The social aspect and peer support of classes is something that appeals to women, in particular. Many a fitness studio becomes a social club, with women spending hours happily chatting over coffee after class and even organizing outings together outside class time, as Lizzie Webb has found with women she teaches.

Don't think that everyone who goes to exercise classes is a lean, mean aerobic machine flaunting their muscular forms in leopard-skin Lycra. Okay, so there are a few around. But real workout pros don't give a hoot about what they wear as long as it is practical, so leggings and an oversized T-shirt do fine. Classes for the overweight and over-fifty are, fortunately, proliferating.

LOOK EAST

Many of the most popular exercise classes today are based on Eastern disciplines like yoga and t'ai chi which are wonderful for people of all ages and can be done well into old age. The benefits of yoga, in particular, cannot be overestimated. It keeps the body supple, improves circulation and strength, and works the muscles hard enough to pull against the bones which stregthens them against osteoporosis. Stand on one leg for a minute (or a few seconds) if you can. Feel how the muscles judder and pull against the bone to try to keep you standing up straight? Apparently that action strengthens the bones and protects against osteoporosis. In other yoga poses, although they may not look too active, the muscles are also pulling strongly against the bone, working against gravity. Try holding this controlled pose, just standing on one leg and then the other for as long as you can every day and you will be strengthening your bones without even breaking into a sweat.

Yoga is the ideal anti-ageing exercise because it is always working against gravity, always stretching, lengthening and opening the body, unlike other exercises which can jar joints and actually shorten certain muscles. You ask a soccer player to straighten out his legs!

LISHA, 52, was a yoga teacher and astrologer who has moved into humanistic counselling work. She demonstrates a few key yoga poses that anyone can master and, like both of us, believes that a bit of yoga a day can help keep ageing at bay.

These poses are terrific for strengthening the whole skeletal and muscular systems while improving concentration, balance and confidence. Check with your doctor before starting any new type of exercise. All asanas, or poses, should be done slowly, gently and carefully. Never force anything. Breathe evenly and deeply through the nose. Strength develops from the duration in poses as well as balancing poses (using forward and backward bending stretches).

1) The Tree

Good for the pelvis, hip joints and shoulders, and may help prevent osteoporosis.

Pick a spot straight ahead of you to focus on at eye level or below – even yourself in a mirror. Shift your weight on to your right leg and gently raise the left foot and place it – with the help of your left hand if necessary – into the inside of your right thigh, the heel digging into the inner thigh as high as is comfortable. (Easier without tights.) Gradually build up the time you can hold the pose to sixty seconds. When confident raise your arms above your head, palms together. Alternate sides.

2) Forward Bends

Help prevent the shrinkage of age. Important for keeping the spine elastic and flexible and for the abdominal organs, kidneys and digestion.

Standing version (sit if you have high blood pressure or back problems). Stand erect with pelvis tucked under. Raise hands above head. Lower the chest down gently towards the knees, stretching out the back and keeping it straight. The head should drop last and the bend is from the hip, not curving the back, the head in a straight line with the body.

Inhale before you begin to drop, slowly exhaling to relax into your stretch. As you complete your descent hold onto your calves, ankles or (if advanced) place your palms on either side of your feet. Hold the pose but not your breath! Inhale and exhale calmly to extend more deeply into the pose. Surrender to gravity. Hold for 30 seconds, then increase to 60 seconds or longer. Slowly unwind, keeping the neck rounded, pelvis in, the head the last thing to come up.

3) Cobra

Good for the spine and hip joints, and for strengthening the abdomen and kidneys. It overcomes backbone stiffness, increasing flexibility.

Lie on your stomach and raise yourself up on your elbows, forearms out straight in front of you on the floor at shoulder width apart. Hold. (Mid pose illustrated.)

4) Bow Pose

Stimulates the circulation, pancreas (said to be good for diabetes) and leg muscles.

This is an advanced posture and not to be tried in isolation (only the mid pose is illustrated). Do not attempt unless you are comfortable in a Cobra.

Start by lying with your forehead on the floor. Bend your legs at your knees and reach behind to hold your ankles, then inhale. On the exhale, bring yourself up slowly by pulling on your feet, which arches your back.

5) Child and prayer poses

The 'antidote' to the Cobra and Bow poses, and counters the effects of sitting all day and incipient osteoporosis.

Kneel, then sit back on your feet and curl your torso forward, relaxing on to your thighs. Stretch your arms forward to form the Prayer pose, or relax your arms back along your legs in the Child pose. Either one of these helps to stretch the spine and lengthen the space between the vertabrae, good for preventing back trouble. Hold for as long as is comfortable, breathing slowly and deeply. You could even fall asleep in this one!

With the discipline of yoga your balance will improve, which will prevent falls and accidents later in life. Certain poses are said to be particularly good for women's reproductive organs as they open up the pelvic region and increase the blood supply there. Others help to nourish the brain. It is quite common to be in a yoga class with eighty-year-olds standing on their heads. But if that seems a remote possibility for you, shoulder stands or the head down dog pose also get blood flowing to the head – and also mitigate the ageing effects of gravity!

The deep breathing integral to yoga and t'ai chi is both calming and invigorating and improves lung capacity. Enhancing the ability of the lungs to take in and hold oxygen improves a range of health conditions from asthma and heart complaints to insomnia. At the Yoga Therapy clinic, which through its Yoga Biomedical Trust researches the beneficial effects of yoga on various diseases, Dr Robin Monro has used yoga to help asthmatics, diabetics, MS sufferers and the generally stressed. He has even devised a programme suitable for wheelchair users.

Don't worry about needing to be 'mystical' or having to adopt a new religion to benefit from exotic disciplines. Most types taught in the West are physical rather than spiritual, concentrating on the poses (the exercises) rather than the meditation, although classes may end on some concentrated relaxation.

Wonderful as an aerobic workout such as swimming can be, it is not enough for post-menopausal women as there is no weight-bearing component and therefore the bones are not strengthened via swimming. But it does increase your lung capacity and, combining swimming with regular walking, you'll be enjoying a balanced and productive exercise regime. But, please, don't think that you can benefit from swimming if you try to keep your hairdo dry, or by floating along or hanging on the side of the pool doing more chatting than lapping. The former will hurt your back (by curving your spine as you try to swim with your neck up) and the latter means you aren't working hard enough. Treat every exercise effort as just that – effort – to get the full benefit.

VARIETY IS THE SPICE OF LIFE

With any exercise routine, no matter how committed you are or how much you excel at it, you can feel jaded by it from time to time. Before you do something so repetitively that you cease to find pleasure in it, try varying your schedule with a few different activities so that you never get bored doing the same thing. The other risk of concentrating on one sport, says the relentless runner, is that you over stress certain muscles, limbs and joints and under work others. So mix your workouts with complementary ones to keep you and your body happy and balanced.

Rest days are essential. Don't build in so few so that you are putting your system at risk of getting run down and over stressed. But also, beware of taking too many days off over a month or you will lose the momentum and never build up your fitness. A good guiding principle is to exercise more days a week than you take off, for example, at least four times.

USE IT OR LOSE IT

Even if you are fit and healthy, you are losing strength year on year of between 1 and 2 per cent, with power slowing up between 3 and 4 per cent. But in a research project directed by Dr Dawn Skelton of the Royal Free Hospital, working with women seventy-five to ninety-three, she found they could increase the strength of the muscles, for example, the thigh muscle, by 25 per cent in only three months with gentle exercise. That's the equivalent of taking off about twenty years of your age in only twelve weeks, she says. And most exercise is free or low cost, unlike other methods of making you look younger. The benefits of exercise are more than superficial.

In Dr Skelton's booklet of exercises, available from Research into Ageing, she points out that regular exercise achieves the following:

✧ Decreases muscular tension and joint pain.
✧ Can prevent falls, broken bones and osteoporosis.
✧ Increases circulation.
✧ Improves lung capacity.
✧ Prevents or lessens the effects of heart disease.
✧ Aids the treatment of many diseases like diabetes and Parkinson's.
✧ Prevents and aids the rehabilitation of arthritis.

✧ Enhances bowel movement and helps control and prevent incontinence.
✧ Lessens lower back pain.
✧ Prevents thrombosis.
✧ Prevents gravitational oedema (swollen ankles).
✧ Generates warmth.
✧ Heightens alertness.
✧ Helps with insomnia.
✧ Increases self-confidence.
✧ Alleviates depression.

'Variety of exercise is the key to keeping at it', according to Lizzie Webb, the pioneer of television fitness in Britain.

One woman who is proof that 'it's never too late' is Daphne Belt, now fifty-eight, who on her fiftieth birthday described herself as 'fat and unfit'. Deciding to take up sports, with the encouragement of Age Resource, part of Age Concern, she took up exercise. At fifty-seven, Daphne came sixth in her age group in the World Triathlon Championships in Australia and now trains about twenty hours a week. She cycles 180 miles, runs 35 and swims. Encouraging other women to follow her experience, Daphne says she is happier than she ever thought possible. 'This is the real me.'

Aerobics guru Dr Kenneth Cooper put three groups of pre-menopausal women into training to walk three miles a day, three days a week for six months. The first group, which walked twenty-minute miles, increased their aerobic capacity by 4 per cent. The second group, which walked a brisk fifteen-minute mile, increased it by 9 per cent, with a third cohort of power walkers doing twelve-minute miles improving by 14 per cent. Hence, getting fitter is easy, do-able, with results as soon as a few months away.

Lizzie Webb, fifty, is one of the pioneering television experts on fitness, who went on to run her own studio for women of all ages with separate classes for men. She warns, 'Don't equate thinness and youthfulness with fitness. Some of the least fit people can be beautiful and slim but survive on coffee, cigarettes and drugs. Look at the fashion models! They have youth on their side, many of them. But eventually their lifestyle will take its toll. A seventy-year-old who exercises can be fitter than a sedentary forty-year-old.' She recommends a variety of exercises to encompass all three important components of fitness: suppleness, stretch and stamina.

'Ideally you should be doing 'cross training – mixing different types of exercise every week, so that you are swimming, cycling, dancing, doing yoga and some gym work. You must keep challenging your body.

You don't have to exercise for longer, just harder. Increase your weight load so that instead of lifting two pounds you lift four,' she explains. 'But too many women think they can just show up at the gym and waft about without any benefit aside from catching up on the latest gossip.'

Even women suffering with osteoporosis can improve. Lizzie talks about one she helped who suffered from a severe dowager's hump. She could scarcely do a sit-up. Lizzie patiently guided her to build up her stomach muscles which would, in turn, strengthen her back. Now the woman is in a much stronger condition. 'You can't undo a dowager's hump, but you can stop things from deteriorating further and improve the quality of life in the process,' says Lizzie.

WHAT WORKS

For exercise to affect body weight it needs to be of thirty–forty minutes' duration minimum and be vigorous, like walking for at least four sessions a week. Dr Skelton warns that people with asthma, angina or other ailments may avoid physical activity because their symptoms become worse during exercise. 'But the loss of fitness can result in new symptoms at progressively lower levels of exercise intensity,' she notes, 'leading to a vicious circle in which a patient with only moderate disease becomes severely disabled, due to low exercise intolerance.'

Dr Skelton recommends the old-fashioned isometric principles as more effective the older we get. 'You won't see much going on but plenty is happening, via resistance, with the muscles. You will certainly feel the impact as well as notice your strength improving with regular practice.'

Always warm up before you do any exercise. Even before a brisk walk, stretch for a bit. And remember that your muscles need lengthening as well as strengthening. So after any workout, allow time to stretch out or your muscles will actually shorten and bulk up. It is better to do a routine slowly and correctly than to do a zillion repetitions wrong. With weights, aim for slow, concentrated movements. Better to do five perfect movements than multiple ones with everything flailing about. Coordinate your breathing by inhaling before you make the effort and exhaling when you are applying the greatest strain.

LISTEN TO YOUR BODY

It is too easy to get swept up in the excitement of exercise. Joining peppy classes with pulsating music and bouncing bodies can lure you

into some moves that might spell disaster if you don't keep in tune with your own body. Modify any and all activities, even when in a class, to suit your abilities and your body. It takes time for the multitude of heretofore complacent muscles to get in shape. Don't rush them and you will improve much more quickly. Never do anything someone else suggests unless you feel you are capable of it.

Overweight people don't listen to their body when it tells them it's satiated. They often eat so fast that they are unaware that they are well past the point of being full. Stressed people don't listen to their body when it tells them that if they don't deal with the cause of the stress it is going to break down. They ignore the little warning signals like sniffles, sore throats, skin rashes and sleeping problems and just collapse in a heap. Overworked people don't listen to their body when it tells them to take a break. They only end up with longer illnesses or worse disease that prevents them from continuing the work that they love. Addicts don't listen to their body when it tells them that what they crave is not what they need.

So learn to listen to your body. It is 'speaking' to you all the time.

So learn to listen to your body. It is 'speaking' to you all the time. Learn its language, its signals, which offer key early warnings of trouble ahead. When in doubt, see a doctor. Err on the side of making a pest of yourself, just in case, rather than overlook a change or signal that just may save your life. Signals to look out for include pain, tiredness, dizziness, headaches, blurred vision, breathlessness, and a pounding or uneven heartbeat.

The Food Dilemma

In the '90s food has become almost sexier than sex! The television schedules are bursting with cookery programmes from the experts sharing their secrets as well as the inexpert making fools of themselves trying to follow recipes. We are voyeurs in the kitchens of superstars, thanks to the minicam, and attend dinner parties as a 'fly on the wall' given by amateur cooks who are so impressive that in previous eras they would have been gourmets in their own right. Our supermarkets offer a full panoply of food no longer native but international with previous seasonal offerings of fruits and vegetables being sourced for

both our convenience and custom year-round. We no longer sit down to just three meals a day but eat all day long, which is good for us in several mini meals but if it is continuous and gluttonous grazing then it is a certain road to developing a weight problem.

The temptation to indulge is ever present in what has been described as a 'toxic food environment' by obesity experts. This is why so many of us suffer from (over) weight problems that feed the multinational, multibillion-pound diet industry. We are deluged daily with diet advice from magazines, newspapers, and the swelling ranks of diet gurus on the bookshelves. Do we go for the low fat Hip and Thigh Diet or with the Hay Food Combining Diet? Is raw food the answer or should we follow our livers (the Liver-Cleansing Diet) or our blood group (the Blood Group Diet)? Why not live it up and follow the Champagne Diet or do as the beautiful people do on the Beverly Hills Diet? On the same day in Britain that one newspaper was touting the GI Diet (meaning 'glucose intolerance', not what American soldiers eat) and claiming that sugar was the major baddie that made us gain weight, another newspaper leaked a World Health Organisation (WHO) report saying that a little bit of sugar makes us healthier than none at all. Who are we to believe?

There is still considerable debate in the world of anti-ageing medicine over the ideal diet. Some specialists, such as Dr Vincent Giampapa, recommend a virtually vegan regime. Others, like Dr Ronald Klatz, believe consumption of first-class animal protein is important for building lean muscle tissue. Dr Michael Perring suggests we should adopt something akin to the primitive diet consisting of meat and fish, and nuts and berries along with fruit and vegetables. The experts do concur that we should not eat too much. Increasing numbers of studies show that rats that eat less live longer than those allowed to stuff themselves. This seems to be true for people, too.

IS SIMPLY EATING LESS THE KEY TO LONGEVITY?

Many people believe that eating a restricted diet is a prerequisite to longevity, since limited rations have been shown to have dramatic effects in increasing the lifespan of rodents. Some keen pursuers of longevity have decided to permanently restrict themselves to a daily caloric intake of 1,500 or less. But Dr Brian Merry of the Institute of Human Ageing, who has researched into and experimented with the effects of diet restriction since 1975, prefers to eat 'a normal healthy diet, with plenty of vegetables and fruit', because, he says, 'I think the level of restricted feeding necessary to get this effect in animals would not be acceptable in humans. You have to get the balance right, and brain and kidney damage can result if the damage is too severely restricted. With humans, too, everyone is different. You can get rodents genetically identical and control their lives to a great extent. But every human is an experiment in themselves.' Like the woman who claims to be a 'breatharian' – living on air – or 'fruitarians' who, more plausibly, exist on fruit.

A restricted diet will only be an advantage to rodents

Naturally, every time research is published Dr Merry gets letters from people asking what diet they should be on. 'I have to tell them this [diet] is not tested on humans,' says he. He points out that restricted diet will only be an advantage to rodents who live in a very restricted, protected environment. 'If you put the diet-restricted rodents in to the wild I don't think they'd survive very well,' he says, encouragingly to those of us who like to go wild from time to time with our food. 'There is a price to pay for longevity – in nature there are always trade-offs. If you start them on a restricted diet early their growth is restricted, too, and thermogenesis is compromised, so that they can't generate enough heat to deal with very cold conditions.'

It is well known that it can be an advantage to carry slightly more fat in a cold climate, but those without much excess thrive in hotter climates. Dr Merry notes that a restricted diet can play havoc with a female's reproductive capacity, but not always necessarily for the worse. While the onset of puberty will be delayed in undernourished rodents, 'We could have rats giving birth to their first litter at 900 days, when the controls would finish being fertile at 550 days,' he says.

So while the jury is still out on the benefits of a restricted diet, it is generally acknowledged that over eating can't be good for us, as we take in more toxins than our bodies can process, along with the excess calories which are turned into fat. And many centenarians, when asked about their secrets of longevity, refer to eating 'moderately' or 'not much' or 'only when hungry', even if they indulge in the odd smoke or tipple, and most are from countries and cultures in which food is not as plentiful as it is in the West.

Our feeling is that it is 'different strokes for different folks' and that every individual is, indeed, an experiment as Dr Merry suggests. There

were reports recently about a young woman apparently thriving on a diet of nothing but chocolate bars; others report losing stones and feeling healthy on the high fat Sugarbusters Diet sweeping the States. No one diet works for everyone and none can claim the moral high ground. We all respond differently to different foods as well as to when and how often we eat.

Every woman has a friend who succeeded with one approach which proved a demoralizing failure for another. One couple we know went on the Hay Diet (food combining) together. For those unfamiliar with its principles, you can eat protein and vegetables at some meals and carbohydrates and vegetables at others but never protein and carbohydrate together. The man lost weight, firmed and toned up and felt his energy levels rise. The woman actually gained weight and felt lethargic and sluggish. She began to thrive when she eliminated yeast from her diet and stopped eating the breads and cakes she adored, after learning from a food allergist that was where her problems lay.

The notion of food intolerances makes many doctors go puce with rage. They simply dismiss it as nonsense. But nutritionists can all tell of quite miraculous results with patients who feel completely different after eliminating a troublesome food. The most frequent causes of food intolerance include: dairy products, sugar, gluten (wheat products), red meat and citrus fruit.

WEIGHT AND SHAPE: IS THERE A CORRELATION?

Your body shape – how you carry your weight and store fat – and your metabolism requires understanding if you are to eat well without worrying about gaining weight. Different body shapes have different metabolisms according to a former consultant of mine, Bel Hislop, author of *The Body Breakthrough*. In her book, Bel cites a study at the University of Gotenburg in which researchers studied a) women who put on weight predominantly above the hips, as most men do, and b) women who put on weight mainly below the waist on the hips, bottom and thighs. The former shape is called android and the latter gynoid.

Women who carry their weight in the middle are thought to have 'bigger' fat cells than women who carry their weight lower. These chunky fat cells also turn out to be the more problematic in terms of health as women, like men, with android shapes and excess weight above the hips have a higher risk of cardiac disease. In other research of over 40,000 women, the Medical College of Wisconsin found that upper body fat increased other health risks: diabetes and gall bladder disease as well as menstrual abnormalities.

Hislop recommends sound principles for anyone wanting to lose weight: keep your fat intake low, eat plenty of fibre, and try to limit sugar in the diet. It is more debatable whether to eat according to your metabolic rate which is linked to your basic shape. Pear shapes are, she believes, kept trim if they eat a main meal at lunch or dinner but should go light with breakfast. Hourglass figures need three balanced meals a day and must resist any proclivity to 'graze' which causes them to gain unwanted pounds. Angular, rectangle shapes, Hislop says, are satisfied most by a rewarding meal in the evening as these women are more inclined to do more aerobic exercise and can afford to scoff more in the evening as they will be burning up more energy during the day.

Hourglass figures are inclined to 'graze'.

But any woman keen to lose excess weight is wise to follow these guidelines: eat only when hungry; stop when you are no longer hungry but not necessarily full; drink plenty of water to feel less hungry and to flush out your system; and eat as much fresh fruit and raw vegetables as you want.

It is now thought that a thick waist is a surer predictor of late-onset diabetes than other factors. A waist measuring more than thirty-five inches is said to be the danger point for women, over forty inches for men, according to a study from the University of Glasgow published in 1998 in the *Lancet*. According to researchers there, waist size is one of the most important predictors generally of the length and quality of life, so anything you can do to whittle it down is important. It may be even more significant than BMI, Body Mass Index, achieved by taking weight in kilograms and dividing by height in metres squared. Normal BMIs are between twenty and twenty-five, the higher ranges acceptable for women who have a higher percentage of bodily fat than men.

MIRROR, MIRROR

Taking a good long look at yourself in the mirror from time to time – more than just a cursory check of the make-up – can tell you a lot about health. Rings around the irises of the eyes indicate high cholesterol as the actor David Suchet discovered through iridology in time to do something about the condition. Dark circles under the eye indi-

cate circulatory problems; pallor and pale insides of eyelids anaemia, etc. Bulging eyes and weight loss can mean an over-active thyroid (hyperthyridism) while dry and thickening skin, hair loss and weight gain can mean an under-active thyroid (hypothyroidism). And looking at your breasts regularly in the mirror will tell you if there are any dangerous changes, like nipples turning inward, or a puckering of the skin, which you might not feel during regular breast examination. Also you can keep an eye on moles for any sinister changes.

It's never too late to make a positive difference in your appearance, even if the stimulus is a negative one. For Victoria's mother the very late onset of diabetes caused her to control her sweet tooth for the first time in her life and look more sylph-like than she ever had in her youth.

The British actress Lynda Bellingham lost nearly 30 lbs. coming up to her fiftieth birthday after the collapse of her sixteen-year marriage, simply by taking up a regular exercise programme and cutting out desserts. Posing in a swimsuit she wouldn't have dared appear in publicly before for a charity 'swimathon', she vowed never to pile on the pounds again because she felt so 'fabulous'. Divorce is often a spur to women to improve their appearance through diet and exercise as well as cosmetic surgery and a complete change of style.

But by the time you've reached your forties you should be past the stage of crash dieting to get into a dress for a specific occasion, and more into cultivating a sensible eating plan for life.

WE EACH NEED OUR OWN LIFEDIET

One of the big problems with a diet is that most people do consider it a means to an end and that end is usually weight loss. This, we believe, along with Dr Geoffrey Cannon who wrote *Dieting Makes You Fat*, is a short-sighted and often unsuccessful goal. For longevity we need to establish a Lifediet that is a sensible eating plan for our life, all our life. It would ideally include many of the power foods which follow, eaten in variation.

Organically grown food is the ideal – pure, unadulterated and real. But many of us can't grow food ourselves and do not have ready access to or cannot afford organic food. An alternative to eating only organic, as a leading environmental health expert advises, is to rotate your food by not eating the same things every day or every week. That means

you are more likely to spread your 'toxic load' inherent in all modern foods from pesticides and herbicides and puts less stress on your system, which in turn helps to avoid the dangers of over ingesting a particular poison.

Scrub and peel your fruit and vegetables if possible, (although if they are organic the peels are healthy), and wash all fish, meat and poultry, paying careful attention to washing all boards and knifes after working with uncooked meats. Limit the use of frozen or convenience foods that get reheated and lose most of the essential nutrients in the process. Preferably steam all vegetables and eat while they are in a crunchy state (*al dente*) rather than mushy at which point they too have been overdone and have few nutrients left although plenty of useful fibre. Increase your intake of fibre through fruit, vegetables, beans and lentils. Fibre helps to process fat more effectively so less hangs around the system and reduces cholesterol. It used to be thought that bran was enough, but too much bran can leach out other nutrients and soluble oat fibre is now thought to be kinder to the system and better on lowering cholesterol, although some bran is still helpful.

Organically grown food is the ideal – pure, unadulterated and real.

Limit the amount of caffeine you ingest to three cups of tea or coffee a day. Watch soft drinks which are also high in caffeine. While caffeine can help boost energy, too much causes lethargy and fatigue. Headaches that you can't attribute to other causes may generate from caffeine overdose. Increase your intake of water to at least two litres a day. Water is essential for good health as well as for looking good and is needed to help fibre do its job of flushing food through our system.

Most nutritionists agree that the key depleters of vitality are refined sugar and saturated fats, in quantity, plus rancid fats; over-heated fats; mouldy foods; pickled and smoked foods (implicated in stomach cancer); processed meats high in nitrates; salt; meats charred and possibly carcinogenic; all synthetic, 'fake' food; anything 'mechanically recovered' like foods presented as 'chopped or shaped'; sugar substitutes; flavour enhancers; and artificially coloured foods. But it's hard to avoid some preservatives.

Think 'fuel' when you eat. Don't put anything into your mouth that isn't good for you (see 'Power Foods') or that you don't enjoy. Mindless pigging out is a sure way to develop a weight problem as well as to clog your system with junk. If something is an indulgence and really not nutritional, allow yourself the pleasure but keep it occasional and indulge very, very slowly so that each mouthful is, well, orgasmic! If you can't honestly say that it gives you that kind of pleasure, resist. You will feel so good for respecting your body and be lighter and more energetic as a result. For Victoria, giving up sugar (except for occasional doses of Häagen-Dazs Chocolate Chocolate Chip) was a huge breakthrough.

POWER FOODS

Over two millennia ago Hippocrates, the father of the medical profession, said, 'Let your food be your medicine, and your medicine be your food.' We would do well to follow that counsel today. The following alphabetical listing of foods gives you a brief reference of the foods that are 'medicinal' to some degree and should be key ingredients of a healthy diet.

Apples keep the doctor away because of their fibre as well as their combination of pectin and Vitamin C which not only helps keep cholesterol levels in check but also binds some of the heavy metals in our body, for example, lead and mercury, and clears them out of our systems.

Avocados are often shunned by women due to being high in fat and, therefore, calorific. But for anti-ageing, avocados are super as they encourage collagen production in the skin, leaving regular eaters with softer, supple, more youthful-looking skin. They also contain high levels of antioxidants (Vitamins C and E) as well as potassium.

Bananas, another good source of potassium, which, when lacking, can lead to tiredness and depression. They also contain high levels of B6 which is good for the nervous system and can help to prevent leg cramps that can attack older people, particularly at night.

Broccoli, and other green, leafy veggies, are perhaps the most useful antioxidant foods you can eat. Others are cabbage and their tops, sprouts, their tops as well, spring greens, kale, spinach, watercress and cauliflower. They contain high amounts of Vitamins C and Beta-carotene (a Vitamin A precursor) that vacuum up free radicals and are high in calcium, essential for building strong bones.

Carrots high in the essential antioxidant Beta-carotene, since they are rich in Vitamin A but like all vegetables are best eaten as fresh as possible

and preferably organically grown. It is possible to overdose on carrot juice, though, so be careful. People have turned orange as Vitamin A is not water soluble like Vitamin C and will not be washed out of the system if you take too much of it. You are unlikely to ingest more than a healthy amount if you eat whole carrots rather than drinking concentrated carrot juice.

Celery, beloved of slimmers because it practically uses up more calories while being chewed than it provides. It is surprisingly high in calcium and benefits the kidneys by acting as a natural diuretic, as do asparagus. Celery enthusiasts also make claims of its aphrodisiac powers. Don't eat wilted celery, though (try not even to use it for soups), as it may then not be so good for you.

Cranberries and their juice protect against urinary tract infections by killing bacteria in the urine. Many American women who grow up with cranberry juice in their diets resort to it, rather than pharmaceutical remedies for cystitis. Cranberries are also high in Vitamins C and A and may have anticarcinogenic effects. Since the berries are very tart, juices and sauces usually contain high amounts of sugar. Hence, better to drink the juice diluted with water (nice with sparkling water) and to make your own cranberry sauces where you can control the amount of sugar. We make an excellent mixture of cranberry and fresh oranges that is sweet enough.

Dates, like figs and prunes, will make sure you don't suffer from constipation and provide many vitamins and minerals. Figs are also high in calcium.

Eggs, 'the source of life', may turn out not to be as harmful for us as previously thought despite a massive industry creating eggwhite omelettes and yolk-free ice-creams for the cholesterol-obsessed American market. Some studies have found no rise in blood cholesterol after eating eggs. Eggs contain both good and bad cholesterol, but the good stuff is damaged when eggs are fried. Better to eat them boiled or poached. Eggs are also a good source of iron, especially for non-vegan vegetarians. The nutritive value of eggs can vary depending on what the chickens that laid the eggs had been fed. Free-range chickens have more natural diets and are free of the foul fishy taste now evident in battery chickens raised on fishmeal. Also high in Vitamin D.

Fish, particularly oily fish like herrings and mackerel, sardines and salmon, are good for both the body and the brain. An excellent source

of protein, oily fish also protect against high levels of 'bad' LDL cholesterol and help the body to produce protective levels of 'good' HDL cholesterol. Fish is packed with Vitamin D which works with calcium to help build strong bones. Non-fattening (except when fried or sautéed), free of saturated fats and cholesterol, fish should feature more heavily in Western diets than it does. But it is wise to eat 'wild' salmon where possible rather than 'farmed' to avoid the excess of pink dyes used in the latter. For the same reason, it is prudent to avoid overly yellow smoked fishes, like haddock, mackerel, and kippers. It is possible to find them without dye. Shellfish is also rich in zinc, which strengthens the immune system, and although it contains cholesterol does not seem harmful. While chicken and meat contain hormones, fish, hopefully, does not. But the pollution of our waterways is making even fish a less tempting proposition.

Garlic is thought to guard against cancer as well as heart disease and other infections. In some countries it is promoted to keep both the vampires and old age at bay! If you can't abide the taste of garlic in your food, try garlic tablets. Cooked garlic is easier on the digestion than raw cloves. Half a clove a day can lower cholesterol by up to 9 per cent. Japanese research also insists that garlic helps with memory and learning ability.

Grapes are high in Vitamin C and prevent gum infections. Since gum problems are now linked to heart disease they are well worth eating.

Grapefruit is high in Vitamin C but the fibre also works to reduce cholesterol and helps metabolize fat. (Remember the grapefruit diet? We wouldn't recommend it but eating grapefruit is a good idea.)

Lentils and pulses are excellent sources of iron and fibre as well as essential amino acids that, when mixed with other foods like rice or potatoes, create complete proteins, which help vegetarians remain balanced, with key B vitamins preventing anaemia.

Milk products, because calcium is so key to women as they age to protect bones from depleting too rapidly. Dairy products such as milk and cheese are a prime source. All milk, whether skimmed or full fat, is high in calcium as well as magnesium, which means a high absorption rate of the calcium. Obviously, skimmed varieties are better as you get the calcium without the unwanted extra saturated fat.

Oats are another, key anti-ageing food. High in calcium and B vitamins, oats lower cholesterol levels and help to regulate the sugar metabolism.

Also high in fibre, oats are a low cost way to fill you up and keep you going for hours. So, start the day with a bowl of porridge to keep fit, healthy, and slim.

Omega 3 and Omega 6 Fatty Acids help to keep the skin and joints well lubricated. You'll find them in fatty fish (mackerel, salmon, tuna, sardines, herring, etc.) and in sunflower, pumpkin and sesame seeds.

Onions have been shown to raise the levels of 'good' HDL cholesterol in the blood and to reduce the risks of strokes.

Oranges are a prime source of Vitamin C but avoid sucking the orange-dyed skins or drinking juices made with them. You're better off eating oranges and apples and other whole fruits anyway than to drink their juice which becomes too sweet as it is full of concentrated fruit sugars, the sugar of several fruit in one glass.

Peppers are very high in Vitamin C, Beta-carotene, iron and potassium.

Pineapples Only fresh fruit should be eaten as it contains enzymes that aid digestion. Also rich in Vitamin C.

Potatoes contain Vitamin C as well as potassium and are a great source of fibre if eaten in their skins. Be sure the skins are well scrubbed before eating as chemicals from the soil are absorbed effectively while they are growing underground. And avoid green, black or sprouted spuds.

Rice, preferably brown and unpolished, is a food that few are allergic to which combines protein, vitamins, minerals and fibres. It is particularly rich in B vitamins which aid the brain and nervous system.

Soyabeans are not only high in protein and B vitamins but also contain lecithin which emulsifies fats which are thought to offer considerable protection against breast cancer as well as minimizing some of the symptoms of menopause (see Chapter Four). They may help to mitigate the progression of osteoporosis. Soya can lower cholesterol and blood pressure and mimics human oestrogens. Approximately 100 grams a day (a glass of soya milk) can go a long way towards warding off cancer, according to Patrick Holford of the Institute for Optimum Nutrition.

Spinach is rich in iron and chlorophyll as well as Vitamins C and E and is excellent for warding off anaemia and tiredness and, possibly, cancer. According to a report in the *British Medical Journal* spinach is the most effective vegetable in preventing cataracts and reducing the onset of macular degeneration, another worrying vision impairment related to ageing, by 40 per cent.

Sprouted seeds of all kinds are even better for you than unsprouted ones since their vitamin levels are higher. If you can't find them at your local supermarket they are simple (and cheaper) to sprout in your kitchen.

Tomatoes are a wonder food filled with antioxidants as well as lycopene which is said to reduce the risk of prostate cancer in men. Curiously, cooked tomatoes work best in this respect (processed ones in ketchup even better!).

Watercress, like all green, leafy veggies, offers protection against cancer but also contains iodine to spark lethargic thyroids into action. Grab a fist full and munch if you are out of puff and feel yourself energized within an hour.

Yoghurt. The 'live' or 'bio' kinds are best as they replenish the good bacteria in our gut that help our digestion. Two particular bacteria found in live yoghurts, acidophilus and bifidus, have been proven to reduce the incidence of some cancers and heart disease and strengthen the immune system. Yoghurt, of course, is also high in both calcium and magnesium.

SUPER SUPPLEMENTS

Most anti-ageing specialists today view ageing as a progressive disease of a range of deficiencies. In our youth, we are firing on all cylinders but slowly our bodies start staggering or worse become depleted of essential nutrients allowing free radicals (see 'Age Accelerators') to take their pernicious grip. Free radicals are aggressive molecules within us that are 'un-paired' and race around gobbling up healthy cells. Caused by smoking, alcohol, heavy metals, medicine, radiation, pollution, chemicals, insecticides, sunlight and stress, free radicals cause a host of problems from benign hassles like lethargy to more sinister, even life-threatening diseases like cancer. Our natural defence against free radicals is antioxidants such as Vitamins like C, A, E and certain B compounds and minerals like selenium, zinc, manganese and copper.

Free radicals not only cause illnesses like arthritis, auto-immune illnesses, cancer, MS, senility and strokes but also premature ageing, which many believe is what these illnesses actually are. These ravaging enzymes attack protective tissue under the skin which weakens its elasticity and causes wrinkles. According to the Danish anti-ageing expert, Dr Knut Flytlie, who studies the effect of lifestyles on health and the

importance of diet in the treatment and prevention of illnesses with particular study into antioxidants, 35 per cent of all cancer cases are directly related to diet. Many studies also show the correlation between low antioxidants and high incidence of cancer.

We have yet to find an antiageing specialist who doesn't agree that the recommended daily allowances (RDA) of vitamins are woefully low when it comes to repairing damage to our systems from both modern diets and lifestyles as well as the progressive deficiencies that set in just from getting older. Many scientists and doctors who are familiar with the astounding power of antioxidants take megadoses (in comparison to the RDA) of vitamins and minerals to mitigate the ageing process for themselves. So, why shouldn't we?

Nutritionists and GPs, of course, recommend caution. They advise that we get all that we need from eating a balanced diet. Ha! Who can put hand on heart and claim that they always eat organic fruit and veg, and always have the recommended five portions daily, get enough of the right proteins, get plenty of exercise and rest, live in a pure, unpolluted environment and, of course, are happy and stress-free? Get real. Besides, with today's intensive farming methods and food processing many of the vital nutrients are depleted from our foods.

Most of us need all the help we can get not just to cope but to thrive as we want to. If a fist full of vitamins can help compensate for the damage we and our lives do to our ageing bodies then let's gobble them up especially when there is no way that we can consume the needed amounts via our diets. Take Vitamin E, which has been shown to reduce the risk of heart disease if we take 200 IU of Vitamin E daily – that's about six whole avocados a day!

However, beware of overdoing it on the supplements because you might not only be doubling up on some things unwittingly (which could be toxic) but some combinations can be harmful to your system. Best to stick to safe levels, for example, the A and B teams recommended below, and get advice before you add too many extra elements to your daily supplement cocktail. But always, as with all treatments, consult your doctor first.

ANTIOXIDANTS: THE A TEAM – YOUR ACES IN LIFE

If you were to take only a few supplements, these should be your prime ones:

Vitamins A (Beta-carotene), C, E, and Selenium

Vitamin A (Beta-carotene) Yellow and orange fruit and vegetables are packed with this essential antioxidant, for example, squashes, apricots, carrots, yellow peppers and sweet potatoes (yams). Also, spinach, kale and leafy green vegetables are good sources of Beta-carotene. If you have an ample supply of Beta-carotene you have a prime defence against cancer. Even smokers have been found to benefit from this vitamin along with Vitamin E and selenium.

Beta-carotene is claimed to prevent cataracts as well as lung, stomach and breast cancer but is an all-round strengthener of the body's immune system. A recommended daily amount, to strengthen your defences against both disease and ageing, is 15 mg.

Vitamin C If you want to add years, possibly decades, to your life, take Vitamin C daily according to the Nobel Prize winning proponent Dr Linus Pauling. And as most Western diets of processed, fake foods are bereft of Vitamin C, many of us are actually deficient in this essential nutrient. But even those responsible folks who do consume five portions of fresh fruit and/or veg a day still need supplemental Vitamin C to help forestall the impact of ageing. If you want rarely or never to have another cold, take 1 g of Vitamin C a day. Both of us can attest that this works. The anti-ageing effects of Vitamin C result from its impact on the white cells, which cause a boost to the immune systems so often weakened and vulnerable in old age. Some have recently suggested that Vitamin C in excess can *cause* cancer, which rather goes against received wisdom, and is certainly quite opposite to Dr Pauling's experience.

For years studies have only shown positive benefits of Vitamin C with virtually no level of toxicity proven. But a 1998 study by the British Leicester University reported that taking 500 mg a day increases the risk of cancer. The 'study' was attacked by experts, like Britain's popular nutritionist turned journalist John Briffa MD as a 'preliminary scientific report'. While one marker for DNA responded by rising with the intake of Vitamin C, another key DNA marker, causing 'damage' and thereby possibly increasing the potential development of cancer, dropped as a result of taking Vitamin C. As Briffa says, 'One would have to question the methods used in the study and the validity of its findings.' The countless studies that report the beneficial effects of Vitamin C should not be diluted by one isolated, preliminary finding, we feel.

Foods high in Vitamin C include citrus fruits, broccoli, sprouts, tomatoes, strawberries, and papaya. Vitamin C is water soluble so best taken with water on an empty stomach. Bioflavonoids enhance the absorption of Vitamin C (whatever is not absorbed is flushed out of our system via our urine). And rather than take one large dose, better to take 500 mg at a time, say morning and night, or use 'time release' formulas.

Vitamin E is the first line of defence against heart disease by breaking down 'bad' (LDL) cholesterol. It is so effective in thinning the blood that anyone planning an operation is advised to stop taking Vitamin E for two weeks prior to surgery! These properties have also meant that Vitamin E is an effective anti-inflammatory remedy so it is effective for anyone with arthritis or aching joints.

As a fat-soluble vitamin, Vitamin E is best metabolized by taking with another fat, for example, after eating a bowl of cereal with milk or with some yoghurt. The recommended dosage is between 100 to 400 IUs daily. (Toxicity is likely in doses over 3,000 IU. Anyone with a blood coagulation problem must consult their doctor before starting a course of Vitamin E.)

Selenium This trace mineral is key to enhance the absorption of the vital Vitamin E but also key in warding off infections, with many scientists claiming its power in preventing pre and cancerous tumours. Selenium-deficient diets are often found in people suffering from colon cancer.

Foods high in selenium are seeds and nuts, especially Brazil nuts, as well as seafood and wholegrains. Selenium is toxic in high doses, causing liver damage, with the recommended and safe anti-ageing level being 100–300 mg. More may adversely affect the thyroid functions.

THE B VITAMINS AND FRIENDS: THE B TEAM – YOUR BACK-UP SQUAD

From an anti-ageing and optimal health perspective, the following vitamins and minerals are worth considering especially if you feel your diet is deficient in them:

B12, B6, B Complex, Folic Acid, Calcium, Magnesium, Carnitine

B12 is found only in meat, fish and dairy products as well as soya, so many vegetarians and women are deficient if they don't get a regular supply of these foods. As a vegetarian myself, I have the brewer's yeast

spread Marmite, which is concentrated B12, almost daily. Without B12, anaemia threatens, making us weak, lethargic and vulnerable to viruses or worse. Along with Vitamin Q, B12 is supposed to enhance the mental faculties which can fray in the ageing process. Most mid-lifers can attest to the frustrating realization that the brain no longer feels as sharp or as quick as it once was. Added B12 may help. It also helps with food absorption, hence is useful for anyone suffering from irritable bowel syndrome or Crohn's disease.

A good multivitamin will have B12 but if you feel you need an extra boost, stick within the anti-ageing limits of 500 mg a day (although some doctors suggest 1,000 mg as fine). Toxicity is not a worry although a skin rash can indicate overdoing it beyond the point of its being beneficial.

B6 A friend of many women, B6 was discovered early as a remedy for pre-menstrual tension which impacts on both mental and physical health. As a mild diuretic B6 helps with water retention, whether related to periods or not. In addition, B6 helps with the absorption of B12 and boosts the immune system in its fight against cancer. Any woman on HRT has an increased need of B6. And, the older you get the more B6 you need due to the decreased ability to absorb it from foods.

B6 is available in a variety of foods like brewer's yeast, chicken, eggs, fish, meat, grains, beans, broccoli, potatoes and soya beans. Most multi-vitamins provide a good dose of B6 (3 mg) to supplement the diet with the anti-ageing specialist recommending up to 50 mg a day. If over 200 mg is taken daily, toxicity is possible and impacts the nervous system for the worse, which is why at one point authorities wanted to ban it from the health food shop shelves, at least in doses over 10 mg. It prompted a furious debate, as many believe high doses to be benefi-cial, but it is arguably best to take your B vitamins in a balanced 'complex' form.

B Complex The B vitamins maintain healthy skin, eyes, hair, liver, gut and mouth and have recognized benefits for brain function as well. Studies of Alzheimer's patients found deficiencies of several B vitamins. To work most effectively, the B vitamins should be taken together, although you can add certain additional doses of specific ones like B12 if vegetarian or B6 if on HRT or suffering from water retention.

Folic Acid aids in the formation of red blood cells and helps to prevent anaemia. Key to foetal cell production, folic acid is recommended for all pregnant women as it may also help to prevent premature births. For

ageing, folic acid is another 'brain food' and may help guard against depression and anxiety. It works best when taken in combination with Vitamin C and B12.

Food sources that are high in folic acid are red meat, brewer's yeast, cheese, dates, green vegetables, oranges, lentils, whole grains, mushrooms and oranges. Many adults are deficient in folic acid and benefit from taking supplements. Without ample supply, the arteries are vulnerable to clogging, according to a study from Tufts Medical School. It also prevents the formation of polyps in the colon, which plague many elderly people.

A good multivitamin contains about 400 mg of folic acid which is a decent daily base to a balanced diet of the foods listed above. If you drink alcohol or are on HRT you need more, with some anti-ageing specialists recommending 1,000+ mg daily. Toxicity is less of a problem in megadoses than the ability of folic acid to mask other problems like anaemia.

Calcium and Magnesium Essential to the continuing formation of bone cells, calcium becomes depleted with age and needs replenishing especially with the onset of the menopause and beyond. Calcium is also needed for healthy teeth and gums, other vulnerable areas.

To be really clever in bolstering your calcium levels you need to consider your foods, what is needed to aid absorption, the best kind of supplement and when to take it. Key foods containing calcium include: dairy products, fish with bones like sardines, leafy green veggies like broccoli, watercress, sprouts, kale, almonds, brewer's yeast, soya beans, sesame seeds and yoghurt.

Supplements vary in absorption quality with the best kinds being chelated calcium tablets and should be taken in a two to one ratio to Magnesium along with Vitamin C. Absorption is aided if you take calcium with meals and in smaller doses twice or three times a day. If you take some with the evening meal, calcium supplements may also help with insomnia. Recommended doses range from 800 to 2,000 mg daily.

Magnesium assists in the absorption of both calcium and potassium. If deficient in magnesium, you might show signs of nervousness and irritability. Correct it and you can feel less stressed. This mineral also helps prevent heart disease and some cancers. If you drink alcohol or are on HRT you will need to increase your intake. Foods rich in magnesium include figs, nuts, garlic, grapefruit, apples, avocados, whole-wheat grains, brewer's yeast, camomile and seeds.

A magnesium supplement of 200 mg to top up the basic 100 mg in a multivitamin is a good anti-ageing prescription. Magnesium can affect the kidneys and heart so if you have had problems with either, get your doctor's advice about the right amount of supplement.

Carnitine The body can manufacture this super substance, related to the B vitamin family, on its own provided that you have enough Vitamin C, iron and B6 in your system. But supplements are also possible.

Carnitine helps to process fat and convert it into energy rather than have it hang around in the liver, heart, or on your thighs. As the main food sources of carnitine come from meats and animal products, vegetarians with sluggish metabolisms might consider a supplement.

THE A AND B TEAM COMBINED

Nutrition guru Patrick Holford, who looks not more than thirty-two at forty, takes: 'a very good all round multivitamin and mineral supplement three times a day – the Optimum Nutrition Formula made by Higher Nature – and an additional 2 g of Vitamin C with bioflavonoids. I also take "Super AntiOxidant Formula", another Higher Nature formulation. So I'm getting 20,000 units of Vitamin A, half beta-carotene, half retinol; around 50 mg of each B vitamin; in total 2.5 g Vitamin C; 300 units of Vitamin E; 150 mcg selenium; 20 mg zinc; 200 mcg chromium. I've recently started taking 200 mg a day of Phosphatidyl Serine (PS) to help my brain function and can already feel mild effects of brain improvement.'

SUPER EXTRAS

Chromium For any woman concerned with her glucose tolerance or who suffers from hypoglycaemia or diabetes, the mineral chromium may help. Thanks to the junk in Western diets (refined white sugars and flours) deficiencies in chromium are not rare. Chromium normalizes the insulin which then processes sugars more efficiently. If you have problems with glucose intolerance, your diet might not be enough to give you the chromium you need. Foods rich in the mineral include brewer's yeast, liver, some shellfish and mushrooms. 200 mg is the recommended supplement.

Diabetics or anyone suffering from hypoglycaemia should discuss the types and amounts of a chromium supplement with their doctor, but it is thought to help these conditions.

Zinc Key to prostate gland functioning, zinc is also key for women for promoting a strong immune system as well as stimulating the production of collagen for youthful-looking skin. Ageing athletes swear by zinc to aid recovery with strained muscles but also to replenish the zinc lost via perspiration. As it protects the liver from damage, zinc is key for any ager who likes her alcohol. Without zinc, Vitamin E is not absorbed as effectively.

Foods high in zinc include brewer's yeast, beans, egg yolks, shellfish (especially oysters), red meat, mushrooms, seeds, whole grains, and soya products. As with some other minerals, getting the balance of zinc right is important. If you take a multivitamin you don't need another supplement like magnesium with zinc. A daily supplement of 30 mg is a good balance, with older women and those with known deficiencies benefiting from 50 mg. Megadoses of this amount should be pursued only under the supervision of a doctor.

Vitamin P – Bioflavonoids The essential benefit of this vitamin is its role in aiding the absorption of Vitamin C, the ace on the A Team. It helps with healing and minimizing bruising but also with gum disease. It is key for menopausal women not on HRT for controlling hot flushes and is best taken in a combined tablet with Vitamin C, with toxicity unknown.

Natural sources of bioflavonoids are citrus fruit, apricots, berries and rosehips.

Vitamin Q – Ubiquinone Q10 An essential part of the cell's energy-producing system, Q10 is a natural substance found in the body which is necessary to extract energy from nutrients. With ageing and illness, the supply of Q10 is depleted, causing problems with the immune system, weight retention, heart and circulation difficulties. It is also effective in treating periodontal problems. Devotees claim an energy surge from taking supplements, hence its popularity among athletes.

Foods high in Q10 include fatty, oily fish like sardines and mackerel, whole grains, nuts, green, leafy veggies, soya products, beef and chicken. A supplement of 30 mg a day is a good insurance policy for the future in preventing heart disease and enhancing brain functioning with old age. It is best to take the supplement with some fat like milk (after a bowl of cereal) or a piece of toast spread with butter or peanut butter. Its toxicity is not known, but it can cause nausea with some people, probably because they take Q10 on an empty stomach.

Glutathione With ageing, the natural production of this tripeptide diminishes and can actually accelerate the way we age. Like carnitine, glutathione is produced from amino acids in the system and is stored in the liver where it processes harmful toxins from all we ingest. Hence, it is key to maintain our supplies of glutathione as we age, especially those of us who live the so-called 'good' life and eat rich food and drink a bit more than we should.

Supplements are possible but some scientists argue that it is better to restock the amino acids that produce glutathione naturally than to take synthetic versions of it. Those are cysteine and glycine.

NATURAL FOODS AND HERBAL SUPPLEMENTS

Acidophilus While most of us consider bacteria as nasty, this natural bacterium is referred to as 'friendly' as it is essential for the maintenance of a healthy gut by helping us to digest proteins and absorb nutrients. There are countless ways that we disrupt the right levels of appropriate bacteria in our systems. Drugs, for example, antibiotics, deplete our stocks, as do conditions like thrush. If you suffer from irritable bowel syndrome or from occasional bloating after a meal, you might benefit from a course of acidophilus. The natural source of acidophilus is via 'live' or 'bio' yoghurts. It is best to eat these first thing in the morning or on an empty stomach for the bacteria to get a chance of taking a grip. Supplements are handy for those who find live yoghurt unpalatable. Store them in the fridge and, if taking antibiotics, take acidophilus two hours before or after.

Bee Propolis The 'natural alternative' to antibiotics, propolis is made from the substance that the bees use to construct their hives. These highly resilient resins stimulate human white cells which destroy bacteria.

Reported to be good for everything from mouth ulcers to bad breath, propolis is an anti-inflammatory and stimulates a sluggish immune system. It is best to get a supply from someone in the 'bee business'. However, if hayfever is your particular weakness, avoid propolis as the pollen contained within might set you off.

Borage An essential plant for those who love to drink 'Pimm's cups' in the summertime, but borage does more than flavour this quintessentially English aperitif. Recognized as an adrenal tonic, borage contains minerals, such as calcium and magnesium, that maintain healthy hair and skin as well as enhance the cardiovascular system.

If you grow it in the summertime, eat the blooms which are high in essential fatty acids. Otherwise, you can find it in a herbal compound.

Camomile As an 'addict' of camomile, I can report from experience of its therapeutic benefits for everything from sleep disturbance and as a digestive aid to being wonderful for headaches. High in calcium, magnesium and potassium as well as other nutrients, adding a cup of camomile tea a day to your diet means you will help body, mind and spirit in one go.

Dong Quai Another herb that is resorted to for relief from hot flushes as well as vaginal dryness. The roots of this plant are what contain all the goodies which include essential oils as well as carotene and Vitamins B12 and E.

Echinacea A herb gaining tremendously in popularity as a natural way to build up resistances to colds and flu. It stimulates the production of white cells, and is beneficial as an anti-inflammatory aid as well as an antibacterial agent. Echinacea contains copper, essential fatty acids, iron, potassium and Vitamins C and E among other useful elements. It is worth having along with your cold remedies. Begin using it if you are starting to feel run down. Many claim it is so effective as to make cold remedies unnecessary.

Evening Primrose Oil This contains the highest concentration of gamma-linolenic acid (GLA) of any food. GLA is essential in our systems for reducing cholesterol, premenstrual tension and maximizing the natural production of oestrogen and testosterone. Additionally it is seen as potentially preventing multiple sclerosis and mitigates the advancement of cirrhosis.

Evening Primrose oil is hailed by many menopausal women who avoid HRT as terrific in helping with hot flushes and night sweats. 1,500 mg Evening Primrose contains 150 mg GLA, the ideal daily intake (in 3 × 500 mg doses) for this condition, although 500 mg Evening Primrose will keep mild pre-menstrual tension at bay.

Kava Kava A herbal 'downer' for the stressed-out woman. Try this when you are feeling edgy or anxious or having trouble sleeping. Don't try during the day as it might be so effective as to make you too drowsy. A bit washed down with some camomile tea is a sure cure for insomnia.

St John's Wort This herb is hailed as an elixir for everything from stress and depression ('Nature's Prozac') to the control of HIV and herpes. It is gaining in popularity because of its antiviral properties mainly, but must be tried with caution and in moderation as it can interfere with the absorption of other key minerals.

Tea Tree Oil God bless Australia for making this essential oil so well known and available around the world. This marvellous substance is terrific for treating many skin conditions including acne, cuts, athlete's foot, and insect bites. It is wonderful added to a bath for soothing an irritating case of thrush or vaginitis, but can also be used diluted in a douche. Gargling with diluted tea tree oil is effective for a sore throat.

But Remember – A Healthy Body Can Be At Least Partly In the Mind!

Before we move on to the sections on a healthy mind and spirit, we should say that a healthy body can be at least partly in the mind. No matter how much exercise you take or how many vitamins and supplements you pump into yourself, if you do it out of hypochondria or fear (see Chapter Three), and without the right outlook, they won't help. Healthy ageing involves a complex recipe of ingredients, as we have said. So far the 'secret' ingredient necessary for immortality may be eluding analysis, thank goodness, but we've got a pretty good idea of the basic mix – individually seasoned to taste, of course – which leads to longevity, and physical fitness may not be, surprisingly, the prime component.

10

An Ageless Mind and Spirit

'The spirit within nourishes, and the mind, diffused through all the members, sways the mass and mingles with the whole frame.'

VIRGIL, *The Aeneid*, 70–19 BC

The Ultimate Age Defiers

If your mind and spirit are ageless, ageing should seem unimportant. Or so we've been told. We haven't reached that enviable state yet but we're working on it. And it can be worked on, we're reliably informed. You may not find 'Nirvana Now', as the saying goes, but you should be able to achieve a state of mental sharpness and spiritual contentment that will make your third (and fourth, and fifth?) age as happy and fulfilling as possible.

It is pretty easy to tell just by looking at someone whether they have found that inner contentment that allows them to be philosophical about the physical changes of ageing because they are at peace with themselves. A man of fifty-something and one half his age were sitting opposite each other on a train. The older man appeared to be enjoying a book; the young one spent the whole journey on his mobile phone, and from his conversations it became apparent, as he actually boasted to one colleague, that 'I work seven days a week, fourteen hours a day, and intend to do that until I retire at fifty with a few million in the bank.' He was a financial trader, clinching several hundred thousand pounds' worth of deals on the journey between Birmingham and London while arguing with a girlfriend who was audibly annoyed he'd scheduled another meeting for ten thirty that night. The older man smiled at the younger one's intensity. He looked at the drawn, white face and asked, 'Do you really think you'll be able to carry on at that pace until you're fifty?' The young man paused in his phoning for a second. 'Of course, why not?' he demanded. 'I thought so, too,' said the older man, before returning to his book. 'But I discovered that if I didn't get a life I wouldn't last until I was fifty.' It was easy to see who was more content.

The well-known author John Updike has written a whimsical book about ageing called *Are You Old Enough To Read This Book?* in which he observes that 'Over fifty, one makes more of less. The muscles of empathy and curiosity strengthen while those of youthful egocentricity weaken . . .'

NEW SEEKERS

When you're young you're sometimes too busy climbing your way up the greasy pole to enjoy your home, your partner, your children – your

life. As you get older, the desire for a better quality of life grows insistently stronger. For some that means having material luxuries. For others that might mean making more time to smell the roses. For a growing group who were never particularly religious before it means finding some kind of spirituality to enhance their existence.

If you've been a mother, you may only have a chance to look around and start questioning the meaning of life when the offspring have left the nest.

It is an age-old and oft-remarked phenomenon that those who sense they are nearing the grave turn to God, even if they never believed they were 'believers' before. Today's 'New Seekers' may not darken the door of a church, temple or mosque, but search for spiritual solace at their therapist's office, by communing with nature, or working for a charity. They delve into books on mysticism and the psyche. The late Diana, Princess of Wales, was probably a prime example of this new seeking, but for many women it comes later in life, when family responsibilities wane and they have the luxury to undertake such a quest.

If you've been a mother, you may only have a chance to look around and start questioning the meaning of life when the offspring have left the nest. Maybe you're left staring at a stranger over the cornflakes every morning. Maybe you start wondering what the point of it all has been. But there is no doubt that mind and spirit are inextricably linked. If one is strong it can help the other, and cultivating a positive attitude can help both. Ageing researchers have found that those who don't expect to become mentally feeble with age usually don't. A positive mindset, agile brain, and a spirit that soars can do more for healthy ageing than scoffing all the power foods and supplements of the preceding chapter.

Brain Fitness

Your mind is one muscle that need never sag. Indeed, brain fitness expert Tony Buzan maintains in his book *The Age Heresy* that 'Many of us still believe the widespread delusions about our mental capacity declining as we age.' He sets about un-deluding us, citing in particular Dr Marion Diamond's work at the University of California which indi-

cates that not only does the brain not necessarily lose cells with age, as was previously thought, but it seems capable of growing new connections if it is continually challenged.

The American ageing researcher K. Warner Schaie found that instead of cognitive abilities declining steadily they could increase and decrease at different stages of life for different people. His studies showed people who had lost mental ability between the ages of twenty and thirty and others who had improved their performance over the age of seventy.

Tony Buzan points out that whereas older people made a bad showing when pitted against younger ones on some timed IQ tests, when the time limit on the tests was removed the older people's results became comparable. He suggests we just get slower as we get older because our brains contain more information for our internal computer processor to sift through. Buzan argues, 'As the brain gets older it must, of necessity, get better and better, until the moment before it dies, as long as it is used well . . .'

That brings to mind a joke told by the actress Sharon Stone at a dinner in the presence of President Clinton. It was set in a futuristic world where brains were being sold, men's brains for $100,000 and women's brains for $25,000. Why the difference in price? 'Because the women's brains were used,' Stone crowed. But by all the evidence available today, it seems as if used brains should be worth much more than unused ones which can atrophy from neglect.

Your mind is one muscle that need never sag.

According to Buzan, and our research reconfirms this, three vital factors in ageing gracefully are: staying socially involved – having an investment in life, work, and people; being mentally active – continuing intellectual interests; and having a flexible personality – being able to thrive on change and to enjoy new experiences.

AGE CANNOT WITHER AN ACTIVE BRAIN

The nonagenarian Countess of Longford, better known as the historian and author Elizabeth Longford, has always been quite an amazing woman. Thoughts of retirement and wrapping herself in shawls have never crossed the mind of this good friend of both the Queen and the Queen Mother. Crimson silk trouser suits like the one given to her by her husband, Lord Longford, on her eightieth birthday and a book always waiting to be written are more her style.

Interestingly, her output proved greatest during the 'post-retirement' years when so many of her peers were out to pasture. It tended to be a book every two years, even though she'd never set herself such a target. And her books are heavy historical tomes, including biographies of the Queen, the Queen Mother, Queen Victoria, the Duke of Wellington and Winston Churchill. Longford explained to Victoria (the author!) that she had 'a need, a very real, physical need, to have a book going' at all times. 'If a day went by without even collecting the notes or making some telephone calls or advancing my book in any way I'd feel thoroughly dissatisfied.'

She worried about a generation brought up in comparative isolation, with microwaved meals in front of the television.

How did she keep her brain in such productive working order? Partly from the constant debates and discussions she and her lively literary family have. The product of a large family herself, and the mother of eight children, she was used to continual cut and thrust. 'Certainly, we've never had a quiet meal,' she reflected. 'You keep your brain exercised by continual discussion and argument,' she asserted, which is why she was a firm advocate of the set family meals of her childhood, when families ate together 'and managed to talk without our mouths full'. She worried about a generation brought up in comparative isolation, with microwaved meals in front of the television.

Lady Longford also undoubtedly benefited from an exceptionally warm and loving family life. The Longfords celebrated their sixtieth wedding anniversary surrounded by their children, grandchildren and great grandchildren. Just remembering the names and birthdays of her twenty-six grandchildren and many great grandchildren was good mental exercise, she joked.

MEMORY TRICKS

But perhaps Lady Longford's brain remained so sharp for so long because she made allowances for it with advancing years. 'Because I know it is not nearly so good as it used to be I don't put so many burdens on it now,' she admitted. 'I'll look up something instead of assuming I know it and I'll use tricks to remember telephone numbers and names. All old people have trouble remembering certain words sometimes and one gets very adept at getting round it with a phrase

– a quick three words instead of the one right one, or perhaps a synonym.'

Lady Longford had many little tricks to aid memory. She kept an engagement diary and a literary one for recording thoughts and recollections. 'But I try not to write everything down because I think if you do, like a friend even writes down the simplest things like "I must change my shoes", you soon wouldn't make the effort.'

If she'd forgotten a name, she would mentally go through the alphabet. 'You get to G and suddenly you see the name! I've got a visual memory and I've got used to thinking of numbers and letters in colours: B was light blue and C green!' She could, in common with others of her age, still remember vividly events that had happened twenty years, or even seventy years before, and the smallest details of her subjects' lives more easily than she can remember matters of the day.

'I sometimes can't remember something important I was supposed to do yesterday,' she confessed. 'I wonder why? I was once queuing up to go to a film and I recognized a woman who'd been at school with me seventy years ago, but if it was someone I'd met at a party last week I wouldn't have known them!'

Short-term memory is like that special fast memory cache you may have on your computer where things can be kept for quick access. 'Short-term memory is considered to be a limited capacity store, a temporary repository of information before it passes to the unlimited, permanent, long-term memory,' reported the Carnegie Inquiry into the Third Age. Although Lady Longford's experience will strike a responsive chord with many, the inquiry's research found little or no age-associated loss in short-term memory.

She could remember events from twenty years ago but not details of yesterday.

Mental deterioration is not evident until the late sixties and then not for everyone. Many older people are able to maintain levels of performance of specific intellectual tests over a seven-year period at age sixty, and even at age eighty-one *a significant proportion* remain around the sixty-mark. Encouragingly, few individuals showed a universal decline on all aspects of their mental abilities. The Inquiry concluded that many enter advanced old age still performing at the level of younger adults.

Dr David Weeks believes that what Lady Longford was going through was quite normal ageing for a healthy brain – possibly because

the earlier events were etched more deeply into the memory from a time when the brain's capacity to store such things was greater. 'Our memories are like mixed-up libraries,' he has found. 'A remote cue may suddenly give you access to a long-lost memory.' Although we don't always bother to cross-reference all our thoughts, it seems, he feels that they are still potentially accessible if we are patient and persevering enough.

TRAIN THAT BRAIN!

Dr Weeks, who works with Alzheimer's patients and has developed brain fitness programmes for them, believes that, like the backup files in a computer, we can eventually access all our memory files if we persevere. This is often demonstrated when, under hypnosis, people can suddenly remember where they've left their car keys, or where the body is buried. 'Remember that the more you practise seeking out a memory with clues and cues, the more likely you are to re-establish the lost connection and re-access your memory,' says Dr Weeks. 'Be confident – all your knowledge is, ultimately, retrievable,' he says. 'We tend to assume that memory loss is an untreatable condition, yet brain exercises and learning to use memory aids – reminders placed around the home to jog the memory – can do a great deal.' One of his exercises involves 'reminiscence therapy', which stimulates an old person's memory by asking them to recount events in their earlier lives which are time-locked in their memory.

'The chief reason the brain declines as people get older is not through age but from misuse and disuse.'

'The chief reason the brain declines as people get older is not through age but from misuse and disuse,' Dr Weeks believes. Loneliness and lack of stimulating human companionship can be as destructive to the brain as alcohol, drugs and tobacco, it seems. And despite advances in the Internet and the possibility of 'virtual' friends, there is no substitute for real human contact. Lack of it can lead to sensory deprivation and, ultimately, adversely affect the brain. Jumbled and scrambled thoughts may have less to do with ageing and more to do with this social problem that confronts the one third of men and one quarter of women estimated to be severely isolated.

Another factor which can affect brain ageing is exercise, or lack of it. A group of middle-aged men (sorry, they didn't test women) working

out for over four hours a week were found to make major strides in ability to process information when compared to a sedentary control group. Exercise brings better circulation to the brain and exercise such as yoga, where the blood is caused to flow to the head in certain poses, can be particularly good. Those same upside-down poses also help to counter the effects of gravity on sagging bits!

Since a plentiful supply of oxygen is vital to good brain function, anything that narrows the arteries bringing oxygenated blood to the brain, like athero-sclerosis as it is called in Britain (arteriosclerosis in the States) is obviously bad for it. Which could be why Dr Weeks's Superyoung all had low to normal blood pressure, and why he recommends a diet low in saturated fat and unlikely to clog up the arteries with cholesterol.

While physical exercise is important in maintaining a healthy brain, mental exercise is paramount.

While physical exercise is important in maintaining a healthy brain, mental exercise is paramount. Brain scans today are able to show up activity in certain areas of the brain as they are stimulated to show that thinking actually is brain exercise. With brain power, as with muscle power, it's a case of 'use it or lose it'. What does that involve?

Well, the brain seems to thrive on variety. So if you have a demanding job in which you have to make important decisions all day, you might like to exercise your brain in other ways when you're off duty, by reading novels or simply daydreaming. If your work is routine and unchallenging, you could try to create challenges for your brain outside work, through a hobby or activity that requires a great deal of concentration. If you are the type of person who habitually throws your bank statements in the bin with scarcely a glance, force yourself to add them up and balance your chequebook for a change. If, on the contrary, you're very mathematically or scientifically inclined, make sure you have plenty of creative communication on other planes. That's why, from the late '80s on, so many stressed-out executives began taking classes in juggling and other circus skills, or joined bellringing groups or took up other hobbies that involved intense concentration of a kind that was very different from that which they needed in their daily work.

In any case you should be exercising your brain through word games, crosswords, quizzes, interesting conversations and debates. Even computer games are not to be sneezed at, as they encourage speed of thought and reaction time. Learning is the most wonderful thing you

can do for your brain, and you're never too old to learn, whether it's a new language or a new skill.

MIND OVER MATTER

One possibly useful way to exercise your brain is by thinking yourself young. Recent developments in the field of psychoneuroimmunology, the study of the links between the immune system and an individual's outlook, could have exciting repercussions to the way we age. If we can, to some degree, think ourselves well, as advocates of the concept believe we can, isn't it possible that we can think ourselves young? Certainly many old people seem to do just that. Mabel James, the eighty-three-year-old cloakroom attendant at Annabel's nightclub in London, voiced the philosophy: 'Make up your mind that you're not going to get old. I have. I live every day to the fullest.'

'People don't grow old. When they stop growing, they become old.'

How we age is intimately linked with our state of mind, according to ayurvedic doctor Deepak Chopra, author of *Ageless Body, Timeless Mind* and rejuvenation health guru to the stars. Many people, he argues, lose vitality and decline in old age simply because they expect to do so, a theory gaining more and more credence. He believes that by programming the mind to have different expectations, youthful abilities and outlook can be retained. He likes to quote one of his eighty-year-old patients who apparently said, 'People don't grow old. When they stop growing, they become old.' He teaches his patients how to calm rapid heart beats, conquer asthmatic wheezing, and restore all body rhythms to their intended functioning which, he says, has enormous implications for ageing.

WHY WE FORGET

The best brain exercises involve mental activities that we love rather than doing tedious exercises for the sake of it, according to Dr Thomas Crook of Memory Assessment Clinics.

There is nothing like keeping yourself involved with people and with work to keep your brain active. A woman we know used to wonder why everybody seemed to remember her name at parties but she could never

remember theirs. The answer was simple – or so it seemed to us. This woman was so self-centred that she wasn't really interested in other people and so didn't bother to absorb information about them. Often she would regret it when the person she was ignoring as she thought about her next appointment turned out to have been, she would discover in retrospect, someone who might have been useful to her had she only paid attention to who they were and what they were saying.

Are you the kind of person who can remember what you were wearing on significant occasions but not what other people were saying? Watch that self-obsession and start taking a more genuine interest in others. Your brain power may suddenly improve when you focus it on something besides your ego. Have you ever noticed how genuinely concerned and caring people can always remember that your husband was unwell, it was your daughter's birthday, or that you needed some help to move house? And don't you appreciate that?

Many of us 'forget' names because we haven't bothered to learn them in the first place. The late Clare Boothe Luce was apparently once introduced to David Burpee, chairman of the seed company Burpee & Co, at a dinner party. As they talked he became aware that she didn't know who he was and said helpfully, 'I'm Burpee.' She reassured him, 'That's all right. I get that way sometimes myself.'

Others forget names they know well, which is a different matter. There's a legendary tale of a woman who met a female acquaintance in a London department store. They chatted for a while and the woman desperately tried to recall her acquaintance's name and what she and her husband did. Finally she hazarded a hesitant, 'And what's your husband doing these days?' to which England's formidable Queen Mary (for it was she!) replied, rather bemused, 'He's still king.'

'The effect of dementia is to make you forget things you know.'

The lady in this second story apparently needed to fear more for her marbles than Clare Boothe Luce for, as Dr Crook puts it, 'The effect of dementia is to make you forget things you know.' So if you're regularly forgetting the names of good friends, or things you should know very well, you may need some urgent brain work or simply a good holiday (see 'Stress' in Chapter Three), because stress can cause a 'brain overload' which may also be responsible for this effect.

Factors which can cause us to forget information we really know include: alcohol or drugs, including sleeping pills, muscle relaxants,

cortisone and some blood pressure medications; depression; smoking, which can cut off oxygen to the brain; stress; vitamin deficiency, particularly the B complex vitamins, and especially B12, found in eggs, fish, meats and milk.

If you simply can't remember the names of new people you meet, it is easier to deal with by learning little tricks and games. 'The effect of ageing is to stop you learning new things. Don't let it!' says Dr Crook. His clinics (which, incidentally, are for research, not walk-in assessment centres for the public) boast some of the best memory-testing facilities in the world but Dr Crook, formerly of the US National Institutes of Health, has devised some far simpler ones which can be practised by anyone at home. He even wrote a book on the subject, *How To Remember Names*. Remember that people of any age can benefit from these tricks, and that there are greater memory differences between individuals than there are between age groups. Although expectations in such tests are generally scaled down by age group because it is expected that a sixty-year-old will be less good at remembering than a forty-year-old, if you start playing these games at whatever age you are now, you will get better at remembering.

BRAIN GAMES

We find that as soon as we write something down we forget it, but if we think we'll never remember something, we do. This is because once we write down a piece of information it goes 'off-line' in our brain computers, which see no reason to remember it – it's taken care of. But if we worry that we'll never remember that name or phone number, we tend to because it becomes imprinted in our memory banks.

We tried the following test and got Dr Crook's test people all right first time, no trouble, although sometimes, to be fair, we can't seem to remember our own names. Why was that, we wondered. Well, it seems we both worked out little tricks to remember them. Our 'Susan' reminded us of a well-known woman called Susan. 'Patricia' looked cuddly, as though we'd like to 'pat' her on the head. 'Ruth' was an old-fashioned, biblical name for a white-haired lady; 'Charles' was an old-fashioned name for an older man, and so on. If you want to remember a name, it helps to think of little associations like that. Meeting Mrs Dawes? Think she looks catty and her name rhymes with 'claws'.

NAME AND FACE RECALL

Draw or get someone to draw for you, or cut out from a magazine, nine faces on separate bits of paper that can be moved around. Write (or stick on Post-Its) names underneath them – first names will do. Study them for a minute. Then cover up the names, move the faces about and see how many names you can correctly recall. Write them down.

If you're between 18 and 39 you should be able to get 8.
If you're between 40 and 49 a good response would be 7.
If you're between 50 and 59 aim for 6.
If you're between 60 and 69 your score should be 5.
If you're between 70 and 89 try to get 4.

On a second try your score should shoot up to nine if you're under sixty, and be up to seven if you're between sixty and sixty-nine, six if you're older.

Introduced to Mr Pritchett? Think he has a spot and might like to itch it, and so on.

Memory note: Remember that it's better to ask someone to repeat their name, even to spell it, when you're first introduced, than to remain talking to them for two hours and then admit at the end of the evening that you don't know who they are. When introduced repeat the name to reinforce it in your brain as most effective communicators do.

First and Last Names

Make a list of six first and last names. Study them for a minute. Then, looking at just a list of last names try to put the first names with their correct companions.

Grocery List Selective Reminding

Write down a list of fifteen grocery items you might need and study it for a minute. See how many you remember and can write down. Keep trying until you improve your score and get them all right. Work out little tricks to remember 'bring home the bacon'; 'tomatoes rhyme with potatoes' (or not, depending on where you live), and so on. Dr Crook suggests imagining the fish swimming in the olive oil or flopping on to the teabags – well, whatever works for you.

Remembering Where You've Put Something

We all forget where we've left our keys, but it's nothing to worry about, says Dr Crook. 'Only worry when you keep losing entire blocks of information, or an entire experience or event is forgotten or only recalled with difficulty.' If you keep losing things, try to be more precise about where you keep them. If you can't do that, and the object you keep losing is something like your glasses which you put down in all sorts of strange places, be aware of your tendency to lose it and make a point of trying to remember where you put it down. Dr Crook says, 'Say you place them on your night stand, near the alarm clock. Mentally imagine the alarm clock ringing loudly as you put them down. If you put them in your purse, imagine the purse coming alive and gobbling up the glasses. Again, the more theatrical or absurd you can make the dramatization, the better your chances of remembering where you put something.' Recreating a scene and retracing your steps also helps.

If you keep losing things, try to be more precise about where you keep them.

Remembering Numbers

Some people have a facility for remembering phone numbers; others hate them. It really has little to do with age, we think. But in order to remember any number successfully make it meaningful. Look for your favourite number within it, patterns (323 3223), dates (4–12–19–49), and so on. We all have to remember so many numbers these days, the PIN numbers to use with different cash and credit cards, our telephone credit card identification numbers, etc., that you could try to memorize certain numbers which are vitally important to you such as your credit card numbers, insurance policy numbers, etc. It's good brain exercise.

Remembering Information

Dr Crook recommends that every time you sit down to read a newspaper or magazine article you pretend that you will be asked to summarize its contents to someone when you've finished, which will make you pay more attention. Practise finding a key sentence in each paragraph.

Developing Awareness

Start being more observant as you walk to work or the shops. Can you make a list of all the shops in your village centre or city block, in the order in which they appear? Pay attention to names and places you pass as if you will be asked to give someone else directions on how to get there for the first time. We know one eighty-year-old who is phenomenal about this and has an almost photographic memory for places, even ones that she hasn't visited for a while. If she says, 'You want a dry cleaner? It's between the "Kittycat" pet shop and "Bighouse" estate agents, on the north-west side of the street about fifty yards past the supermarket,' she's always absolutely right.

'In general we neglect our brains and concentrate too much on body fitness.'

Victoria's grandmother was like that. When she was in her eighties the family was going to France to visit the tiny village from which she had emigrated to America when she was a small child. She told them, 'You'll recognize our house because it has windows that are not evenly underneath each other like the others on the street. It's the only house like that.' Sure enough, she was right (and it was such a sleepy little village that progress hadn't changed things beyond all recognition). Victoria, on the other hand, admits she is clueless when it comes to directions, even if she's been somewhere fairly recently. She's working on it.

Professor Siegfried Lehrl of the University of Erlange, who noticed that the brain seems to atrophy, producing a measurable drop in IQ, when we take a mindless holiday of the 'sun, sea and sangria' sort, recommends a daily 'brain workout' of at least ten minutes to prevent any loss of IQ. Such a workout could, he suggests, even increase IQ by as much as 15 per cent in as little as a month. 'The brain needs to be kept active, so if you are on holiday you could, for example, play cards, speak to foreigners or practise a different language. This is some-thing new and keeps the brain active.' He believes that 'in general we neglect our brains and concentrate too much on body fitness. Our research has shown that people who kept fit but neglected their mental health were just as likely to end up dependent on others in their old age, but those who kept their minds active remained independent for much longer.'

If all else fails, rely, like Lady Longford, on a little notebook or, better still, some stick-on 'Post-It' notes to remind you of things. Victoria writes urgent reminders on her hand when she's racing about during the day and too busy even to get out her diary and was delighted when meeting Virgin Airlines boss Richard Branson to discover that even a famous, rich, successful and comparatively youthful business tycoon like him scribbled on his skin!

FEED YOUR HEAD

It is vital to 'feed your head' or 'feed your mind', expressions most Baby Boomers will recognize from the old Jefferson Airplane song 'White Rabbit' and from the Beatles' 'Revolution', although not quite in that spaced-out sixties way. The brain needs to be well nourished in order to perform its best. Like the rest of your body it needs top quality fuel, custom-tailored to its needs. Fortunately, most of the foods that are good for the brain are good for the rest of your body too, and the power foods and supplements in the last chapter are for the most part beneficial to the brain. The better nourished you are the better your brain will work, and Tony Buzan feels it's partic-ularly useful for the brain if you drink the recommended eight glasses of water a day, so that it doesn't dehydrate and shrink.

If you've heard the old wives' tale that fish is good for the brain, remember that old wives are often right.

If you've heard the old wives' tale that fish is good for the brain, remember that old wives are often right. Certain fish oils contain decosa-hexaenoic acid (DHA) which has been shown to aid vision and brain development. Many fish also contain choline, which can improve the rate at which the brain processes information.

Carrots, said to be good for the eyes, contain copious supplies of Vitamin A, good for scavenging up the free radicals that can attack the brain. Vitamin E is also excellent for that purpose.

B Vitamins which are water soluble, unlike Vitamins A and E, and therefore very easily lost in the system need to be taken regularly. Try a good B Complex supplement that contains B1, B6, and B12 in partic-ular.

Since most of the brain's energy comes from burning up carbohy-drate, thiamine (Vitamin B1) is important for this process. You'll find it in wholemeal bread and cereals, vegetables, nuts, meat and yeast, which also supply the Vitamin B6 needed for the nervous system gener-ally. Iron, in liver, eggs, wholegrains and leaf vegetables, assists in bringing oxygen to the brain. Linoleic acid, part of the make-up of brain membranes, is to be found in polyunsaturated fats.

The high antioxidant properties of olive oil, which contains high quantities of natural Vitamin E, are thought to make it a possible preventer of premature senility, as well as helping to ward off other diseases in which the activities of free radicals, which can damage cells and even DNA, are implicated, such as cancer and cardiovascular disease.

Phosphatidylserine (PS), a phospholipid naturally present in the body, is a 'nutrient building block that accelerates all brain functions', according to promoters pushing it in supplement form at the 1998 conference of the A4M in Las Vegas. It is said to reverse memory loss due to ageing and to benefit Alzheimer's and Parkinson's disease patients as well young, healthy adults struggling to cope with stress, and to be 'safe to take with negligible adverse effects'. It is synthesized from soya lecithin instead of the potentially dangerous cow brain material it once was taken from. Dr Crook, who is sceptical of many other supposedly anti-ageing treatments, says he has no qualms about taking this.

St John's Wort is one of a number of herbs and natural remedies said to enhance brain power and beat depression. But it can have adverse effects if taken in conjunction with some medicines, or if pregnant, so, as always, don't take such things without consulting a doctor.

Age with Attitude

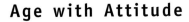

The eminent British gerontologist Professor Sir John Grimley Evans, based at Oxford's Radcliffe Infirmary, believes that 'Those who insist on staying in control of their own lives, the wilful and cantankerous, live longer than the more compliant, sweet old folk who make good patients favoured by doctors and nurses. The first imperative for those wishing to be a healthy hundred, therefore, is to be informed, to stay in command and to be thoroughly obstreperous.'

'Rage, rage against the dying of the light'

DYLAN THOMAS

Victoria had a ninety-year-old neighbour who she thought initially was a 'sweet old lady'. She soon learned that the neighbour, whom she grew to like and respect enormously, wasn't sweet but shrewd, assertive and not at all shy about asking for, even demanding, things that she needed. That seemed to be connected with her survival, and right up until her death at a very

late age she continued to tend her huge garden, harvest her fruit and vegetables, bake apple pies for the friends with whom she enjoyed outings and live alone without even the company of a telephone.

Some of the 'sweetest' most uncomplaining people, sadly, die of cancer. It has been suggested that there is a 'cancer personality' and that part of this is being self-effacing and very accommodating to others. Whether or not this is true is very controversial and understandably offensive but some studies have found that patients who were assertive, even unpleasantly so, survived better after breast cancer than those who were meekly accepting of whatever fate had in store for them. Dylan Thomas's advice to 'Rage, rage against the dying of the light – do not go gentle into that good night' seems as good a rallying cry as any when the end appears imminent, but perhaps we should all get into 'survivor' mentality long before we need to. Having the sort of positive outlook that seems to be a factor in longevity doesn't mean being a Pollyanna or a doormat. It means not wasting time in the nega-tivity of fretting and looking back, and you are less likely to need to do this if you are assertive enough to make sure that things are right for you in the first place.

... if you mentally try to fight a physical disease, you are more likely to beat it than if you politely give way to it.

Also, if you mentally try to fight a physical disease, you are more likely to beat it than if you politely give way to it. (Think of the horror movie symbolism of inviting the vampire in rather than warding it off with a firm belief in the existence of a higher power.) It is on this prin-ciple that positive visualization exercises are suggested to cancer patients, who are told to imagine that their cancer is being eaten up or destroyed in some other way by their immune system.

Recent evidence that people who simply imagined themselves to be exercising showed actual benefits from their fantasy workouts gives even greater credence to this theory. Researchers at Manchester Metropolitan University in 1998 asked one group of, yes, male, students to perform twenty contractions of their little fingers eight times over a four-week period. Another group was asked only to imagine performing these contractions. At the end of the month the strength of all the students' little fingers was tested on a force-measuring device and while those who had done the exercises had fingers that were

30 per cent stronger, those who had only imagined them had an improvement of 16 per cent. No wonder fantasy lovers are said to be good for the libido!

'Ageing disgracefully' has its advantages. Don't feel you have to be 'good' when you're old. Be like the old woman in Jenny Joseph's poem 'Warning', written when the poet, now in her sixties, was only twenty-eight, who wanted to wear purple, run her walking stick along railings and learn to spit.

Think of the artist Beryl Cook's wonderful paintings of middle-aged, and older, women behaving 'disgracefully' and enjoying it – dancing, drinking, joking together, often in too-short skirts and fishnet tights. While we wouldn't necessarily recommend the too-short skirts and fishnet tights, we would concur that the best thing you can do is have a good time, particularly if it involves fun and friendship.

DON'T CLUTTER UP YOUR MIND OR YOUR LIFE

You need to have the guts, as we admit we don't always, to clear your life of the useless and the dead, from old papers you're never going to read again or that '60s mini skirt you'll never fit into again to relationships that hang like dead albatrosses around your neck, pulling you down with them. You have to be slightly ruthless sometimes to be a survivor. Feng Shui practitioners, increasingly fashionable in Western society, teach that clutter blocks energy and potential. So does cluttering your life with draining relationships and cluttering your brain with fruitless worries and regrets.

> *You have to be slightly ruthless sometimes to be a survivor.*

One possible reason the better off in society live longer could be not just because they eat more healthily, take more holidays and have fewer money worries but that they're not afraid to get divorced, as the number of divorces proclaimed in the English peerages should prove. Of course it's easier to get divorced if you both know where your next meal is coming from, and you're only arguing about who gets the villa in the south of France and who the Aspen ranch rather than frantically trying to figure out if the two of you can survive in separate households on what you could barely exist in one. But Dr David Weeks' Superyoung, not all of them wealthy, were quick to realize if they'd made a mistake with

partners, and equally swift to ditch them and find another rather than suffering in martyred silence. Often their new partner was considerably younger than them, reflecting their youthful outlook on life.

If it's any comfort to you to know, divorced women of a certain age seem to get an extra surge of energy that allows them to start new businesses and new lives successfully. In fact, surveys have shown that divorced women do much better than divorced men in many respects. They tend to take themselves in hand, lose weight, have a new hairstyle and go out to conquer the world whereas men, unless they fall immediately into some other woman's loving arms as all too often they do, tend to mope around and lose interest in their work, ambition and initiative.

REJUVENATING RELATIONSHIPS – AND YOURSELF

But before you throw away the relationship in which you've invested so much of yourself, why not try to rejuvenate it? It may not be a fashionable idea in our 'throwaway' society, but Boomers are old enough to remember, just, the era when things could be repaired rather than replaced with an upgraded model at the first sign of trouble. How do you do this?

First recognize that the relationship needs redefining. If trying to tackle the whole thing is beyond you, then work out little ways to improve your communication and/or time spent together: change the routine – have a walk on a Sunday morning instead of fighting over the Sunday papers; make a 'date' to meet for lunch during the working week – a sandwich somewhere quiet like the park can be better for talking than a restaurant meal where you spend half your time talking to waiters.

We sometimes regard our 'other half' as we do the furniture or the wallpaper.

If the sex side of things is under par, don't just moan about it, introduce a new sensuality, whether it's a massage or just cuddling up together with a favourite film. There are lots of books (see 'Further Reading') that suggest sensual massage techniques and other ideas for spicing up a long-term relationship. Try to move the conversation subtly around to sensual matters rather than nagging and putting additional pressure on your partner who may be suffering from mid-life insecurities or inabilities in that area.

Try to make time to really listen to your partner and encourage them to talk. It is important to make prolonged eye contact during this communication, rather than continuing to watch the telly or reading the newspaper. We sometimes tend to regard our 'other half' as we do the furniture or the wallpaper – always there, functional, but not very exciting. Really look at them again as a human being – imagine meeting them for the first time at a party and chatting them up, and treat them with the same interest and attention you would in such a situation!

Avoid vexing areas which usually start an argument. Try, instead, to remember those occasions when you have had fun together and try to recreate situations like that. (See 'Small Adventures' in Chapter Eleven.)

Try getting together with good old friends who bring you out of yourselves.

Try getting together with good old friends who bring you out of yourselves and remind you of what you saw in each other originally.

Bring the 'surprise' element into your relationship again: don't go to bed in your sweatpants and woolly socks as usual, but wear something sexy for a change, or nothing at all.

Play games with each other or just play. Too often relationships stagnate because people become totally bogged down in the day-to-day running of life and are so busy running it that they don't actually have a life. One fun idea we saw in an episode of the television programme *Friends* is to quiz each other to see how much you really know about each other as if it's a session of *Mastermind* with your 'specialist subject' your other half. For example, ask 'What is my favourite television programme? Who was my first boyfriend? What do I eat for breakfast? What turns me on?'

Once you have become happier with your partner, be frank about wanting change and encourage them, in a peaceful setting and in a non-confrontational manner, to say what they would like to have changed in the relationship. Don't use the accusative 'YOU always do that. . . .' Say instead, 'I would really like it if we could do more of such-and-such.'

Be aware that there are numerous books (see 'Further Reading') devoted to helping you to spice up an existing relationship, in addition to relationship counsellors trained to do so, so don't ditch it until you're sure it's not salvageable. You might be surprised!

BUT IF YOU DO DECIDE TO BAIL OUT

Don't worry about the rumour that it's supposedly more likely that a woman of forty-plus will be shot by a terrorist than find another man. First of all, that was disproved. Secondly, remember that most centenarian women are unmarried while most centenarian men are married. What does that tell you? That marriage is not necessarily the healthiest state for a woman if she is not in a healthy marriage of mutual support, as so many women, alas, are not. If she's a victim in a marriage where she is ministering to someone else's needs without getting support for her own, all the indications are that she's better off out. Take Tina Turner as a role model: look at how her career really took off when she left the abusive Ike and had the courage to set out on her own! You can be a victim at any age, but by middle age you should have wised up enough not to allow yourself to be one for any longer.

Don't believe it's supposedly more likely that a woman over forty will be shot by a terrorist than find another man.

One of the great ironies among the many surrounding the death of Diana, Princess of Wales, was, as her biographer and media friend Richard Kay noted, that she had just cast off her 'victim' mantle and was becoming a strong and independent woman when her life was so abruptly ended. As he put it, 'The moment that the Princess of Wales stopped thinking like one of life's victims and began to be an independent woman happened as she watched her belongings arrive at Kensington Palace from Highgrove and Prince Charles's being carted off in the opposite direction.' That she was able to laugh and quip to a friend 'I'm surprised he didn't take the light switches,' demonstrated this, he feels. That may be, but undoubtedly the princess was taking control of her life as she had taken control of her eating disorders, and as a stronger body visibly emerged so did a more empowered mind.

She might have benefited, in the normal course of events, with an increased lifespan. As psychologist Jenny Reeves notes, 'In the psychological literature we see over and over again that the "survivors" are those who have taken control of their lives enough to end any relationships in which they do not feel themselves to be thriving.' Why not take a long, hard look at those in your life. You don't necessarily have to dump your boring partner like you do an old sweater if you

can find ways to find or rekindle positive elements in the relationship. Just don't let things stagnate!

If you hate your job, ask yourself why. Is it something you can change or should you be thinking of changing jobs? Don't just suffer and seethe in silence. If you consider your work boring, try to find ways to make it interesting for yourself. Set yourself personal goals and targets. Plan interesting activities in your lunch break. Network constructively and develop social contacts. Think of how you can move towards something that would interest you more.

Go for Goals

Have you ever noticed how it is often the people who wrote down their life's ambitions on the back of an envelope while they were at school or college who seem to achieve them? That's because they keep challenging themselves, keep focusing and visualizing the positive outcome that they want.

It is all too true that the person voted 'most likely to succeed' at high school has, more often than not. Returning to her university for a reunion twenty years after graduating, Victoria found it amazing how unsurprising it was, with one or two notable exceptions, what people had turned into. Those who had strong goals during their college years had, by and large, achieved them and seemed satisfied with their lives. The drifters were still drifting. Goals keep us going, keep us ambitious, keep us involved with life. One lively octogenarian we know whom everybody thinks is in her sixties confided, 'I still think about what I'd like to do when I grow up – I've got so many ambitions still and plans for the future!' Another is planning her next holiday before she's come back from the previous one. This seems to keep her young.

Goals should be realistic, aspirational and visual.

Goals should be realistic, but also aspirational and visual. See yourself starring in the annual pantomime, clinching that business deal, sitting at a tidy desk. Keep on moving the goalposts if you want to get anywhere. Okay, so you've learned French in two weeks. Why not move on to Japanese and Greek, lambada dancing or deep sea diving? Never say never. Never think you're too old. Keep reaching for the sky. Astronaut John Glenn went to the moon

again in his seventies. Ex-president Bush decided to go parachute jumping in the lull after the thrills and spills of office. Keep challenging your body and your brain!

THE ROLE OF RELIGION

It is easy for an ex-convent girl to become areligious but never to lose her respect or understanding of the magnet of traditional beliefs and forms of worship. Visit any church, mosque or temple on its day of worship and they will be filled predominantly with greying or balding heads. Houses of worship draw us back in the winter of our lives and fulfil an important role of solace and spirituality when the rushing is over and the need to make sense of our brief time on this planet becomes acute. I find myself seeking out a cathedral near my office just to sit from time to time in a way I would never have done just a few years ago. I am not exactly praying – just being something other than I can be anywhere else, and feeling at peace.

'Nearer my God to thee' takes on new meaning in middle life.

Born-again believers might make you recoil with their evangelical fervour but can only fill us with admiration when you appreciate their sense of purpose and self-less giving of their time, efforts, even material wealth to aid others less fortunate. Several of my own consultants are very commited Christians and Jews and amaze me how they balance their work as glamorous image consultants with raising money and sourcing medical supplies for war-torn regions in Europe. One even jumps aboard a lorry and shares the driving to deliver much needed clothing and food to Bosnia shortly after wowing audiences with a slick presentation on how to present yourself better in business. She sees no dichotomy and takes joy from her work but finds life's purpose from her faith. Those of us without such conviction we can only applaud her efforts, harbouring an un-Christian dose of envy.

Victoria has a close friend who regularly takes food to the homeless. That is the kind of positive action that can help many people feel prepared to face the future when the words 'nearer my God to thee' take on new meaning in middle life. Another woman we know, in her late seventies but looking at least fifteen years younger, lives on her own in a country community, her children grown and far away. The Church has become her family and social life all rolled into one. She doesn't have much money but enjoys a rich and rewarding life in that

close community, bringing a casserole to communal suppers, baking for coffee mornings, enjoying a wealth of companionship.

Therapy: New Opiate of the Masses?

They say that children and grandchildren are our immortality, and they serve that function not just because, through them, our genes are continuing in the world, but because their existence keeps us alert and interested in the future. Few but the very altruistic would care about the future of the planet if there wasn't going to be a little part of them left on it. We worry about these things, we say, for our children and our children's children.

But an increasing number of people are becoming concerned about leaving the world in a better condition; being 'at one' with nature; tapping into the universal 'Qi' life force; saving the planet; purifying their bodies and their souls.

The runaway success of books such as *The Celestine Prophecy* and others with a mystic, New Age appeal, 'help' guides promising how to find personal and emotional fulfilment, and books and 'mind/body/spirit' festivals featuring complementary therapies shows how interested people are in alternative pathways.

'Therapy' has been called the new religion, as increasing numbers of people seek from Reiki (Japanese spiritual healing) or reflexology what they used to get from religion, or seek salvation through gurus rather than God. While it is of course worrying if people are worshipping false prophets, particularly those who will exploit them for profit (as so many 'New Age' therapists did, it seems, with Diana, Princess of Wales, the quintessential 'New Seeker'), there seems to us nothing wrong in seeking comfort anywhere you can find it.

The nice thing about spiritual healing is that spiritual belief is not a prerequisite!

Victoria has benefited greatly from Reiki. She had her first treatment for a story she was writing shortly before she was due to have an ovarian cyst, which had shown up on a scan, removed during an exploratory laparoscopy. When the practitioner Stewart Ivory, who practises at Champney's health spa and also in London, put his hands above her pelvic region she had a sudden sensation as if something burst, and

an image of yellow waves washing against a shore. The feeling was gentle and subtle, nothing painful, but she was not surprised when her surgeon told her the following week that no ovarian cyst had been found, despite the clear evidence of one on her scan. 'There are more things in Heaven and Earth, Horatio, than are dreamt of in your philosophy,' as Hamlet said.

What's the harm if these non-invasive techniques make people feel good?

She has also felt benefits from the effects of spiritual healer Mevagh Horton. (The nice thing about spiritual healing, as with Reiki, is that spiritual belief is not a prerequisite!) A spiritual healer will not usually charge but might ask for a donation to a special cause. Indeed, over the years we have both tried an array of 'complementary' medicines for the dual impact of being both therapeutic and a treat!

No longer are homoeopathy, acupuncture, aromatherapy, and the like only options for the well-off or the indulgent. These are not 'religion substitutes' or even substitutes for conventional medicine. These complementary therapies help to make people feel good, and that can't be bad. It is no surprise that spiritual healers and aromatherapeutic masseurs are now available in hospitals and hospices, sometimes covered by private health insurance or under rationalized health systems, and acceptance of these often Eastern therapies in the West is growing at a phenomenal rate. Many of us have access almost daily to knowledgeable gurus via the popular press, day-time television and the internet who can teach us many new things to improve our sense of wellbeing.

At the Yoga Therapy Centre in London, an outgrowth of the Yoga Biomedical Trust which looks into the health effects of yoga, yoga is used to treat a range of conditions from arthritis to asthma. The Kailash Centre recently opened in London offering a variety of unusual Eastern therapies including Mongolian warrior massage of the kind apparently favoured by Genghis Khan. Current devotees include the Marquess of Bath. What's the harm if these non-invasive techniques make people feel good? They have fewer side-effects than the conventional drugs doled out by over-worked doctors and appeal to the egocentricity of the 'Me Generation' since they focus on the individual and are an excuse for indulging in the 'Me-time' that is actually important for us all as long as we don't become too self-obsessed!

Go to your doctor and say you have a headache and the chances are you'll be prescribed a painkiller. Go to a homoeopathic physician

with the same problem and you'll have a detailed discussion about the type of headaches you have, and what you feel brings them on, and will go away with a homoeopathic preparation specifically tailored for that type of headache and no other.

BEATING A RETREAT

It is important to realize that you can go on relaxing and refreshing 'retreats' run by different groups without actually committing yourself to their philosophies, or feeling them forced upon you. Victoria had a very pleasant weekend a while ago with the Friends of the Western Buddhist Order. She was doing an article on the experience, but relaxed totally and found it very soothing after her frenetic lifestyle. Okay, she found it hard to meditate in front of a buddha that had been Westernized to look disconcertingly like Elvis Presley, but by the time she got in her car to go home on the Sunday evening, driving twenty miles an hour seemed fast to her. She had never been so relaxed. She felt her soul had been soothed and nourished even though it hadn't been a religious experience and no one had attempted to convert her.

In the same way holy orders like The Little Sisters of the Cenacle, whom I counselled on what colours to wear when they were 'coming out of the habit' a few years ago, are seeing increasing numbers of burnt-out business people seeking sanctuary and solace in a short-term retreat with them right near a famous health club, which attracts another type of pilgrim also looking for a change of life.

Health spas have a full range of alternative therapies and exercise classes such as t'ai chi. They have become a late twentieth century retreat for a privileged few. They may help you lose a few pounds too but they cost many pounds more, whereas some religious groups like the Woodland Hermits at their Grail Centre offer you your own little wooden cabin (without running water, and only a shared portable toilet outside) for about £15 a day, and the Vipassana Trust runs utter silence retreats during which you cannot talk for ten days but meditate for ten hours a day with breaks for vegetarian meals, for a mere donation at your discretion. Seek and you shall find, if you want one, a reasonably priced retreat where you can lick your wounds or simply recharge your

Retreats allow plenty of time for contemplation and planning life changes.

batteries in peace or maybe get the inspiration to embark on that new career as a novelist, philosopher or New Age therapist!

The ballerina Bryony Brind is one of many women who have retrained in mid-life for a career in the therapies that are becoming an important part of so many people's lives. Always interested in aromatherapy, she trained in aromatherapeutic massage as well as moving into acting, knowing that a ballerina's career is, of necessity, brief. The actress Lori Fox trained as a Reiki therapist after experiencing its benefits for herself, but continues to act.

Retreats allow plenty of time for contemplation and planning life changes. However, if you haven't yet had a revelation on the road to Harrods it might cheer you to know that Dr David Weeks found that his 3,500 Superyoung were neither more nor less spiritual than the population as a whole.

Make your own Luck and Longevity

Over several years Hunter Davies has interviewed twenty-six people born in the year 1900 for a book on the millennium. He found that most had drunk alcohol all their adult lives and many still drank a whisky every evening or a Guinness every day, but that 'On the whole they have been fairly moderate in their food and drink.' Several did smoke but gave it up years ago. All considered themselves fairly independent and had a social life they valued. And 'The quality of their life was still strong enough to keep them positive and cheerful.' One was still working – Len Vale-Onslow who ran a motorcycle repair shop in Birmingham and, at ninety-six, was still riding motorbikes as well as driving a car.

'Trust in the Lord and keep your bowels open.'

One common thread that united them was that all had maintained a great interest in other people and in the world at large, which Hunter Davies became convinced was the vital prerequisite for longevity. When he asked each one of the twelve men and fourteen women for their secret of long life, his ninety-six-year-old father-in-law said, 'Trust in the Lord and keep your bowels open,' while one woman swore by 'lots of suet pudding'. Several mentioned the need for moderation in all

things, others said it was important to stick to routines. All emphasized the importance of being independent and not moaning. Almost all mentioned luck.

'In the end,' Davies concluded, 'I decided there is no common denominator for long life, apart from good luck and some good genes. In a way, that's reassuring. It means almost all of us have a chance. If, of course, we want to reach a hundred.'

We'd heartily agree with him, except to add that we believe you can make your luck with positive thinking and proper planning and assist those genes through exercise, nutrition and sheer determination. We predict that more and more people will be doing this successfully in the new millennium.

11

The Pleasure Principle

'Tell me where is fancy bred,
Or in the heart or in the head?'

SHAKESPEARE, *The Merchant of Venice*

Fancy That

'A little of what you fancy does you good,' the saying goes, and after all our research we've concluded that this is probably as good a precept as any to follow. So why not read this chapter soaking in a hot bath scented with soothing aromatic oils, a glass of champagne or your favourite drink, a box of chocolates or what you will and someone to scrub your back, if you can find such a paragon, by your side? Or maybe that wouldn't be pleasurable to you. One person's pleasure can be another's chore. And vice versa. Remember how Prime Minister John Major's wife Norma once rashly admitted that she got some of her greatest kicks in life from ironing?

Before you read any further, why not make a list of your 'fun-da-mentals' – the pleasurable things in your life. It should include the free and natural ones like looking at a starry sky or a beautiful landscape; the cultural ones such as going to concerts and art galleries; the sporty ones, even if you're just an armchair athlete; the homely, like the scent of freshly laundered sheets or home-baked bread; and the purely hedonistic such as breakfast in bed or a full body massage (see our pleasure quiz, p. 360). Don't forget to include pleasures such as learning, as well as loving, and the pleasure that comes from making other people happy as well as yourself. By the end of this chapter we hope you'll agree that you should try to work as many of these as are practically possible into your life every day. You owe it to yourself to do what makes you feel good as long as it doesn't hurt anybody else. There is positive proof that pleasure will do your immune system good. Have fun and live longer!

From what we've read and seen we're convinced that positive thoughts will go further than any miracle potion that's likely to be invented in the next few years in keeping people young. Not only is it important to find pleasure in your work and daily routines, but it's essential to keep dreaming and planning for future pleasures and adventures, even if they're only inside a library book – or your imagination.

Once it was just a gut instinct but nowadays pleasure can actually be proven to boost our immune systems and do us good. A complex battery of tests can measure our hormone and enzyme levels as well as our blood pressure and composition. When we are happy or experiencing pleasure the levels of positive substances in our systems are demonstrably high.

When we are unhappy, stressed, or depressed, levels are quantifiably lower. And scientists believe they have discovered an actual 'pleasure pathway' through the brain which is observable in animals as well as in humans. When it is travelled by pleasurable impulses our cholesterol levels drop and more natural killer cells are present in our blood to fight off infections. Immunoglobin A, which protects us against upper respiratory infections such as colds, is present in greater quantities. Figuratively speaking, when our pleasure pathway is left untravelled it gathers 'weeds' which hastens our 'going to seed'.

The effect of pleasure on the pleasure centres of the brain is being studied by scientists all over the world. The German sociologist and former physicist Rainer Bramer, based at the University of Marburg, discovered in 1998 that looking at beautiful landscapes gives such pleasure that it can actually be measured in the change of brainwaves from gamma to the more calming alpha waves. Many relaxation tapes used by therapists while they are performing massage or healing work in the same way have been shown to change the brain waves into a less frenetic state. Dr Vincent Giampapa of Longevity Institutes International believes very firmly in the value of such tapes, which are now available from virtually every health food store as well as from record shops.

Just smiling, even if you don't feel like it, can send impulses along this pleasure pathway, so that you may feel better even if, like the smiling Pagliacci, your heart is breaking. Try it sometime. Remember that smiley crinkles around your eyes are much more attractive than deeply etched frown lines, and that your whole face lifts when you smile – an added benefit!

LEARN THE FUN-DAMENTALS

It is our fun-damental belief that no matter now many vitamin pills you pop, how carefully you stay out of the sun, how intense your exercise regime, how rigorous your diet or how many hormones you ingest, if you don't have love, joy and laughter in your life you're not really living. Without these vital ingredients, you may not live as long as less body-obsessed folk who do.

An Italian study, reported in 1998, showed that elderly people who had loving human contacts, whether with a partner or with children, grandchildren and close friends, lived longer than technically healthier counterparts with a dearth of loving contacts. Happiness was also

shown to be linked to longevity by a long-term study [by Winokur and Tsuang] reported in the *American Journal of Psychiatry* as long ago as 1975. At the end of a thirty-year trial period, two-thirds of the 'depressed' group in the survey had died (8 per cent were suicides) whereas only one third of the control group had, and none of them from suicide. In between these two studies have been numerous experiments indicating that petting animals can lower blood pressure and that people with pets tend to be healthier and/or live longer than those without. For pets, however, we believe you can substitute any pet pleasure.

Dr David Weeks' research into, first, eccentrics, who tended to live longer and be healthier than the average population, and, later the Superyoung, who looked younger, showed that both of these groups benefited from happiness and humour. They also both derived considerable pleasure from what they did as their day-to-day work or, in the case of eccentrics, an obsessive hobby or interest. In the same way Pat York's study of seventy-five over-seventy-fives still 'Going Strong', many of them in their nineties, showed that all these people, while having a strong sense of humour which shone out in their interviews, derived a great deal of pleasure from the work or activities in which they were still enthusiastically involved.

THOSE WITH VOCATIONS DON'T NEED VACATIONS

'Business or pleasure?' is a common question but the two needn't – shouldn't – be mutually exclusive. To be able to earn a living doing what you love is one of life's greatest pleasures, and a sense of vocation, of loving what you do for a living, is a huge health benefit, since most of us spend more waking hours working than we do playing. Clearly 'clock-watching' for fifty years until you get your gold watch is not going to be nearly as exhilarating as doing a job you revel in so much that the passage of time seems irrelevant. In Victoria's book *Working It Out* she discovered huge health differences between downtrodden, wage-slave workaholics and work enthusiasts buoyed up by their work who enjoyed it so much they would have done it almost without pay.

She found that those with vocations seldom need vacations and often don't take them, since they feel continually refreshed and invigorated by their life's work. But she also found it was beneficial to have a 'hinterland' to escape to, whether a literal one like a country cottage or a

figurative one like participating in amateur dramatics, or reading or writing escapist novels. Today's oldest woman, the diminutive Maria Geronimo from Brazil whose baptismal certificate gives her birth as 5 March 1887, says that her secret of longevity is singing.

DON'T STOP THE WORLD. YOU DON'T WANT TO GET OFF . . . YET!

Keeping in the rat-race keeps you young, that's the bottom line from recent multi-billion-dollar research by the US National Institute on Ageing into the effects of ageing and how to minimize them. Testing rodent rats to theorize about humans in the rat race showed that if you stayed in work you lived up to 50 per cent longer than those who opt out. Researchers reported their honest surprise over the results as they assumed that a steady decline due to ageing would be inevitable regardless of whether you were working or not.

You don't have to opt out or downshift to enjoy a mid-life change.

But while the rats that were left unstimulated became indolent with age, the rats who continued on active programmes showed far fewer effects of ageing as well as living up to half as long again. The message, he said, seemed to be that people who stayed involved in work they enjoyed, and not necessarily in the rat race but the human race, will last longer and be fitter.

Professor Janet Spence of the University of Texas, Austin, did a major study of those she dubbed work enthusiasts versus workaholics and found that they experienced fewer psychosomatic and actual illnesses than workers who didn't enjoy what they were doing. When you're not getting pleasure from your work you can be stressed or bored or overwhelmed by it, and health consequently suffers. 'Those who love what they're doing are sick much less than other types of workers due to the phenomenon known as psychoneuroimmunology, by which pleasure boosts the immune system,' agreed 'futurist' and management consultant Christine MacNulty of the international consultancy Applied Futures.

Psychoneuroimmunology is the fancy word for mind-over-matter in matters of health which even the most sceptical have now been forced to acknowledge probably does exist. It could account for the phenomenon that people who love their work tend to be ill in their own time,

during holidays, while those who hate what they do tend to be ill on company time. If the fun factor is not in what you are doing for a living, or if you're starting to feel ill a lot of the time, it's probably time to change jobs, which is exactly what many people are now deciding to do in mid-life.

Pam decided to go back to college and train as a teacher when her children were teenagers, abandoning her part-time work as a receptionist for a full-time career which brings her the job fulfilment she never had before. Kate was working at a corner shop that sold sandwiches. She noticed what types of sandwiches were most popular and started making some of her own to supply the store with. Now she has a good-sized little business she loves, supplying beautifully wrapped sandwiches on freshly baked baguettes.

IS IT A VOCATION OR A SLOG?

It's easy to know if you're happy in your work ... you bound out rather than drag out of bed Monday to Friday. You are early many mornings and rarely count the minutes to clocking-off time. You aren't a desperately driven, work-obsessed drone who doesn't have time for meaningful personal relationships. Being happy in your work means enjoying it as part of a balanced life. And being women, great jugglers that we are, we often feel we can balance the various aspects of our complex lives better when we are the boss, even if we are our only employee. I am the head of an international image consultancy, Victoria self-employed, and we are both experts at fitting several quarts into the proverbial pint pot. It might mean working until midnight some nights, but you can usually make time for a child's sports day, an important doctor's appointment or just a little light relief when you need it.

Research shows that you are most likely to be happy and unstressed if you have a sense of control over what you're doing, which the self-employed may enjoy more easily than those who feel nothing more than pawns in a corporate game plan they don't quite understand. But it's up to you to create that sense of control in your working life. You can do this without becoming a fascist but by questioning what you don't understand, by taking the initiative when you have the opportunity to, by organizing your own routines as much as possible. If you can't find the right amount of control to feel empowered in your job then it's essential to find a new environment where you can. To do so

is essential for your health and happiness and might just affect how long you live.

POSITIVE THOUGHTS, A PLEASURE IN THEMSELVES

Looking back in anger is a very negative, ageing pastime which can give you a crick in the neck, a permanent scowl on your face and numerous stress-related ailments. Looking forward in anticipation is a pleasure in itself, as well as the kind of positive visualization which can help you make pleasurable things come to pass. It's a technique taught by corporate motivators, the coaches of world-class athletes and some holistic healers but there's very little mystique about it. Just visualize things that would give you pleasure to do and see yourself doing them. Business people use this technique to visualize positive outcomes for meetings or successful presentations.

When you are depressed so is your immune system.

Sports people are taught to see themselves winning, and never to admit the possibility of defeat. If you have a good enough imagination, this technique may not just be effective but pleasurable as an end in itself.

One woman of eighty-two we know still travels the world and actively runs her own business. She bubbles with plans to see the few countries she hasn't yet visited, and considers herself to be having a quiet week if she's not out till late, going to theatre, concerts and parties at least five nights. She's usually planning the next event before she's finished the last, and the anticipation seems to keep her going. Another woman of a similar age is largely housebound yet she, too, manages to have great adventures through escapist books she borrows from the local library. Although in real life she can't walk very far, through them she can wander through the mountains of the Lake District and explore famous gardens of the world. A delightful conversationalist, she also derives a great deal of pleasure from the visits of friends and relatives who enjoy coming to see her. She seems to have boundless energy as she bustles around her immaculate home making them welcome, possibly because she never wastes an ounce of it on self-pity.

These women are very different but, like others of their age, realize that time is precious and to be enjoyed, and that all time can be 'quality time' if you make it so. Only teenagers have the luxury of being bored. Someone who takes no interest in forward planning, who can't summon

up joy at the prospect of a day out with a friend, a visit from a grand-child or a beautiful piece of music may be seriously depressed, and when you are depressed, so is your immune system.

NAUGHTY CAN BE SO NICE

But what constitutes a pleasure, and what if the things we find plea-surable are supposedly 'bad' for us like cigarettes and chocolate? Can what is 'bad' be 'good'?

Twin sisters Rhea Spohner and Ruth Emblow of New York state, who celebrated their hundredth birthday together in February 1988 in the company of their ninety-four-year-old kid sister, confessed to being partial to chocolate and figure-skating. They clearly enjoyed life and didn't waste much time worrying. Canadian Marie-Louise Meilleur, born in 1880, rolled her own cigarettes daily until her nineties while Lebanese Ali Mohammed Hussein, born in 1862, remains a sixty ciga-rettes a day man!

Professor David Warburton and his colleagues in ARISE, Associates for Research into the Science of Enjoyment, believe that it is good for us to stimulate our pleasure centres, even with some supposedly 'bad' things. Professor Warburton, a professor of human pharmacology and the founder of ARISE, an inter-national affiliation of interested academics, doctors and scientists who meet annually over a gargantuan soup-to-nuts feast washed down by fine wines, can provide ample scientific evidence that enjoying ourselves is good for us.

ARISE has found that even such 'naughty' plea-sures as chocolate and alcohol can be beneficial as long as they are unaccompanied by guilt, which produces as many negative physiological reactions as pleasure does positive ones. The least healthy option is to indulge and then feel anxious about it. 'Guilt is basically stress,' Professor Warburton warns, 'the heart beats faster, the blood pressure rises, the palms sweat, the blood vessels dilate, causing flushing. The stress hormone cortisol increases with the level of guilt felt, the choles-terol level rises and Immunoglobin A, which protects against upper respiratory infections, measurably drops. Fewer lymphocytes and natural killer cells are present to fight off infections.'

> *'Naughty' pleasures such as chocolate and alcohol can be beneficial as long as they are unaccompanied by guilt.*

Precisely the opposite effect occurs when we are experiencing pleasure, whether that pleasure is a favourite chocolate bar or a fantasy lover. While the advantages of fantasy lovers have not, to our knowledge, been analysed, good, dark chocolate (not over-sugared confections) is a source of protein, iron, magnesium and valuable B vitamins. Eating it has been shown to trigger the release of endorphins, the body's natural opiates, which make us feel good. Chocolate, craved by so many, is not just the ideal combination of sweetness and creamy, mouth-watering texture, but contains theobromine, a potentially psychoactive stimulant of the central nervous system. However, Professor Warburton cautions, because of the release of endorphins chocolate causes, a cycle of craving can be set up.

It is the rare smoker who lives to have the last laugh.

ARISE can find advantages in even the wickedest of pleasures in the effect they have on our immune systems and, ultimately, it is thought, not only on our health but on our appearance and longevity. Caffeine and nicotine, Professor Warburton notes, 'elevate mood by acting on the dopamine pathway in the brain'. Dopamine is the neurotransmitter found to be essential for stimulating the 'brain reward' mechanism which has been monitored in rats. These substances can also enhance performance and productivity.

'Nicotine produces an improvement in information processing, attention and memory,' says Professor Warburton. 'Caffeine seems to create an absolute improvement in work output. Alcohol may impair performance but produces relaxation and therefore can provide a welcome escape from problems.' A recent study showed that the effect of a single daily bottle of beer on each of thirty-four senile patients was dramatic. 'Compared with a control group on orange juice they were measurably less morose and distant and more talkative and alert', ARISE notes.

But with these substances there is a danger that people think they feel better when indulging but actually their systems are under increasing strain from them. Cigarettes and coffee are often cited as relaxing yet they are actually stimulants because of the nicotine and caffeine. It is the rare smoker who lives to have the last laugh.

ARISE recommends pleasure in moderation: less of very good chocolate, a small piece of which may satisfy as much as a sweeter, fattier concoction several times the size; wines as good as you can afford so that you will savour them rather than simply knocking back the plonk, and so on.

DON'T KID YOURSELF

Avoid deluding yourself that you're only indulging in a simple comfort habit when you're really addicted to something that is bad for you. There is a vast difference between a comfort habit and an addiction. Going back to that packet of biscuits, having two and enjoying them with a cup of coffee when you feel you need a little solace may fill you with a warm, comforting glow and get those positive enzymes flowing. Scoffing the lot is probably due to a deeper hunger that biscuits cannot sate. Comfort habits are comforting; addictions are usually avoidance habits, and seldom are.

Shopping with a friend for frivolities can be a fun way to spend a day and forget some of your worries, unless your worries are of a financial nature and you're a shopaholic. Although a shopaholic's addiction isn't written all over her body like a drug addict's needle tracks, the toll it takes in terms of negative emotions will ultimately be visible and may affect the balance of her life as well as her bank balance.

An art lover can derive tremendous pleasure from a single picture; an art collector may be an obsessive acquirer whose huge collection never seems enough. There is a saying we once read on a calendar that said, 'If you're not happy with what you've got, why do you want more?' Addicts don't often enjoy the collections they accumulate, the substances they use, the thrills and supposed pleasures they experience. They crave them, which is a very different matter. The highs get fewer and further between and they need more and more of whatever it is and can all but lose themselves in the process.

True pleasures are different from feeding addictions. The feeling you get from a long country walk or maybe even a bracing city run is pleasurable because these activities, like all exercise, produce endorphins, pleasure enzymes, but also because they are beneficial to your body and brain in other ways. Some pleasures are not, and it's important to recognize the difference. You will if you're in tune with your body and spirit, and being in tune with them is important for your wellbeing. Take time to listen to your body. Is it hungry? Does it need a stretch, need fresh air, a hug? Treat it right, be a team and it will serve you well. Ignore it and the conflict between you and your body can become palpable, manifesting itself in lethargy, irritability, skin rashes, digestive problems or worse.

True pleasures are different from feeding addictions.

Go back to that list of personal pleasures you made at the beginning of this chapter.

How many of them are positive pleasures, and how many, do you suspect, are negative ones that will do you more harm than good?

Think about how you can change them. Only a slight 'twitch' might be needed. Like try going for a walk without the pub or shops at the end of it, and see if it's really the walking you enjoy or if it was just a means to an addictive end. Does chocolate truly give you pleasure or are you scarcely tasting it in your desperation to cram it down? Are you using it to avoid asking yourself what you're really hungry for, for example, love or companionship? What is it that you want truly? Be honest about that and devise a real plan of attaining it or altering your dreams to be more realistic and attainable.

GREAT ADVENTURES

Sometimes, as Dorothy learned in *The Wizard of Oz*, 'The happiness you seek is in your own back yard.' We may be so busy searching the shops and travel brochures for adventure and excitement that we fail to generate them from within where it counts. How many couples go to fancy restaurants or on expensive holidays but have nothing to say to each other when there? It's important to realize that pleasures are not the same as luxuries. Whether you live somewhere beautiful or overlooking a sewage plant, you can make sure that you give yourself plenty of pleasure and stimulation. Even if you can't afford the luxury hotel or exotic holiday of your dreams, there are plenty of cheap, and even free, adventures to be had that can give a great deal of pleasure.

All learning should be a great adventure.

Long before there were 'virtual' worlds to explore on the internet, as there are now, and so much learning accessible to those with the facility to 'surf' and 'download', there were adult education classes in everything from Afrikaans to Zen Buddhism to keep you in touch with the rest of the world. Why not consider the range of adventures from Alexander Technique to yoga to keep you in touch with your body and yourself? Maeve Binchy's wonderful book *Evening Class* shows how new worlds and new friendships can open up from such things. Now that libraries have computers for readers' use, and schemes to put 'grannies on the net', as the headlines screamed, it's getting ever easier to have great adventures at the press of a button.

But all learning should be a great adventure, and the day you think it's not, or think that you're too old to learn, is the day you should probably start packing your cases for that final journey.

Manchester College of Oxford University is just one of an increasing number of centres for further learning around the world that have recognized the desire of older people to savour the delights of the full or part-time undergraduate experience when they are mature enough to appreciate it. (Youth is wasted on the young, as we now know.) Grants were eagerly applied for from a wide cross-section of students when Manchester announced its new programme for mature students in the early nineties. The first intake included a chief of police coming up to retirement age, a former slimming club counsellor and several mothers leaving young teenaged children for the year so that they could live in student digs and totally immerse themselves in the learning and social life of the college.

Most had a whale of a time, just enjoying learning for learning's sake, without a thought of where it would lead. For one, a wife and mother in her fifties, the whole experience was 'pure pleasure', and having the luxury to worry about nothing but intellectual debate instead of all her normal wifely and motherly tasks was a sheer delight. She loved riding her bicycle through cobbled streets and having late night arguments about changing the world. This was truly learning for learning's sake, although some of the students did put their degrees to professional use.

•

LAUGH YOUR HEART OUT AND LIVE LONGER

One of life's greatest pleasures, of course, is laughter, which often arises as a result of pleasure but is a pleasure in itself. *Reader's Digest* has long called one of its joke columns 'Laughter, the Best Medicine' and it may well be. *The International Journal of Humour Research*, dedicated to promoting that theory, published a study by Dr William Fry of the Stanford University School of Medicine in California which demonstrated how laughter boosted the cardiovascular, respiratory, muscular, hormonal, central nervous and immune systems, not least simply by drawing more oxygen into the lungs.

'A child of six laughs 300 times a day,' Professor Warburton points out, 'while the average adult has fifty laughs and for a depressed person less than six. We should all laugh a great deal more, if just the act of

smiling can produce demonstrably lower levels of stress hormones.' That's why so many consultancies have sprung up in recent years holding 'laughter clinics' (one of them, started by Robert Holden in Birmingham, even available free to patients referred through the British National Health Service) or teaching 'the art of clowning'. Clowns go out to hospitals to cheer seriously ill patients, getting those in stitches into 'stitches'. The Holy Fools, an international group of clerics, believe that foolishness is next to godliness and that they can reach out to people better through laughter than through serious sermons.

Certainly the sense of humour is one of the first things that disappears from depressed people.

Certainly the sense of humour is one of the first things that disappears from depressed people, and is a precious commodity to cultivate. It will not desert you with age like your looks eventually will, and may be a truly saving grace. The ability to laugh at yourself, and even at tragic events that touch you, can help to get you through the toughest times intact. Women often put 'GSOH' , as the personal ads abbreviate 'good sense of humour', top of their list of requirements for a man, whereas men inevitably put 'slim'. Hmmm.

Shared senses of humour can keep marriages going when little else remains of what you lusted for in each other in your youth. As one woman whose face and figure bore little relationship to those her husband had courted, but whose wicked sense of humour had remained unscathed, said, 'I knew we were heading for divorce when he said "You stupid cow," when I accidentally knocked over a can of paint as we were doing up the kitchen. When we were younger he would have laughed and we would probably have ended up on the floor together, rolling around in it instead of tetchily looking for the turps.'

Our close friends are a diverse lot of all ages, scattered all over the world, some from schooldays, others acquaintances from our work. But the one thing we all share is a sense of humour and the ability to make each other laugh. When Victoria's with an old friend they giggle together like six-year-olds and the years seem to drop away. They feel so good afterwards that any problem somehow doesn't seem so bad. Laughter is cathartic in that way. With seven sisters all I need to do is ring one and start bantering and within minutes we are sparring with one-liners, determined to see who will wet themselves first, our pelvic floors not being what they used to be!

Boy did we have some laughs about my facelift, even though Victoria was trying desperately to dissuade me from it. Whoever has the last laugh, the other will undoubtedly join in. When I came back from the hospital and Victoria phoned to ask my younger daughter how I was, because I was unable to speak, Lucy said, 'Mummy's all right. At least she's still got her sense of humour.' That's one thing that can't be surgically removed or implanted. At least not yet. And it is good to know that my children have their priorities right – they are more interested in my humour than my cooking!

Okay, so you might not be able to tell a joke. But that doesn't mean you can't be giggling more than you do. Try whatever it takes from watching slapstick comedies to lurking with a video camera in the hope that someone falls off a ladder so you can send it to one of those silly television programmes in which people laugh at other people making fools of themselves. It has been proved that just forcing a grin will fool your body into feeling more cheerful.

PLAYTIME REQUIRED

You don't have to be into the Californian notion of 'finding your inner child' to enjoy the health bonuses that the ability to play can bring. 'Play', says Professor Jeffrey Goldstein, an American expert on toys and play based at the University of Utrecht in the Netherlands, 'can be doing anything you enjoy. But we have found that it can be highly beneficial for older people to play *imaginative games* with younger ones, and have been working on several inter-generational playschemes around the world to encourage this. We have also studied the effects of playing games on the reaction time, cognitive/perceptual adaptability and emotional wellbeing of twenty-two non-institutionalized elderly people aged sixty-nine to ninety in the Netherlands. After playing video games for five hours a week for five weeks they had significantly improved in all these areas, and seemed to benefit longer term in memory, concentration, coordination, attention span and general mental health and wellbeing.'

Professor Goldstein found that playing board games helps with problem-solving skills in adults as well as children, that inter-generational play with dolls, puppets and soft toys promoted fantasy and language skills which older people could benefit from while computer and video games enhanced reaction time and memory. Using toys with

moving parts helped to keep fine muscles working smoothly in older people, while using science and craft kits encouraged creativity and imagination. 'Let go of the adult notion that play is only for children,' Professor Goldstein advises. 'Adults can regain the playful attitude of a child.' Would you know what to do if you were told to go and play? Maybe it's time to rediscover how to.

Have you ever noticed how the teenaged babysitter was better at playing with your child(ren) than you were? It wasn't just because she was willing to get down on the floor and muck in with them, it was because she was still young enough to remember how to play games and young enough to enjoy playing them. So the next time your child, or grandchild, is crouched uncommunicatively in front of a computer, why not insist on joining in the game? You will, according to Professor Goldstein, benefit on every level personally and, with a second person involved, both of you will.

Making up stories for children is not only a pleasure, it's one of the best brain exercises there is, and really keeps you on the ball, particularly when they ask why.

LOVE . . . THE ULTIMATE PLEASURE

Love can be one of the greatest pleasures – when it's not being one of the greatest pains. The sensation you get from being part of a loving, sexual relationship should be qualitatively different from a 'wham, bam, thank-you ma'am' of simply sexual relief. But orgasm sets off a chain of positive neurochemical reactions that should leave you feeling an afterglow of pleasure and bubbling with health-giving hormones.

The very act of sex brings many health benefits. It:

✦ is excellent exercise: tones muscles and burns calories, though how much depends on how long and rigorous the procedure!

✦ stimulates the pleasure centres of the brain. Sex is the ultimate stimulate, releasing endorphins which are the body's natural opiates.

✦ provides the ultimate relaxant – that is, once orgasm has been achieved.

✦ is 'the best painkiller since hurtin' began' as some country and western singer wailed. Sex takes the mind off other worries and is a great stress reliever.

✦ releases human growth hormone thought to be rejuvenating.

Dr Jack Dominion, founder of the first marriage research centre in Britain, found that the loss of a loving relationship caused minor psychiatric symptoms such as poor sleep, irritability, anger and anxiety, which in turn could lead to more serious problems such as depression and increased drinking.

On the other hand, Ben Bradshaw of the 'Happiness Project' (no joke) warned that the type of infatuation where you cannot eat or sleep, have butterflies in the stomach, a pacy heartbeat and dry throat may not, indeed, be good for us. 'Adrenaline addicts are always looking for that euphoria, that excitement. And some people can get hooked on it as much as on a drug,' he says. 'But the body can't sustain it. Some relationships break down because people wrongly equate that feeling with true love which is much more based on mutual respect, humour, trust and loyalty.'

However, doctors do warn men with coronary problems to enjoy sex only with the wife because sex with an established partner is more relaxing than with a new lover!

Britain's fastest-growing new publication is, apparently, *The Erotic Review* – a pruriently playful publication designed to titillate the sexual sensibilities of the over-fifties. An offshoot of the Erotic Print Society and started by two art dealers in the early nineties, it has articles by such *eminences grises* as Auberon Waugh stylishly set amidst the erotic drawings of bygone eras. Proof that although there may be snow on the roof . . .

Although this magazine carries ads for many more primitive types of impotence 'cures' than Viagra – the first, no doubt, of an avalanche of aids to erection and orgasm for men and women – it could help to ensure that active, pleasurable and penetrative sex goes on well into old age.

WHAT ABOUT THE SINGLETONS?

Don't think, well, sex is okay for everyone with a partner. What about me on my lonesome? You don't have to wait for someone else to give you pleasure. Discover it for yourself. There is nothing wrong with it and it's eminently justifiable as an anti-ageing remedy! The high-minded and righteous tried to convince us many years ago that masturbation causes blindness. If it did, there would be a lot more men walking around with white sticks or guide dogs!

Since women are often less adept at the technique of what was bravely referred to in the television sitcom *Veronica's Closet* as romancing yourself, there are even courses in masturbation techniques for women in America (of course!). Eager participants arrive for weekly sessions with pillows and bean bags, strip down and learn the 'art'. You might not be ready for that but if you can get over your inhibitions about it, generating regular orgasms may lower your blood pressure and your stress hormone levels, raise your levels of HGH plus help to keep your vaginal area supple and lubricated. Some women can do it while reading a book, in the bath or while watching a film. For some just pressure on the pubic bone will suffice. Others will require direct stimulation of the clitoris. Special equipment is optional – all that's needed is you and your imagination. (And maybe a dream lover.)

SEXERCISE!

There are numerous exercises a woman can do to enhance sexual pleasure and strengthen her pelvic floor to prevent urinary problems and prolapse at the same time. But Dr Anthony Harris, author of the book *Sexual Exercises for Women*, like sexologist Anne Hooper, author of many books on sexuality (see Further Reading), argues persuasively that such exercises can be regarded as a pleasure in themselves rather than simply a preparation for sex with a partner. Different ones can serve different purposes, from relaxation to energizing, increasing muscle tone to providing sexual stimulation.

You could begin with some self-massage, Sitting somewhere comfortable, stroke up from your knee along your inner thigh into your groin and then on to your stomach and breasts. Work on the backs of the thighs and, for stronger pressure, stand up and use your whole hand rather than just your fingertips. Work on your buttocks, too. Relax!

Dr Harris, a PhD, not a medical doctor, who researched and taught female biochemistry for many years, suggests massaging along the 'sexual meridians' with hands that have been dipped in moisturizing cream or aromatic oil. To start, stand with your feet apart and press firmly along either side of your crotch, up over your pubic hair and on either side of your navel. Continue up and over your nipples and repeat the procedure, sweeping your hands this time. Such massage may be able to act as a satisfactory substitute for sexual intercourse or masturbation, and has the benefit of relieving tension, too.

Rocking on your stomach, bending your legs up at the knees and holding on to your ankles with your hands, can also be good for this purpose, using a cushion on your pubic bone if the action is uncomfortable. This is very similar to a yoga position that is good for the back and brings circulation to the genital area. In a relaxed squat, the anus and vagina relaxed and supported by your hands, Dr Harris notes that 'Most women experience pleasure in the pit of their tummy' and says that 'Waves of relaxation will go up the inside of your legs and up from your crotch to your breasts.'

STAY SENSUAL!

Remember that sensuality is a vital part of life which is all too often lost as we get older and no one wants to run their fingers through our white hair or lose themselves in our wrinkled bosoms. It's important to keep sensual pleasure in your life through people and activities, having a bath with a baby, giving a friend a head massage or brushing their hair. Remember how sensuous moulding clay was made to seem by Demi Moore and Patrick Swayze in the film *Ghost*? Maybe a local pottery class will release the same feelings in you! Grooming an animal, polishing the leaves of your houseplants or even letting a favourite piece of music really release you into another dimension, all are non-sexual opportunities for feeling, so important to our vitality.

I love the sensual feeling of soil on my hands as I work in my garden and nurture plants as I nurtured my children when they were little. Whispering sweet nothings to my seedlings makes my kids roll their eyes but makes me feel terrific. Victoria feels wonderful kneading dough for bread or having her feet kneaded by a reflexologist. You don't have to pay for expensive treatments. Persuade a friend to rub your back, or feet, if you'll rub theirs.

DON'T ACHE FOR IT . . . HAVE IT

The marvellously moving book *Love in Later Life* by eighty-three-year-old gerontologist Dr Hamilton Gibson poignantly describes the aching yearning older people can experience to be part of the sensual world. In it Cicely, a sixty-one-year-old woman, recalled how she used to 'watch groups of young men with sun-browned arms and legs jogging in packs past my garden' thinking 'they have no idea an ageing woman is watching them, harmlessly enjoying their display of youthful vigour and high spirits. Elderly women are not expected to show such interest.' She also remembers wanting to linger with her head on the shoulder of a male colleague who gave her a hug of thanks for a birthday present.

Sensual people have what sex therapist and anti-ageing specialist Dr Michael Perring describes as a 'moist' look about them. They don't tend to become dried-up old prunes but keep a sparkle in their eye and a spring in their step, he has noticed. That is possibly one of the reasons why the Superyoung keep finding themselves new partners. Dr Weeks noticed that his Superyoung didn't waste too long mourning the passage of one partner before looking for another, often a younger one better suited to their mindset.

Despite worrying about 'the defects of my body, my dereliction in the arts of love', as she put it, Cicely found sexual love again in her sixties and was filled with wonder and joy at her luck. Love in later life, she discovered, was more about gratitude than gratification, and she was profoundly grateful for it.

'It is difficult to put into words the marvel of loving consummation in old age,' she said. 'The warmth, the glow, the gentleness from mutual consideration, the actuality of loving arms enfolding one away from a menacing or indifferent world; to be succoured by embraces and loving kindness at a time when one is vividly aware of the inevitable invasion by infirmity and death.' Those of us who are not fortunate enough to have partners to succour us with loving embraces must make doubly sure to be surrounded by good friends and sensual pleasures.

If you answer mostly a's and b's to our highly pleasurable questions opposite, you're pretty hopeless in the pleasure stakes. Give yourself one point for each c answer only, and c how you did. Hope it's been a bit thought-provoking. Compiling silly quizzes is one of our small pleasures!

Do you have enough pleasure in your life?

1. What 'small pleasures' did Nancy in *Oliver Twist* want?
   a) honey still for tea
   b) a new dress
   c) gin toddies, large measures

2. What did Eliza Doolittle want to keep her happy?
   a) hot water bottle
   b) a million pounds
   c) a room somewhere far away from the cold night air with one enormous chair, plenty of chocolates to eat, etc.

3. What are your favourite pleasures? List your top ten. Go on, really think about it. Then you can leave the book open to this page for the right people to see and get the hints.
   1.............. 6 ....
   2.............. 7 ....
   3 .... 8 ....
   4............. 9 ....
   5............. 10 ....

4. How many of them have you enjoyed today?
   a) none
   b) fewer than three
   c) I'm in such a state of constant ecstasy I can't bother with silly quizzes

5. Seriously. How many of your ten top pleasures are in your power to give yourself?
   a) none   b) fewer than half
   c) the majority

6. Then why aren't you?
   a) too shy   b) too busy
   c) I am, not that it's any business of yours

7. How many are free, or cost relatively little?
   a) none   b) fewer than half
   c) the majority

8. How many are really, if you're honest, addictions or cravings that you suspect don't do you any good?
   a) well, only the smoking and the drugs and the gambling
   b) if Hollywood stars can be sex addicts, what's wrong with it?
   c) cross my heart, none. You can't be unhealthily addicted to bubblebaths and Beethoven, can you?

9. Has your idea of pleasure changed with age?
   a) no, I still like the Rolling Stones, but I do buy good seats for their concerts instead of standing
   b) a little; we've traded the tent for a caravan
   c) I'll say, from cold duck to Bollinger, cupcakes to caviar

10. Do you think your pleasures are selfish?
    a) yes   b) not sure
    c) no – just self-indulgent

11. Can some of your pleasures be shared?
    a) No, I want the whole cake to myself
    b) Maybe. I suppose I could worry about his orgasm too.
    c) Of course. Would you like to?

12. How would you describe the feeling you get after partaking of your pleasures?
    a) guilty
    b) bloated and burpy
    c) Ummm . . .

12

Future Perfect?

'I wanna live for ever!'
SONG FROM *Fame*

New Age Expectations

Ageing itself, and our expectations of it, will change tremendously during the first decade of the new millennium. Those who can last thirty years into it, predicts Dr Ronald Klatz of the American Academy of Anti-Ageing Medicine (A4M), will probably last a long time more due to medical advances.

Those involved in the fast growing field of anti-ageing medicine stress that it is not an alternative medicine but, as Dr Klatz puts it, 'at the cutting edge of conventional medicine'.

Already, without medical intervention, people are looking and feeling younger, as we have discussed. This is due in part to improved diet and health awareness, and in part to changed perspective and aspirations. But now we really do seem to have the technology to turn back the clock at least a little, for those who are tempted to risk fate and try it.

We have slightly different perspectives on this – Victoria frightened of the 'hubris' of messing with nature, worried about tempting fate and troubled by images of *The Picture of Dorian Gray*, Dr Faustus, Goldie Hawn and Meryl Streep's characters in the film *Death Becomes Her* and others who have unhappily sought eternal youth; while I am happy to give modern technology a go within reason. Would God have given us cosmetic surgery if we weren't meant to use it? Although I don't think I'd go as far as some and have myself frozen in the hope of future resurrection.

But we are both fascinated by the ageing process and why it affects people so very differently, with some ageing visibly more rapidly than others and some minding desperately and feeling out of synch with their mental age while others don't seem to care and feel in step with the rhythm of time.

Organizations such as the A4M, the US National Institute of Ageing; and Research Into Ageing in Britain are eagerly funding research into the following questions, as outlined by Research Into Ageing:

✧ Why do some individuals age more 'successfully' than others?

✧ What are the processes involved and what are the factors influencing healthy ageing?

✧ What conditions are due to the 'normal' ageing process and what are due to the presence of disease?

✧ How does ageing at the cellular level contribute to age changes at the tissue and organ level and eventually to ageing of the body as a whole?

Research has also only recently begun to investigate whether the rate of ageing slows, as it seems to, very late in life, so that some ninety-year-olds don't look very different from seventy-year-olds.

There is an old saying that 'Growing old is like being increasingly penalized for a crime you haven't committed.' Some Baby Boomers, many of them lawyers, are refusing to take such a 'bum rap' but others argue that they are condemning us all to a more difficult life sentence. The British Centre for Policy on Ageing has made the point that the emphasis is on:

> keeping going as before, not retiring, not falling ill, maintaining a macho sex drive and other cavortings usually attributed to the healthy fledgling. The danger is that society will create another dogma, almost as dangerous as the conventional one that we are so anxious to correct. We risk pressuring older people into an ageless mould, with the consequence that those worn down by life's strictures will feel unhappy because they are no longer able to sustain the lusty energetic activities of their former years.

We hope that will not be the case. We hope we will not feel pressured into competing for 'the most glamorous granny' prize, but will genuinely feel and look better, be more mobile, less retiring and more active than previous generations. We also feel it's fun to speculate (while keeping a sense of humour) about what the future may have in store for us – if we let it.

Our Body Ourselves?

The eminent Cambridge University physicist Stephen Hawking predicts the 'birth of superman' in the new millennium, with the human race likely to 'redesign' itself within 1,000 years. The 1998 science fiction film *Gattaca* shows just that, with bio-engineered 'perfect' people ruling the world and a sub-class of 'normal' human beings by today's standard who are considered only fit to clean up after the master race. (But in it the human spark of individuality triumphs over rigidly conformist perfection.)

Superbrained but feeble-bodied Hawking, confined to his wheelchair due to motor neurone disease and unable to communicate without a computer, told a gathering of scientists at The White House in 1998, discussing what was likely to happen in the new millennium, that 'Genetic engineering on plants and animals will be allowed for economic reasons and someone is bound to try it on humans. Unless we have a totalitarian world order, someone will design improved humans somewhere.'

But there are conflicting views on this. At the Edinburgh Science Festival in 1998, it was predicted that we would be turning into a race of overweight couch potatoes, with only our fingers becoming more dextrous due to the keyboard and keypad skills necessary to operate computers. Another panel suggests that superwomen may come sooner than supermen. A group of scientists writing in the science magazine *Focus* in 1998 noted that women are already outperforming men in most areas and that men 'could soon find yourselves surplus to requirements'.

Not only are girls now outperforming boys at school, they are doing so in endurance sports where their stamina can outstrip men partly because of the additional fat a healthy woman carries compared to a healthy man. And it's female management skills that are wanted, we are told, in the workplaces of the new millennium, so more women are putting off starting families in order to establish their careers. For the first time in decades more women are having babies in their thirties than in their twenties.

Of course, women tend to look after their health better than men do, taking preventative measures rather than waiting for a breakdown. (They also look after their men's health, which is another reason married men are better off than single ones.)

Is the Secret All in our Genes?

Cracking the DNA code was probably the most exciting development of the late twentieth century. In the twenty-first we should be able to reprogramme our body's building blocks, geneticists believe, to weed out disease and many of the disabilities that come with age. Will it be a brave new world or a horror story like the science fiction film *Gattaca* and so many others? Already parents can choose the sex of their children, if they want to, and can have them genetically screened against certain diseases. The next step is to 'design' the blonde-haired, blue-eyed, disease-, dyslexia- and delinquency-free offspring of your dreams, capable of living almost for ever. In the world of *Gattaca* you can hand in a hair of your lover and get a complete health check on your prospective partner. That will not only soon be possible, but companies may start screening and only hiring the fittest. It is both an exciting and terrifying prospect – exciting for its potential and terrifying in what it will mean for humanity which by its nature is *imperfect*.

'It is now within our reach to design ways to grow hair, remove hair, even dye hair, genetically.'

But soon any diseases we might be likely to get could be wiped out in the womb as sophisticated, sensitive and accurate genetic screening becomes possible. In the meantime it is known that what happens to us in there, and immediately after birth, may determine much of our future health. Underweight babies are more likely to get heart disease, diabetes and strokes when they are adult, and overweight babies and children are now thought to be more prone to cancer. Mothers who smoked more than half a pack of cigarettes a day during their pregnancies were recently found to be four times as likely to have sons with behavioural problems.

The probable gene for baldness has just been discovered, with Dr Angela Christiano in New Jersey, suffering from female pattern baldness herself, saying excitedly, 'It is now within our reach to design ways to grow hair, remove hair, even dye hair, genetically.' It is thought that genes hold the answer to 'life, the universe and everything' (Douglas Adams' ultimate question in *The Hitchhikers' Guide to the Galaxy*), and that if we can learn how to turn off the genetically programmed self-destruct mechanisms in our cells we will live for ever. But do we really want to?

We Have the Technology . . .

In science fiction books and films they have been working on this for eons. Remember the robots in *Metropolis* of the '20s and *Forbidden Planet* from the '50s? Already the 'bionic' capabilities exist to largely rebuild human beings, making television's Six Million Dollar Man of the '70s

almost a realistic possibility in the late '90s and certainly likely early in the twenty-first century.

Laboratories are growing new skin that can be used in transplants, titanium limbs can replace those lost to accidents or bone cancer, synthetic bladders have been developed, and even regenerated or replacement livers and pancreases seem in the offing. Artificial knee and hip joints are becoming more efficient and should soon be able to last for fifty years rather than ten or twenty. Now that a mouse has been able to grow a human ear, grafted on to its back in a rather gruesome experiment, restoration and regeneration seem more plausible prospects.

Professor Susan Greenfield, a brain researcher at Oxford University, believes that soon it will be possible to alter the mind with electrical implants. Artificial eye and ear implants that will allow the blind to see and the deaf to hear are predicted. Already there are cochlear implants which do this to some degree. It has just been proven possible to regenerate motor neurons in severed spinal chords in rodents in experiments that hold the first glimmer of promise for paralysed people. Womb transplants are now thought possible, and breasts may be 'regenerated' thanks to experiments in Boston.

Can the Unborn Keep us Young (and Should We Use Them)?

Swish Swiss clinics such as La Prairie have long been using foetal cells from sheep, not humans, as ingredients in 'rejuvenating' treatments. The ageless Eleanor Lambert is one of many devotees of such treatment. As she explained, 'I have diabetes so they take the cells that relate to the pancreas and inject them into me. If you have problems with your liver or with some other part of the body, they'll use those.' The idea is that the foetal cells can stimulate the growth of healthy new tissue – a 'regeneration' effect is not possible in adult cells. Certainly, she said, she always felt better and more energetic after her treatment and could tell when it was time for another, every couple of years, because she felt she was 'slowing down'.

While the idea may revolt some, it is not so far fetched. Placental elements are thought to be healthy and, indeed, many mother animals eat their placentas to compensate for energy lost during the birth process. Obviously the debate over using cells from aborted or miscar-

ried human foetuses is hot and the subject is very controversial. But their potential will continue to be explored despite attempts to control or ban such experiments as many believe that the secret of immortality is carried by the foetal cells which are programmed to differentiate and create different body parts. Cloning is also an ethically fraught area of exploration, but scientists will do it, it is believed, simply because they can once they have the capability. It is only a matter of time. If cloning humans eventually becomes a possibility the theory is that we will all be able to keep a clone in the cupboard, or rather deep freeze, to plunder for spare parts when we need them! NOT a vision that appeals to us, we have to say.

Dr Klatz thinks that in the next two or three years we will see:

✧ foetal cardiac cell transplantation that can grow new revitalized heart tissue.
✧ implantable hormonal pacemaker devices pumping out a custom tailored combination of hormones in a cyclic rhythm to mimic the body's own.
✧ blood tests to screen for biochemical markers of DNA damage and early cancer growth.
✧ technological advances which 'will extend life span to virtual immortality in the coming millennium'.
✧ brain preservation after serious accidents.

Menopause Men

Work going on in a Boston laboratory with rodents could hold the key to ending the menopause for ever, and making Chapter Four irrelevant. Just think, no more menopausal symptoms and moist skin, and a moist vagina, for life. No need to squeeze having children into the most pressured time of your life as you thrust your way up the career ladder. You'll be able to have them at your leisure as a fit forty- (or fifty- or sixty) something. Think of how much pressure that will relieve, not having to have your biological clock ticking ever louder in your ears!

Dr Jonathan Tilly at Harvard Medical School was deluged by telephone calls from desperate women when it was reported that he may have found a way to make menopause a thing of the past. He, like a good research scientist, was appalled, and stressed that his research is still in its early stages and that 'It's a long way from laboratory experi-

ments with mice and test tubes to working with real women in a clinical setting.' But it's hard not to get excited by the possible implications of his work for fertility and longevity.

He has discovered how to stop the death of egg cells in female mice. 'My work shows that the female eggs were actively taking part in their suicide,' he explained. 'So if we could block even one of the three signals that set off this process we could block virtually all the deaths.' His work has shown that cells die from a process called apoptosis. One of the cell death triggers is ceramide, a fat molecule which he has been able to inhibit with another naturally occurring compound in the body – if you must know, it goes by the name of sphingosine-1-phosphate. It should have no unpleasant side effects on healthy women, he says. 'We've flooded mouse eggs with sphingosine-1-phosphate and found that if it is present, ceramide can't activate the death machine.'

Think of how much pressure that will relieve, not having to have your biological clock ticking ever louder in your ears!

His work at the moment is aimed towards trying to preserve fertility in female cancer patients, whose apoptosis is set in train by the powerful anti-tumour drugs used in treating them. But it could also be used eventually to stop or at least postpone menopause in healthy women. He agrees that being able to delay or prevent the menopause, 'not necessarily to provide fertility into great age but to prevent health problems from lack of functioning ovaries' such as bone density loss and a greater tendency towards heart disease, could be a valuable application of his work.

In the meantime, women who want to be fertile in later life must rely on donated eggs from younger women, as it is still at the time of writing impossible to successfully freeze a woman's ova like a man's sperm can be. This may change rapidly. Eventually, however, there should be 'ova banks' as there are sperm banks, where a woman can store her own eggs when she's at her peak of fertility in her twenties until she meets the man, or chooses the sperm, she wants to fertilize it. She needn't even worry about interrupting her career or ruining her figure with pregnancy, as she will surely be able to find a surrogate to carry the baby to term, or perhaps, by then, it will all be done in a laboratory. Then women will no longer, as they do today, have to spend half their reproductive lives trying not to have babies and the other half worrying that they will be too late.

One British hormone and fertility expert has boasted that even at the moment he could 'prep Cleopatra's mummy's womb for childbirth' by giving the fertility hormones which have made it possible for women in their late fifties and, now, even over sixty, like Elizabeth Buttle, to give birth.

The Dream Teams

MAKING ALL CELLS IMMORTAL

In 1998 huge excitement was generated worldwide when it was reported in *Science* magazine that 'Scientists find clue to the secret of eternal life.' Scientists from the anti-ageing research company Geron together with those at the University of Texas Southwestern Medical Centre in Dallas had come up with the theory that the enzyme telomerase could halt the biological ageing of cells.

Telomerase is the substance that seems to allow cells to carry on dividing rather than going into self-destruct mode, transforming a senescent cell into one that is virtually immortal. Dr Woody Wright, one of the leading researchers, had noticed that the telomeres, located at the tips of chromosomes, seemed to act somewhat like the tips on shoelaces, preventing the chromosomes from fraying at the edges. The telomeres would shorten as the cells divided. But the enzyme telomerase appeared to prevent this. They found it was present in 85 per cent of cancerous tumours as well as in the 'immortal' cells that could be cultured in test tubes.

The results of this research have phenomenal implications. It implies that if the telomerase in cancer cells is blocked, it could kill the tumour, and that if telomerase is added to healthy cells, it could stop them from dying off.

But Professor Tom Kirkwood, an expert on the theory of ageing, was only cautiously optimistic about the potential because he believes that cellular senescence is just one part of ageing, and that 'telomeres don't get shorter in brain cells', confirming Tony Buzan's belief that the brain can continue to improve with age if it is used well. Dr David Kipling, an expert on telomerase at the University of Wales College of Medicine, issued the graver warning that 'You might stay younger for longer, but your chances of cancer might shoot through the roof!'

WE DO NOT LIVE BY BREAD ALONE, BUT COULD YEAST CELLS HOLD THE KEY TO IMMORTALITY?

Meanwhile, scientists at the Massachusetts Institute of Technology (MIT), working with yeast cells, believed they, too, had discovered the ageing mechanism. 'It is remarkable that this mechanism of ageing in yeast cells is so simple at the molecular level,' Leonard Guarante and David Sinclair reported in the journal *Cell* in 1998. They found that the yeast cells seemed to become clogged up with broken-off coils of DNA from the chromosomes known as 'extrachromosomal ribosomal DNA circles' or ERCs. They found that the older the cell the more ERCs it would have. The ERCs seemed to gum up the cell works somehow and interfere with the process of cell division so the cell would eventually die. 'Once an ERC is formed or inherited, the period of time until a lethal number of ERCs has accumulated may be the clock that determines the lifespan of the cell,' was their conclusion. ERCs seem to form when the DNA is damaged as it can be in humans from disease or environmental elements. The yeast cells studied are said to be similar to the 'stem' cells of humans which are in our bone marrow and blood.

Working along similar lines Dr Seth Schor and PhD student Jackie Banyard completed a project for Research into Ageing that demonstrated that a specific 'control module' influences cell migration to the site of a wound, improving healing. Since repair of tissues following injury is impaired in older people, often leading to pressure sores and ulcers, this could be a major breakthrough in slowing age-related changes in 'fibroblast' migration in wound healing.

RING OUT THE OLD; BRING IN THE NEW

Dr Judith Campisi and her team of the University of California's Berkeley National Laboratory have just developed a test that can distinguish between youthful and old cells in our bodies. This has caused so much excitement because it should greatly enhance our understanding of the mechanisms of ageing and of cancer, which in a curious way seem to be linked, since cancer cells, which don't die when they're supposed to, make many people die long before they're supposed to.

It is believed that being able to identify the old, senescent, cells that have stopped dividing will make it possible to get rid of them before they drag the rest of the system down with them, so to speak. Already a cream is in preparation to try to block the effects of ageing on the

skin through this method, since Dr Campisi said she had used the test to show that senescent cells accumulate in our skins and other tissues as we get older. 'The long-term goal should be to try to kill these senescent cells rather than block the many molecules they expel,' she said. She believes they could eventually be targeted in much the same way cancer cells can be because of their particularly fast dividing properties. Yet her goal isn't to extend lifespan, just 'healthspan', she has said.

A GENETIC CURE FOR CANCER?

Professor Ronald Wolf, who heads the Imperial Cancer Research Fund's laboratory at Ninewells Medical School in Scotland, and his team of scientists supported by those from the Cancer Research Campaign's Beatson Laboratories, believed, in April 1998, that they may have identified a single gene that protects against cancer 'triggers' like carcinogenic chemicals. It is the gene that seems to determine whether a smoker will get lung cancer or not, and could pave the way for producing a genetic 'antidote' to protect us against the second biggest killer in the developed world. Whereas studies have concentrated on mechanisms that make cancer cells multiply out of control, Professor Wolf's team decided instead to look at how cells interact with their environment.

Thanks to what they discovered, he told the National Academy of Sciences, 'I would hope we could have a serious programme, at least in trial form, of cancer chemoprevention by manipulating these types of genes specifically in the next ten years. I guess you might take it like you take a vitamin pill.' Although that pill is a long way from being available at our health food shops or even on an expensive prescription, the research led Professor Wolf to say that he will continue to look at ways to produce the protective enzymes that some cells genetically contain and others don't. Its implications for healthy ageing are huge.

'LOOK, MA, NO MORE CAVITIES!'

Boomers may remember that line from a toothpaste commercial in their youth as we seem to. But a new vaccine developed after twenty-five years' work by a team at Guy's Hospital Dental School could mean an end to tooth decay once and for all. Professor Tom Lehner, head of immunology at the hospital, says it could become widely available to

both children and adults within the first two years of the new millennium, initially only administered by dentists but eventually possibly for use in the home in the form of toothpaste or mouthwash.

Once teeth have been rigorously cleaned and disinfected with strong mouthwashes the vaccine, which comes in the form of a clear solution with no unpleasant taste, would be applied to dry on the teeth. Teeth would need to be covered with the vaccine solution twice a week for three weeks for complete protection from bacteria and decay for around half a year. The vaccine contains an antibody to the streptococcus mutans bacteria which triggers tooth decay when it comes into contact with food, particularly sugary food. Curiously it has been produced from genetically modified tobacco plants so this might mollify the tobacco industry, panicking in case cigarette smoking is ever banned. It could also mean an end to being 'long in the tooth' (see Chapter Three), false teeth and a diet of mushy food in old age, not to mention all that drilling and filling!

CHILLING OUT

One of the most frightening faces of anti-ageing medicine has always been cryogenics. Celebrated or, most likely, cautioned against, in science fiction films and in the recent Mel Gibson tearjerker *Forever Young*, 'freezing' people into a state of suspended animation seems somehow scary and barbaric. Yet experiments with dogs and baboons have shown that it is possible to resuscitate a brain (and body) that has been chilled to a low enough temperature to put it into a state of stasis. While the technique has not yet progressed far enough to allow reanimation of the dead, experiments are now underway using what has been learned to protect victims of accidents and traumas. This has been made possible by the development of new blood substitutes which can function at temperatures far below those at which blood is viable, research that has come from the growing organ transplant field, where hearts and lungs and livers and kidneys need to be 'nourished' by these blood substitutes when they are having an out-of-body experience.

Dr Ronald Klatz of the A4M and his team at Life Resuscitation Technologies in the States are developing what he calls a Brain Resuscitation Device (BRD) which would allow the brain of an accident victim to be quickly cooled to give surgeons a chance to repair other damage without risk of the brain dying due to lack of blood.

Similar principles are being tested in Britain during heroic surgery at one major hospital.

The idea is to cool and nourish the brain with the blood substitute solution so that dramatic blood loss or even a stopped heart doesn't destroy it. A heart can be restarted or transplanted but once the brain has died from as little as four minutes without oxygen there is no hope. The American military are very keen on the idea, and Dr Klatz believes that it should prevent many deaths not only on the battlefield but from car accidents, surgery carrying a high risk of blood loss and other traumas. He says the technology could soon be easily carried on ambulances in a form no bigger than a briefcase. It could have huge repercussions. But Dr Klatz points out, 'We're not talking about freezing, we're talking about chilling. While we have the technology to freeze a human being, defrosting one would still be sort of like trying to defrost a lettuce, which will come out all soggy and not in the state in which it was frozen.' A chilling thought.

Redefining Our Allotted Span?

'Threescore years and ten' was considered a generous allotted lifespan for centuries. Now ageing experts are talking about one hundred and forty as a fairer slice of life's cake. 'The genetic potential for longevity in human beings is 120 to 140 years but only a few cultures reach this,' says Nobel Prize for Medicine nominee Dr Joel Wallach. He cites a Dr Li on the Tibetan border with China who was supposedly born in 1677 and died 256 years later, being written up as a phenomenon in both the *New York Times* and the *London Times* in the thirties when he died. He was, according to Wallach, partly the inspiration for James Hilton to write *Lost Horizon*, made into a film in 1937 and remade in colour in the 1970s. In it the lady from Shangri-La lived an enchanted, ageless, existence in her isolated cocoon, but when love made her try to leave she turned agonizingly and horrifyingly into a desiccated mummy.

In his lectures Dr Wallach talks admiringly of the Titicaca Indians of South America, the Hunzas in Pakistan and the Georgians in Russia, apparently once used in a Danon yoghurt advertisement to imply longevity from eating yoghurt, who are also known for living to between 120 and 140. In Nigeria a 126-year-old chieftain was eulogized by one of his wives for still having all his own teeth and, it seemed, all his other faculties as well! A Syrian man died at 133 who had married again at the age of eighty and then fathered nine children, some after the age of 100; and a *National Geographic* article on centenarians a few years back featured a 136-year-old woman with a large cigar and glass of vodka. 'These were people who enjoyed life – they weren't sitting in an old folks' home waiting for someone to take their money,' said Dr Wallach.

Dr Wallach has a simple prescription for reaching great age: 'If you want to live to 120 to 140, remember to avoid the pitfalls – not step on the landmines, play Russian roulette, smoke or drink excessively or wear a black sweatsuit and run down the highway at three o'clock in the morning,' he advises. 'And avoid going to doctors.' He points out that 'Ralph Nader's [consumer] group in January 1993 put out a news release on the causes of death in US hospitals. The bottom line says "300,000 Americans are killed each year in hospitals alone as a result of medical negligence." In Vietnam we lost only 56,000 in ten years on a field of battle!'

He maintains that everyone who dies ultimately does so because of a nutritional deficiency and that the way to keep out of doctors' clutches and out of the graveyard is to make sure we are well protected by supplements. 'Margaret Skeet of Radford, Virginia, died at 115 from the complications of a fall which were due to osteoporosis which was due to a nutritional deficiency,' he notes. But with cell death mechanisms being discovered, this might not necessarily be the case. Perhaps we are pre-programmed at birth for an allotted span and nothing we do will change that? In that case we might as well 'eat, drink and be merry'. Geneticists are still pondering that question.

The problem is, we can't be sure, and the benefit of good nutrition, exercise and the other anti-ageing strategies we've talked about in this book is that they make you feel better now and improve your quality of life even if no one can guarantee they will improve your quantity.

Pioneers Exploring the Final Frontier

The couples who came out of the biosphere in Arizona who were supposed to eat the perfect food, drink pure water and have no pollution, were examined by medical gerontologists from UCLA after they emerged from their sealed pod. Apparently the medical computers

projected that they could live 165 years if they continued to do what they were doing. But obviously they didn't want to and were happy to rejoin the human race.

Astronaut-turned-senator-turned-astronaut-again John Glenn, despite knowing that going into space accelerates ageing, not least because the lack of gravity weakens the bones and can lead to early osteoporosis, went back up there in his seventies to help scientists study the ageing effects of space travel, and suspected he would be no worse affected than younger astronauts. We await the long-term results of this experiment with great interest but, as Dr Merry said (see Chapter Nine), every human being is an experiment.

Dr Ronald Klatz and his colleagues in the A4M, which in 1998 managed to get anti-ageing medicine classified as a specialist medical subject in the States, are also pioneers in this field. They practise what they preach and pop the pills and inject in some cases the hormones that they prescribe to those who consult them.

If you were at one of the conferences held by the A4M, you'd find everyone carries their little zip-lock plastic bags of pills and powders with them for every meal. Dr Klatz himself takes something like sixty pills a day, he says, adding hastily, 'But I'm not a health nut.' He swears by deprenyl, selenium (although he found it was making his thyroid sluggish), antioxidant vitamins and amino acids such as arginine and lysine, but most of all by HGH, the subject of his book *Grow Young with HGH*.

HGH – the Elixir of Youth?

Everything seems to point to Human Growth Hormone (HGH) as being the elixir of youth if there is such a thing. Dr Klatz says that the right levels will help you lose fat and wrinkles, gain muscle, enhance your sex life and prevent disease. Once it had to be extracted from cadavers and was only used to help children who were not growing. Now it is expensively synthesized to feed the growing anti-ageing industry.

You need to have your production of HGH stimulated if you are in poor health, depressed, lacking in energy or experiencing 'a reduced sense of wellbeing and a lessened capacity for work,' says Dr Klatz. One of the reasons that sex is supposed to be so good for the health

is possibly because orgasms stimulate the release of HGH, but so does exercise of any kind. While it is difficult to ignore the growing mass of evidence about the benefits of HGH (Professor Purdie of the British Menopause Society even points out that 'oestrogen doesn't work in rats without growth hormone in the pituitary') we believe it is probably only prudent to stimulate its production by means such as exercise, sex and sleep.

We are convinced that it is enough for most people, except the truly age obsessive quite late in life, to exercise and eat healthily, laugh a lot and enjoy an active sensual life, for these habits will encourage the production of more growth hormone. Or, going one step further, to take some of the essential amino acids and 'nutrient precursors' that encourage our own bodies to produce more HGH. Getting a good night's sleep and exercising sometimes first thing in the morning on an empty stomach can also stimulate HGH production naturally.

We are still wary of taking injections of hormones which, if the right balance is not obtained, can lead to liver and other damage. The National Institute on Aging at the US National Institutes of Health issued a report on hormone therapy in 1997 which stated that 'Side effects of HGH treatment can include diabetes and pooling of fluid in the skin and other tissues, which may lead to high blood pressure and heart failure. Joint pain and carpal tunnel syndrome may also occur.' As growth hormone, naturally, causes things to grow, there are concerns about its effect on cancers, as well as its ability to enlarge organs in a potentially hazardous way. This doesn't deter its enthusiasts, any more than fears about steroids have stopped athletes determined to maximize their physical potential from taking them. But Dr Giampapa says, 'What's very exciting is that within the next few years out-patients will not need to be giving themselves growth hormone injections. We're on the verge of having growth hormone secretagogues in capsule form that will stimulate the pituitary to produce more growth hormone.'

We've also noticed that many of the people on these hormones, which are also beloved of the body-building industry, have bulked out with muscle in a way that we would not want to. We feel it is better to encourage the body to produce its own hormones, and Dr Giampapa and the other anti-ageing experts agree that this is the most desirable state of affairs. But sometimes it may need a little outside assistance.

So I have already started taking some of the amino acid precursors of HGH which Dr Klatz recommends, arginine, ornithine, lysine and melatonin, which isn't available in the United Kingdom. The list of amino acids is readily available from health food stores but should only be taken in consultation with a doctor, as they require careful balancing and only work well when 'stacked' intelligently together.

The Star Amino Acids

Arginine, an essential amino acid that stimulates the secretion of HGH from the pituitary gland and is also said to speed up healing and enhance exercise performance. Although test subjects in their seventies had lower responses than younger people, arginine was still shown to be able to boost their levels of growth hormone to triple the average for their age group, says Dr Klatz. His recommended dosage? Two to five grams on an empty stomach one hour before exercise and before sleeping. It can cause nausea.

Ornithine, a non-essential amino acid similar in structure to arginine, which some argue is even more effective in stimulating HGH. Dr Klatz says it is 'best used as a stack with other amino acids like arginine, lysine or glutamine'. His recommended dosage? Two to three grams at bedtime. It can cause diarrhoea in high doses.

Lysine, another essential amino acid that has been shown to boost arginine and, together with it, partially reduce the immunodeficiency that comes with ageing. It is said to help bone formation and genital function. Dr Klatz's recommended dosage? One gram on an empty stomach, one hour before exercise and before sleeping. It is well tolerated.

Glutamine, one of the immune system's major fuels, and high levels of it in the blood have been linked with having fewer illnesses, lower cholesterol and lower blood pressure. Dr Klatz's suggested dosage? Two grams at bedtime. It is well tolerated.

Tryptophan is an essential amino acid that increases a sense of well-being by increasing serotonin production and encourages restful sleep which helps to stimulate the production of HGH. This mind–body regulator is best used at night and never before driving. Dr Klatz's suggested dosage? 500 milligrams to two grams at bedtime. It can cause drowsiness, headaches, sinus congestion and constipation.

Dr Giampapa recommends starting with two grams of arginine, two grams of ornithine, one gram of lysine and one gram of glutamine, and then gradually working up to two grams each. 'We don't start

people on growth hormone,' he says. 'We use these releasing agonists which only cost about $15 a month whereas growth hormone is extremely expensive.' It can cost up to $18,000 a year in America or around £8,000 in Britain. Only as a last resort will he start HGH injections, and then only about three times a week rather than every day, with two weeks off after the first month of treatment. Dr Giampapa is the first to tell his patients that simply relaxing and listening to one of the soothing audio tapes he has available can increase their production of HGH, and that sometimes this, combined with exercise and proper nutrition is all they need.

Other substances you might be offered at an anti-ageing clinic

HGH, hailed as the 'miracle' anti-ageing hormone. It does almost everything theoretically that you could dream of. It is supposed to increase bone density, maintain mental alertness, and favour muscle development over fat. That it is said to have a positive effect on hair growth could be why so few male delegates at the A4M conferences are bald despite their high supplemented testosterone levels. It is

It does almost everything theoretically that you could dream of.

taken by injection, usually twice a day in a dose of 0.5 international units, says Dr Perring. 'But we're still unsure how to set the levels. Do we want to give a sixty-year-old the physiological levels of a forty-year-old? It is controversial!' He prescribes it, tentatively, to older patients only if they have an IGF-1 (see below) factor of less than 350 units per litre.

Dangers? There are many, and a very vocal lobby of distinguished doctors has been speaking out against its use for any but children with growth problems. It can cause diabetes and increase the risk of heart disease and various types of cancer. It can also cause a thickening of the skin which some welcome as thick skin is supposed to be a sign of youth, but others find worrying. And a report in the *British Medical Journal* (April 1998) of a French study found that high levels of growth hormone could lead to enlarged organs and was associated with premature death. Personally, at the time of writing, we wouldn't touch it with a bargepole despite the promise of renewed vigour, fewer wrinkles and a lively libido! But we are happy to find ways to stimulate our natural production of this essential hormone, through healthy patterns of exercise and sleep, or even (in my case) through taking some of the essential amino acids which seem to do this.

According to Professor John Wass, an endocrinologist at the Radcliffe Infirmary in Oxford and spokesman for the Royal College of Physicians, 'To give too much HGH can increase the body's resistance to insulin and increase the risk of mortality from cardiovascular disease and colon cancer. That's why it's only licensed for patients with growth hormone deficiency.' The cost can be offputting too.

IGF-1 is almost as potent as HGH and, like it, needs to be injected. It stands for insulinlike growth factor-1 and is said to increase lean body mass, reduce fat and build bone, muscle and nerves while bypassing the pituitary gland which produces HGH and may be burnt out with ageing. Like HGH and many of the other hormones in the anti-ageing arsenal it is favoured by body-builders who want to build muscle. It may be better for diabetic patients than HGH, high doses of which can increase insulin resistance. It has had some exciting effects on regenerating nerves after accidents. If it can regenerate spinal cord motor neurons in lab animals, its potential for human beings like ex-Superman Christopher Reeve, paralysed from the neck down after a riding accident, is tremendous.

Testosterone is needed by women as well as men and is the main basis of libido in both sexes, as well as maintaining muscle mass in both men and women. It can cause liver damage in high doses.

Dehydroepiandrosterone (DHEA): a testosterone precursor, formed from cholesterol and now available in health food shops. 'I gave myself DHEA for about eighteen months and had no doubt that it helps you to cope with more stress than usual,' says Dr Perring. 'I went off it because it is contraindicated for prostate problems, which I have had, but decided on the weight of the evidence for and against it to go back on. In women it appears to increase testosterone production, which they need for strong bones and libido.' On the down side, it could cause facial hair in women.

Pregnenolone is another of the steroid chain, with benefits in mental functioning, memory and attention span.

Melatonin, readily available in the States but not in Britain, is a hormone produced by the pineal gland in the brain which controls long-term sleep/wake cycles. It is a powerful antioxidant and protects against stress. Doses can range from 0.5 to 1 mg, and should be taken two hours to half an hour before bedtime. If patients feel groggy in the morning, they are told to reduce the dose by 0.5 mg; if they have trouble sleeping,

raise it by 0.5 mg. Melatonin should never be used by pregnant or nursing mothers, Dr Klatz warns, or by women trying to conceive, who are on prescription steroids or who have allergies, depression, autoimmune diseases or immune system cancers.

Thyroid hormone controls the metabolism, and a lack of it seems to be linked with a lack of growth hormone. Symptoms of hypothyroidism are a lot like the worst symptoms of ageing, including lack of energy, weakness, and moving slowly.

Seligiline Hydrochloride: a nootropic usually used in the treatment of Parkinson's disease but which can increase concentration and memory.

Deprenyl is another anti-Parkinson's disease drug that has been shown to extend the lifespan of rodents and slows down the loss of the brain chemical dopamine whose loss may slow down the production of HGH.

Centrophenoxine, another nootropic, commonly prescribed in France, which increases cerebral circulation and improves protein synthesis in the brain.

To give you an example of the daily 'diet' of an anti-ageing expert, Michael Perring takes 50 mg daily of DHEA which he says gives him 'energy and the ability to cope with stress, and some conversion into testosterone'; two tablets daily of ginkgo biloba 24 per cent, a standardized extract from Solgar, 'for alertness and mental function. Forgetting names was concerning me'; nine tablets daily ('they recommend fourteen a day, so I'm slightly underdosing!') of 'Life Extension' vitamins, a mix by Prolongevity, with a broad range of contents including a vegetable complex, lycopines, genestin and various other 'anti-cancer' agents plus standard antioxidants and minerals and vitamins including 3,000 mg (3 g) of Vitamin C a day; and an ascorbate citrus antioxidant complex before meals. And that's modest compared to what some of the American anti-ageing enthusiasts, the actor Nick Nolte among them, were wolfing down before each meal at the A4M's big conference in Las Vegas.

At anti-ageing clinics you will also get advice about diet, some of it conflicting.

Whereas Dr Klatz recommends a 'high protein, low fat, moderate carbohydrate menu for optimal body contour', Dr Giampapa recommends more of a vegetarian regime with 40 per cent protein, 40 per

cent carbohydrate and 20 per cent fat. 'We don't recommend avoiding fish or dairy products, just limiting them. North Atlantic salmon and halibut and trout are excellent. So is chicken organically raised, in moderation,' he says.

Both agree, however, with the general consensus that fried foods, carbonated drinks, sugar, chemicals and processed flours seem to accelerate the ageing process and raise the insulin and cortisol levels which in turn seem to increase ageing.

Mood Foods, the Foods of the Future?

So-called functional foods, also known as nutriceuticals or foodaceuticals, are becoming more and more prevalent in health food shops and supermarkets. A functional food can be anything from a chewing gum that promises to clean your teeth or give you a buzz to a mood-altering drink made of guarana, a tropical herb. The loaf of bread designed for menopausal women (see Chapter Four) is a prime example. Such custom-tailored foods for specific purposes will increasingly be on our supermarket shelves and in our corner shops. Many have been there for years, although not all their boasts are to be believed. The humble Mars Bar that promises to help you 'work, rest and play', the cereal that says it will keep you regular, the glucose drinks implying improved sports performance – all are, theoretically at least, functional foods.

Smart foods and psychoactive drinks go a step beyond this because they fall into a category somewhere between food, dietary supplements and drugs. Whereas in the '80s the big thing was taking something away from foods, giving us a huge array of reduced-fat crisps, sausages and spreads, decaffeinated coffee and low-calorie drinks, in the '90s, and the millennium, the trend has been and will be to put something extra into foods so that they can be said to increase cognitive abilities, boost sporting or sexual performance or improve the immune system. This has become one of the fastest-growing sectors of the food market, worth $7.5 billion in America in 1991 according to a survey of American food consultants, and no doubt worth hugely more now.

One major management consultancy, PA, with food industry clients, set out to discover, in the early '90s, what European manufacturers could learn from the functional food phenomenon in Japan, where it

originated. Products on the market there included calcium-enriched chewing gum with cinnamon to aid digestion, sports drinks with 'electrolytes, iron and vitamins', salad dressings containing Omega 3 fatty acids believed to lower cholesterol, and drinks and biscuits containing oligosaccharides to stimulate the growth of healthy bacteria in the digestive tract and possibly prevent cancer.

'Functional food is a marketing term rather than a technical one,' an industry spokesman explains. Ginseng and guarana are frequently used ingredients in so-called elixirs and tonics. One, called Gusto, contained two types of ginseng and was marketed as something that could 'strengthen the body's ability to resist illness, degeneration and fatigue' and another called Mind Peak became a favourite with brokers and traders in the financial markets for its ability to keep them awake.

Drinks with names such as Choline Cooler and Fast Blast have become commonplace, available from special super-market coolers as well as from certain night clubs. London's Brain Club was one of the first to specialize in these in the late eighties. Choline Cooler was said to be a memory improver; Fast Blast to provide a quick dose of noradrenaline, the body's natural stimulant.

Everyone is calmer after a meal, but a meal high in complex carbohydrates seems to have the best effect.

Which? magazine in Britain, which published a report, at the dawn of the '90s, on 'Foods of the Future', explained that the development of some of these foods grew out of research into Alzheimer's disease, and the balance in the brain between acetyl choline and dopamine. Alzheimer's victims have too little of the former and too much, it seems, of the latter.

Many foods are natural mood foods such as chocolate, whose ingredients include theobromine to stimulate the nervous system and phenylethylamine which seems to improve the mood. But unpleasant mood changes can be brought about by cravings or vice versa, it seems.

Everyone is calmer after a meal, but a meal high in complex carbohydrates seems to have the best effect. But if a meal is too calming, too full of refined carbohydrates and sugars, it can be soporofic, leading to reduced performance at work in the afternoons, and falling asleep in front of the television at eight o'clock in the evening at home, with a feeling of lethargy. Learn, by trial and error, which foods are the right mood foods for you and listen to what your body tells you by the way it reacts.

Keep a chart if you're unsure, writing down everything you've eaten and how you feel afterwards. That way you should be able to start isolating the baddies in your diet, which might not be the same as those in anyone else's. This is different from having a serious food allergy, for which you might consult a specialist. It may just be that eating bread makes you feel tired and sluggish, or that certain foods make you unable to perform at your peak. If you stick to the foods that make you feel good and energetic, you will have created your own positive mood food menu.

Anti-ageing Cosmetics

New skincreams and lotions coming on to the market use a combination of retinoic acids such as Retin-A with growth factors. Biosyn, in the States, claim their product Agera can improve the effects of sun exposure and ageing. Dr Giampapa is looking into the matter at the National Skin Institute near his headquarters in New Jersey. Ingredients he is working with include RNA for skin springiness; hyaluronic acid for moisture and collagen regeneration and retinyl palmitate which promotes faster cell division. Growth hormone (see below) can plump out the skin, improve its colour and increase the circulation so that the 'ageing clock of the skin' is reset to run at a slower speed. Some skin creams already contain foetal cells and other 'futuristic' ingredients.

Biomarker Feedback

You may have heard of biofeedback, a trendy term of the eighties, but have you heard of biomarkers? These are the markers that can tell you your body's biological age which can be very different from its chronological one. Biomarkers, a word tossed around by anti-ageing specialists, can be enzymes, skin cells and biochemicals produced by the body which indicate when the body is approaching 'a critical change of function' as Dr Giampapa describes it, and for predicting the risk of developing certain age-related ailments.

At Dr Giampapa's Longevity Institutes, 144 separate tests are done to establish a patient's biological age.

✧ Level 1 Physiological tests to ascertain 'surface indicators' of ageing include:
    muscle mass/body fat ratio; flexibility; aerobic capacity; tactile response time; forced expiratory volume; visual and auditory tests.

✧ Level 2 Cellular level tests on the skin include:
    basement membrane changes
    collagen ratios
    sebaceous gland architecture
    microvascular changes
    elastic fibre content

✧ Level 3 Molecular level tests include:
    levels of key biomarker hormones such as DHEA, HGH, thyroid hormone, testosterone, oestrogen, progesterone, cortisol
    melatonin
    cellular co-enzyme Q10
    other phytochemical compounds

✧ Level 4 Chromosomal level tests include:
    DNA damage assessment

He often does tests on the saliva that patients post him from all over the world! These sophisticated tests will show the levels not only of hormones but of trace minerals such as copper and iron in your body.

At the Cenegenics anti-ageing centres run by Dr Alan Mintz, headquartered in Las Vegas, the tests are performed in highly luxurious surroundings with marble halls and Romanesque pillars. There is an entire room dedicated to gauging reaction times, the room itself a giant computer that tells you where to place your feet and your hands. There are sophisticated and expensive pieces of scanning equipment for bone density and other tests.

Going through these programmes and following the recommendations for supplements and 'nutrient precursors' of hormones can set you back up to $8,000 a year in the States and each company usually has its own proprietary products. For Longevity Institutes International these products include ProHGH (an HGH and IGF-1 secretagogue that makes the body step up its own production of these anti-ageing hormones) and SynchroPower, said to be a 'body composition and anti-ageing hormone regulator'.

A DIY Diagnosis

A few simple home tests can tell you how you are ageing. Dr Klatz suggests the following, originally devised by Dr Roy Walford:

The Skin Elasticity Test Pinch the skin on the back of your hand between thumb and forefinger for five seconds. Time how long it takes to flatten out completely. The average rates are 0–1 second for those aged between 20–30; 1–2 seconds for the 30–40 age group; 2–5 seconds for those between 40 and 50; 10–15 for those aged 60; and between 35 and, yes, 55 seconds for those aged seventy. Less than these figures and you're doing well for your age; over your age range and your skin is ageing faster than it should.

Reaction Time Test Have someone hold an 18-inch wooden ruler at the top (larger numbers down) between your fingers. The thumb and middle finger of your right hand, or your left if you're left-handed, should be three and a half inches apart and equidistant from the 18-inch mark on the ruler. Tell the other person to let the ruler go without warning. You catch it between your fingers as quickly as you can. Try three times and average your score, scoring by the numbers at which you catch it. The average score at age 20 is the 11-inch mark; for 40–50-year-olds the 8-inch mark; for sixty-year-olds the 6-inch mark.

Balance Test Stand on a hard surface with both feet together, barefoot or wearing a flat shoe. Have someone standing by to catch you if you fall. Close your eyes and lift your left foot if you are right handed, otherwise the right, about six inches, bending your knee. Stand on the other foot without juddering for as long as you can. Try it three times and average your performances. Someone of 20 should be able to hold this pose for over 30 seconds; someone of 40–50 for 12 and someone of 60 for only about 3 or 4 seconds.

Visual Accommodation Test Slowly bring a newspaper to your eyes until the print begins to blur. Have someone measure the distance between your eyes and the paper with a ruler. At 21 the distance should be within 4 inches; at 30 within 5½; at 40, 9 inches; at 50, 15 inches; and at 60, 39 inches, longer than your arms. Do this without reading glasses, of course.'

In England, without the high-tech centres of his American counterparts, Dr Michael Perring performs similar tests on his patients. He measures lung capacity (can you blow out all the candles on your birthday cake?), blood pressure, grip strength and manual dexterity. These tests clearly demonstrate that different body systems age at different rates. Dr Perring, sixty, found he had the blood pressure of a fifty-year-old, the manual dexterity of a thirty-five-year-old but the hand-grip of a seventy-year-old.

One of his patients, a fit and attractive sixty-six-year-old who takes regular exercise and still works full time, was surprised that these tests showed her to be no younger than her chronological age, although she looked it. Yet her husband, who looked every one of his seventy-six years, came out at sixty-nine on the tests. She believed her arthritis held her back.

Another forty-five-year-old woman came out as forty-six on the tests while her husband, forty-eight, came out at forty-three, making him intolerable to live with for a short time. 'I found out I had a toyboy,' she joked, but was clearly hurt that despite the blood pressure of a twenty-eight-year-old and the dexterity of a forty-year-old her lung capacity and grip, that of a fifty-six- and fifty-eight-year-old respectively, let her down. And she trains regularly at a gym! These tests clearly show how different systems age separately and not always compatibly.

Is Ageing a 'Treatable Condition' or an Inevitable One?

Is ageing a natural process or a disease? That question is still being argued among the anti-ageing community. A4M members consider ageing 'a treatable condition' like other minor illnesses and, like them, an irritation to be ended as quickly as possible. Whether we were meant to become more infirm with age or whether it's the way we age that leads to the infirmities we experience is a question that is as keenly being debated today as 'how many angels fit on the head of a pin' was centuries ago. Certainly it is true that rodents who lived on restricted diets were fairly free of diabetes, cancer, heart disease and other ailments associated with ageing, as well as living long lives. Jeanne Calment, Dr Klatz points out, 'rode a bicycle until age hundred and smoked until age 118', and yet was remarkably free of illness until her death.

In support of those who argue that the down side of ageing is 'treatable' is the evidence that substances such as HGH that seem to retard ageing also have a positive effect on the so-called diseases of age. It has been shown to improve the ability of the heart to pump out blood, and to prevent cell damage after heart attacks and strokes. It seems to stop shrinking with age, and to prevent osteoporosis. That makes us conclude, as the anti-ageing specialists have, that many of the problems associated with age are actually due to dysfunction rather than normal ageing.

Defining, or rather redefining, 'normal ageing' will be one of the tasks of the UltraAgers in the new millennium.

Defining, or rather redefining, 'normal ageing' will be one of the tasks of the UltraAgers in the new millennium. And it will be fascinating to see if our children and grandchildren, born into a world that understands so much more about preventing the ravages of time than it did when we were born, will age very differently from us. (Yet with smoking on the rise among young women even as older women give up, and with drug abuse, junk food and other threats to the positive ageing of young people today, it seems they won't always learn from our mistakes.) In the meantime, we can at least enjoy 'virtual' immortality right now (see below)!

Virtual Youth

It is just one small step for man, but possibly a large one for mankind, to make use of new technologies such as virtual reality to give us at least the sensation of youth. Armchair adventures of all kinds are now possible, so that we can stroll down the streets of ancient Pompeii, visit the world's great museums and have all kinds of 'virtual' experiences without moving. Brain researcher Professor Susan Greenfield of Oxford University has said that we might soon be able to 'buy a basic experience for the day' on Virtual Reality.

We can even, it seems, be made to look virtually young. Computer generated images of Hollywood stars can now be used to allow old Clint Eastwood and Sean Connery to make films featuring their younger selves, a wonderful way for film stars always at the forefront of anti-ageing techniques to stay for ever young. Marlon Brando even appar-

ently had his image fed through, notably slimmed down, by a computer for a 'life' appearance on the *Tonight Show*, and hotelier Leona Helmsley famously 'younged up' her pictures in advertisements for Helmsley hotels, so much so that it was quite a shock to see her real appearance at her trial for tax evasion.

Virtual reality may shortly also be able to restore lost libido in older people (although with the potential of virtual libido, do we need to maintain actual libido?) by sending them on a 'virtual journey' back to their lost youth. An Italian team is claiming impotence can be cured by this method, which has been trialled on fifty men, some as old as seventy-five, with a success rate of 84 per cent. The patient is apparently taken on a virtual trip back to his youth, to when he first began to get interested in sex. But nobody seems interested in testing this technique on older women, for whom a lack of libido is generally considered a bonus by society, since older women who are sexual creatures can be very disconcerting – until society changes its views on that, as UltraAgers will make it do!

Where Do We Go From Here?

To immortality, Dr Klatz and the A4M would say. To a healthy and contented old age, we would say. Neither of us has any desire to be immortal. But we would like to lead long, fit and fulfilling lives. We're not anti-ageing and, in fact, approve of the British Advertising Standards Authority's suggestion that anti-ageing remedies and clinics should not be advertised as such, but use the term 'healthy ageing' instead. That sounds better to us too.

We hope that you will live as long as you want to, and be healthy and happy while you do. We know that time is precious, so we thank you for spending so much of yours sharing what has been a journey of exploration and learning for us, and will continue, we hope, to be an exciting voyage of discovery for our generation in the new millennium.

Now, Over to You

If you have stayed with us this far, or just dipped in and out of the book from time to time, we thank you. We hope it has been a journey of discovery for you as it has been for us. We have undergone some changes along the way. I started out very gung-ho about HRT and ended feeling I'd rather get along on natural progesterone cream. Victoria began the book convinced that she would never entertain HRT and now suspects she would be tempted by some of the latest 'natural' combinations – should she feel the need, of course. She also said she'd rather die than try cosmetic surgery. Now she's less sure about that!

We hope it has been a journey of discovery for you as it has been for us.

Should you meet us please don't discount our advice if you think we look our age or older. As we hope we've explained, we haven't got things right in the past and have been bumbling along like most people, hoping for the best. We trust, however, that if you meet us some time in the future, we'll have taken more of our own suggestions on board and be even healthier (and more youthful in many ways) than we are today. We are thrilled to learn that we can better ourselves and improve our fitness at any age.

From the bubbling melting pot of information, filling so quickly it seems about to overflow, we have distilled our own recipe for healthy ageing. We have served it up to you, in different courses, during the course of the book and hope you have digested at least some of it and found the messages palatable.

While there are many contradictions and exceptions, and people who because of their own peculiar mix of ingredients react differently from the majority, our basic recipe is made up of the elements you see in our UltraAge acronym opposite:

Fuel – the right mix to keep your body functioning on all cylinders, and to replace any deficiencies we acquire when we've been running for a while untended;

Exercise – the right kind to keep our hearts, lungs, muscles, and joints in shape and able to continue to serve us for a long time to come;

```
            L
            a
            u
      V     g
      o     h
      c     t
F     a     e
U  L  t  r  A  t  t  i  t  u  d  e
e  o  i     G  o  a  l  s
l  v  o     E  n  e  r  g  y
   e  n
```

Vocation – a sense of commitment to our job or to an interest we enjoy, not working for the pay packet alone but getting fulfilment from what we do;

Love – a vital part of the recipe, although it doesn't have to be conventional love. Love for your neighbours, your friends, your pets, the environment, your work and your children and grandchildren are just as important as love for a partner. But love of yourself is paramount, because if you don't love yourself you won't be kind to yourself and will weaken your immune system.

Relationships – links to love but means staying connected with other people and involved with life and commitments, therefore having a stake in the future. Those who have nurtured relationships have been shown to be far healthier in later years than those who shut themselves off. But the ability to cast off 'dead' relationships is equally important.

Laughter – just smiling can immeasurably boost your immune system; laughing regularly is one of the best medicines and should help to render other medicines unnecessary. Be able to laugh at yourself and at what life throws at you!

Attitude – encapsulates the others to a large degree, because a positive mental attitude will want to make you eat healthily and exercise as well as ensuring that you stay interested in what you're doing and the world

around you. This is worth more than all the anti-ageing prescriptions when it comes to staying youthful.

'Immortality is my short-term goal,' said one delegate at an anti-ageing conference recently. We laughed. Immortality isn't our goal in the short or long term. We just want to age actively and healthily and to be around to enjoy our children and our children's children if we're lucky. And we want to waste less time on worry and negative emotions and to really revel in the time we have left, however much or little that may be.

Further Information

Books

Inspiration

Blackman, Honor. *How to Look and Feel Half Your Age for the Rest of Your Life*, Virgin, 1997

Carlson, Richard. *Don't Sweat The Small Stuff*, Hodder & Stoughton, 1998

Coleman, Vernon. *Mindpower*, Century, 1986

Collins, Joan. *My Secrets*, Boxtree, 1994

Cottin Pogrebin, Letty. *Getting Over Getting Older*, Berkley Books, 1997

Csikszentmihalyi, Mihaly. *Living Well*, Weidenfeld & Nicolson, 1997

Doress-Worters, Paula B., and Laskin Siegal, Diana. *The New Ourselves, Growing Older*, Simon & Schuster, 1994

Downes, Peggy, Tuttle, Ilene, and Mudd, Virginia. *The New Older Women*, Celestial Arts, 1996

Gibson, Dr Hamilton. *Love in Later Life*, Peter Owen, 1998

Gurley Brown, Helen. *The Late Show*, Avon Books, 1993

Holden, Robert. *Laughter, The Best Medicine*, Thorsons, 1993

Leshan, Eda. *It's Better to be Over the Hill Than Under it*, Newmarket Press, 1990

Miles, Dr Rosalind. *The Woman's History of the World*, Michael Joseph, 1988, Grafton, 1989

Sheehy, Gail. *New Passages*, Random House, 1995

Storr, Anthony. *Solitude*, The Free Press, 1988

Updike, John. *Are You Old Enough to Read This Book?*, Reader's Digest Books, 1998

Warburton, David, and Sherwood, Neil. *Pleasure and Quality of Life*, Wiley, 1996

Weeks, David, and James, Jamie. *Superyoung*, Hodder & Stoughton, 1998

York, Pat. *Going Strong*, US, Arcade, 1991

Beauty and Style

Fairley, Josephine, and Stacey, Sarah. *The Beauty Bible*, Kyle Cathie, 1996

Forever Beautiful with Rex, Clarkson Potter, 1994

Hislop, Bel. *The Body Breakthrough*, Vermilion Books, 1993

Hutton, Deborah. *Vogue Futures*, Ebury Press, 1994

Kingsley, Philip. *Hair: An owner's handbook*, Aurum Press, 1995

Loren, Sophia. *Woman and Beauty*, Aurum Press, 1984

Spillane, Mary. *Makeover Manual*, Macmillan, 1998

Brain Fitness

Buzan, Tony. *Make the Most of Your Mind*, Pan, 1988

Buzan, Tony, and Keene, Raymond. *The Age Heresy*, Ebury Press, 1996

Crook, Dr Thomas, Allison, Christine, and Boswell, John. *How to Remember Names*, Harper Collins, 1992

Kidd, Parris M. *Phosphatidylserine: the nutrient building block that accelerates all brain functions and counters Alzheimers*, Keats Good Health Guide, 1998

Work

Bronte, Lydia. *Longevity Factor; The New Reality of Extended Careers and How They Can Lead to Richer Lives*, Harper Perennial, 1993

Davies, Phillipa. *Total Confidence*, Piatkus Books, 1994

Johnson Gross, Kim, and Stone, Jeff. *Chic Simple: Work Clothes*, Thames and Hudson, 1996

McKee, Victoria. *Working It Out*, Robson Books, 1991

Spillane, Mary. *Presenting Yourself*, Piatkus Books, 1992

Health and Wellbeing

Benjamin, Harry. *Better Sight Without Glasses*, Thorsons, first edition published 1929; sixth edition 1992

Kenton, Lesley. *Ultrahealth*, Vermilion, 1994

Kahn, Farrol. *Arrive in Better Shape*, Thorsons, 1995

Marantz Henig, Robin, and the editors of *Esquire Magazine*. *How a Woman Ages*, Ballantine, 1985

Marks, Prof. Ronald. *The Sun and Your Skin*, Macdonald Optima, 1998

Marks, Prof. Ronald, and Dunitz, Martin. *Sun Damaged Skin*, Scovill Paterson, 1992

Marks, Prof. Ronald, and Dunitz, Martin. *Skin Disease in Old Age*, 1998

McPherson, Dr Ann (ed.). *Women's Problems in General Practice*, Oxford University Press, 1993

McPherson, Dr Ann, and Durham, Nancy. *The Woman's Hour Book of Health – By Women, For Women*, BBC Publications, 1998

O'Connell, Dr David. *Jetlag and How To Beat It*, Ascendant Publishing, 1997

Payne, Dr Mark. *Superhealth: The Complete Environmental Medicine Health Plan*, Thorsons, 1992

Sapolsky, Prof. Robert. *Why Zebras Don't Get Ulcers,* US, Stanford University Alumni Association's 'Portable Stanford' Series, 1994

Smith, Angela, and Jones, Dr Hilary (ed.). *Gentle Medicine, Thorsons' Concise Encyclopaedia of Natural Health*, Thorsons, 1994

Watts, Murray, and Cooper, Prof. Cary L. *Stop The World: Finding a way through the pressures of life*, Hodder Headline, 1998

Menopause

Coney, Sandra. *The Menopause Industry*, Penguin Books, 1991

Cooper, Wendy. *No Change*, Arrow Books, 1988
Glenville, Marilyn. *Natural Alternatives to HRT*, Kyle Cathie, 1997
Greenwood, Sada. *Menopause the Natural Way*
Greer, Germaine. *The Change*, Hamish Hamilton, 1991
Kenton, Leslie. *Passage to Power*, Vermilion, 1996
Klatz, Dr Ronald. *Grow Young With HGH*, Harper Collins, 1997
Sheehy, Gail. *The Silent Passage: Menopause*, HarperCollins, 1993
Stewart, Maryon. *Beat PMS Through Diet*, Vermilion, 1994
Wilson Robert A. *Forever Young*
Weed, Susun. *Menopausal Years, The Wise Woman Way*, Ash Tree Publishing, 1992

Diet and Nutrition

Balch, James F., M.D., and Balch, Phyllis A., M.D. *Prescription for Nutritional Healing*, Avery Publishing Group, 1997
Cannon, Geoffrey, and Einzig, Hetty. *Dieting Makes You Fat*, Sphere, 1984
Carper, Jean. *Stop Ageing Now*, Thorsons, 1996
Chopra, Deepak. *Ageless Body, Timeless Mind*, Harmony Books, 1993
Clark, Jane. *Body Foods*, Weidenfeld & Nicolson, 1996
Courteney, Hazel. *What's the Alternative?*, Boxtree, 1996, 1998
Flytlie, Dr Knut T. *Q10 Body Fuel*, Norhaven Rotation, A/S, 1994.
Frank, Benjamin. *The No Aging Diet*, Dial
Holford, Patrick. *The Optimum Nutrition Bible*, Piatkus Books, 1997
Holford, Patrick. *100% Health*, Piatkus Books, 1998
Lockie, Dr Andrew, and Geddes, Dr Nicola. *The Women's Guide to Homeopathy*, Hamish Hamilton, 1992
Marsden, Kathryn. *Hotline to Health*, Pan, 1998
Rodin, Judith. *Body Traps*, William Morrow, 1992
Van Straten, Michael, and Griggs, Barbara. *Superfoods*. Dorling Kindersley, 1990

Exercise

Chopra, Deepak. *Boundless Energy*, Rider, 1995
Corvo, Joseph. *Zone Therapy*, Arrow, 1993
Dancey, Dr Elizabeth. *The Cellulite Solution*, Coronet, 1996
Fraser, Eva. *Eva Fraser's Facial Workout*, Penguin, 1992
Hodgkinson, Liz. *How To Banish Cellulite For Ever*, 1992
Maggio, Carole. *Facercise*, Boxtree, 1995
Robinson, Lynne, and Thomson, Gordon. *Body Control The Pilates Way*, Pan, 1998
Scaravelli, Vanda. *Awakening the Spine*, HarperCollins, 1991
Silva, Mira, and Mehta, Shyam. *Yoga The Iyengar Way*, Dorling Kindersley, 1990
Iyengar, B. K. S. *Light on Yoga*, Unwin, 1968, constantly reprinted

Love and Sex

Botting, Kate and Douglas. *Sex Appeal*, Boxtree, 1995

Chopra, Deepak. *The Path to Love*, Rider, 1997

Grant, Ellen. *Sexual Chemistry – Understanding our Hormones, The Pill and HRT*, Cedar, 1994

Harris, Anthony, M.Sc., Ph.D. *Sexual Exercises for Women*, Carroll & Graf, 1988

Hooper, Anne. *The Ultimate Sex Guide*, Dorling Kindersley, 1992

Hooper, Anne. *Sexual Intimacy*, Dorling Kindersley, 1996

Markman, Howard, Stanley, Scott, and Blumberg, Susan L. *Fighting For Your Marriage: positive steps for preventing divorce and preserving a lasting love*, Jossey-Bass, 1994

Cosmetic Surgery

Bransford, Helen. *Welcome to your Facelift*, Doubleday, 1997

Imber, Gerald, M.D. *The Youth Corrider*, William Morrow, 1997

Haiken, Elizabeth. *Venus Envy: a history of cosmetic surgery*, Johns Hopkins University Press, 1998

New Age Ageing

Heinerman, John. *Dr. Heinerman's Encyclopaedia of Anti-Aging Remedies*, Prentice Hall, 1977

Klatz, Dr Ronald, and Goldman, Dr Robert. *7 Anti-Aging Secrets*, ESM Publications, 1996

Klatz, Dr Ronald, and Goldman, Dr Robert. *Stopping The Clock*, Keats Publishing, 1996

Rifkin, Jeremy. *The Biotech Century: Harnessing the Gene and Remaking the World*, Putnam 1998

Smith, Timothy J. *Renewal: The Anti-Ageing Revolution*, Rodale Books, 1998

Yanick, Paul, Jr, Ph.D., and Giampapa, Vincent C., M.D. *Quantum Longevity: Living to 100 and beyond with the Longevity Institute International's Anti-Aging Program*, Promotion Publishing 1997

Inspirational Fiction

First Wives Club, Olivia Goldsmith, Mandarin, 1993

How to Make an American Quilt, Whitney Otto, Ballantine, 1991

Ladder of Years, Anne Tyler, Chatto & Windus, 1995

Evening Class, Maeve Binchy, Orion, 1996

Under The Tuscan Sun, Frances Mayes, Bantam, 1998

Warning, Jenny Joseph, Souvenir Books, 1998

Useful Organizations

Age Concern England (incorporating
Age Resource and The National Council
on Ageing),
Astral House,
1268 London Road,
London SW16 4ER
Tel: 0181 679 8000

**The American Academy of Anti-Ageing
Medicine** (A4M),
1341 West Fullerton,
Suite 111,
Chicago, Illinois 60614
Tel: 001 773 528 1000

Alcohol Concern,
305 Gray's Inn Road,
London WC1X 9QF
Tel: 0171 928 7377

The Amarant Trust,
56 St John Street,
London EC1M 4DT
Tel: 0171 490 1644

**ARISE – Association for Research Into
the Science of Enjoyment**,
PO Box 114466,
London SW18 5ZH
Tel: 0181 874 5548
Fax: 0181 874 3755

**The Association of Image Consultants
International** (AICI),
1000 Connecticut Avenue NW,
Suite 9,
Washington, DC 20036–5032
e-mail: aic@worldnet.att.net
website: www.aici.org

**Association of Retired, and Persons
over 50**,
4th Floor, Greencoat House,
Francis Street,
London SW1 1DZ
Tel: 0171 828 0500

**Association of Sexual and Marital
Therapists**,
PO Box 62,
Sheffield S10 3TS
No telephone service available

**British Association for Cancer United
Patients**,
121–123 Charterhouse Street,
London EC1M 6AA
Tel: 0171 608 1661

**Breast Care and Mastectomy
Association**,
26 Harrison Street,
King's Cross,
London WC1H 8JG
Tel: 0171 833 0908

British Heart Foundation,
14 Fitzhardinge Street,
London W1
Tel: 0171 935 0185

British Longevity Society,
PO Box 71,
Northampton NN1 5HJ
Tel: 0850 221796

British Menopause Society,
36 West Street,
Marlow,
Bucks SL7 2NB
Tel: 01628 890199

Cancerlink,
17 Britannia Street,
London WC1X 9JN
Tel: 0171 833 2451

Carers' National Association,
11 John Street,
London WC1N 2EB
Tel: 0171 404 2900

Cenegenics,
851 South Rampart Boulevard,
Suite 210,
Las Vegas,
Nevada 89128
Tel: 001 702 240 4200

Centre for Policy on Ageing,
25 Ironmonger Row,
London EC1
Tel: 0171 253 1787

CRUSE,
126 Sheen Road,
Richmond
Surrey TW9 1UR
Tel: 0181 940 4818
Bereavement Helpline: 0181 332 7227

CMB Image Consultants UK, Europe,
Africa, and Middle East,
66 Ingate Place,
London SW8 3NS
Tel: 0845 603 3408 / 0171 627 5211
www.colormebeautiful.co.uk

The David Lewis Consultancy Ltd,
15A High Street,
Tunbridge Wells,
Kent TN1 1UT
Tel: 01892 542 825

Eating Disorders Association,
First Floor, Wensum House,
103 Prince of Wales Road,
Norwich,
Norfolk NR1 1DW
Tel: 01603 621414
Youth Helpline (under 18s): 01603 765050

Employers Forum on Age,
1268 London Road,
London SW16
Tel: 0181 679 1075

Health Education Authority,
Hamilton House,
Mableon Place,
London WC1H 9TX
Tel: 0171 383 3833

Imperial Cancer Research Fund,
Dept NFD,
61 Lincoln's Inn Fields,
London WC2
Tel: 0171 269 3413

Institute of Complementary Medicine,
PO Box 194,
London SE16 1QZ
Tel: 0171 237 5165
(for lists of registered practitioners in
various fields)

Institute of Optimum Nutrition,
121 Deodar Road,
London SW15
Tel: 0181 877 9993

Institute of Human Ageing,
University of Liverpool.
L69 3BX
Tel: 0151 794 2000

Longevity Institutes International,
89 Valley Road
Montclair, New Jersey
Tel: 001 973 783 6868

Macular Disease Society,
PO Box 247,
Haywards Heath,
W. Sussex RH1 7FF
Tel: 0990 143573

Menopause Helpline,
Tel: 0181 444 5202
Fax: 0181 444 6442

National Centre for Eating Disorders,
54 New Road,
Esher,
Surrey KT10 9NN
Tel: 01372 469 493

National Heart Forum,
Tavistock House,
Tavistock Square,
London WC1
Tel: 0171 383 7638

National Osteoporosis Society,
PO Box 10,
Radstock,
Bath BA3 3YB
Tel: 01761 471771

Natural Progesterone Information Service,
PO Box 24,
Buxton SK17 9FB
No telephone.
Fax: 01298 70979

Optimal Health *at*:
114 Harley Street,
London W1N 1AG
Tel: 0171 935 5651

and:
41 Elystan Place,
London SW3 3JY
Tel: 0171 589 3389
(incorporating Jetlag Clinic)

Prowess,
Silchester House,
Silchester RG7 2LT
Tel: 0118 9701 901

RELATE,
Herbert Grey College
Little Church Street, Rugby,
Warwickshire CU21 3AS
Tel: 01788 573241

Research Into Ageing,
15 St Cross Street,
London EC1
Tel: 0171 404 6878

Mr Jan Stanek,
Cosmetic Surgeon,
58 Harley Street,
London W1N 1AP
Tel: 0171 637 3310

Woman Returners' Network,
344–354 Gray's Inn Road,
London WC1X 8BT
Tel: 0171 278 2900

Women's Nutritional Advisory Service,
PO Box 268,
Lewes,
East Sussex, BN7 2QN

Yoga Therapy Centre and Yoga Biomedical Trust,
60 Great Ormond Street,
London WC1N 3HR
Tel: 0171 833 7267

Acknowledgements

Our gratitude to our special consultants Professor Cary L. Cooper of the University of Manchester's Institute of Science and Technology, Dr Thomas Crook of Psychologix, Dr Vincent C. Giampapa of Longevity Institutes International, Mr Patrick Holford of the Institute of Optimum Nutrition, Mr Joseph Jordan FRCOG, chairman of the Birmingham and Midland Women's Hospital Trust, Dr Ronald Klatz of the American Academy of Anti-Ageing Medicine, Mr Philip Kingsley, trichologist, Professor Ronald Marks, professor of Dermatology at the University of Wales in Cardiff and the University of Miami in Florida, Dr Michael Perring of Optimal Health Centres, Professor Craig Sharp of Brunel University, Dr Dawn Skelton of Research into Ageing, Dr David Warburton of ARISE, Lizzie Webb, Dr David Weeks of the Jardine Clinic in Edinburgh.

We would also like to thank the others who shared research or life experiences with us, or who simply provided inspiration for this book. They include Jane Asher, Dr Neil Lawson Baker, Daphne Belt, Katie Boyle, Isla Blair, Ursula Bornstein, Tony Buzan, Barbara Cartland, Joan Collins, Pat Chambers of Stockport College of Further and Higher Education, Julie Christie, Jo Cutmore and Mark Scott of Jamieson Scott and Prowess, Pamela Davenport, Hunter Davies, Dr Dee Dawson of the Rhodes Farm Clinic, Rosa della Tolla, Catherine Deneuve, Dr Jan de Winter, Professor Sir Richard Doll, Michael Durtnall of the Sayer Clinics, Margaret Evison, Dr Knut Flytlie, Becky Sue Epstein Gerovac, Elizabeth King George, Dr Hamilton Gibson, Professor Jeffrey Goldstein of the University of Utrecht, Professor Sir John Grimley Evans, Newby Hands of *Harpers & Queen*, Sydney Rice Harrild of The Coaching Company, Dr Anthony Harris, Fiona Harrold, Shere Hite, Professor Malcolm Hodkinson, Philip Hodson, Anne Hooper, Mevagh Horton, Dr Gerald Imber, Deanne Jade of the National Centre for Eating Disorders, Liz Keeble, Vivian King, Dr Mario Kyriasis of the British Longevity Society, Eleanor Lambert, Jane Lapotaire, Dr John Lee, Dr David Lewis, Elizabeth (the Countess of) Longford, Sophia Loren, Lucy Lowther, Dr Brian Merry of the Institute of Human Ageing, Nancy McKee, Dr Rosalind Miles, Nanette Newman, Jane Orton, Jilly Pengilley, Professor David Purdie, Margaret Read, Louise Reed,

Jenny Reeves, Professor Robert Sapolsky, Helen Sher, Lisha Spar, Professor Janet Spence, Dr Jan Stanek, Sharon Stone, Dr Jonathan Tilly of Harvard Medical School, Tina Turner, Alix Williamson, and our stunning models used throughout. Color Me Beautiful stylists Juliet Yasher and Caroline Bennett are responsible for the pictures looking so superb. Clothes throughout provided by Kenzo, Donna Karan, Ghost, as well as models' own wardrobe. Special thanks for clothes go to Debenhams, and especially to Jean and Mark Pallant, who have dressed me for over a decade. Special thanks are due to our tireless, ageless editor Gordon Wise and the whole dynamic team at Macmillan Books.

Illustration Acknowledgements

Principal original photography for *UltraAge* by Sanders Nicholson, make-up by Sarah B and hair by Dottie Monaghan, both of Joy Goodman.

p.11 Anita Corbin

p.14 Sanders Nicholson

p.19 Authors' own

p.23 Goldie Hawn – left: © Associated Newspapers/Popperfoto; right: Shawn Baldwin/Popperfoto/Reuters

Tina Turner – left: Popperfoto; right: Graham Whitby/Sportsphoto/Popperfoto

Catherine Deneuve – left: Popperfoto/Reuters; right: Reinhard Krause/Popperfoto Reuters

Lauren Bacall – left: Popperfoto; right: Robert Giroux/Popperfoto/Reuters

p.34 Sanders Nicholson. Models: Caroline and Rosalind Bennett; Minnie Stevens

p.42 Left: Graham Whitby/Sportsphoto/Popperfoto; right: Des Jenson/Rex Features

pp.47, 51 David Gadd/Sportsphoto/Popperfoto

p.54 Alex Oliveira/Rex Features

p.55 Rex Features

p.63 Fred Prouser/Reuters Popperfoto

p.66 Swanson © Sipa Press/Rex Features

About the Authors

Mary Spillane is world renowned as an image consultant. The founder of Europe's first image consultancy, CMB, she has written numerous books including *Makeover Manual*. A Harvard graduate and, like her co-author, American born, her career has spanned management consulting and PR, and US Government and the United Nations. She is noted for her image advice for politicians, sports personalities and business leaders as well as women of every shape, size and age.

Victoria McKee is an internationally known journalist who has written extensively on health, women's and work issues, contributing to *The Times*, *The Sunday Times*, *The New York Times*, *Harpers & Queen* and other publications in Britain and around the world. She has an MA from the University of Birmingham in England, is the author of *Working It Out* and is a Fellow of the Royal Society of Arts.

Index